WHY 565?

Various sources mention different numbers of princely states. While the count in the *Report of the Indian States Committee*, also called the Butler Committee (1929), is 562, a *Report of the Joint Committee on Indian Constitutional Reforms* (1933–34) refers to nearly 600 states. Meanwhile, the number listed in the Appendix of the White Paper released by the Government of India (1948) is 584.

In his book *The Great Divide: Britain - India - Pakistan*, H.V. Hodson mentions Sardar Patel stating the number **565** when speaking of the princely states with the then viceroy, Lord Mountbatten, a few weeks before 15 August 1947.

In his address to the Chamber of Princes on 25 July 1947, Viceroy Lord Mountbatten said, '**Out of something like 565 states**, the vast majority are irretrievably linked geographically with the Dominion of India.'

Several other references also state the number as 565. This number (565) was hence chosen for the title of the book.

Praise for the Book

'Veiled as they are behind the drudgery of textbooks, some of the most enthralling episodes from the making of modern India fail to reach a majority of young Indians, who will go on to helm our future. One of these episodes is the integration of more than 500 princely states into the Union of India. As an impoverished and soon-to-be-liberated India ran the gauntlet of infernal communal violence and armed invasion, the venerable Sardar Vallabhbhai Patel and his sagacious aide, V.P. Menon, strove to cobble together, one challenging maharaja a time, the India we see on the map. Were it not for these two patriots and their valorous crusade against formidable odds, India's fate would have been wholly different. This is their story.

An outstanding volume, woven into a spellbinding yarn by Mallika Ravikumar and brought to sparkling life by Ishan Trivedi's excellent illustrations, 565: *The Dramatic Story of Unifying India* is sure to enthral readers, introducing them to the glory of independent India's founders and the cataclysms they surmounted to leave behind the nation we boundlessly treasure.'

– ***Dr Shashi Tharoor***, *author and Member of Parliament*

'565: *The Dramatic Story of Unifying India* is a compelling narrative that unravels the intricate negotiations, strategic manoeuvres and powerful personalities involved in integrating over 500 princely states into the Indian Union, both pre- and post-independence.

A well-researched book, with vivid storytelling, interesting snippets and a note on sources called 'Did it Happen This Way', it brings alive a pivotal yet overlooked chapter of Indian history.'

– ***Rana Safvi***, *author and translator*

565
THE DRAMATIC STORY OF UNIFYING INDIA

Winner of the Atta Galatta Bangalore Literature Festival Award for Best Children's Fiction 2023, and the Binod Kanoria Children's Book Award 2023 in the Young Adult category, Mallika is a lawyer turned writer. An MA in Ancient Indian History and Culture, her study of, and interest in, the accession of princely states, began when she was the curator and chief content writer for the Government of India's National Virtual Library of India portal on Sardar Vallabhbhai Patel's life and legacy.

Mallika also loves learning about trees, conducting tree walks and creating videos about trees on her YouTube channel, *Tree Talk with Mallika Ravikumar.* You can find out more at www.mallikaravikumar.com and reach her on Instagram at mallika.ravikumar.

565
THE DRAMATIC STORY OF UNIFYING INDIA

Mallika Ravikumar

Illustrations by Ishan Trivedi

First published in 2024 by Hachette India
(Registered name: Hachette Book Publishing India Pvt. Ltd)
An Hachette UK company
www.hachetteindia.com

SRD

Illustrations by Ishan Trivedi
Maps by Syed Salahuddin; Text divider on page xxi: vecteezy.com; Attribution: panadesignteam;
All coats of arms of princely states sourced from Wikimedia Commons Public Domain
Newspaper clipping on page 5 from www.indianculture.gov.in, Ministry of Culture, Government of India
Map of India on page xx roughly based on map of India before Partition in
The Transfer of Power 1942–47, Volume XII and Survey of India boundaries.

ISBN 978-93-93701-13-8

Hachette Book Publishing India Pvt. Ltd
4th & 5th Floors, Corporate Centre
Plot No. 94, Sector 44, Gurugram – 122003, India

Typeset in Lora 9.5/14.5 by Manmohan Kumar, Delhi

Printed and bound in India
by Manipal Technologies Limited

To
Appa
for the love of reading,
and
Amma
for the love of research

Contents

HOW TO READ THIS BOOK

Unlike a typical history-based book, events in this story do not unfold in a strictly chronological order. Events in each chapter are often occurring at the same time as those in other chapters and multiple fires are put out at once. Readers can therefore choose to jump to the story of any princely state that interests them, after reading the Prologue and initial sections to understand the background. That being said, the story does begin with Travancore (the first princely state to declare its independence) and ends with Hyderabad (among the last princely states to join India). Because the story has been narrated in this manner, you may find a few details repeated, as every chapter is meant to stand on its own as a separate unit, while at the same time being one part of the larger narrative.

Prologue

As the British prepared to leave India in 1947, India was not a single political entity. Although geographically one land mass, politically, India comprised two distinct portions:

1. British India
2. Princely India

British India was that part of India which had been directly annexed by the British and was administered by a government in Delhi. Divided into various provinces such as Bombay, Bengal, Sind and so on, it formed roughly half of the Indian subcontinent.

Princely India was that part of India which the British ruled indirectly through hereditary rulers, who were known by various names like maharaja, nawab, nizam and so on. Comprising over 500 kingdoms – some larger than nations in Europe; others, small landholdings barely visible on a map – this part formed about half of the Indian territory.

The indirect rule in Princely India (also called princely states) was facilitated through treaties, which were agreements the rulers had signed with the British Crown. Under these treaties, the rulers had been provided with security and various privileges by the British; and in return they had accepted the

British monarch as their supreme or paramount power (the arrangement was hence called *paramountcy*).

When, on 20 February 1947, British Prime Minister Clement Attlee announced in the British Parliament that Britain would withdraw from India by June 1948, two processes were required to be undertaken:

1. In British India: Transferring power to the successor government of independent India; and
2. In Princely India: Ending the arrangement of paramountcy with the hereditary rulers.

On 3 June 1947, the deadline for Britain's withdrawal was arbitrarily advanced by Lord Mountbatten, India's last viceroy, when he suddenly declared that India would become independent on 15 August 1947, leaving less than three months for the mammoth task.

In British India, the transfer of power was a challenge because the two principal political parties in India back then – the Indian National Congress (or Congress) and the Muslim League – were at loggerheads. Most of us are familiar with that story, and the saga of the Partition of India that followed.

Little, however, is written or discussed about the dramatic events that occurred during the same period in Princely India; despite the fact that the princely states constituted about 45 per cent of the total territory, and 24 per cent of the total population of pre-Partition India. In fact, sixteen of those princely states had a population of over 1 million.

These princely states – 565 in all (by several accounts) were given three options:

1. Join India; or
2. Join Pakistan; or
3. Remain independent.

Several rulers were nervous about these developments. Over the years, many had helped Britain in her war efforts, even sided with the British in the Revolt of 1857, and were jittery about being left in the lurch. Some distrusted the Congress, as its leaders, such as Jawaharlal Nehru, were avowedly opposed to monarchy; hence the rajas and nawabs feared that their powers and privileges would be taken away in independent democratic India. Some negotiated with Muslim League leader Muhammad Ali Jinnah about joining Pakistan; others deliberated with one another about forming a third front and calling themselves Princestan; while some others preferred to simply stay out and declare their independence.

It was in these circumstances that a States Department was formed and placed under the charge of Sardar Vallabhbhai Patel and V.P. Menon to convince the over 500 princely states, scattered across the length and breadth of the subcontinent, to join India. With less than three months in hand – moreover, with other upheavals like Partition happening simultaneously – this was going to be an impossible race against time.

While every state had its own challenges and priorities, and tense events took place in some other princely states as well (such as in Alwar), it was not possible to include the story of every state in this book. With an effort to neither vilify nor idolize any of the personalities involved, or their decisions, the states featured in this book have been selected for the dramatic quality of how events unfolded there, and the far-reaching impact they had on the outcome. The stories of these states encompass nearly all the major events concerning the episode of the accession of princely states while providing a glimpse into this complex and colossal task.

This is the story of that immense endeavour, that unparalleled achievement in history, in which more than 500 princely kingdoms were threaded together into a union – in record time and against all odds – to create the India we now have.

The Key Personalities

JAWAHARLAL NEHRU

Interim Prime Minister and first Prime Minister of Independent India

Fifty-seven-year-old Jawaharlal Nehru was the head of the interim government and was set to be the first prime minister of free India.

Nehru played a key role in supporting the States Department/ Ministry in the impossible task of uniting 565 princely states.

SARDAR VALLABHBHAI PATEL

Minister of States

Vallabhbhai Patel, then seventy-two, headed the States Department that was given the responsibility to convince the princely states to join India. Many saw the pragmatic Patel as the best man for the challenging task.

Despite his age and failing health, Patel would become the deputy prime minister, and head the Ministry of Information and Broadcasting and the Ministry of Home Affairs, while also being on many committees drafting India's Constitution.

V.P. MENON

Secretary, States Department

I HAVE A PLAN! LET'S USE THE PAUCITY OF TIME TO OUR ADVANTAGE!

Fifty-four-year-old Vappala Pangunni Menon had had a long bureaucratic career, at the end of which came his posting as the reforms commissioner to the viceroy. After Independence, he looked forward to a quiet retirement, but Patel insisted that he take up the position of secretary in the States Department under him.

The critical agreement under which the princely states joined India, known as the Instrument of Accession, was Menon's brainchild.

LOUIS MOUNTBATTEN

The Last British Viceroy; First Governor General of Independent India

I AGREE TO HELP APPROACH THE RAJAS AND NAWABS TO JOIN INDIA.

The representative of the British king in India, Lord Louis Mountbatten was given the humongous responsibility of overseeing the transfer of power. Although he had to remain strictly neutral, he played a key role in bringing the princely states into India upon the suggestion of Menon and Sardar Patel.

MUHAMMAD ALI JINNAH
Leader of the Muslim League

Seventy-year-old Muhammad Ali Jinnah, leader of the Muslim League, was on the verge of carving out of India a separate country for Muslims. But contrary to his expectations, the map of Pakistan was much smaller than what he desired (with only half of Bengal and half of Punjab). As August 1947 neared, Jinnah hoped to compensate for this loss by luring various princely states into Pakistan's fold – even those located deep inside India's territory, and those with a Hindu-majority population, despite that being completely against the principles of his two-nation theory.

PRINCELY STATES AND THEIR RULERS

The kingdoms called princely states were ruled by hereditary rulers who were known by various names such as raja, maharaja, maharawal, nawab, nizam and so on. As 15 August 1947 approached, these rulers had to make a decision about joining India. The states were ranked by the British and the more important ones, known as salute states, were ranked by the number of gun salutes given to the ruler – the higher the number of gun salutes, the more important the state. Occupying the highest position in this pecking order were the states of Baroda, Jammu and Kashmir, Gwalior, Mysore and Hyderabad – all of which were 21-gun-salute states.

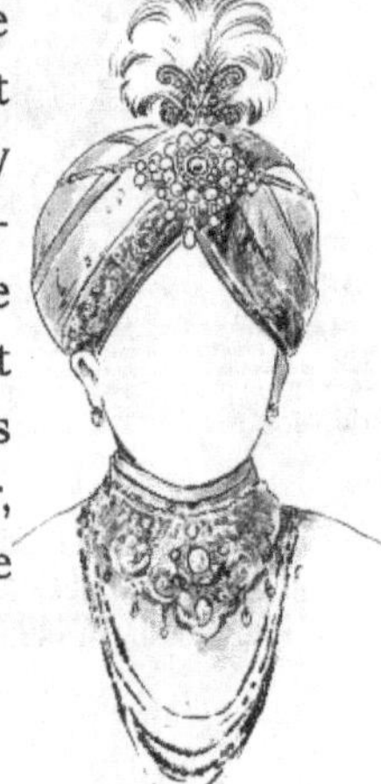

PRIME MINISTERS/ DIWANS OF PRINCELY STATES

Rulers of princely states appointed ministers or advisers: 'diwans' or prime ministers. The diwans of the princely states advised the ruler, and helped him administer and manage the state. Many of them played a decisive role in the saga of accession.

CHAMBER OF PRINCES

The Chamber of Princes, also called Narendra Mandal, was a forum formed in 1921 as an association of rulers of princely states. It was an advisory forum where princes got together for mutual consultations on matters that affected them as a whole. In early 1947, the nawab of Bhopal was the chancellor of the Chamber of Princes.

ALL INDIA STATES PEOPLES' CONFERENCE (AISPC)

This was an all-India association of people living in the princely states. Initially, the Congress party did not want to interfere in the princely states, but gradually the national movement started having an impact among the people living there, who began demanding that their rulers provide them with a responsible government. The AISPC, also called the Praja Mandal, became the voice of the people in the princely states. In early 1947, Jawaharlal Nehru was the president of this association.

THE POLITICAL DEPARTMENT AND ADVISER

The political department maintained links between Princely India and British India by appointing 'residents' or 'agents' in the princely states. The department was headed by a secretary, also called the political adviser, who worked under the viceroy. In 1947, the political adviser was Sir Conrad Corfield.

Pre-Partition India: 1947

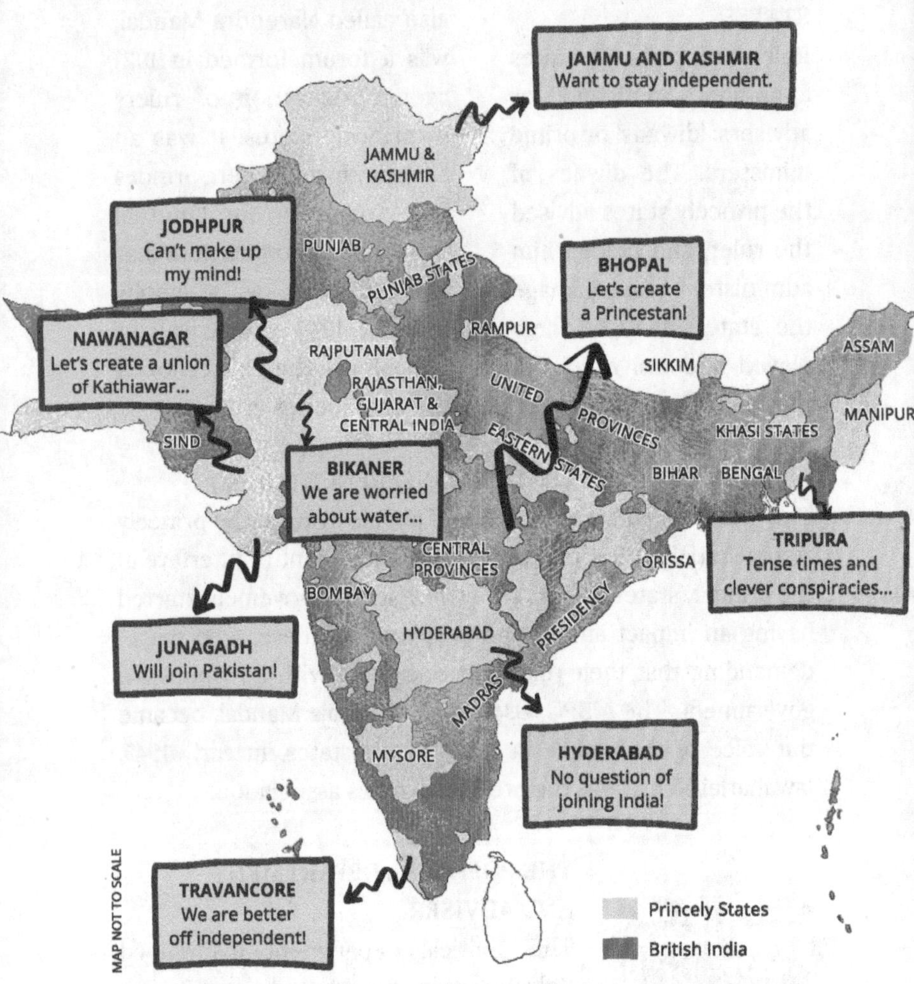

In 1947, princely states occupied approximately 45 per cent of Indian territory. Together, they had a population of 93.2 million, constituting about 24 per cent of the population of pre-Partition India. As the British left, every princely state was given the choice to join India, or join Pakistan, or remain free.

The Final Countdown

WHO?
The princely states

HOW MANY?
Approximately 565

WHO DECIDES?
The ruler of each princely state

DECISION TO MAKE:
Join India; or
Join Pakistan; or
Stay independent

BY WHEN?
15 August 1947 – about two months!

WHY DOES IT MATTER?
Princely India constituted roughly 45 per cent of pre-Partition India. The states' territories were contiguous with and criss-crossed with British India

HOW?
Accede to India by signing two documents:

1. **Instrument of Accession:** To hand over powers on matters of external affairs, defence and communications to the Government of India

2. **Standstill Agreement:** To allow matters like postal services, railways and so on to continue to function as before, until further arrangement

If a princely state acceded to Pakistan, or declared itself independent, India would have had pockets of Pakistan, or other nations within her borders – and would not have been the single, consolidated nation we now have.

A Basketful of Apples

'Look,' Viceroy Mountbatten said, interlacing his fingers and leaning on his desk, 'you have asked me to help you with the princes, and I am ready. I have spoken to some of them and I feel that if the Congress can agree to some of their conditions, perhaps I can persuade them to sign the Instrument of Accession to join India...'

'What conditions?' asked Sardar Patel.

'If you can get the Congress to agree that the princes may retain their titles and palaces,' replied the viceroy, 'and keep some of their rights such as immunity from arrest, their British decorations and so on, I can help you get them on board.'

Sitting back in his chair, Patel inhaled deeply as he mulled over the proposition. While he had nothing but contempt for the titles of the maharajas and nawabs, he couldn't deny that the offer was tempting. No doubt the privileges were elitist, but those ranks and titles meant a lot to many in the pomp-loving, prestige-brandishing princely order. And, as a man of royal lineage, the viceroy's word held great sway among the Indian royalty. If, by allowing them to retain their hollow perks, he could get Mountbatten to work his persuasive charm on the princes, perhaps that would work to India's advantage.

'I am prepared to accept your offer...' Patel scratched his chin.

Mountbatten raised his eyebrows, startled by the swiftness of Patel's response.

'...provided,' Patel cocked his head, 'you give me a full basket of apples.'

'I beg your pardon?' asked the puzzled viceroy.

'I'll take the basket...' clarified Patel, 'provided it has all 565 apples.'

'Ah!' Mountbatten grinned, a tad amused by Sardar's apple-basket metaphor for the princely states scattered across the subcontinent. But suddenly he didn't feel quite as confident about the idea. 'What if I can't manage to bring in everyone?' he asked. 'Would you give me the leeway of a dozen states?'

'That's far too many.' A stoic Patel shook his head, as a surprised V.P. Menon and bemused Hastings Ismay watched their bosses bargain over states like fruit sellers haggling in the marketplace. 'Perhaps I can leave you two.'

'Oh, that's impossible, Mr Patel,' the viceroy raised his hands in the universal gesture of surrender, 'we have less than two months.'

'Okay...I'm prepared to accept six less,' shrugged Patel. 'Any fewer and the deal is off.'

'All right,' the viceroy held out his hand. 'I cannot guarantee it...but I will do my best.'

As the men shook hands to seal their unusual deal, Menon who had mooted the idea of reaching out to the viceroy for his help, looked up at the special calendar on the wall that showed the countdown to the date of the transfer of power. The number of days left to 15 August 1947 stared back at him in bold print. Menon heaved a nervous sigh.

Fifty days. Five hundred and sixty-five states.

The race was on!

1

Breaking Free

THE STORY OF TRAVANCORE

PRINCELY STATE OF TRAVANCORE IN 1947:
about half the size of present-day Kerala
AREA: 7,662 square miles (19,844 square kilometres)
POPULATION: 6,070,018
RULER: Maharaja Chithira Thirunal Balarama Varma
DIWAN: Sir C.P. Ramaswami Aiyar
19-gun-salute state

❋ The Wizard of Travancore ❋

'In law as well as in fact,' declared Sir C.P. Ramaswami Aiyar, Travancore's brilliant and erudite prime minister, 'Travancore will become an independent country from 15 August 1947.'

Dressed in a crisp black *bandgala* paired with a white dhoti and turban, Chetpat Pattabhirama Ramaswami Aiyar, known to most simply as CP, was addressing a large press gathering in the inner courtyard of Bhaktivilas, his official residence, with the authority and confidence that came with experience and excellence.

'Travancore will not be a protectorate of any other dominion or dominions,' CP triumphantly proclaimed the grand vision, one he shared with the kingdom's young maharaja, Chithira Thirunal Balarama Varma, and the maharaja's mother, Maharani Sethu Parvathi Bayi – for both of whom he was more than just a prime minister or diwan.

'While we are prepared to enter into arrangements as required with India for purposes such as postal services, railways, water and so on,' continued the diwan, loved by few and reviled by many, 'there is no question whatsoever of Travancore joining India.'

Scribes, scribbling away furiously on their notepads, stopped to gape at the man on the podium. With his almond-shaped eyes, aquiline nose, delicate lips, unruly mop of thick, curly hair, phenomenal memory and oratorial flair, CP could well have been a fêted theatre artiste. But this performer had moulded himself for a far greater stage. Journalists from local dailies such as *Malayala Manorama* and *Kerala Kaumudi* to national newspapers like *The Hindu* and the *Hindustan Times*

THE PATH OF INDEPENDENT TRAVANCORE!

had turned up at the press conference expecting a momentous announcement, but this was beyond anything they had foreseen – *Travancore was going to be an independent nation?*

Murmurs rippled through the courtyard as CP paused for the full import of his words to sink in. The news would soon reach New Delhi, he mused, looking around at the reporters with satisfaction.

'I ask the people of Travancore today...' CP raised his pitch as he gazed at the grand arches above him as though he was envisioning a dream, 'do you wish to cherish your freedom, or do you prefer to be submerged in anonymity in a divided India? His Highness, the maharaja, has decided that Travancore must remain independent, and I implore the people to stand by him in solidarity. Travancore is destined to be the saviour of south India.'

The kingdom of Travancore was the only Indian power ever to have defeated a European naval force when one of its most illustrious rulers, Marthanda Varma, vanquished the Dutch fleet in 1741.

Years ago, CP had crossed paths with the Indian National Congress, and his commitment to the national cause had brought him into close contact with party stalwarts such as Annie Besant and Motilal Nehru. But those days were long gone. As things stood on that overcast day in June 1947, he harboured no love or reverence for the Congress triumvirate – not for Gandhi's unconventional methods, not for Nehru's socialistic leanings and, most certainly, not for Patel's authoritative ways. And he had no intention whatsoever of gifting his prized kingdom to them.

'From 15 August,' the diwan said, holding up his forefinger, 'no power on earth – short of open war, for which we are prepared – can prevent Travancore from asserting its independence. The path of necessity and the path of duty, the path of destiny and the path of glory'—he paused, as reporters jotted down his every word—'is the path of independent Travancore.'

❋ At Daggers Drawn ❋

Springing up from his chair, Jawaharlal Nehru, his eyes tired and weary, flung the newspaper on the table in front of the viceroy. 'CP has announced that Travancore will become an independent nation,' he fumed, his face as red as the rose on his lapel. Viceroy Mountbatten turned to Nehru.

Dressed in his trademark cap, well-cut churidar-kurta and polished Peshawari sandals, the leader of the Congress appeared to have aged several years over the last month, vacillating between sudden displays of temper and long, moody silences. Having experienced one of Nehru's outbursts first-hand in Simla only a few weeks ago, which had compelled him to rework the plan for the transfer of power, the viceroy braced himself for yet another explosion.

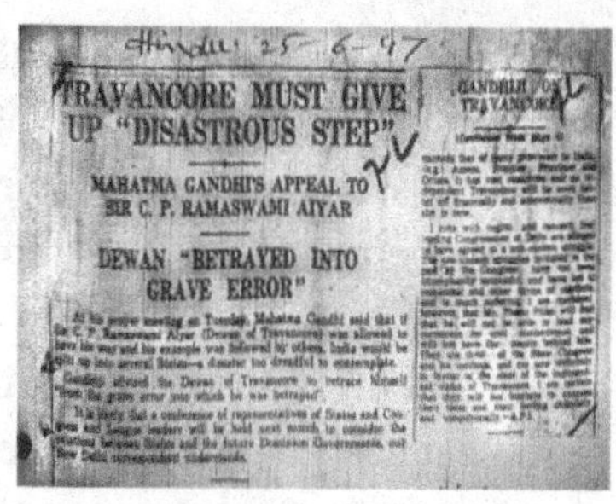

TRAVANCORE MUST GIVE UP "DISASTROUS STEP"

MAHATMA GANDHI'S APPEAL TO SIR C. P. RAMASWAMI AIYAR

DEWAN "BETRAYED INTO GRAVE ERROR"

At his prayer meeting on Tuesday, Mahatma Gandhi said that if Sir C. P. Ramaswami Aiyar (Dewan of Travancore) was allowed to have his way and his example was followed by others, India would be split up into several States—a disaster too dreadful to contemplate.

Gandhiji advised the Dewan of Travancore to retrace himself from the grave error into which he was betrayed.

It is likely that a conference of representatives of States and Congress and League leaders will be held next month to consider the relations between States and the future Dominion Governments, our New Delhi correspondent understands.

GANDHIJI ON TRAVANCORE

[illegible]

'TRAVANCORE DECLARES INDEPENDENCE.'

Seated to his left in a crisply tailored brown suit, a frail Muhammad Ali Jinnah, leader of the Muslim League, peered at the news article that had infuriated Nehru. Liaquat Ali Khan and Rab Nishtar, his colleagues from the League, exchanged telling glances.

'Travancore has declared its independence,' Nehru reiterated, this time with more vehemence. 'This is impossible. If the other princely states follow suit, India will disintegrate into hundreds of pieces.'

'Well...Travancore has every right to declare its independence,' retorted Jinnah matter-of-factly, adjusting the monocle on his bony face.

Seated beside Nehru, with the bearing of a Caesar, Sardar Vallabhbhai Patel cast a grim sidelong glance at the Congress president, Acharya Kripalani. Weary of the constant bickering with Jinnah and his Muslim League, the Congress had finally agreed to Partition. But clearly more thorns lay strewn on the long road to freedom.

'Absolutely,' concurred Sir Conrad Corfield, head of the political department that oversaw the princely states, as he drew forward his copy of the Cabinet Mission Plan. 'According to the terms here,' he indicated the document, 'the void resulting from the withdrawal of the British from India will have to be filled either by entering into a relationship with the successor governments, or by forming particular political arrangements as they, the states, deem fit.'

'That does not mean the possibility of their remaining independent,' thundered Nehru, throwing up his arms.

'What else could "particular political arrangements" imply?' demanded Corfield, tapping the words in the memorandum with his pencil.

'I agree,' Jinnah shrugged again. 'Surely, after the lapse of British paramountcy, every princely state is sovereign and can do as it pleases.'

'I do not see matters as you do,' Nehru countered Jinnah, making no attempt to hide his dislike for the head of the Muslim League. Just a week earlier, Jinnah had quibbled over yet another clause, arguing that *agreement* to a proposal did not necessarily mean *acceptance* of the proposal. Jinnah and his histrionics exasperated Nehru. 'As a lawyer, my views

IF THE PRINCELY STATES DECLARE INDEPENDENCE,
INDIA WILL DISINTEGRATE INTO HUNDREDS OF PIECES...

differ entirely on the interpretation of the phrase "particular political arrangements".'

'I speak as a lawyer too,' Jinnah shot back in his heavily accented English, heartily reciprocating the mutual dislike. 'Every state has the right to choose,' he insisted, 'to either join India or Pakistan, or remain free. And CP has made his state's position quite clear. In fact,' Jinnah pressed on, 'Travancore has even appointed its representative in Pakistan.'

'How extraordinary!' Nehru huffed, turning to the viceroy in dismay. 'There *is* no Pakistan as we speak. I wasn't aware envoys were now being sent off to non-existent countries.'

Turning to his chief adviser, General Hastings Lionel 'Pug' Ismay, the viceroy heaved a sigh. As if presiding over the dissolution of the empire of his great-grandmother, Queen Victoria, were not demanding enough, he was often tasked with having to officiate at meetings where grown men squabbled like schoolboys.

Exasperated, Nehru flopped back in his chair. The nation was on the brink of civil war. Punjab was in turmoil. Bengal was being torn apart. Riots. Arson. Looting. Mayhem. Food shortages. And now this!

Convinced that the princely states were being encouraged by the political department, Nehru turned next to Conrad Corfield. 'I'm told you have been burning records related to the princes and offering the Crown's police force to rulers,' Nehru snickered. 'What right does the political department have to take such unilateral action that could prove detrimental to the Government of India?' he demanded. 'My colleagues and I have not been brought into consultation at all,' he bellowed before turning to the viceroy again. 'A judicial enquiry at the highest level needs to look into this misfeasance.'

'I take strong exception to this...' remarked Corfield, glancing at Lord Mountbatten. But the viceroy said nothing to refute

Nehru's charge, leaving Corfield seething over Mountbatten's patent partiality to the Congress leader. Nevertheless, mindful of Nehru's immense capacity for speaking, Corfield harboured no desire to leave the floor open to him. 'The states have a perfectly good case to opt out of joining either India or Pakistan, and that has been made clear by His Majesty's government.'

An astute man of few words but decisive action, Sardar Patel tapped Nehru's arm, urging him to simmer down. The sixteen-hour workdays were taking a toll on all of them, and Nehru's frayed nerves had made him particularly irritable.

'This is all the result of your lobbying for the princes,' Nehru continued his tirade, pointing an accusing finger at Corfield. In Nehru's view, most princely states were backward, feudal and autocratic; and most rulers, neither competent nor benevolent. He believed the princes had survived this long solely due to the indulgence of the British Crown that they enjoyed through the political department. 'You have been conspiring with them,' he added, 'and encouraging the sad ambitions of the maharajas to turn their kingdoms into independent countries.'

'And what if I have?' countered Corfield, wondering why Nehru was so riled up about allowing the rulers to retain their independence, when Jinnah didn't appear worried. It seemed to him that Nehru was only feigning anxiety to improve India's bargaining position with the rulers. However, as chief of the political department responsible for the princely states, he felt duty-bound to stick up for them. 'Europe has small efficient nations like Denmark and Switzerland,' he said, 'so there is no reason Travancore cannot replicate that model here.'

'That way, India will be balkanized...fractured into hundreds of pieces!' Nehru protested. 'This is...'

There was a knock on the door, followed by the entry of Eric Miéville, Lord Mountbatten's private secretary.

'My apologies for the intrusion...' said Miéville and then quickly walked across the room, whispered into the viceroy's ear and handed him a note. The viceroy's face paled as he read the message.

'The nizam of Hyderabad has issued a *firman*...' the viceroy broke the news hesitantly.

'What now...' Nehru's face clouded with worry. Head of a 21-gun-salute state, the nizam of Hyderabad was the richest and most prominent of the Indian rulers. Anything he did would undoubtedly produce a ripple effect.

'The nizam has declared that on 15 August 1947, Hyderabad too will become an independent sovereign nation,' announced the viceroy.

Jinnah suppressed a slight smile.

Liaquat Ali Khan nodded in approval.

Nehru sank back into his chair.

Patel closed his eyes in despair.

Independent India was yet to be born.

And already, every day, she was dying a thousand deaths.

❋ Rogue-Elephant Politics ❋

As the sun began to set on the most precious jewel in Britain's vast empire, it prepared to rise over the city of Delhi, casting long, early morning shadows on the grassy lawns of 1 Aurangzeb Road, the official residence of Sardar Patel, where an animated discussion was already underway.

Patel, pragmatic veteran of the freedom struggle and devoted disciple of Gandhi, had been appointed as minister of the new States Department and entrusted with solving the challenge of the princely states. To bring in, within a mere six weeks, about 565 kingdoms into the new Indian dominion –

some of them larger than England; others too small to be easily located on a map – a task the likes of which had never been attempted anywhere else before. But even before he could saddle up his horse and take charge of the reins, the ground had started shifting beneath their feet with Travancore and Hyderabad declaring their independence.

'CP has already applied to the United Nations to accept Travancore as a member,' K.M. Panikkar, the suave diwan of Bikaner, informed the motley group seated on cane chairs around the coffee table in the garden. 'I believe he has also appointed a trade agent in Pakistan, and sought recognition from America and Britain.'

'Tell me...' said Sardar calmly, resting his elbow on the armrest, 'is this the maharaja's own decision?' In his trademark khadi kurta and dhoti, hand-spun by Maniben, his daughter, seventy-two-year-old Sardar Patel knew he needed to tackle the Travancore situation head-on and looked to men like Panikkar for their wise counsel. Like CP, Panikkar too was the prime minister of a princely state. But, unlike CP, Panikkar's loyalty to the Congress and the nationalists was undisputed. He had been canvassing for closer relations between the princes and the Congress, and as a Travancorean, he had an intimate understanding of events in his home state.

'Maharaja Chithira Thirunal is young, and controlled by his mother and the diwan,' Panikkar explained. 'The maharaja comes across as diffident and shy,' he lamented, 'perhaps because he is a mild-mannered and pleasant young man, very much like his introverted father. His masterful mother is all-powerful, and CP even more so. They have placed the maharaja's father under house arrest, claiming that he is of unsound mind. The son is wholly in the iron grip of the maharani and the diwan.'

'I see...' Sardar nodded, making a mental note that it was the diwan he needed to woo in the southern state, rather than the maharaja.

'Sardar, this has encouraged other princes who are dreaming of establishing a third force, a union of princely states,' said K.M. Munshi, the Bombay-based lawyer and trusted Congressman in Sardar's inner circle. 'They are inspired by the wizard of Travancore.'

'This kind of rogue-elephant politics makes my blood boil,' Panikkar exploded, referring to CP's sensational announcement. 'The people of Travancore will give a fitting reply at the right time to save the state and the maharaja from the stewardship of the *Sachivottama*,' Panikkar declared, folding his hands in mock reverence to the title 'Supreme Counsellor' that the maharaja had bestowed upon CP.

Sardar clicked his tongue and was about to say something, but Panikkar had not finished, 'The man is a practised acrobat! Depending on the direction of the wind, he will somersault to suit his agenda. I am prepared'—he stood up abruptly—'to resign from my my position as diwan in Bikaner and return to Travancore. I will join the State Congress in Travancore.' Panikkar continued to ramble and grumble as he paced the lawn. 'I will put up a fight. I will expose CP and resist him.'

'CP's attitude is most disturbing,' interposed T.M. Varghese, in charge of Congress propaganda in Travancore. 'A few days ago, CP called for a press conference in Trivandrum and insulted all the Indian leaders,' he updated Sardar and the others at the meeting, about the shrill media battle underway in Travancore with the eloquent and masterful CP engaging the Congress in a war of words. 'We have to work towards setting up a popular government in the state. If needed, CP must be removed by force.'

'Have you seen CP's onslaught against me in the Malayalam press?' Panikkar spat, when Varghese paused for breath. 'And for what?' he demanded rhetorically, spreading out his hands. 'For exposing his misdeeds? Do you know what they call him in Travancore? An adopted son of the British,' he ended on a note of withering scorn.

Panikkar then weighed in with a blistering attack on how CP and his administration had gagged newspapers and crushed media liberties in Travancore.

'It is not just you,' remarked V.P. Menon, the viceroy's constitutional adviser, slated to take over soon as secretary to the States Department under Sardar Patel, 'CP spares nobody. Ayyangar, Ambedkar – everyone who opposes him has had to face his wrath.'

'What's that slogan he raises?' Panikkar sneered. 'Travancore for Travancoreans! Bah! Perhaps he needs to be reminded that he is not a Travancorean himself.'

Panikkar was miffed, much like many other Travancoreans who resented Tamil domination in their state. CP, a Tamil Brahmin who had at one time been the most illustrious lawyer of the Madras High Court, had eclipsed all other voices and stood alone now as the maharaja's close confidant and trusted lieutenant.

'The truth is the creation of Pakistan is not as much of a damaging blow to India's prestige or influence,' mused R.K. Shanmukham Chetty, former diwan of Cochin, who had been a quiet listener thus far. The raja of Cochin had taken a progressive and cooperative stand of joining India, making its neighbour Travancore stick out like a sore thumb. 'The real danger to our unity is the attitude of the princely states. If the others follow Travancore's example, it would usher in the balkanization of India, and the country will be splintered into smaller nation states. It is truly ironical that CP, a champion of nationalism, should now ally with Jinnah.'

Sardar listened patiently. They were all consumed by the same fear: if Travancore were allowed to have its way and others followed its example, India could be fragmented into several pieces.

'Well...Hyderabad has already followed Travancore to the party,' scoffed Panikkar.

'Goondas armed with lathis and knives roam the streets of Travancore, wrecking public meetings,' said Pattom T. Thanu Pillai, president of the Travancore State Congress. 'They parade around the streets, harassing Congress workers. The police support them. There is utter chaos in the state.'

'I must...I must give up my post in Bikaner...' Panikkar muttered. 'I must go to Travancore.' He clenched his fists, outraged at Travancore's intransigence.

'You will do no such thing,' said Sardar emphatically, tossing one end of his shawl over his shoulder as he rose from the wicker chair. Teetering on the edge of peril, there would be some princes who would not hesitate to stab the nation in the back... He was prepared for that blow. 'I will do whatever needs to be done...I will handle this. As long as the Congress continues to have a foothold there,' he declared, 'there is no question of Travancore's independence.'

❋ The Travancorean Trio ❋

'The millionaire Seth Dalmia has deposited five lakh rupees into the Travancore State Congress fund,' a visibly edgy CP informed his maharaja, who sat leaning against plump bolsters on a silken mattress. 'No prizes for guessing what that means.'

The diwan was at the magnificent Kowdiar Palace for his daily briefing with the maharaja. The spectacular three-storeyed palace, with its rising steeples and over a hundred rooms, topped with the quintessential Kerala-style gabled roof, had been built by Maharaja Chithira Thirunal as his official residence for his sister's wedding a decade ago. His mother, Maharani Sethu Parvathi Bayi, in her off-white saree and high-necked blouse, long, dangling gold necklaces bedecking her throat, sat beside the maharaja.

THE CONFIDENT KING-MOTHER

'Seth Dalmia?' the maharaja enquired, turning to his mother. 'The owner of the cement businesses and airlines?'

THE YOUNG MAHARAJA

'Hmm...I'm sure it's all Sardar Patel's doing,' grumbled Sethu Parvathi Bayi, cracking a betel nut with her silver nutcracker. A uniformed attendant in a red turban stepped forward and bowed low. She waved him away. The 'Junior Maharani', as she was known, was no ordinary King-Mother. After the throne had passed to Chithira Thirunal at the age of twelve from his uncle, Sethu Parvathi Bayi's elder cousin – Sethu Lakshmi Bayi – had been appointed as regent to rule on behalf of the young monarch until he came

THE RESOURCEFUL DIWAN

of age. But even before the regency was due to terminate, Parvathi Bayi had wrested power from her cousin, with CP's intelligence and resourcefulness, establishing herself firmly in a position of control over the docile maharaja.

'This means more trouble,' said CP, glancing at Sethu Parvathi Bayi. 'The Congress is strong and well organized at the grassroots. The money will be used for organizing agitations by its supporters. There will be chaos.'

'Let them try...' the maharani said through gritted teeth, 'we will give them a fitting answer.'

'They've already gone all out to malign me in the press,' the diwan exclaimed, handing a sheaf of newspaper cuttings in a folder to the maharaja. 'Just look at this nonsense!'

The maharaja leaned forward and took the folder from his diwan. He winced at the crude remarks and unflattering caricatures. The reports were full of mud-slinging and name-calling. He pushed the folder away in disgust.

'They are making a mockery of us,' the diwan shook his head.

'Tell me – the people...are they really against us?' the maharaja asked, his gentle features furrowed with worry. His gold earrings glinted in the soft sunlight filtering in through the wooden window slats. Travancore had been the first state to proclaim equality in temple-entry rules, allowing people of all castes into temples. It had been a revolutionary change, eliciting praise from Mahatma Gandhi himself. Education, industrialization, food security, irrigation, reform – his kingdom had spearheaded progress in almost every field. Revenue in the state had quadrupled during his reign. 'Surely,' the maharaja voiced his thoughts, 'the people realize we have done so much for their welfare.'

'It is no doubt disconcerting,' reflected the diwan, marvelling at the fickle nature of public memory. He had been a brave and dynamic administrator for nearly ten years. All the good they had done for the state had been forgotten, erased, wiped out – drowned out in the aggressive and noisy propaganda drummed up by the Congress mouthpieces. 'I would advise Your Highness to reconsider your stand about holding out,' he said. 'I must warn you that you are treading on quicksand.'

'Does nobody support my decision?' asked the maharaja, genuinely perplexed.

'Well...Mr Jinnah supports us,' the diwan shrugged. 'We have also received a letter of support from Mr Savarkar of the Hindu Mahasabha. The nawab of Bhopal and the nizam of Hyderabad – they are holding out as well.'

'Travancore doesn't belong to the people, nor to us, to simply hand it over to Mr Patel on a platter,' pointed out Sethu Parvathi Bayi, her face taking on a mutinous look. 'Travancore belongs to Sree Padmanabhaswamy.' She raised her reverently folded hands above her face. Maharaja Marthanda Varma, who had ruled Travancore nearly 200 years ago, had surrendered the kingdom to Lord Padmanabhaswamy, the titular deity of the royal family. To Sethu Parvathi Bayi there was no question at all about handing over their sacred kingdom to India.

'Precisely,' agreed the maharaja, following his mother's lead. 'I am only the Padmanabha-*dasa*, a servant, a humble custodian, who

Two features made Travancore unique amongst the princely states. Firstly, as was the custom in the region, kingship was passed on matrilineally from uncle to nephew, and not patrilineally from father to son. So, a ruler's heir was his sister's son, and not his own child. Secondly, Lord Padmanabhaswamy was regarded as the head of the kingdom and the maharaja considered himself to be a trustee, ruling on behalf of the deity.

governs the state in the name of the Lord. How can I hand over something that is not mine?'

'I've been hearing about an economic boycott by India if we don't accede,' the diwan informed the maharaja in a sombre voice, his approach practical and realistic as always. 'India is threatening to stop all supplies to us. A trade embargo will affect us badly.'

'Make alternative arrangements, then!' snapped the maharani, tucking her long, fragrant tresses behind her ears as she rose to walk to the window.

'India may cut off supplies of steel and cement to us...' said the diwan. 'I am trying to arrange a trade agreement with Pakistan and England to take care of that. I am leaving for Delhi tomorrow to meet the viceroy. I will take it up with him.'

'Very well, then,' the maharani said, throwing open the window's shutters and inhaling the soft scent of the earth released by the pre-monsoon showers, 'our decision remains unchanged. Travancore will soon be an independent nation.'

❋ Friend of the Friendless ❋

Sardar Patel waited at his desk as Shankar, his personal secretary, tried to put the telephone call through.

After much coaxing and cajoling, CP had agreed to come to Delhi to meet the viceroy, and Sardar was keen to mend fissures and build bridges. Much water had flowed under the bridge since the time CP had been a Congress member and an ardent nationalist. They now inhabited worlds that were poles apart. Sardar owed his allegiance to democracy; CP had bent the knee to monarchy.

The call came through. Shankar handed Sardar the receiver and sat down by his side, as he often did on important calls, leaning into the earpiece to assist Sardar, who was slightly hard of hearing.

'I believe you are expected in Delhi to meet the viceroy,' said Patel after exchanging pleasantries with CP. 'I will be pleased if we could have a short meeting.'

'Hmm...' CP sounded cold and non-committal.

'It is in my nature to be a friend of the friendless,' Patel remarked, pressing the telephone to his ear. 'You have become one by choice. I will be glad if you can come and have lunch with me tomorrow at 1 p.m. What do you say?'

CP mulled over the backhanded courtesy. A man of the arts as much as one of politics and law, CP revelled in the realm of literature. For someone who quoted Shakespeare and Wordsworth as effortlessly as he recited verses from the Upanishads and Vedas, not a single word was employed without intent. He would not let the seemingly gracious barb pass without a rebuttal.

'I appreciate your invitation,' replied CP after a deliberate pause, 'and the kind thought underpinning it, but it so happens that the friendless person you refer to,' he enunciated each word slowly, 'has an engagement with someone else for lunch tomorrow.'

'Ah, I see...' mumbled Sardar.

'Therefore, I'm afraid he cannot avail of your friendly and generous invitation,' CP continued speaking of himself in the third person to roughen the blow.

Sardar suppressed a wry smile. In the three decades he had spent in public life, he had come across people of all shades. From vainglorious princes to cantankerous officials, earnest nationalists to desperate despots, morally bankrupt sycophants...to even bumbling fools. But seldom had he clashed with a man of CP's stature and chutzpah.

'But since you've reached out,' continued CP, 'may I take this opportunity to remind you that Travancore is nominally ruled by the maharaja, as a trustee of the Lord. The real ruler, as you know, is Sree Padmanabhaswamy. And surely you understand that the Lord cannot be compelled to negotiate a treaty submitting to India.'

'Is that so?' scoffed Sardar, unimpressed by the argument. 'Then please tell me how Lord Padmanabha could negotiate a treaty with the British and become subservient to them!'

It was CP's turn to retreat to the back foot. 'Anyway...' he sighed, feigning regret, 'let me thank you once again for your extremely kind act of friendliness. Let's hope for better luck next time.' He disconnected the call.

Sardar exhaled heavily and handed the receiver back to a bewildered Shankar. Few men had the audacity to snub Patel. In Sir Chetpat Pattabhirama Ramaswami Aiyar, Sardar Patel had met his match.

❋ Iron Fist in Velvet Glove ❋

'We have everything a nation needs: A strong economy. Exportable products. A highly literate population. A long coastline with our own ports. An established trade link with the world. Joining India would mean surrendering our huge revenue from customs and import duties to Delhi. We will be reduced to a fifth-grade state.' CP drowned V.P. Menon in a deluge of words as he picked at sliced fruit with a silver fork as they sat face to face at the well-appointed breakfast table in the tea room at Travancore House in Delhi.

V.P. Menon, secretary to the States Department – or the velvet glove on Sardar's iron fist, as some would call him – nodded, playing along as he dabbed his lips with a napkin, glad to have managed to squeeze in a quick meeting with the diwan of Travancore before his luncheon with the viceroy.

'India asks you to accede with respect to three aspects alone, sir,' Menon clarified. 'Defence, external affairs and communications – that's all. We do not seek to interfere in the other affairs of the states.'

'Hmm...I see...' CP took a sip of his coffee, before pushing his cup away in disgust. The coffee in Delhi tasted nothing like the freshly ground filter brew in his home in Madras. He gulped down some water to wash away the unpleasant aftertaste.

'On 15 August, when the princely states reclaim their sovereignty, they will be literally released from the Centre, with no contact either with the Centre or with each other,' Menon presented the picture of things to come. 'This is a dangerous position, sir. Transitions are always risky,' Menon continued, trying to draw CP into a mind game, 'and if we do nothing to secure the situation, there will be complete chaos.'

'My dear Menon,' CP replied, 'you may recall that a few years ago, Mr Nehru said he recognized no treaties between the Crown and the states. He said anybody speaking of treaties is either a lunatic, a knave or a fool! And you want me to put my faith in an administration headed by him?'

'Sir, unless safeguards are put in place,' Menon argued, drawing his chair closer to broach an angle he knew would appeal to CP. 'There is a great danger of undesirable elements rearing their heads...you know what I mean,' Menon whispered conspiratorially. 'If you wish to counter the communist threat, joining forces with the Congress is your best course of action.'

CP cocked his head. It was no secret that he detested communists. A year ago, his administration had come down heavily on a communist uprising in Vayalar, drawing ire in the press, which had alleged that the state police had killed over a thousand people. Communist ideology, he had made clear, had no place in Travancore.

'Well, Mr Menon, you say that joining hands with the Congress will help us keep the communists at bay,' CP said, buttering his toast, 'but I hear Nehru's sister, Vijaya Lakshmi Pandit, has been appointed ambassador to Moscow.'

'I...I beg your pardon?' Menon looked puzzled, unsure how that had anything to do with anything.

'The maharaja has the overwhelming support of his people, a highly educated populace in South Asia,' CP replied stridently. 'They cannot be coerced to join a dominion whose leaders have diplomatic relations with communist powers like the Soviet Republic. For all we know, there will soon be Russian embassies mushrooming all over India.'

'Sir, now you are letting your imagination—' Menon began, scratching his receding hairline while he made a mental note of CP's dramatic reaction. Clearly, this was what the diwan feared most. He would have to press the viceroy to exploit this fear.

'Imagination?' CP cut him off. 'Don't you know the main centres of communist influence in India are within 50 miles of Travancore?'

'And a strong, united Centre will help you fight it,' Menon countered. 'Joining forces with India will make you stronger.'

CP put down his knife and fork. His disagreement with Gandhi and distrust of Nehru were both common knowledge. The Congress party, in his view, was an accident waiting to happen.

'Look, sir,' said Menon in a conciliatory tone, 'among all the politicians in the country, there is no one I respect more than you. It ought not to be said of you that at India's most critical hour, you did not make your contribution towards building the nation when it was within your power to do so.'

Crafty and cheeky, thought CP, smiling slightly. Menon had tried reasoning, then played to his fears and followed it up with unabashed flattery. He was impressed. 'I'll think it over...' he replied, leaning back. Despite his differences with Sardar, CP found himself admiring the states minister and his squad. Victory is surely within reach for a captain who chooses his team wisely, he thought to himself; and Sardar, it seemed, had taken great care in selecting his partners - Menon, the self-effacing bureaucrat sitting before him at the breakfast table, and Lord Mountbatten, the pomp-and-pageantry-loving viceroy, whom he was due to meet next.

❋ A Secret Agenda ❋

The large French windows in Viceroy Mountbatten's study overlooked the splendid Mughal Gardens and made for a spectacular setting. Nevertheless, hardly anyone who stepped into the stately green room in the last days of the British Raj had the time or the inclination to enjoy the stunning view.

Among the many tense and harrowed visitors to the viceroy that summer was John Wilmot, minister of supply for the Labour government in London, entrusted with delivering a top-level secret message to the viceroy.

'On the Travancore issue'—Wilmot got directly to the point, dabbing at the perspiration on his forehead with a handkerchief—'His Majesty's government wishes that you do not commit anything.'

'What do you mean?' The viceroy was intrigued. The diwan of Travancore had travelled all the way to Delhi to meet him and they were to have lunch shortly, over which he intended to cajole CP into joining India. His private secretary, Abell, had just handed him a note from V.P. Menon, with tips on how to approach the matter. These instructions from London were both sudden and befuddling.

'Let me explain,' Wilmot said, taking off his coat. 'The richest known deposits of monazite sand are in Travancore. As you know, monazite sand is a source of thorium. And thorium is a nuclear fuel, for atomic energy...likely to be as significant as uranium.'

Lord Mountbatten raised his eyebrows. When he had agreed to his appointment as viceroy, he knew he had taken on a very thorny job. With Britain's economy in a shambles, Prime Minister Attlee had announced Britain's withdrawal from India by 1948. But, with the Congress and Muslim League perpetually at loggerheads, working out the modalities of the transfer of power had turned out to be a formidable challenge. And yet, nobody had warned him of the most complex problem of all – the knotty tangle of the princely states. And even as he tried to unravel the snarls one at a time, they seemed intent on getting into a matted mess of petty politics all over again.

'Germany has had a monopoly on Travancore's thorium supplies for many years,' Wilmot went on, 'and we have been buying thorium from the Germans at several times their buying price. We have finally made a breakthrough and signed an agreement with Travancore for thorium. We don't want that to be jeopardized.'

Viceroy Mountbatten leaned forward to rest his elbows on the desk and cupped his chin. Although she was withdrawing from India, Britain wanted to retain her influence in the subcontinent as it was strategically important – both in countering Russia and to secure her own future interests. He pursed his lips, recalling the promise he had made to Patel to help resolve the issue of the princely states. This was going to be a tightrope walk!

'And as per the terms,' Wilmot went on, 'Travancore can cancel the agreement in case of a change in Britain's policy. The secretary of state for India fears that they might actually do so if we fail to support them in their quest for independence. Travancore requires careful handling.'

The memory of the day he had taken over as viceroy suddenly flashed back to Lord Mountbatten. On that day, his predecessor Lord Wavell had handed him a file on the transfer of power which he had codenamed 'Operation Madhouse'. Mountbatten was now beginning to see why. 'So...do you want me to support Travancore's stand to remain independent?' he asked, leaning back in his chair.

'Avoid making any statement that gives either Travancore or India any leverage,' advised Wilmot, handing the viceroy the secret memorandum from their India Office in London. 'Be neutral. Be evasive. Let the tide run its course.'

Mountbatten glanced through the memorandum and handed it to Hastings Ismay. 'Secret and Confidential', he scribbled across it, wondering how he ought to deal with CP now, given this new angle to the tangle.

'I may as well add,' said Wilmot, leaving no room for doubt as he rose to leave, 'that it would be to Britain's advantage if Travancore remained independent.'

❋ In the Shadows ❋

As the viceroy prepared to meet CP in Delhi, the kingdom of Travancore prepared for the birth centenary celebrations of Swathi Thirunal, one of their most glorious kings. As huge crowds arrived at the Trivandrum railway station, three burly shadows lurked in the dimly lit corridor of GBR Boarding and Lodging nearby – three men on a deadly mission.

'Here's the money for your rent,' said Velayudhan Nair, thrusting some soggy, rain-soaked notes into the hands of the portly K.C.S. Mani, who had journeyed over a hundred miles from Ernakulam for the special task.

'And here's the payment for the job,' whispered Chellappan Pillai, counting out some more money before handing it to the hitman. 'CP will be back from Delhi tomorrow morning. Don't mess it up this time.'

Mani swallowed hard. After the unsuccessful attempt at the Victoria Jubilee Town Hall, he was determined not to fail this time. Having completed a thorough reconnaissance of the location, he was certain the plan was foolproof.

'Do you have what you need?' asked Nair, as a railway engine tooted in the distance.

Mani nodded, pointing to the large, curved knife in his bag as he looked over his shoulder. Sometimes, he was filled with confidence; at other times, with a deep sense of foreboding.

'Here, keep this carefully...' Pillai handed Mani a small rectangular slip of paper. 'It's the music academy pass for tomorrow,' Pillai whispered. 'I managed to get it from a student.'

Mani slipped it into the pocket of his khadi *jubba*.

'Remember, the place will be heavily guarded,' Pillai reminded Mani as he turned to leave. 'Stick to the plan. Finish him off!'

❋ The End of Me ❋

Miles away from the plot to assassinate him, CP placed a copy of the *Bharat Jyoti* newspaper on the viceroy's desk. 'May I draw Your Excellency's attention to this outrageous and perverse piece...' he said. 'A part of the continuous, scurrilous attack on me by the Congress-influenced press.'

The viceroy suppressed a smile as he glanced cursorily at the cartoon before him, depicting CP being spanked by him like a naughty schoolboy for demanding independence for Travancore. The Malayalam press, it seemed, was having a field day, humiliating the diwan of Travancore as payback for his excesses against them over the years.

'The Congress-supported agitation has not abated despite your assurances,' said CP, turning to the folder he had placed upon the table. 'Here...' he said as he extracted a newspaper clipping, 'they speak of Travancore being put in its proper place...and here, Nehru's speech of 1 July,' CP pulled out another article. 'He says states cannot be allowed to be independent, that the Congress will not recognize the independence of any state in India... What does this mean?'

CP was beside himself with rage. 'The Cabinet Mission Plan and His Majesty's government have assured us that paramountcy will revert to the states after 15 August, and that the states can choose to remain independent. Our decisions and actions are perfectly legitimate. It is the Congress that is indulging in unconstitutional means to grab the princely kingdoms.'

The viceroy glanced at the articles laid out on the table.

'And here...' CP whipped out one more clipping, this time a cutting from the *Hindustan Times*. 'What is all this talk of unpatriotic princes, I ask. This paper is a mere mouthpiece for Sardar Patel—'

'On that note,' the viceroy cut in, 'I wish you could meet Sardar Patel to discuss your grievances. I can tell you that Patel is a complete realist. If you could discuss these matters, the whole situation may be changed.'

'No...I do not wish to see him,' CP replied firmly. 'There is a fundamental difference in my outlook and theirs. I do not see eye to eye with Gandhi or his so-called disciples,' he said, making a derisive reference to Patel and Nehru. 'And I have no faith in the Congress treating its opponents fairly or equitably. In fact, this whole business of accession is being steamrolled by the central leaders.'

'But, Sir Ramaswami, you have always insisted on a strong Centre all these years when the federal structure of government was under consideration...'

'Undoubtedly...but that was when India was to be one country. That is no longer so. India is going to be divided. And besides,' CP said, leaning forward, 'a state like Travancore must keep its commerce and foreign-trade position intact. Our state lives by customs earned through import and export. Without it, Travancore would be nowhere.'

'That is precisely why you need to work out at least some sort of a working relationship, even if it's a loose one, with the Indian government,' the viceroy replied, Wilmot's instructions to stay evasive and neutral ringing in his ears. 'You are linked with them geographically whether you like it or not.'

'Yes, I understand that,' CP responded. 'I grant that certain flexible relationships would need to be established with India for that reason. I met Menon earlier today and he has explained that India seeks accession on the three subjects of defence, external affairs and communications. If there is a possibility of coming up with a formula by which these can be worked in alongside the internal independence of the state...maybe a treaty of some kind...then I can take it to the maharaja.'

'I hear you have deployed a trade agent in Pakistan?'

'Yes, we have,' CP nodded, 'and we plan to send out trade agents and representatives not only to India and Pakistan, but to all the countries in the world.'

'As you know, I have called all the states for a conference on 25 July. I hope to lay out the terms before all the rulers and have a discussion on—'

'Travancore will not attend this summit,' cut in CP tersely. 'As we have decided not to join India, there is little point in it.'

'Look...you spoke of a special treaty,' the viceroy pointed out. 'Let me tell you, the other states will not like Travancore being treated differently. So it would be unrealistic to expect a special treaty or agreement in place of accession. I request you to take this to the maharaja. I am told he will ratify anything you decide.'

'That is not so,' CP protested, affronted by the viceroy's remark. He abhorred their perception of the maharaja as an obedient boy following his mother and diwan submissively, making CP out to be a ruthless puppeteer. 'His Highness confides in me, but the decision will be his own,' CP stated to clear any misconceptions. 'All policies and actions formulated by me are the result of close and daily consultation with His Highness, who is highly educated and cognizant of public affairs. He is the sovereign; I am merely his diwan.'

'Nehru and Patel tell me that there are serious differences of opinion between you and your maharaja,' parried Lord Mountbatten, 'and that he may well ask you to resign shortly...'

'Hah...won't Sardar like that!' CP scoffed. 'Well...perhaps you can point out to Sardar that were I to resign at this moment, the very thing he wants to avoid will surely happen. The hub of communist activity, which he fears so greatly, is not far from Trivandrum. And if I am gone, they will sweep across the region.'

Elbows on the table, Viceroy Mountbatten laced his fingers thoughtfully.

'And let me also remind Sardar,' CP went on, 'that I did resign of my own accord a year ago. I returned to my post only at the maharaja's behest.'

'I take it you are aware that Seth Dalmia has pumped in about five lakh rupees into the Travancore State Congress to start some sort of a subversive agitation there after 15 August, and I am sure there is more to follow,' the viceroy pointed out, 'perhaps to overrun the administration.'

'Well, if the Congress can spend five lakhs,' CP mounted a spirited defence, 'the government of Travancore is more than capable and prepared to counter this. Do convey this, along with my warmest regards, to Sardar Patel and Pandit Nehru.'

The viceroy sighed. If Nehru was a master of words and Sardar a man of steel, C.P. Ramaswami was a bit of both.

'The bullet may make an end of me...' CP stood up to leave, his words heavy with prophetic undertones as a clap of thunder rumbled across the skies. 'And perhaps the Congress thinks that will solve the whole problem, but let me make it very clear,' he added, undaunted by rumours of threats to his life, 'the Congress will not get the result they want by eliminating me.'

❋ Blood on His Hands ❋

'It is my privilege to stand before you on this special occasion,' CP began his speech on a flower-festooned stage, addressing a packed gathering at the Music Academy Hall in Trivandrum after his return from Delhi. 'Sree Swathi Thirunal was one of Travancore's greatest sons, and as a devoted and lifelong *shishya* of Carnatic music, I say with confidence that few composers have surpassed him.'

Raja Ravi Varma, the famous artist, was born into the Travancore royal family in the late nineteenth century and was the grandfather of Sethu Parvathi Bayi. Swathi Thirunal, the illustrious early-nineteenth-century music composer, is another famous name from the dynasty. Continuing the rich tradition, Aswathi Thirunal Rama Varma, a great-grandson of the last maharaja, is a reputed contemporary Indian classical musician.

Maharaja Chithira Thirunal nodded at CP in agreement. Resplendent in a fine silk tunic and turban, he was seated in a gilded, throne-like seat behind the diwan. A musician-king, Swathi Thirunal was indeed one of the finest composers of all time, one among the many great artistes the royal family of Travancore had produced.

'Maharaja Swathi Thirunal had a troublesome and uneasy relationship with the British.' CP said, casually tossing his *angavastram* to drape it over his shoulder. 'And it is only befitting that his centenary celebrations coincide with the end of British paramountcy when we are about to usher in a new era of a sovereign and independent Travancore.'

The auditorium erupted into rapturous applause. *Rasikas*, royals, musicians, officials, special guests, students, all rose as one to give CP a standing ovation, as Semmangudi Srinivasa Iyer, one of the finest singers of the day, came on to the stage, bowing to the royals before he began his performance.

The maharaja, his mother and CP descended from the stage and took their seats in the front row. Semmangudi began his *alapana*. Down the passageway, Mani took up his position behind a cylindrical pillar.

As the audience swooned over Semmangudi's masterful musical rendition, CP closed his eyes in bliss, little knowing that death lurked in the shadows.

Mani rested his hand reassuringly on the weapon tucked into the khaki shorts under his *mundu*, waiting to strike.

Semmangudi finished the *charanam*. The audience applauded heartily. The maestro bowed and thanked his enthralled listeners.

Taking leave of the maharaja and his mother, CP rose from his seat. His secretary, Chidambaram, stood up to follow him. The inspector general of police jumped to attention, insisting on escorting the diwan to his car.

Behind them, the Alathur Brothers – Srinivasa Iyer and Sivasubramania Iyer – came on to the stage to perform next. Pleasantries were exchanged between the artistes. The mridangist began tuning his instrument. The violinist cracked a joke. They all laughed.

The inspector general, who was escorting CP, paused at the end of the aisle to speak to an acquaintance at the door.

CP reached his car and just as he was about to get in, a thickset youth, brandishing a pointed hooked knife, blocked his path and shoved the diwan to the ground. Chidambaram stood by, paralysed with fear.

Pinning the diwan down with his left arm, Mani slashed at his torso with his weapon. With remarkable agility and presence of mind, the diwan twisted to his left, the first blow lacerating his fingers. Mani retracted the dagger to strike again, this time gripping the diwan's throat.

The lights went out. The street was plunged in darkness.

'Help!' rasped CP, struggling for breath.

'Police...torch...help!' Chidambaram gasped from somewhere behind him.

'HELP!' RASPED CP.

CP tried to wriggle free of Mani's grasp, instinctively twisting away each time the weapon came down. Its sharp edge grazed the bridge of his nose and cheek. He let out a howl of pain. The mridangam and violin swallowed his screams.

Mani struck again. And again. And again.

CP gasped and then slumped to the ground.

Shuffling footsteps. Cries. People. Voices. Police. Stretcher. Doctors. Hospital.

A blur.

❋ Death or Democracy ❋

As dark rain-bearing clouds threatened to burst over the emerald kingdom - a picturesque domain dotted with windswept coconut groves and paddy fields - Bhaktivilas was abuzz with activity. Doctors and nurses bustled about carrying trays of medicine and bandages. Attendants tiptoed in and out with food and drink. Well-wishers dropped by, bearing fruits and making enquiries. Officials and bureaucrats waited in the corridors, clutching files and paperwork.

'My staff cannot but marvel at the way you braved the surgery without anaesthesia,' said Dr Keshavan, smiling as he changed the diwan's dressing. 'How fortunate that you had the *angavastram* around your neck, but for which the dagger would have sliced through the jugular vein.'

CP lay back and closed his eyes. Talk of all kinds of conspiracies had been doing the rounds along with rumours of the involvement of high-ranking officials: Congress party workers, the electricity department and even the police. Questions whirled in his mind. Mere seconds before the attack, why had the inspector general stopped short of escorting him all the way to the car? Why had there been a power outage just at that moment? The lights had come back on immediately after the assailant's escape. How had the killer managed to flee from right under the nose of the police force? Answers were hard to come by, but the good news was that, despite his age, CP had managed to thwart his assassin.

BHAKTIVILAS: HOME BECOMES OFFICE

'Fortunately, no bones or cartilage were damaged,' said the doctor as he finished his examination. 'The flesh wounds will heal soon.'

'Thank you for all you have done for me, doctor'—CP sat up to begin work. The bedroom in Bhaktivilas had been temporarily converted into his makeshift office and all senior government staff reported to him there.

Krishnamurthi, the maharaja's private secretary, who had been waiting in the anteroom, entered with a basket of dry fruits and healing herbs. 'His Highness and the maharani are worried about you,' he said, pulling up a chair beside CP's bed.

'I must convey my thoughts to the maharaja and maharani immediately,' CP told Krishnamurthi, propping himself up by his elbows, recalling his discussion with the viceroy.

Meanwhile, the viceroy had agreed to negotiate for certain concessions for Travancore. 'My formal letter of advice will come later, but first tell the maharaja,' CP drew in a breath, 'that I reiterate what I told him after my return from Delhi. It is either accession or independence – there is no middle ground. No special treaty. No face-saving formula.'

Krishnamurthi nodded, pulled out his pen and began jotting down CP's every word.

'It was clear from my talk with the viceroy,' CP went on, 'that if we give way, we will get some advantages just like the other states. But if we do not comply, it will be a hard battle. I would go so far as to say civil war may break out within the next six months, and I am willing to bet that the Congress leaders will be gone by the end of the year.'

Still reeling from the impact of the blow at the back of the skull, CP paused to sip water with his attendant's help. He opened his mouth, then winced – the stab injury behind his lower palate made eating and drinking painful. 'We can hope for some assistance from Mr Jinnah in case of trouble,' he continued, scrutinizing his bandaged fingers. 'Those who survive the terrible confrontation that is in the offing will emerge as rulers, but there is great risk of a threat to life and property... And whatever we decide, we will need to inform the nawab of Bhopal and the nizam of Hyderabad.'

A bearer entered with coconut water for the diwan and fruit juice for his visitor. As the attendant held the glass to CP's lips, Krishnamurthi continued to scribble in his notepad, taken aback by the diwan's remarks. CP had always been a great advocate of India's unity, vociferously opposing Jinnah's 'two-nation theory'. However, suddenly now, Jinnah, the nawab and the nizam – all of whom had set their faces against a united India – appeared to have become confidants and allies.

'It is either death or victory,' CP said prophetically. 'The events of the last few days have made me realize that the maharaja's life is also in jeopardy, as well as the lives of those near and dear to him. If the maharaja feels that his people are not ready for battle or they are not worth fighting for, compromise is inevitable.'

Flopping back on the pillow, CP looked out through the window at the ominous, overcast skies. The weather seemed to reflect his sombre mood.

'Tell the maharaja'—he sighed deeply—'that accession to India is his only option.'

❋ In with India ❋

As his diwan lay recuperating at Bhaktivilas, Maharaja Chithira Thirunal Rama Varma fiddled with his fountain pen at the desk, casting another glance at the two letters before him. One had been sent by the viceroy, allaying their fears and promising no interference from the Government of India in Travancore's customs, tariffs and taxes or its internal jurisdiction. The other was from his diwan, writing to him from his sickbed, advising him to take the plunge.

Standing beside him, her face solemn and grim, Maharani Sethu Parvathi Bayi nodded slightly.

The maharaja took a deep breath and brought nib down to paper. He paused. The bruised face of his diwan, a father figure, appeared before his eyes. That a man as powerful and protected as CP had been attacked sent a chill down his spine. He gripped the pen tightly, said a silent prayer and began writing to the viceroy.

> *Your Excellency's letter of the 22nd July has been handed over to me by Sir C.P. Ramaswami Aiyar.* He has also *told me of the discussions he has had with Your Excellency ... Having regard to the assurances conveyed by Your Excellency, I have decided, though not without hesitation, to take this step of accession to*

the Dominion of India subject to the conditions adverted to in your letter.

Putting down the pen, the maharaja gazed at the tall palace spires framed by the window. They appeared to reach for the skies through the gabled roof. Would the Lord approve, Chithira Thirunal wondered, weighed down by the enormous legacy he carried. *Would his glorious ancestors approve*?

Maharani Sethu Parvathi Bayi placed her hand on her son's shoulder; their dream of a sovereign Travancore was perhaps not meant to be. They looked on, mother and son, watching the monsoon clouds loom large over their beautiful land, a land that generations to come would call 'God's own country'.

♦♦♦♦♦♦♦♦♦♦♦♦♦♦♦♦♦♦♦

Postscript

♦♦♦♦♦♦♦♦♦♦♦♦♦♦♦♦♦♦♦

On 19 August 1947, C.P. Ramaswami Aiyar stepped down as diwan after holding the reins of power in Travancore for twelve long years. Soon thereafter, Maharaja Chithira Thirunal announced a fresh constitution and, in 1948, a popularly elected government came to power in which several Travancore State Congress workers earlier imprisoned by CP, such as Thanu Pillai and T.M. Varghese, became ministers.

CP, a man of multiple talents, had contributed greatly to Travancore – from bringing hydroelectric power to the state to industrialization and education; from ushering in social reforms like the historic, first-of-its-kind all-caste Temple Entry Proclamation, which allowed people of all castes entry into temples, to cultural activities like reviving art and music.

However, having been sidelined from politics due to the accession episode, he spent the last decades of his life pursuing literary interests and serving as vice chancellor of universities. Compelled to eat his own words, months later, he wrote to Sardar Patel, conveying his sincere felicitations and paying tribute to the leadership talents of both Nehru and Patel.

K.C.S. Mani, who had been paid sixty-five rupees to carry out the assassination, was a member of the Travancore Socialist Party. Although he went into hiding after the attack, he was eventually captured by the police. However, he was set free by the court due to lack of evidence. Years later, some hailed him as a hero and a memorial was erected in his honour in front of the Music Academy Hall for his role in making Travancore a part of India.

All assurances from Delhi granting special concessions and exemptions to Travancore, based on which the maharaja agreed to sign the Instrument of Accession, were eventually withdrawn. The maharaja was appointed the first *rajpramukh* of the state after its merger with Cochin.

Travancore was subsequently erased from the map of India and integrated into Kerala in 1956 by its merger with Cochin and British Malabar.

♦♦♦♦♦♦♦♦♦♦♦♦♦♦♦♦♦♦♦

Did It Really Happen This Way?

♦♦♦♦♦♦♦♦♦♦♦♦♦♦♦♦♦♦♦

On 11 June 1947, Travancore did announce its intent to become an independent nation and the opening scene of the chapter draws from the declaration and other speeches made by the diwan in this regard. In his book The Princes of India in the

Endgame of Empire, Ian Copland refers to large sums of money being transferred by the diwan of Travancore to the nawab of Bhopal in support of their campaign for independence.

The scene describing the explosive meeting where Nehru accuses Sir Conrad of misfeasance is drawn largely from the viceroy's record of the meeting of 13 June 1947, modified slightly with a few creative liberties. In his autobiography, Corfield mentions that Nehru later apologized to him for the outburst.

The scene in Patel's garden has been dramatized with inputs that Patel received from K.M. Panikkar, T.M. Varghese, Thanu Pillai, K.M. Munshi and others through letters and telegrams. The phone conversation between CP and Patel was actually a set of letters exchanged between the two.

Sir Conrad's role and his perspective have been drawn from his autobiography titled The Princely India I Knew.

The diwan's meetings with Menon and Mountbatten took place largely as described. The conversation about Britain's interests in monazite in Travancore is drawn from part of a letter written to the viceroy by John Wilmot from London, which can be found in The Transfer of Power 1942–7, Vol. XII.

The diwan's letter to the maharaja subsequent to the attack, advising him to accede to India, is rendered here as an oral conversation.

The details of the assassination attempt, the assailant and the actual attack on the diwan in the Music Academy Hall are all based on records describing the same. India's Bismarck by B. Krishna, Triumph and Tragedy in Travancore: Annals of Sir CP's Sixteen Years by A. Sreedhara Menon and The Ivory Throne: Chronicles of the House of Travancore by Manu S. Pillai are other sources for the events described in this chapter.

Some timelines have been compressed to maintain the pace of the narrative. Descriptions of the maharaja, the maharani, *the diwan and their relationships are drawn from historical sources. While archival records appear to suggest that the decision to remain independent was that of the maharaja and his mother, some narratives paint Diwan C.P. Ramaswami Aiyar as the one who opposed accession.*

2

Oysters at a Tea Party

THE STORY OF BHOPAL

PRINCELY STATE OF BHOPAL IN 1947:
in present-day Madhya Pradesh
AREA: 6,921 square miles (17,925 square kilometres) approx.
POPULATION: 7,85,822
RULER: Nawab Hamidullah Khan
ADVISER: Sir Muhammad Zafarullah Khan
19-gun-salute state

❋ One, Two, Three ❋

'I absolutely abhor the Congress!' Nawab Hamidullah Khan vented his frustration as the Chevrolet sliced through the thick mist, below gigantic sal trees; a convoy of cars tagged along behind them with gun-toting *shikaris*. 'I want to have nothing – nothing at all – to do with a Congress-dominated India.'

'The Cabinet Mission Plan makes it very clear,' replied Sir Conrad Corfield, political adviser to the viceroy, Lord Mountbatten, 'that Britain will not transfer paramountcy to an Indian government. All rights surrendered by the princely states to Britain will return to the princes,' he explained. 'The states can negotiate terms about their future with the Indian government.'

'You want us to negotiate with those *dhotiwallahs*?' demanded the nawab, speaking contemptuously of the Congress leaders. 'I am so unhappy about everything in this country. The British are abdicating power and – what's worse – they intend to hand it over to the enemies of all their friends. I look upon it as one of the greatest, if not *the* greatest, tragedies that has ever befallen mankind,' he lamented, his voice partly swallowed by the roar of the engine as the vehicle climbed a steep incline, with bewildered *chital* and *nilgai* peeping from behind mist-curtained bushes.

'I would recommend you set up a committee to negotiate on behalf of the princes,' suggested Sir Corfield, clutching the support handle above the window as the car bumped over a rough patch before screeching to a halt. 'The political department will do its best to assist you.'

A uniformed orderly opened the door while a dozen others stood bowing by the car. 'Everything is ready, Your

Highness,' said the officer in charge of the hunt, holding out a shikar chart with information on tiger counts received from signallers stationed in various zones of the jungle. 'Trackers have found fresh pugmarks not far from here this morning,' he said, ushering the nawab towards the bamboo platform secured high above the ground.

'Excellent!' the nawab stretched his stiff legs, inhaling the sweet scent of *mahua* flowers. 'Shall we?' he turned to his guest.

Corfield followed along, reminiscing about the splendid days he had spent in India. Tiger hunts in Rewa, trout fishing in Kashmir, grouse bagging in Bikaner, duck shooting in Bharatpur, pig-sticking in Kathiawar. How he would miss

WHY NOT HAVE A STATISTAN FOR THE PRINCES?

Shikar or hunting was a wildly popular pastime for the royals. To provide a snapshot - Maharani Gayatri Devi (Princess of Cooch Behar), who married the maharaja of Jaipur, went on a shoot when she was only five years of age and shot a panther when she was just twelve. It is said her grandfather shot 365 tigers, 311 leopards, 207 rhinos, 438 water buffaloes, 318 antelopes, 259 sambars, 133 bears and 43 bison in a span of thirty-seven years.

these wondrous adventures. As they trotted up the steps to the machan, a platoon of *shikaris* in khaki coats, and drumbeaters in yellowed dhotis, fanned out into the thick jungle.

'The princes, the Muslims and all the people who relied on British justice and their sense of fair play,' the nawab whispered, casting a glance at the rifles laid out on the dry grass, 'suddenly find themselves helpless and unsupported. What should a prince who has some life and honour left in him do?'

'You mustn't lose heart,' Corfield consoled the nawab, reaching for the leather-cased thermos filled with *nimbu-pani* as they settled down in the shooting tower to begin the long wait. 'Remember we spoke about a third front? Hindustan for the Congress; Pakistan for the Muslim League; a Statistan for the Princes. Rajastan... Princestan...call it what you will!'

Eyeing a swamp filled with partridges, the nawab mulled over the suggestion: the trifurcation of India. It wasn't the first time the idea had been mooted. Former viceroy Linlithgow had proposed it to Jinnah a few years ago and the nawab himself had suggested it to the Cabinet Mission. *If India could be divided into two, surely there was no reason it couldn't be sliced into three!* And if he managed to get all the princes together to back his scheme, their Princestan would be almost as large as Pakistan. 'It has been discussed before... but nothing's come of it,' he mumbled.

'Press for it,' urged Corfield, as the fluty call of treepies filled the air. 'Create Bhopal's own independent militia against India; rally the princes around to support your cause...' he urged the nawab, wiping the beads of sweat off his face. 'With the Congress and Muslim League at each other's throats, the balance of power will be in your hands. The next few months will be the most crucial in the history of the states,' he said as a steady drumbeat was heard in the distance. 'The time for action is here and now.'

Spotting a slight movement in the tall grass ahead, the nawab tapped Corfield on his shoulder, then picked up his long-range rifle. The fog was lifting, and his vision cleared as the sunlight shone brightly through. The nawab steadied himself and held his breath. *Would he bag the coveted prize?*

❋ Damming the Atlantic ❋

A silvery blue Rolls-Royce came to a halt outside the Art Deco-style Faridkot Palace, set to host a meeting of the princes, on Copernicus Marg near India Gate in New Delhi. A uniformed guard, sporting a bright red sash, opened the door, bowing low, as Nawab Hamidullah, the chancellor of the Chamber of Princes, stepped out, looking dapper in his Savile Row suit.

A sparkling black Daimler pulled up behind them. Another guard rushed forward to hold open the door for the arriving dignitary. Maharaja Sadul Singh of Bikaner, a lavish and colourful turban adorning his head, disembarked along with his diwan, K.M. Panikkar.

The two rulers stood facing each other for a few moments as the grandfather clock in the lobby struck eleven, its Westminster chime echoing down the hallways.

To Sadul Singh, Hamidullah was the root cause of the divided views among the princes. They exchanged cold greetings and made their way in – the leaders of the two rival groups of princes, the Bhopal and the Bikaner camps, as they had come to be known – each wondering how the day might unfold.

A uniformed aide-de-camp (ADC) bowed as he announced their arrival; another led them inside, along a carpeted corridor. They emerged into a large hall where resplendently dressed maharajas sipped fragrant tea, sitting around an ornately carved table. Scarlet-liveried bearers fussed about the guests, serving delicacies, as diwans and ministers huddled about discussing the chancellor's plans.

TAKE OFF YOUR BLINKERS!

'I say it's time to take the blinkers off!' The nawab of Bhopal began the meeting with a clarion call to the rulers, after the initial formalities. 'Make no mistake, we do not intend to hamper the attainment of India's freedom,' he clarified, 'or do anything that is unpatriotic. And yet we cannot submit meekly to Indian leaders usurping our special powers, our historical legacy and our ancestral inheritance.'

His words were greeted with applause. Freedom was dear to the princes, but so were their rights and privileges. They owned dozens of palaces, had prized collections of cars, splurged extravagantly on foreign trips. Their pleasure paradises were attended to by hundreds of workers. Their treasuries were stashed with the choicest collections of diamonds and gemstones. Armed guards protected them; large armies marched at their command. It was too much to relinquish.

'We wish to see India as a great and honoured nation, but that does not mean we should not demand our due,' the nawab thundered. 'We had an arrangement of paramountcy with the British. It is unfair, improper and unacceptable for the agreement to be terminated unilaterally.'

Once again, there was a roar of consensus. Stout, chubby palms with bejewelled fingers thudded enthusiastically on the teak tabletop. Dark clouds had gathered, heralding the approach of a storm. Unless the rulers constructed solid embankments, they were sure to be swept away.

'Let us decide here, today, that we shall not join the Indian Constituent Assembly,' he egged the princes on, 'not unless we are able to secure for ourselves certain guarantees from the Congress to protect our future.'

Convinced by Sir Corfield's suggestion, the nawab had decided to go all out to put the Princestan plan into action. The expectation was that the Muslim League would not participate in the Indian Constituent Assembly, which had been tasked with drafting a constitution for independent India. If he could get the princes to boycott it too, the assembly would be reduced to a mere Congress party conference.

'With this intent,' said the nawab, holding out a sheet of paper, 'I propose a resolution seeking a guarantee that they will not touch monarchy in the states. There will be no impairment of our powers, no interference in our internal affairs.'

'Hear, hear!' another roar welcomed the nawab's words.

'I second the proposal,' said C.P. Ramaswami Aiyar, the diwan of Travancore, standing up in support of the nawab. 'These guarantees are essential.'

'We are with you,' declared Ramaswami Mudaliar, the newly appointed diwan of Mysore.

'This is non-negotiable!' the nawab thundered, very pleased with the response.

'Non-negotiable,' the princes chorused, following his lead and the hall reverberated with the echoes of their words.

'Non-negotiable,' the nawab reiterated, his lips curving into a smile. If the Congress disagreed with his terms, which they were very likely to do, given Nehru's staunch anti-monarchy and pro-republican stand, the blame for the breakdown in talks would fall on them, not him. 'These conditions are absolutely non-negotiable.'

***

Sitting with his back to a large oil painting at the far end of the table, K.M. Panikkar, the diwan of Bikaner, winced. To him, this was all a ruse, a strategic move by Nawab Hamidullah to block negotiations between the princes and the Congress. Having served as secretary to the Chamber of Princes, Panikkar had known the nawab at close quarters.

It was clear to him that the nawab was using the princes as a cat's paw to aid the Muslim League, which was meeting under Muhammad Ali Jinnah in Karachi on the very same day.

He exchanged glances with the diwan of Jaipur, seated beside him. 'Part of this grand plan is a front for the nizam, I suppose,' Panikkar whispered. The nizam of Hyderabad was the richest and most powerful of the Indian princes and the nawab, it seemed, had a pact with him to use the Chamber to rally the princes to undermine the Congress. Why CP, who had been an avowed nationalist in years past, was now siding with the nawab was a mystery to him.

Yet, just as the nawab thought his proposal would sail through, T. Vijayaraghavachari, the aged and ailing diwan of Udaipur, stood up to speak, leaning uncertainly on his wooden cane. 'This is a historic moment when India is about to attain independence,' he said firmly. 'The princes should support this cause rather than obstruct it.'

The excited murmur in the room died down. The nawab's face turned pale.

'If the princes don't support the Congress, they will be destroyed...and our descendants will consider this an unpardonable crime,' continued Vijayaraghavachari hoarsely, between bouts of coughing. 'The Indian people...the future generations...they will look upon the princes as the accursed tribe. Even your own offspring,' he said, pointing an accusatory finger at those around the table, 'will not forgive you.'

V.T. Krishnamachari, diwan of Jaipur, spoke next. 'The Indian princes have not enjoyed sovereignty even under the British,' stated the senior statesman, his commanding presence reminding many of Bhishma Pitamaha from the Mahabharata, the grand epic. 'Even premier states such as Hyderabad and Mysore or Gwalior and Kashmir,' he looked around at the representatives of the 21-gun-salute states, 'were not wholly independent.'

'And, besides,' interjected Panikkar so as to support his colleagues, 'the people of the Indian states have also fought for India's independence – how can we now hold them back from that freedom?'

Together with C.S. Venkatachar, the diwan of Jodhpur, the four south Indian premiers of Rajputana shared a great rapport, bonded by their common devotion to the cause of a free and united India – an able match for the two Ramaswamis at the opposite ends of the table. Panikkar looked around expectantly at the faces in the room – it appeared as though the scales were beginning to tilt. 'I do not, for a moment, doubt the nawab's patriotism,' he continued. 'I know he is not motivated by communal bias, that he remains untainted by such prejudice. But the unintentional result of his scheme would be the strengthening of one community. I think you all ought to keep that in mind.'

Saddened by Panikkar's remarks, the corners of the nawab's lips curled downwards. The communal frenzy tearing British India apart hadn't touched his state; Hindus and Muslims of Bhopal lived together in harmony. The words pained him.

'What you now contemplate is like the action of the foolish man who tried to dam the Atlantic Ocean with a broom,' declared Vijayaraghavachari. 'Whether you obstruct it or not, whether you oppose it or support it, freedom is coming to India.'

The nawab expelled a laboured sigh, feeling like a complete misfit among princes blind to their own interests.

Down but not out, over the next few months, Nawab Hamidullah would try again – to rally the princes together, to promote his idea of a third front, to give a fillip to his dream of Princestan. But the Bikaner camp would thwart his every effort, rise to his every challenge, undermine his every move, often in collaboration with the powers in Delhi, strategizing with Nehru and Patel over dinner meetings into the thick of the night – forcing the nawab repeatedly on to his back foot.

Still, as spring made way for summer in 1947, the nawab would find his hopes rising again – for a dear friend was on his way to India to take over as India's last viceroy.

❋ Oil and Water ❋

'This,' said the viceroy, tapping the sheet of paper on the table, 'is the general outline of the announcement I propose to make on 3 June.'

Nawab Hamidullah picked up the document. Few people had a close enough relationship to call the viceroy by his nickname, Dickie. Fewer still had the privilege of being shown his plans in advance. 'I pledge to keep this a secret,' he assured his friend. 'You have my word.'

In two days, the viceroy proposed to make a historical broadcast that would set off India's final countdown to independence. A proclamation that would tear apart an ancient civilization and sever it into two nation states, putting an end to the uncertainty and speculation. Britain would leave soon. India would be bisected. And Pakistan would become a reality.

The nawab gulped in dismay. 'So...dominion status for India and Pakistan...' he handed back the statement.

'Somehow, people seem to have doubts about this phrase "dominion status",' said the viceroy. 'I assure you it means absolute independence in every possible way, with the sole exception that the nation will be a part of the British

Commonwealth,' he explained. 'And that is a completely free association of peoples where member nations are linked together only by bonds of mutual trust and affection, so that we may all draw support from one another.'

'Your statement makes no mention of the princely states,' pointed out the nawab.

'That's because this decision concerns only British India. The position regarding the states remains the same as stated before in the Cabinet Mission Plan. British paramountcy will lapse when Britain withdraws.'

'Tell me, Dickie,' the nawab said, leaning forward, 'if the states choose to remain free, will they be recognized as independent dominions by Britain? Will we be allowed membership of the British Commonwealth?'

'I am expecting that certain states, particularly Travancore, might seek recognition as independent dominions,' noted the viceroy, 'but, to be honest, I do not see the possibility of Britain allowing the states to enter the Commonwealth as separate entities.'

'I can't help but feel let down once again,' complained the nawab. 'Through three crises – the Indian uprising of 1857 and the two World Wars – we, the rulers, did our best to assist the British Crown. Bhopal has a proud heritage of loyal friendship with Britain, and that is being broken unilaterally by His Majesty's government. We wish to retain our relations with the monarchy in Britain, rather than merge ourselves with an unfriendly political party in India, which may be ousted by communist elements in the future.'

'Look, I realize the princes place a high value on their relationship with Britain,' said the viceroy, 'but we have repeatedly made it clear that paramountcy will end upon the transfer of power. For the future, it is important that the princes negotiate terms with either India or Pakistan.'

'The central governments of both countries will retain tight control over everything and eat up state resources,' sighed the nawab. 'If I join them, Bhopal will stand to lose nearly 60 per cent of its revenue.'

'I understand this is a difficult decision,' said the viceroy, and then offered his advice. 'I would suggest the states cast their minds forward ten years and consider the situation before coming to a decision. And, in such a scenario, I do hope that most states will decide to join either India or Pakistan.'

'I too would ask you to think about the time to come,' retorted the nawab. 'There is no guarantee of what the future of India will be. How can the rulers throw in their lot with a political party that resolves to turn India into a republic? You cannot, my dear Dickie, mix oil with water. No'—the nawab shook his head, feeling betrayed and bitter—'Bhopal shall not join the Constituent Assembly of India.'

❋ A Carrot from Pakistan ❋

'Do you see this? Do you see this, Zafar?' the nawab asked his constitutional adviser, leaning over his desk in the study in his palace in Bhopal. 'Subscriptions to Britain's war bonds, assistance for materials, contributions to the Prince of Wales Relief Fund, Imperial Relief funds...' he rattled off from the files containing the records of expenses from his royal treasury for the World War that had concluded a few years ago. He picked up another file pertaining to the costs Bhopal had incurred to fund Britain's campaign in the First World War. 'Ambulances, aeroplanes, hospital ships, clothing for wounded soldiers, horses, fodder for the horses, petrol for vehicles, telephones, subscriptions to the Red Cross...material of every kind!' He rose in a huff. 'We covered their wartime expenses - can you see this? It runs into tens of thousands of pounds.' The nawab's ancestors had aided Britain in her every need, stood by her monarchs in her every peril. He felt hopelessly short-changed.

A bearer entered carrying a silver salver loaded with butter cookies and coffee for Bhopal's constitutional adviser, along with the nawab's special paan that he had once every two hours.

'It is preposterous,' the nawab continued. 'The Congress has opposed the British all along, has always been a thorn in their side, while we princes have supported them and stood by them through their every trial. And yet, they turn their backs on us...they...they throw us to the wolves.'

Zafarullah Khan gave the nawab a patient ear, waiting for the right moment.

'I abhor the insidious suggestions made by some that misrepresent princes as opponents of India's freedom,' the nawab sighed. 'Never was there a greater distortion of the truth. We yield to none in patriotism and love for our country.'

'What of your plans to form a third front?' asked Zafarullah Khan, sipping his coffee. 'Are you getting a favourable response from the other princes?'

'I am tired...just exhausted from leading a team that has neither the will nor the desire to survive,' the nawab lamented. 'Like Sisyphus, my endless labours are washed away without a trace. The intrigue. The calumny... Oh! It fills me with sadness... It drives me to a rage...' He felt a sudden rush of emotions. 'Communal feelings of the worst type are rife among the princes and their diwans.'

The paan halfway to his lips, the nawab stopped short, carried away by another thought. 'And this turnaround by the Congress,' he said agitatedly, 'they opposed Partition, tooth and nail, and now they make a sudden volte-face and accept it. What did Gandhi say? Partition over his dead body? What happened to that?' He threw up his hands. 'How can I trust what they will do after independence? How can I just hand over my kingdom to such people?'

'Spilt milk...water under the bridge...a closed door...' remarked Zafarullah Khan, delighting in the nawab's tirade. More than Bhopal's constitutional adviser, Khan was also the former president of the Muslim League and a trusted confidant of Muhammad Ali Jinnah. 'No point in trying to go back through a jammed door, Nawab Sa'ab,' he said. The question is...what do you propose to do now?'

'I resign!' said the nawab emphatically. 'I shall resign as chancellor of the Chamber of Princes. I want maximum sovereignty for Bhopal. Joining India is simply out of the question!'

'Your Highness, joining India is not your only option...' Zafarullah Khan put down his coffee cup. 'Jinnah Sa'ab sends you his *salaam*, and he has asked me to convey a very special message to you.'

The nawab's eyes narrowed.

'Should Bhopal join Pakistan,' said Zafarullah Khan, 'Jinnah Sa'ab proposes to offer you a very senior position in the new state.'

'I beg your pardon?' The nawab was greatly surprised by the offer. *Bhopal was in the middle of India. The borders of Pakistan were likely to be over 500 miles away.*

'Perhaps the secretary general of Pakistan...' Zafarullah Khan stroked his chin thoughtfully, 'or perhaps the Quaid has something else in mind for you – a position befitting your exalted stature...'

The nawab gaped at his constitutional adviser.

'Perhaps,' suggested Zafarullah Khan slowly, 'the Quaid has you in mind for the post of governor general of Pakistan – who, as you know, will be Pakistan's head of state – the highest constitutional position in the country.'

ZAFARULLAH KHAN: IF BHOPAL JOINS PAKISTAN, JINNAH SA'AB WILL OFFER YOU A VERY SENIOR POSITION...

The nawab sat back and exhaled a long breath. With every passing day, circumstances were compelling him to abandon his attacking mode and forcing him to adopt a more defensive style instead. But perhaps he had yet another innings to play. He comforted himself with the thought and finally reached for his paan. The game was not over, until it was over.

❋ Operation Scuttle ❋

'I believe the nawab of Bhopal has resigned as chancellor of the Chamber of Princes.' Nehru linked his hands behind him as they walked out of the viceroy's rectangular office into the expansive Mughal Gardens outside.

'I was sorry to hear of his decision,' said the viceroy. Of all his friends in India, the viceroy counted Jawahar as the dearest; Hamidullah came in a close second. 'I accepted it with great regret.'

'I also believe,' noted Nehru grimly, 'that, as soon as paramountcy ends, Bhopal proposes to become independent.'

Lord Mountbatten nodded, his eyes scanning the garden's blossoming flowers. 'That is what I have been given to understand...'

'Tell me,' Nehru said, 'are trains to stop when they cross state boundaries? Or is the postal system not to operate in the states?'

The viceroy's brow furrowed.

'The states are not geographically isolated.' Nehru shrugged. 'Their boundaries criss-cross with the rest of India. I fail to understand how they can be allowed to become independent. Is it not apparent how many difficulties that would cause?'

The viceroy said nothing as they approached the terraces bursting with colourful climbers and shrubs, recalling Nehru's eruption only weeks earlier over the issue, when he had accused the viceroy's political adviser of misfeasance.

'It is impossible for us to admit the right of any state to independence,' stated Nehru, the sweet birdsong in the garden doing little to calm his frayed nerves. 'Impossible for us to allow them to do just what they will. While we are willing to deal with them in as friendly a manner as possible, we simply cannot admit their declaring independence – as Bhopal clearly intends to do,' he carped, angered by the nawab's persistent attempts to sway the princely states into his camp. 'It will affect all of India's administration and defence, not to mention create a host of other problems.'

'Look,' said the viceroy, 'I have made every effort to convince Hamidullah of the folly of his actions—'

'There are so many common matters,' Nehru interrupted him, 'the railways, customs, posts, telegraph, food distribution... The political department under your office is the only link between the Centre and the states,' he stressed. 'Now, if the states start declaring themselves independent just as the political department begins to wind up, won't there be chaos? Innumerable pockets will be created within India. The country will splinter into pieces...not to mention all the various illegal activities, such as smuggling, it would give rise to.'

Mountbatten walked on in silence. Three months ago, when he had reluctantly taken charge as India's last viceroy, he had been aware of the formidable task he had taken on but hadn't quite realized that the princely states were going to give him such a headache.

'The policy of the political department has made us very uneasy,' said Nehru candidly, seething over the news that great bonfires were being lit across the country to destroy secret records of the maharajas. 'The department is covertly setting ablaze the confidential files of the Indian royalty, winding up residencies and transferring forces to the princes. And now the princes are being encouraged to declare their independence,' he protested. 'Their actions seem deliberately intended to break up the unity of India and introduce anarchy by the back door. If I may borrow Winston Churchill's words,' he said, 'it deserves to be labelled "Operation Scuttle"!'

'Now, now,' remarked the viceroy pacifyingly, 'the political department has proposed that each state deal directly with the Government of India to sort out these matters.'

'That is a truly extraordinary proposal,' Nehru said, rolling his eyes. 'Every department of the Government of India will be flooded with hundreds of letters from hundreds of states! How can one permit an entire administrative structure dealing with such vast and complicated matters to be wound up all of sudden?' he demanded, baffled by such unfeasible ideas.

The viceroy, no great friend of Corfield himself, gave Nehru a patient ear. It was no secret that, behind his back, the political department was shoring up the princes, fanning their monarchic pretensions and aspirations of sovereignty. Some of the princes, on their part, were expanding their armies, openly buying arms and stacking up military supplies.

'It seems clear to me,' said Nehru, 'that some mechanism will be required to deal with the states if we are to avoid descending into complete and utter chaos. You need to give your urgent attention to this matter, else, I'm afraid, it's going to lead to a great deal of friction.'

While neither chaos nor friction were in short supply in those challenging times, Nehru's persistent complaints would soon fructify into a special unit called the States Department (later named the States Ministry). Placed under the charge of the tenacious Sardar Vallabhbhai Patel and the indefatigable Vappala Pangunni Menon, the department would then embark upon a historical journey of corralling, not just Bhopal but more than 500 princely states – some reticent, some pliant, some belligerent – into the Indian Union.

And to accomplish this mammoth task, they would have a little under fifty days.

❋ Pagalistan! ❋

'A part of Pakistan, in the centre of India...' complained Sardar, walking down the palm tree-flanked avenue of Council House. 'That is what we will have if the nawab allies with Jinnah. India can live even if she were to lose her limbs in the west and east...' he remarked, referring to the portions that would become West and East Pakistan, 'but she cannot survive without her heart!'

'We have more than enough on our plate with our eastern and western frontiers on fire,' sighed Nehru. 'The last thing we need is another volcano erupting in the centre.'

'The nawab is going to town with his demand for Princestan,' Sardar said, his hands clasped behind him. 'Some want Jatistan, others are asking for Sikhistan, Nagastan, Pathanistan, Meostan – these dreamers need to be disabused of their delusions, otherwise we will all soon find ourselves in a Pagalistan – a land of the insane!' he bemoaned.

'Corfield and his political department are fuelling these princely ambitions.' Menon gritted his teeth. 'I have told the viceroy categorically that I cannot continue if Corfield is

going to run the show from behind the scenes. I said to Lord Mountbatten – it is either him or me.'

Sardar couldn't help chuckling, unaccustomed to seeing Menon consumed by rage. But Menon's outburst appeared to have done the trick. For even as they spoke, Conrad Corfield had resigned and was on his way out of the country.

'Why don't we ask Lord Mountbatten to help us approach the princes?' suggested Menon. 'He is, after all, the king's cousin. His "blue" blood will help break the ice with the rulers.'

Sardar and Nehru exchanged telling glances, drawn in by the thought.

'Menon, I think that is an excellent idea,' said Nehru.

'Hmm...I agree,' Sardar nodded determinedly. 'We shall not let the grass grow under our feet.'

❃ Death Warrant ❃

'Your grandmother, Sultan Kaikhusrau Jahan, was a remarkable woman,' said the nawab to his daughters Abida, Sajida and Rabia, gazing at the photograph of his mother's strong face beneath its intricate golden crown topped with a sprightly white plume. 'She had the foresight to make education free and compulsory for her subjects. One day,' he added, turning to his eldest daughter posing before the camera, 'when you inherit this kingdom, you must follow her lead.'

'Inherit...the kingdom, Abba?' Abida looked at her father in surprise, then turned her enquiring gaze to Maimoona, her mother.

'Please look at the camera, madame,' pleaded the French photographer who had been commissioned to photograph the royal family. 'Please, this way...' He tried adjusting the frame to capture the leopard skins and bison heads decorating the high walls behind the princess.

'I'm sorry...' The princess, dressed resplendently in a heavily embroidered pink ensemble with gold threads woven into the fabric, turned her head demurely. The sunlight filtering in through the lace curtains lit up the *maang tika* and the *jhoomar* on her young, delicate profile.

'Why are you so surprised?' smiled her younger sister Sajida, as two maids fussed about her, adjusting a mint-green *odhni* over the princess's shoulders. 'More begums than nawabs have occupied the throne in our family.'

'And what a legacy the begums have left us too,' noted Nawab Hamidullah, turning to the portrait of Begum Sultan Jahan swathed in a blue burqa, seated confidently beside the Prince of Wales. Adhering to strict Islamic traditions, the begum had ruled from behind a purdah screen. 'She was an inspiration. She...'

'But...' cut in Princess Rabia, straightening out her finely embroidered mauve *farshi gharara*, 'I thought there is no longer going to be...'

'Don't even utter such inauspicious words,' the nawab snapped at her. 'And what do you mean by "no longer"? "No longer" – what?'

'As soon as the British leave, India is to be a democracy, is it not?' Princess Abida reasoned with her father, turning away from the camera once again. 'So where is the question of my inheriting the throne?'

'That may be so – but Bhopal is not part of India,' the nawab thundered crossly.

'May I request you to focus on the camera, madame...' the photographer repeated in broken English, as Maimoona led her husband by his elbow into the corridor so that the girls could carry on with the photoshoot.

'How much longer will you resist?' Maimoona asked the nawab. 'The other rulers are joining either

India or Pakistan. We will be isolated.'

'It is not as simple as that...' The nawab looked pale and worried.

'I understand you are tense'—Maimoona placed a gentle hand on her husband's arm. A few days ago, they had received the viceroy's invitation to a grand reception for the rulers; the nawab had turned it down, pledging to hold out. 'But you do realize, don't you, that you're fighting a lone battle?'

NAWAB HAMIDULLAH: I WILL NOT CEDE BHOPAL TO INDIA...

'Look...' said the nawab, visibly annoyed, 'I shall not cede my kingdom to anyone. Bhopal is ours. And so it shall remain.'

They stood in silence, staring at the portraits and photographs, trophies and titles lining the long corridor. Holiday pictures in front of the Eiffel Tower and the Big Ben. Hunting pictures over carcasses of tigers and leopards. Receiving kings for durbar, hosting viceroys for shikar. Turning to look out of the window, the nawab watched the sun's glint reflecting off the beautiful *jali* work on the façade of the Qasr-e-Sultani, the palace built by his late mother. *Was this glorious past going to be reduced to a fading silhouette? Was this heritage about to crumble into ruins?*

'I will go and meet Dickie again,' said the nawab. Mountbatten was, after all, of royal lineage – the great-grandson of Queen

Victoria and cousin to the king of England. 'I'm certain he will help me.'

Little did Nawab Hamidullah know that the star batsman, upon whom he had pinned his hopes, had crossed over to the other team.

❋ The Walrus's Tea Party ❋

The viceroy's study had the only working air conditioner in Delhi, and yet it did nothing to comfort the nawab, who sat gaping at the viceroy in dismay.

'I am disappointed that you did not attend the meeting of the princes on 25 July,' said the viceroy, as bearers served tea. 'I had hoped to clarify all your doubts about accession then.'

And I'm disappointed you have shifted your allegiance to the Congress party, the nawab wanted to retort.

'Well, this invitation makes me feel like the Oyster summoned by the Walrus and the Carpenter to the tea party!' he sniggered instead.

The viceroy laughed at the *Alice in Wonderland* reference. 'Come, come, now...it isn't as bad as all that.'

'Look...let us speak frankly,' the nawab cleared his throat, glancing at the framed picture of the viceroy with his royal cousins. 'Through every crisis and war, we princes have supported the British. Funds, weapons, soldiers...we have given whatever you needed. And after all that, you treat us like this?'

'The British Crown appreciates your efforts...'

'We seek no special favours,' the nawab said, holding up his hand. 'All we ask is that there be no discrimination against us and no interference in our internal affairs. His Majesty's government has left us princes in the lurch. You must at least let us regroup and recognize us as a separate union.'

'But, Hamidullah, you will not be losing complete control by joining India,' the viceroy argued. 'Only over defence, communications and external affairs.'

'My people will never agree to joining India,' the nawab remonstrated. 'Becoming part of India can only harm Bhopal.'

'The only abiding harm you can do to Bhopal is to throw down the gauntlet,' the viceroy warned him, 'and take on a straight fight with the Congress, as Travancore is doing.'

'Any state joining India would be relegated to a powerless minority at the mercy of the Congress,' the nawab said. 'You may feel I'm expressing matters strongly, but I'm sure you have seen the recent malicious propaganda against the princes.'

'I understand you have your reservations about the Congress,' the viceroy said persuasively. 'You have ample justification for feeling bitter and disappointed. But...'

'If you were going to be here permanently, Dickie,' the nawab interjected, 'to ensure fair play, I'd have no hesitation in standing by you. But unfortunately, it is the Congress. They make no secret of their intention to destroy the princes. They are at present busily engaged in liquidating zamindars and *jagirdars*. The fate of the princes, I'm afraid, will be the same.'

'If my word carries any weight for you, Hamidullah, I must tell you that I have the highest regard for both Nehru and Patel. I can assure you that they will be true to their word.'

'I'm sorry, Dickie, but I think I know Gandhi, Nehru and their colleagues better than you do. They have done nothing to inspire confidence and friendship.'

'But, as I've told you, Sardar Patel is in charge of the States Department.'

The nawab sighed. 'Frankly...' he pursed his lips, 'that offers me some solace and alters my outlook somewhat...but...if I may draw a parallel'—Hamidullah paused—'Switzerland remained neutral during the World Wars. Why can't we do the same? Look at the communal frenzy in other parts of India. My state has remained quiet, and both my Hindu and Muslim subjects are at peace. Impartial forces, such as us, will act as brokers of goodwill between warring communities.'

'Hamidullah, we are at a stage in time when it is necessary to forget the past and think dispassionately of the future in the common interest of all sections of the country.'

'History will record its verdict on Britain's unfriendly act to a friendly state,' said the nawab, his shoulders drooping. He stood up to leave. 'That leaves me with no choice in the matter!'

'So...you will accede?' The viceroy raised his eyebrows.

'No! I will abdicate.'

'What?' The viceroy stood up with a start.

'Yes, Dickie,' the nawab sighed. 'I cannot make this decision. I cannot throw away the legacy of my ancestors without a care in the world. I shall vacate the throne, and leave both the crown and the decision to my daughter.'

❋ Take It or Leave It! ❋

The diminutive build and ordinary appearance of the self-effacing Malayali across the table may have been enough to fool the world, but the nawab knew that this simple man, most trusted aide and adviser to Patel, the fuel in his fire - V.P. Menon was the silent conductor of this grand orchestra. If India were to emerge unscathed from this chaos it had been plunged into, it would owe a great debt to this man.

'I must inform you at the outset,' Menon said, letting out a laboured sigh, 'that Sardar has heard about your meetings with Jinnah, not to mention your efforts in instigating the other princes to stay out of India. He is far from pleased.'

Almost sensing the heat of Sardar Patel's steely disapproving gaze, the nawab drummed his fingers nervously on the armrest.

Menon eyed the nawab. He knew that Hamidullah was not only a respected figure, he was also a good and tolerant ruler. The palace in Bhopal, he had heard, celebrated Holi with as much fervour as it did Eid, and it was not communal concerns but panic that was at the root of the nawab's actions. The end of the Second World War, the transfer of power, Partition, accession – the rapid pace of events over the last few months was enough to send anybody into a tizzy. Menon decided to shift gears. 'The viceroy has conveyed that he does not agree with your plans to give up the throne,' he said, taking a less confrontational approach.

The nawab nodded. 'Yes...he told me so.'

'If I may say so, Your Highness, I agree with the viceroy,' said Menon. 'I feel it is unfair to your daughter – to put such a burden on a young girl at this critical time. Besides, it would show you in poor light if you were to abdicate now, almost as if you tried to escape the situation at her expense.'

Menon placed a set of documents on the table between them. 'I hope you have reached an agreement to sign,' he said, pushing the Instrument of Accession and the Standstill Agreement towards the nawab.

'We need more time,' sighed the nawab.

'Unfortunately, that is the one thing we cannot give you,' replied Menon.

'I am sure an extension can be granted.'

'We cannot make an exception for you.'

'But Hyderabad has been given an extension.'

'That had the Cabinet's approval.'

'Why not do the same for me?'

'Because the Cabinet does not meet again before 15 August. It is impossible.'

'Then, I will sign after 15 August...' The nawab leaned back in his chair.

'In that case, we cannot guarantee that you will get the same terms.' Menon leaned across the table.

'I'll sign the Standstill Agreement, but not the Instrument of Accession.' Hamidullah looked for a way out.

'The Standstill Agreement cannot be signed with rulers who refuse to accede,' Menon pinned the nawab down.

'I have objections to a few of the clauses and would like them modified.'

'Bhopal will have to join on the same terms as the others. As I said, we cannot make exceptions.'

'I'll sign, but subject to certain conditions.'

'I'm sorry, but Sardar has made it clear that accession must be unconditional,' Menon countered.

The nawab threw his head back and closed his eyes. If Jinnah had dangled a carrot before him, Sardar was going for the jugular. No negotiation. No extension. No exception.

It was either all...or nothing.

❋ The Trump Card ❋

'It troubles me,' the viceroy said to Sardar in dismay, glancing at the calendar on his desk with the countdown to D-Day, 'that Hamidullah still hasn't made up his mind. What disturbs me most is that he should behave like a friend to my face and foil all my plans behind my back!'

'Mmm!' Sardar grunted. The basket of apples that the viceroy had promised him was rapidly filling up. However, Bhopal, right in the centre of India, was still hanging in suspense.

'Sardar...as a friend of Hamidullah,' the viceroy said, 'may I take this matter into my hands? If you are willing to give him one more chance, that is...'

'What do you mean?'

'I will propose to him,' said the viceroy, standing up and walking over to the French windows overlooking the gardens, 'that he should sign the Instrument of Accession before midnight on 14 August and hand it to me. I will then keep it in my custody and undertake not to deliver it to you for ten days.'

Sardar exchanged a puzzled glance with Menon.

'So, in effect,' Menon threw his arm around the back of his chair, swivelled around and said, 'the nawab will get the ten-day extension he has been wanting...and—'

'...And it won't cause any loss of face to you,' the viceroy completed the sentence, 'as it will not appear like an extension.'

'What if he changes his mind in ten days?' asked Sardar.

'If the nawab does that, I'll return the documents to him,' replied Mountbatten. 'If not, I'll give them to Menon on 25 August. He gets his ten days, and you get your accession before 15 August.'

'What if the other princes get to know of this?' asked Menon.

'Nobody should get to know about this,' Sardar said, shaking his head.

'Undoubtedly,' the viceroy nodded, encouraged by Sardar's response. 'Hamidullah will want to keep it under his hat as well. So...' he said, rocking on his heels, 'shall I make the offer to the nawab?'

Sardar drummed his fingers on the table, giving the matter some thought. Sometimes an ace was not enough to win; one needed to pull out a trump card as well. 'You have my approval,' he nodded. 'Go ahead.'

❋ Never Play False ❋

Nawab Hamidullah leaned on the balustrade, gazing at the flower-decked terraces at the edge of the Mughal Gardens, his mind still grappling with the blistering pace of events. India was no longer a British colony but a free nation. Lord Mountbatten was no longer India's viceroy but her governor general. And Bhopal was no more holding out but had acceded to India. He turned to Sardar, grateful for the special favour he had been extended.

'I do not disguise the fact that, while the struggle was on,' he said, 'I used every means in my power to preserve the independence of my state. But now that I have conceded defeat,' he added, taking Sardar's hand, 'I hope you will find I can be as staunch a friend as I have been an opponent.'

'My dear Hamidullah,' Sardar pressed the nawab's hand in his, 'quite honestly, I do not look upon your accession to India as either a victory for us or a defeat for you. It is only rightness and propriety that have triumphed in the end, and in that triumph, you and I have played our respective roles.'

'I wish for you to know that I have no ill feelings towards anyone...' said the nawab, his voice sincere. 'Truth be told, I once had ambitions to play a big role in the Muslim world, but...' he paused, watching Mountbatten hand over to Menon the sealed envelope containing the accession papers signed by him ten days ago, 'I feared that if I acceded to India, Mr Jinnah would denounce me as a traitor to the Muslim cause.'

'You deserve full credit for your courage and honesty, Nawab Sa'ab,' said Patel, shaking his hand warmly. 'I'm disappointed your talents were not at the country's disposal during the critical times we passed through in the last few months,' he added 'but looking to the future, I value your assurance of cooperation and friendship.'

'Sardar, you have extended your hand in friendship to me,' the nawab placed a hand over his heart, 'and I'm prepared to hold it firmly. Now that we are united, I promise I will never play you false.'

Postscript

Back in 1930, the nawab had reminded the Muslim residents of Bhopal that, as subjects of a Muslim-ruled state, it was 'their duty' to be 'extra-magnanimous, large-hearted, tolerant and sympathetic towards those of their fellow subjects who may belong to other communities'.

Tolerant and open to political reform, the nawab grew increasingly apprehensive about losing identity in a new India ruled by the Congress, which was pro-republican and anti-monarchy.

In hindsight, the nawab's fears were not altogether unfounded. The Indian government did gradually take over all powers from the princely states, which were integrated into India in a few years. Bhopal was merged with other princely states such as Gwalior and Indore into the state of Madhya Bharat, later called Madhya Pradesh. In 1971, the titles, privy purses and privileges of princes were abolished on the basis that all Indian citizens ought to be treated as equals.

Nawab Hamidullah Khan died in 1960. His daughter and heir, Abida Sultan, had by then chosen to migrate to Pakistan. Thereafter, the nawab's second daughter, Sajida Sultan, was recognized as the titular head of Bhopal. She was married to Iftikhar Ali Khan, the nawab of Pataudi, who played cricket for both England and India between 1932 and 1946. Their son,

Mansoor Ali Khan, better known as Tiger Pataudi, was one of India's most iconic cricketers in the 1960s.

Nawab Hamidullah Khan's adviser, Zafarullah Khan, was relieved of his duties and he moved to Pakistan in December 1947, where he was appointed Pakistan's first foreign minister. Khan later represented Pakistan's case in respect of Kashmir in the United Nations between 1947 and 1954.

♦♦♦♦♦♦♦♦♦♦♦♦♦♦♦♦♦♦♦

Did It Really Happen This Way?

♦♦♦♦♦♦♦♦♦♦♦♦♦♦♦♦♦♦♦

The conversation between Nawab Hamidullah Khan and Sir Conrad Corfield in the opening scene is based partly on the nawab's correspondence with Corfield, reproduced by Ian Copland in his book The Princes of India in the Endgame of Empire, 1917–1947. *The setting of a tiger hunt has been added to give readers a glimpse into this aspect of princely India. In their book,* Lives of the Indian Princes, *Charles Allen and Sharada Dwivedi describe royal hunts and speak of how rulers made use of hunting trips to discuss important matters with British officers.*

The meeting in Faridkot Palace is a compressed composite of several meetings between Nawab Hamidullah Khan and other princes. The words of the nawab have been culled from his speeches and letters. The words of the diwans of Udaipur, Jaipur and Bikaner, opposing the nawab, are based on the narration of these events in K.M. Panikkar: An Autobiography.

The scene where Nehru cautions Mountbatten about the impending chaos, pressing him to create a separate department for states, is based on Nehru's correspondence with the viceroy, to be found in The Transfer of Power 1942–7, Vol. XII. *Ian Copland also wrote: 'It was Jawaharlal Nehru, Mountbatten's* closest ally in the interim government, who initially drew his attention to the fact that important questions about the future of the states remained pending.'

Menon mentions his idea to seek the viceroy's help in resolving the problem of the princely states in his book Integration of the Indian States. He sought the consent of Sardar and Nehru separately, but it has been captured here as a single scene. Menon's complaint to the viceroy against Corfield has been referred to by Narayani Basu in her book V.P. Menon: The Unsung Architect of Modern India.

Subsequent to this, Corfield disagreed with Mountbatten over his decision to help the Indian leaders, and decided to step down and leave India, which he mentions in his autobiography, The Princely India I Knew, from Reading to Mountbatten.

The conversations between the nawab and Zafarullah Khan, and later between the nawab and his family, have been imagined to offer a peek into the nawab's inner thoughts and introduce his family. These are based on his letters and speeches.

The conversations between the nawab and Lord Mountbatten are based on records of their letters and meetings to be found in The Transfer of Power 1942–7, Vol. XII. The conversation between the nawab and Menon is a dramatized version of the requests made by the nawab regarding accession.

The decision by Patel to grant the nawab an extension of time, at the behest of the viceroy, is mentioned by Menon in his Integration of Indian States and in The Transfer of Power, Vol. XII. The last scene where Patel and the nawab make efforts to reconcile is based on a set of letters, rendered here as a conversation.

3

A *Race to the Finish*

THE STORY OF GWALIOR

PRINCELY STATE OF GWALIOR IN 1947:
in present-day Madhya Pradesh
AREA: 26,008 square miles (67,360 square kilometres) approx.
POPULATION: 4,006,159
RULER: Maharaja Jivajirao Scindia
DIWAN: M.A. Sreenivasan
21-gun-salute state

❋ Collision Course ❋

'Nehru's car has been attacked!'

M.A. Sreenivasan, the diwan of Gwalior, pressed the phone to his ear. 'Could you speak a little louder, please?'

'There's been an attack on Pandit Nehru's vehicle,' Marsh Smith, Gwalior's inspector general of police, repeated from the other end. The poor telephone connection crackled with static. 'Black flag demonstrators hit Nehru's car with a pole.'

'What? Is Panditji all right?' Sreenivasan's pulse quickened. 'Hello...hello?' The connection went dead.

'Yes...he's fine,' a familiar voice answered from behind him. 'May I come in, please?'

Sreenivasan whirled around. The interim prime minister of India, Jawaharlal Nehru, stood in the doorway, dressed in his trademark achkan and churidar, a red rose tucked into his buttonhole. Congress member Ram Sahai was by his side, rubbing his wrist.

'Panditji! Thank heavens, you're all right.' Sreenivasan hurried towards them. 'Please...please come in. Are you hurt?'

'Sahai's wrist is injured – he needs help,' Nehru replied, panting slightly. 'I'm quite all right, thank you.'

'I had alerted the police about your attending the conference here today,' Sreenivasan felt compelled to explain, as he ushered his guests into the living room. 'I am sorry... I did instruct them to take adequate security measures.' He offered his guests a seat. Knowing Nehru was to be in Gwalior to attend the annual session of the All India States Peoples' Conference (AISPC), Sreenivasan had anticipated trouble from those opposed to the Congress.

'They did,' Nehru replied, reassuring his anxious host. 'I decided to take an alternative route. It's not their fault.'

'Even so, I'm so sorry about this...' Sreenivasan repeated, disturbed that one of the tallest of Indian leaders should be attacked in his state. 'Please make yourself comfortable. Some tea?'

'I'd be happy with a tall glass of cold orange juice,' Nehru replied, sinking into an armchair.

'Just some water for me...' replied Sahai, massaging his injured hand.

'Sure...sure...' Sreenivasan moved purposefully towards the kitchen, pausing to turn back to his guests. 'Sorry, I nearly forgot to ask. How was the conference? Did everything go smoothly?'

'Yes...it went well,' said Nehru, surveying the bookshelf by the wall. 'Sheikh Abdullah will be the next president of the AISPC, now that my term has ended,' he said, referring to the Kashmiri leader jailed by Maharaja Hari Singh in Srinagar. 'And I made my position quite clear regarding this whole states' affair. Those who don't join the Indian Constituent Assembly will be considered as hostile states and will have to bear the consequences of being treated as such.'

Sreenivasan stared at Nehru, his eyes begging for an explanation. *Hostile*? It seemed a very harsh word to use. The Constituent Assembly was setting out to draft a new constitution for independent India and, so far, only a few states had joined this effort. Most were bystanders, watching the situation unfold, playing a game of wait-and-see. But to be treated as an enemy state by India for treading cautiously seemed outrageous. 'I beg your pardon, sir?' the diwan of Gwalior asked. *Had he heard right*?

'That's right...' Nehru nodded, picking out a book containing a collection of Robert Frost's work from the rack. 'A princely state,' he repeated, 'that does not join the Indian Constituent Assembly will be treated as a hostile state.'

Sreenivasan drew in a sharp breath. Even as the maharajas deliberated their next move, Nehru, it seemed, had decided to take up the cudgels against them.

This was going to be a fight to the finish.

❋ At the Crossroads ❋

A pale blue Mercedes cruised past the crowds gathered at the racecourse and pulled up outside the owners' special entrance of the Royal Western India Turf Club in Bombay. There were men in crisply tailored suits and women in glistening silk sarees, their sunglasses glinting in the bright sunlight. Fashionable European ladies in wide-brimmed hats clutched little handbags; aristocratic Indians glittered in rubies and sapphires. Trainers. Breeders. Jockeys. Bookies. All looking forward to the season's last race at the Bombay Derby. Pushing through the crowd, an orderly rushed ahead to hold open the door of the Mercedes.

Jivajirao Scindia, the stocky, sunburnt and suave maharaja of Gwalior stepped out. Maharani Vijaya Raje, dressed demurely in a mint-green saree, diamond solitaires in her ears and a string of elegant pearls around her neck, followed. The maharaja's ADC and racing staff crowded around them, doffing their caps. The couple nodded in acknowledgement and the entourage made its way in.

Educated at Eton in England and Mayo in Ajmer before being cloistered within marble palaces and sandstone fortresses, Indian royalty aspired to be very much like their colonial masters. Participating in sports like cricket and polo, hunting and racing, took them one step closer to mirroring the lives of Englishmen. And of all the royals who descended upon the racecourse for Bombay's famed derby each year, the Scindia of Gwalior was the indisputable doyen. Owner of over 200 thoroughbreds and Arabian racehorses, the largest and most passionate horse breeder in the country was out on the course every morning before sunrise, personally training his steeds. As he ascended the steps of the stands, exchanging polite greetings with his royal brethren that day, he noticed that they seemed somewhat uneasy, troubled no doubt that the British bubble that cocooned them was about to burst.

'Maharaja Hari Singh looks unwell,' Maharani Vijaya Raje whispered, as they settled down in the Gwalior Box.

'Hmm...tense times...' the maharaja whispered back. As he watched the horses being led around the enclosure one by one, he was reminded of the dinner at Bikaner House in Delhi a few months ago, during which Nehru had assured the princes that nothing grievous was likely to happen to them. And yet, the princes were worried about their future.

'What do you expect will happen after the British leave?' asked the maharani, as her aide handed her the race card with the day's schedule. Information came in almost daily about Britain's departure and the prospect of the division of the country, but it was impossible sometimes to sift news from rumour.

'There is no saying...' the maharaja mumbled, reaching for his binoculars. 'The viceroy is in talks with the leaders...and an announcement will soon be made.'

'And what about us?' asked the maharani. 'What is to become of the princely states?'

The maharaja watched the horses being saddled and the jockeys weighing in before taking their positions, his eyes searching for his three horses running that day, even as Nehru's words echoed at the back of his mind. If the monarchs were approved by the people, Nehru had declared, he would

THE RACE IS ON: A BATTLE OF NERVES!

not interfere in the administration of the princely states, whether he liked it or not. *But given Nehru's anti-monarchy views, would he stay true to his word?*

'What is to happen to the princes?' the maharani repeated, placing her hand gently on the maharaja's knee.

'Your guess, my dear,' replied the maharaja glumly, his eyes fixed on his favourite steed, 'is as good as mine.' His horse seemed a tad off colour, as was he. A gust of wind had thrown up puffs of dust, blurring the racetrack. But this was momentary, the dust would settle. There was no saying the same, though, about Gwalior's future.

❋ This Shopkeeper Mentality ❋

'Look...I admit not all princes are alike,' Nehru said, taking the glass of orange juice from the bearer. 'Some have done the right thing and come into the Constituent Assembly. They deserve to be congratulated.'

Sreenivasan sat down beside a distressed Ram Sahai with a first-aid box.

'But you see, others are putting every possible obstacle in the way,' Nehru went on, 'not to mention finding all manner of excuses and demanding all sorts of conditions. I do not like this "shopkeeper mentality". This bargaining mindset and short-sightedness will do no good...but only create enmity with the rest of India.'

Sreenivasan listened silently, cleaning the wound on Sahai's hand, wary of making any remark that might rub Nehru the wrong way. The princes wanted to march along with India. *Could they be faulted for also wanting the best deal for themselves?*

'Most of the princely states are known for their backwardness, the feudal nature of the administration and autocracy,' Nehru continued berating the princes. 'Strange things occur there because power is concentrated in a few hands and the general populace is kept in the dark. Not to mention the rampant injustice and inefficiencies.' He shook his head disapprovingly. 'A new era beckons, Sreenivasan. This medieval, feudal set-up has simply got to end.'

'Panditji...Gwalior has never taken a stand opposed to India,' Sreenivasan protested, a tad defensively.

'No...no, I did not mean the maharaja of Gwalior, or you,' Nehru brushed aside the remark lightly. 'I'm tired of the Nawabs and the Maqbuls, the Alwars and Khares, and all the rest.'

Winding the bandage around Sahai's wrist, Sreenivasan knew fully well whom Nehru was alluding to. The nawab of

Bhopal topped the long list of those Nehru considered hostile to the plan for an Indian Union. Sreenivasan wished to convey that Gwalior was not a part of their clique. *But could he be absolutely certain*? After all, the Scindia was close to the nawab of Bhopal and even addressed him as 'Uncle'.

'You know how rapidly the situation is changing...' Nehru snapped shut the book he was browsing through. 'There's simply no time left for anyone to just wait and watch from the sidelines. We are on the verge of great changes, but disruptive forces are at work at every step.'

'Sir, the Cabinet Mission Plan makes it clear that the princely states are free to stay out of India or Pakistan,' Sreenivasan argued, hoping Nehru could see that the stance taken by the states was not unreasonable, and certainly not hostile. 'It is quite natural then that some states – particularly the larger ones – may opt to stay independent.'

'There is no future for any state, however big it might be, if it stays outside of India,' Nehru dismissed the proposition. 'You must understand that if the states do not enter the Constituent Assembly, the gap between them and the rest of India will only increase. I cannot conceive of any state staying out. Nor of a state having an authoritarian government when the rest of India has a democratic one.'

Sreenivasan sighed as he finished putting the dressing on Sahai's hand. Nehru appeared in no mood for a compromise. The maharajas and nawabs were clearly in for a tussle.

'Anyway,' Nehru said, putting down the glass and springing to his feet like a young boy, 'thank you for your help and hospitality, Sreenivasan. We shall now be getting on our way.'

'I...I will call the police right away, Panditji,' said Sreenivasan 'and have them escort you on your way back.'

'Not required.' Nehru waved away the offer. 'Rest assured that no power on earth can prevent me from going anywhere in India unless I am arrested or forcibly removed.' Stepping close to his host, he said in a mellow voice, 'Maratha history is not unknown to you, Sreenivasan... The story of India could have been different...very different... had the Marathas stayed united. I only hope the Scindia has not forgotten history.'

Jawaharlal Nehru was known as a man of letters, a lover of literature and a great orator. American poet Robert Frost's famous poem, 'Stopping by Woods on a Snowy Evening', was found on his table when he died.

'Panditji, as you say... things are changing rapidly,' Sreenivasan tried once again to shine a light on the other side of the story. 'It is hard for the princes, who are accustomed to a different way of life, to accept so quickly that the world as they know it might end.'

Nehru nodded slightly and replaced the book on the shelf. Pausing for a moment at the door, he turned, replying in verse, drawing his words from Robert Frost:

'Ah! When to the heart of man,
Was it ever less than a treason,
To go with the drift of things,
To yield with a grace to reason,
And bow and accept the end
Of a love or a season?'

❋ Charting a Clear Course ❋

'So...what headaches have our friends in the press cooked up for us today?' Sardar sat down in his airy living room to browse through the newspapers as was his daily routine after lunch.

'Quite a migraine.' Shankar handed him the *Dawn*, a league newspaper founded by Jinnah himself, which often took an anti-Congress stance. 'Nobody has taken kindly to Nehru's statement in Gwalior. Least of all the princes and the Muslim League,' pointed out Sardar's private secretary. 'They claim the Congress is threatening the rulers.'

'Hmm...to tell you the truth, I am not so pleased with that statement myself,' said Sardar, putting on his glasses before reading from the article:

> Liaquat Ali Khan of the Muslim League has taken strong objection to Pandit Nehru's statement at the All India States Peoples' Conference in Gwalior. 'What does Mr Nehru mean to suggest by labelling states not joining the Indian Constituent Assembly as hostile states?' Liaquat Ali Khan demanded. Liaquat Sahab has urged the rulers not to succumb to pressure from the Congress.

Sardar clicked his tongue. 'Now the League is going to make capital out of it,' he lamented. Even as he had taken one step forward in reaching out to the princes, Nehru's statement had pushed them two steps back. 'I don't deny that the conditions in several princely states are regressive; the rulers are autocratic and their subjects suffer. Change is needed. But it cannot be brought about by picking a fight with the princes. A conciliatory approach is required.'

'Already we have some disruptive elements among the princes...' Menon pursed his lips, having noticed a similar news item in another newspaper. 'This will only add fuel to the manoeuvres and machinations of those out to sabotage our efforts.'

'Although Nehru has been elected as president of the Congress for the fourth time,' bemoaned Sardar as he turned the page, 'he often acts with childlike innocence...and that puts us all in great difficulty.'

'Do you think Panditji's statement is likely to cause a problem?' asked Maniben, sitting down on a mat by her father's feet with a sheaf of letters in Gujarati. Draped in a white saree, a bunch of keys tucked at her waist, Sardar's petite daughter was actively engaged in every step of his journey. From managing his health and household, to handling his schedule and correspondence, Maniben was on top of it all – even joining Gandhi and her father earnestly in the freedom struggle and spending time in jail. 'Will the princes feel threatened by it?' she asked, placing her draft replies before him for his approval.

'They most certainly will,' replied Sardar, his thoughts drifting. Of late, Nehru had done many things to cause embarrassment to the party, putting a strain on the rest of them to put out fires and set matters right. Only last year his statement about not being bound by the Cabinet Mission Plan had sent Jinnah into a tizzy, completely altering the course of events. But Patel knew that these were innocent indiscretions, and recognized Nehru's unparalleled enthusiasm and burning passion for freedom. He understood that it was Nehru's zeal and sense of commitment that made him so restless, making him forget himself at times.

'Jawahar's actions are governed by his desire to reach the cherished goal at electric speed,' he explained, displaying a tender affection for his colleague, despite several causes for friction. 'His mind has been exhausted with overwork and strain. He feels lonely and reacts emotionally sometimes. We just have to bear with him in the circumstances.'

Shankar turned to Sardar, his eyes filled with admiration. Just a year ago, Patel had withdrawn his candidature for the presidency of the Congress, despite having popular support, because Gandhi had asked him to back out in favour of Nehru. Patel was the senior of the two, the grassroots worker, the organizer. Most importantly, the choice of the party. But, just as he had quietly relinquished the opportunity to study law in England in deference to his brother many years ago, he had once again stepped back without a fuss to make way for Nehru. And yet, he spoke of his colleague's follies with no trace of bitterness. Despite all their differences, Shankar realized, there was undoubtedly a bond between the two men, a commitment binding them to a greater cause.

'Sardar...I have an idea,' said Menon, putting down the newspaper. 'The Cabinet Mission Plan clearly says that the states need not join India or Pakistan. Naturally, the princes believe they have a free hand.' He leaned forward. 'Why don't we prepare a statement from you to the princes? Something that will appeal to them – allay their fears, explain our policy, convince them that the Congress is not their enemy?'

Sardar threw back his head in thought. The current situation did hold dangerous possibilities. If they did not act promptly, their hard-earned freedom could well disappear through the door of the princely states.

'The statement can explain that we do not seek to subsume them or take away all their powers; tell them they needn't feel threatened by us; and convey to them that all we ask is that they cede their power over defence, external affairs and communications to the Government of India, and nothing more. A statement directly from you is sure to help. What do you think?'

'Hmm...' Sardar nodded, convinced by the idea. It was going to be impossible for him to reach out to nearly 600 states in six weeks. A joint appeal to all of them seemed the best way forward. 'I agree. Prepare a draft.'

'Right away.' Menon jumped up and dashed into the study. There was not a moment to lose.

Watching Menon bolt enthusiastically to the door, Sardar chuckled. 'You know...' he said, turning to Maniben, '...last week, when I asked this fellow to join as secretary to the States Department, he told me he was getting old, growing tired, and that he wanted to retire after 15 August. That he wasn't sure we'd hit it off together as a team.'

Pausing for a moment at the entrance to the veranda, Menon smiled slightly. Yes...he had been apprehensive about working with Patel. Not because he feared him or did not get along with him, but because he held a deep reverence for him and did not wish to jeopardize that in any way. Sardar, on the other hand, had been certain he wanted Menon - and only Menon - as his deputy.

As he made his way to the study and settled down by the typewriter, Menon's mind was already abuzz with ideas; Abraham Lincoln's words from his famous inaugural address swirled before him. He would write Sardar a grand speech, he told himself. Like many a document that had stemmed from his hand, this speech too would shape the course of India's history.

❋ Off Track ❋

'CP, have you had a look at Sardar's statement?' the diwan of Gwalior asked the diwan of Travancore, who was watching, with childlike fascination, the little serving train chugging along the dinner table in the resplendent Banquet Hall of the Jai Vilas Palace of Gwalior.

The diwan of Travancore, C.P. Ramaswami Aiyar, or CP as everyone called him, was one of India's most respected statesmen, and his opinions were highly sought after and valued by Indians and Englishmen alike. Sreenivasan too hoped to gain some insight from the man

COULD THIS ARISTOCRACY FIT INTO NEW, DEMOCRATIC INDIA?

currently putting up a brave front against Sardar Patel's grand unification plan.

'This train delights me'—CP grinned, looking at the approaching silver wagon relaying port wine to the guests seated around the table.

'It was designed by the maharaja's father,' Sreenivasan explained, halting the serving train before them. CP peered into it and lifted the decanter. He sniffed the contents, nodded in approval and replaced the bottle on the carriage, chuckling as the train resumed chugging along the table on its route once again.

'The late maharaja loved locomotives - well, anyway...' Sreenivasan tried steering the conversation back on track. 'Sardar has stated that the Congress is asking the states to accede only in respect of three subjects. There is likely to be no encroachment on the rights of the princes otherwise. What does Travancore propose to do?'

'My dear Sreenivasan...' - CP turned to him quizzically - '...do you really trust the Congress triumvirate? We are at long last going to throw off the British yoke and become free, and you want to bind yourself down once again?'

'But Nehru and Patel have declared that the Cabinet Mission proposals have been accepted in full,' Sreenivasan argued. 'There is to be no change in the monarchical form of government in the princely states. Things can continue the way they are.'

'The Cabinet Mission Plan was for a united India,' CP replied, 'not for two dominions. Things have changed now. Even Gandhi's protests against Partition have been set aside. What could prevent them from making yet another U-turn?'

Sreenivasan sat back. That the Congress had agreed to Partition had hit everyone hard. That Gandhi's pleas had been bypassed had grieved many deeply. *Would the Congress renege on their*

The ornate Durbar Hall of the Jai Vilas Palace, built by Maharaja Jayajirao Scindia of Gwalior in the late nineteenth century, is said to be one of the largest in India. Its crystal chandeliers, sourced from Vienna were so huge that it was feared they would make the roof collapse. To test its strength, a wooden ramp had been constructed and a dozen elephants marched on to the roof over this ramp. When the roof withstood the weight of the elephants, it was certified safe for the chandeliers.

promises to the princes too? He turned to look at the members of Indian royalty seated around the enormous dinner table in the magnificent Banquet Hall. Dressed in brocaded, diamond-encrusted suits, dining off gold platters and sipping from silver goblets, they proudly displayed the badges of honour conferred upon them by the British; owners of vast acres of land and fabulous pieces of property, with their coffers overflowing with the choicest of gems...could this aristocratic class fit into the new India to be built on the foundations of democracy and equality?

'Look here...' CP dabbed his mouth with a napkin. 'Some years ago, Nehru said that the princes were lunatics, knaves and fools. In February this year, he swore that the monarchical governments will not be touched. In a matter of months, he turns around and claims that sovereignty rests with the people and not the rulers, and declares that he has no faith in monarchy. A few months ago, right here in Gwalior, he called us hostile states. Hostile states! He calls us the enemy!' CP emphasized each word, his arms spread out in bewilderment. 'For what? What have we done to be called India's enemy? Then, at the meeting of the Constituent Assembly, he says that the Congress will not solve any problem by force. Now you tell me...how are we supposed to trust this man?'

'But Sardar has made the position quite clear now...' Sreenivasan tried playing devil's advocate.

'Forget Sardar's statement! It is historically untrue to say that sovereignty resides anywhere else other than in the ruler. Doesn't that tell you enough about Nehru's dislike for the princely order,' CP demanded, dipping his hands in a finger bowl, 'of his contempt for them? Nehru is the leader. He is going to be the head of government. Naturally, the Congress will follow his lead!'

'So'—Sreenivasan prodded him—'would you advise us to stay out of India?'

'Absolutely.' CP shrugged. 'Else, the Congress will wipe out the princes.'

'And you've decided that Travancore will stay out then?'

'No doubt about that.'

'Well...what do you know!' exhaled the diwan of Gwalior, drumming his fingers restlessly on the table. 'The longer the night, the more the dreams one has.'

Sreenivasan realized then that it was down to one question. Nehru or Patel? Whose writ would run? Both were defining faces of the Congress, both had the same core ideals, but they often stood for different things. Nehru disliked and distrusted the princely order and the princes. Patel was more conciliatory, more willing to befriend them. Nehru appeared to want nothing but the annihilation of princely India. Patel's approach seemed more tempered.

He turned to the ceiling, as if seeking an answer in the lights glittering above him. However, not even the dazzle of 200 lamps in the world's largest chandelier in the adjoining Durbar Hall would help him find his way out of this fog. That beacon of light would have to come from within.

❋ A Step in the Right Direction ❋

Maharaja Jivajirao Scindia bowed his head before the marble memorial, feeling the force of his mother's cold stare. Her statue, draped in a bright blue saree, complete with diamond necklace and adorned with garlands, stood atop the platform decorated with beautifully carved stone *chhatris* and elephants. It seemed to be judging her son today, even as the band of musicians behind him sang paeans to the glories of his dynasty.

The stony eyes of his father's large statue in the centre of the shrine made him even more uncomfortable, a grim reminder of the legacy that weighed heavily on his shoulders. At one point the only significant contenders to the British, the Scindias had Delhi and Agra, Jaipur and Jodhpur, Bharuch and Berar under their sway. Two centuries on, the little region around Gwalior was all they had left. Accession to India would mean losing even that last remnant of past glory.

A priest entered and applied a sandalwood tilak on the maharaja's forehead, blessing him with life for a hundred years and eternal happiness for his offspring. Many a Scindia had died without a male heir in the past and Maharaja Jivajirao had been pleased that he would leave behind a successor. Only two years ago, guns had boomed from the battery point at the fort to announce the birth of his son, Madhavrao. His worry now seemed ironical. *He had left his kingdom with an heir; but would he leave his heir with a kingdom?*

Prostrating before the *shivalinga* first and then circumambulating the family shrine, the Scindia emerged in a disturbed frame of mind after paying homage to his forefathers. 'I do not want to fail my ancestors, Sreenivasan,' the maharaja said to his diwan, as he slipped on his footwear and proceeded to his Daimler. 'This decision about accession weighs heavily on me.'

'I understand, Your Highness,' said Sreenivasan, aware that the moment of reckoning was upon them. 'Sardar Patel has made a statement to the princes...and frankly that fills me with great confidence,' he said, getting into the car beside the maharaja.

The maharaja gazed out of the window as they drove past bullock carts and pack animals herded by wrinkled old men who bowed low as the maharaja's car passed by them.

'Sardar has admitted that there appears to be a great deal of misunderstanding about the attitude of the Congress towards the states,' Sreenivasan apprised the maharaja, 'and has clarified that the Congress will not interfere in any manner in the domestic affairs of the states...'

Vast multitudes flanked the street outside, their heads bowed in obeisance. They had waited in the hot sun for hours just to catch a glimpse of their beloved maharaja whom they considered to be God's representative on earth. They idolized him, worshipped him, loved him. 'I have read Sardar's statement,' he said, as he waved to his subjects, 'and yes, I admit I am somewhat reassured by it.'

The Gwalior Fort atop the hill, from where the 21-gun salute boomed for the maharaja whenever the occasion demanded, came into view. And then came the white colonnades of the magnificent Jai Vilas Palace, which was spread across vast

AT THE CROSSROADS OF THE PAST AND THE FUTURE...

acres of green, dotted with elegant fountains and tranquil ponds. Peacocks danced in the courtyard; partridges and quails strutted about its lawns. Sambar, *chital* and barking deer called from Harivan, the woods beyond the palace premises. The maharaja gazed at the dynasty's flag fluttering atop the palace. *Was the sun about to set on the Scindias?*

'I want to know your thoughts,' the maharaja said, turning to his diwan. Sreenivasan had spent several years as minister in Mysore, which was known to be one of the more progressive princely states. The Scindia valued his opinion. 'Do you think Gwalior should accede to India?'

Sreenivasan took a deep breath. He had weighed his words, consulted his seniors and considered the options. 'Yes, Your Highness,' he said confidently, 'I would advise you to sign the Instrument of Accession with India.'

❋ Two Roads in the Woods ❋

Persuaded by his diwan's inputs, the Scindia made an announcement that Gwalior would soon accede to India. But as the old adage goes, there is many a slip between the cup and the lip. And so it was in the summer of 1947, when assailed by second thoughts, Maharaja Jivajirao Scindia summoned Sreenivasan urgently to his study one morning. Face pallid, expression sombre, hands unsteady, the Scindia handed his diwan the telegram he had just received. 'From Hamidullah…' he mumbled in a feeble voice.

Looking enquiringly at the maharaja, Sreenivasan took the missive from him and read it aloud.

> Have seen the proclamation through which you have agreed to accede to India. I believe you have been wrongly advised to do so. Withhold your consent and telegraph me in Bhopal.

Eyebrows raised, Sreenivasan looked at the Scindia's ashen face.

'This has put me in a predicament, Sreenivasan.' The maharaja shook his head, leaning forward on his desk. 'As you know, Uncle is a well-wisher...Bhopal is our neighbour... I cannot take this decision in isolation.'

Sreenivasan was taken aback. So *the nawab was still fantasizing about his Princestan – a union comprising the princely states that stood apart from both India and Pakistan.* Whether one looked at it geographically or politically or economically, this idea of a third front of princes seemed completely impractical to Sreenivasan. The nawab, it appeared, was only clutching at straws.

'What...what is your view?' the Scindia asked his diwan.

Placing the telegram back on the desk, Sreenivasan looked the maharaja in the eye, untroubled by this new development. 'I stand by my advice, Your Highness,' he replied, undeterred. 'Gwalior is in the heart of Indian territory. Unlike Travancore or Kashmir, we are not a border or coastal state. We will be surrounded by India on all sides. Joining India is the right thing to do.'

'So is Bhopal'—the maharaja shrugged—'but Uncle seems to have other plans.'

'I'm not sure those plans are viable, Your Highness,' Sreenivasan replied with candour and clarity, 'but perhaps you can take a day or two to have a word with him. And meet with the local Sardars too. They have guided your ancestors through difficult decisions.'

Resting his elbows on the table and leaning his forehead on his steepled hands, the maharaja considered the suggestion. The hereditary Sardars had supported his forefathers through their ups and downs, and had held his hand as he ascended the throne as a boy of nine. Consulting them would not only give him an insight into the wishes of his people but also accord them the respect they deserved. 'Thank you, Sreenivasan...that is a good idea.'

Pushing back his chair, Sreenivasan walked over to the writing desk by the window where the maharaja's stationery was neatly stacked in little wooden drawers. Flipping open the official palace notepad, he pulled out his fountain pen and scribbled swiftly.

Agree with you. Consent to join India withdrawn.

Tearing off the page, he wrote once again on another sheet.

Decision to join India taken after due deliberation and careful consideration. I see no reason to change decision.

Placing crystal paperweights over both sheets of paper, he walked back to the maharaja. 'Your Highness, I have drafted two replies from you to Nawab Hamidullah.'

The maharaja looked at him curiously.

'Both replies are on the desk. Take your time and decide which one you want to send to Bhopal.'

❋ End of the Road ❋

The Sardars filed out one by one, bowing before the maharaja. Each one – even those old enough to be Jivajirao's grandfathers – bent to touch the maharaja's feet with their right hand, raising it thrice to their chest, offering the *mujra*, the traditional salute among the Marathas for their rulers.

Shitoles. Angres. Phalkes. Others. The consultation with the hereditary Sardars at the Usha Kiran Palace, where the maharaja lived, was completed and the ball was now firmly in Jivajirao's court.

Stepping through the double doors, Jivajirao made the long walk to his study, overlooking the lawns and the Mughal-style pavilion outside. As he passed the portrait of Mahadaji, the Scindia who had captured Delhi from the Mughals, Jivajirao adjusted the *pagri* on his head. It felt unusually heavy today, balancing, as it did, the weight of the glorious past with the promise of an unknown future.

Opening the door to his study, the Scindia went over to the desk by the window and picked up the two sheets left by Sreenivasan. He read the first.

Agree with you. Consent to join India withdrawn.

He picked up the second.

Decision to join India taken after due deliberation and careful consideration. I see no reason to change decision.

Walking over to his desk, he rang for his aide, glad that this decision would be finally behind him. His ADC entered.

'Arrange for a telegram to be sent to the nawab of Bhopal,' said the maharaja, handing the aide a sheet, his hand steady, his voice firm. Crumpling the other sheet, the maharaja tossed it into the wastepaper bin.

Decision to join India taken after due deliberation and careful consideration. I see no reason to change decision.

The aide read the message handed to him, to confirm its contents.

'Yes...that's right,' the maharaja sank into his chair, his shoulders suddenly feeling lighter. 'Have it sent to the nawab. My decision remains unchanged. Gwalior will join India.'

♦♦♦♦♦♦♦♦♦♦♦♦♦♦♦♦♦♦♦

Postscript

♦♦♦♦♦♦♦♦♦♦♦♦♦♦♦♦♦♦♦

Gwalior was a leading Maratha-ruled principality of north India. In 1818, following the Third Anglo-Maratha War, the Scindias accepted the supremacy of the East India Company and came under British control. It was one of the 'big-five' princely states, whose ruler was accorded a 21-gun salute. Their original family name was Shinde, and it was the British who began calling them Scindia.

While Ujjain, the former capital of the Scindias, is the land of India's great poet Kalidasa, Gwalior, which was made their capital in 1810, was home to the legendary Tansen and is the famed birthplace of the Gwalior *gharana* of Hindustani music.

Maharaja Jivajirao Scindia (who had been given the English name 'George' by his father) passed away in 1961. His wife, Vijaya Raje Scindia, entered politics and became a member of Parliament. Their children – the late Madhavrao Scindia, Vasundhara Raje Scindia and Yashodhara Raje Scindia – and their grandson, Jyotiraditya Scindia, were/are actively involved in politics.

♦♦♦♦♦♦♦♦♦♦♦♦♦♦♦♦♦♦♦

Did It Really Happen This Way?

♦♦♦♦♦♦♦♦♦♦♦♦♦♦♦♦♦♦♦

The attack on Nehru's car in Gwalior with which the chapter opens, followed by his visit to Sreenivasan's home, has been mentioned by Sreenivasan in his book Of the Raj, Maharajas and Me. *The content of the conversation between Nehru and Sreenivasan is drawn from various speeches and letters of Nehru.*

The conversation between Sreenivasan and C.P. Ramaswami Aiyar, the telegram from the nawab of Bhopal, the meeting with the hereditary Sardars and the incident about the two draft replies have all been mentioned in Sreenivasan's book. Creative liberties have been taken with the settings and dialogues in these scenes.

The conversation at the racecourse has been imagined to provide readers a glimpse into the lifestyle of the royals as the Scindia was known to be the largest horse breeder in the country and a regular at the Bombay Derby. The conversation at the memorial has also been imagined to throw light on the kind of dilemma the princes might have faced.

Patel's decision to prepare a statement to the princes upon Menon's suggestion has been mentioned by Menon in his book Integration of the Indian States. *His thoughts about Nehru in that scene find mention in his correspondence after Nehru's controversial statement in 1946 about the Cabinet Mission Plan created a stir. Gandhi's request to Patel to withdraw his candidature as Congress president to make way for Nehru has been recorded in several sources.*

There is no record of Nehru's reciting Robert Frost's poem during the meeting as described in this chapter. These harmless liberties have been taken to add nuances to the personalities involved in the events covered in the book.

4

Foot in the Door

THE STORY OF INDORE

PRINCELY STATE OF INDORE IN 1947:
in present-day Madhya Pradesh
AREA: 9,934 square miles (25,729 square kilometres) approx.
POPULATION: 1,513,966
RULER: Maharaja Yashwant Rao Holkar II
DIWAN: Horton
19-gun-salute state

❋ The Die Is Cast ❋

'It is the lesson of history,' Sardar's voice crackled through the radio set, stately, sagacious and senatorial, 'that India succumbed to successive waves of invaders owing to the country's fragmented condition. Due to our inability to take a united stand, our internecine quarrels and jealousies have been the cause of our downfall and the reason for our falling victim to foreign domination over and over again. We cannot afford to fall into those errors and traps again.'

Patel's daughter, Maniben, and personal secretary, Shankar, exchanged glances with V.P. Menon, as they listened in to Sardar's speech. The statement, a common appeal to all the princes straight from Sardar, had been Menon's idea – to clear the murky air, erase the many misunderstandings and strike a mutual chord.

'It is an accident,' Sardar's voice continued through the radio, 'that some of us live in the princely states and others in British India...but we all partake of the same culture and are all knit together by the same bonds of blood,' he said, emphasizing to the princely order that they shared a common heritage with the rest of India and would be among their own. 'No one can segregate us into segments, nor impose insurmountable barriers between us.'

Shankar pictured the many rajas and nawabs, diwans and their underlings, listening in to Sardar's speech all across India. While Pakistan had only a handful of princely states to deal with, India had more than 500 to bring together, in a matter of a few weeks. He wondered how the princes would react.

SARDAR PATEL: LET FUTURE GENERATIONS NOT CURSE US...

'To our bitter disappointment and sorrow, some parts have chosen to go out of India and set up their own government,' Sardar noted regretfully, referring to areas that would be ceded to Pakistan, 'and it is thus true that we have not been able to preserve the unity of the country entirely unimpaired in the final stage...'

The Congress had done its utmost to walk along with Jinnah and the Muslim League – but the League had scuttled every plan, thwarted every effort and stamped out every hope, rendering it impossible to step forward together. Parting ways was now the only solution.

Drawing the *pallu* of her saree over her head, Maniben leaned forward on the chair, recalling her trip to Birla House five weeks earlier with her father to meet Gandhi. 'India will be divided over my dead body,' Gandhi had once famously declared. But Sardar had managed to make Gandhi swallow the bitter pill. If he could convince Gandhi to accept Partition, Maniben mused, surely her father could prevail upon the princes to accede to India.

'We are on the threshold of independence,' Sardar's voice lifted, 'and a vast majority of the princely states have already come into the Constituent Assembly. To those who have not done so, I appeal that they join now. And we ask no more of the states than accession on the three matters of defence, external affairs and communications. In other matters, we will scrupulously respect their autonomous existence.'

Exhaling deeply, Menon removed his spectacles and wiped them clean with his kerchief. As the chief architect of this plan, he could have had no better spokesperson to take it to the world. The deal was simple, really; and Sardar had made it crystal clear.

'There appears a great deal of misunderstanding about the attitude of the Congress towards the states,' Sardar said, getting to the heart of the issue. Nehru's scathing remarks about the princes some months ago had created a rift between the Congress and the princely order. It was necessary to undo the damage. 'I would like to make it clear that it is not the desire of the Congress to interfere in any manner whatsoever in the domestic affairs of the states,' Sardar clarified. 'We are no enemies of the princely order, and we wish them and the people under their aegis all prosperity, contentment and happiness. There will be no domination of one over the other. If there is to be any domination, it will be one of mutual interest and welfare.'

Sardar's words reminded Shankar of a story he had once heard about Patel's father, Jhaverbhai. On his way from Gujarat to join forces with the Rani of Jhansi to fight the British in 1857, Jhaverbhai had been taken hostage by Malhar Rao Holkar of

Indore. Legend had it that while watching the Holkar play chess, Jhaverbhai had suggested some great moves, leaving the ruler of Indore impressed, which led to his earning his freedom. Years later, Sardar's father had told his children about his adventures in princely India, warning them about the pettiness and vanity of some of the royal class. Clearly, Sardar was no admirer of the princes, but he had decided to play fair.

'We are at a momentous stage in the history of India,' Sardar said, raising the stakes. 'The alternative to cooperation in the general interest is anarchy and chaos...let not the future generation curse us,' he implored the princes. 'Instead, let it be our proud privilege to leave them a legacy that would raise this sacred land to its proper place among the nations of the world, and turn it into an abode of peace and prosperity.'

As the speech ended, Menon closed his eyes and wiped his sweaty palms on his trousers. The die had been cast; the clock was ticking. How was this going to end?

❋ Half a Dozen Princes ❋

As the July sun rose over Indore in the centre of the Indian subcontinent, six Maratha rulers prepared to descend upon its maharaja as emissaries of the viceroy.

'I've got a bad feeling about this whole affair,' said Pratap Singh Rao Gaekwad, maharaja of Baroda, over the whine of the aeroplane's engines as it taxied to a halt. 'I'm not too sure the Holkar is going to appreciate all six of us turning up, uninvited, on his doorstep like this.'

Jivajirao Scindia, the maharaja of Gwalior, adjusted the boat-shaped *pagri* on his head, as he stepped off the plane, Sardar's appeal still ringing in his ears. 'I understand...' said the Scindia, 'but the viceroy has tasked us with the responsibility to speak with Yashwant Rao in Indore. As you know, we are answerable to the viceroy, so we must try.' Indore and Gwalior were some portions of what was left of the once powerful and immense Great Maratha Confederacy, a vast empire that had crumbled because of petty jealousies, constant infighting, backstabbing and treachery. Its chiefs had been perpetually in conflict – just as Sardar had said. It was time to avoid those mistakes and move on.

'It is a tad disturbing,' said the Pawar of Dhar, as the six rulers made their way to the waiting Rolls-Royces at the edge of the tarmac, 'that even after reading Sardar's statement and hearing of the viceroy's reception for the rulers, Yashwant Rao remains untraceable, and has not even bothered to reply or get in touch with Delhi.'

'Look...as Maratha rulers, we must stand together,' said Chhatrapati Shahaji Bhosale II, the maharaja of Kolhapur, who had rallied them all together. Traditionally, the ruler of Kolhapur occupied a high rank among the Maratha princes. He alone was permitted to carry the hereditary title of Chhatrapati before his name, symbolic of his direct line of descent from Chhatrapati Shivaji Maharaj, the founder of the Maratha Empire.

'August is nearly upon us – only a few weeks remain,' he reminded them. 'We must strive to be united and take Yashwant Rao along.'

MANIK BAGH PALACE, INDORE

The six maharajas got into the waiting luxury cars and sped away, their ministers and staff in tow. As the convoy made its way through the imposing archway of the Manik Bagh Palace in Indore and on to its gravel driveway, everyone had only one question in mind.

Why was Indore, situated as it was in the heart of the subcontinent, vacillating over acceding to India?

❋ In the Net ❋

'Uh...I'm afraid Maharaja Yashwant Rao is not here,' a bewildered aide politely informed the royal party, not quite sure what protocol he was expected to follow in this unprecedented situation. Royals were sticklers for ceremony and formality, never calling on one another in this unscheduled manner. He gaped at the large retinue of ministers, ADCs and staff behind the six maharajas.

'We will wait,' said the Gaekwad of Baroda, curiously examining the contemporary chrome-fitted light fixtures and lacquered fittings in the drawing room. 'When is he likely to return?' he asked, peering at an oddly shaped mantelpiece.

'No...er...I mean, His Highness is...not in Indore,' replied the aide.

'Where has he gone?' asked the Scindia, also taken in by the unusual design and décor of the palace, which stemmed from the peculiarly modern aesthetic taste of Yashwant Rao Holkar II.

'I am...I...don't...quite know...' the aide mumbled, uncertain how much he could reveal to the royal party that had shown up unannounced.

'Where is your prime minister?' demanded the Chhatrapati of Kolhapur crisply, annoyed with the aide's evasive responses.

'Prime Minister Horton? Uh...I'm afraid he...he too is away.'

'Where have they gone?' asked the Pawar of Dhar. 'And when are they expected to return?'

'I don't quite know...I...uh...we have no information...' repeated the aide.

'We have an important message from the viceroy – it is crucial that we see your maharaja,' said Chhatrapati Shahaji Bhosale tersely.

'I am sorry...but...'

'If you don't tell us where he is, we will be compelled to complain to the viceroy about your maharaja,' threatened the Gaekwad.

'Bhopal,' the aide blurted out. 'The maharaja has gone to visit the nawab of Bhopal.'

'Hamidullah?' asked the Scindia, exchanging anxious glances with the others. It was no secret that the nawab had been encouraging the princes to stay out of India and to form a joint third front called Princestan instead. *Was Indore ensnared in the nawab's net?*

'We have to get hold of the Holkar before he makes a rash decision,' said Srimant Yeshwantrao Hindurao Ghorpade, the raja of Sandur, his forehead crinkled with worry lines.

'How do you propose to do that?' asked the Gaekwad. 'For all you know, the Holkar has already signed a pact with the nawab to stay out of India.'

'Still...we can make one last attempt,' suggested the raja of Sandur.

'How?'

'By sending word to Yashwant Rao in Bhopal.'

'Is it not enough that we have come all the way here?' muttered the Gaekwad. 'Do we have to chase after the Holkar all over the country now?'

'I will send my prime minister to Bhopal with this,' the maharaja of Kolhapur waved the envelope containing the viceroy's letter. 'Surely this will make Yashwant Rao reconsider.'

The six rulers looked at one another. The viceroy had sent them to Indore with a simple task. Failing to deliver a message to one of their fellow princes would be a grave loss of face. They simply had to get the job done.

'I suppose we have nothing to lose.' The Scindia shrugged. 'All right, let's give this another shot.'

❃ Game Plan ❃

'No! He is my guest. I cannot let you disturb him.' Nawab Hamidullah of Bhopal said, deeply displeased to find the diwan of Kolhapur camping in his drawing room, demanding to see the Holkar urgently. The nawab had kept him waiting for over three hours and then had tried to fob him off. But the diwan was unrelenting and dead set on delivering his message.

'Your Highness, I am sorry to intrude,' the prime minister of Kolhapur apologized yet again, 'but, as I said before, I bear an urgent message for the maharaja. The Bhosale, the Gaekwad, the Scindia and three other princes are waiting for him at present in Indore.'

'If they haven't informed Yashwant Rao about their visit in advance, he can hardly be expected to receive them when they show up without notice,' the nawab snapped, piqued by this interruption of his critical discussion with the Holkar.

'Your Highness, they have been sent by the viceroy.'

'The viceroy?' Nawab Hamidullah's jaw dropped. The viceroy was a dear friend, and they went back many years to when Louis Mountbatten had first visited India, over two decades ago, to accompany his cousin Prince Edward, then Prince of Wales, on his India tour. Hamidullah was one of the few people close enough to call the viceroy by his nickname,

Dickie. 'All right then...tell me, what is the message?' the nawab relented slightly.

'I am sorry, Your Highness,' demurred the diwan respectfully, 'but the viceroy has asked the Chhatrapati and his brother princes to deliver the message personally to the maharaja of Indore.'

'I see...' The nawab sighed, finding himself in a quandary. How hard he had tried and wished for the rulers to display more foresight and solidarity, instead of aligning their fates with the Congress. His grand vision of floating a third front of princely states was crumbling with state after state falling into Sardar Patel's accession basket. 'Wait here,' he said, turning towards the corridor. 'I'll send for the Holkar.'

The nawab walked back to his study, torn between personal ambition and friendship. On the one hand, the maharaja of Indore was one of his last remaining allies in his risky game plan. On the other hand, he could not hinder Dickie's messenger. He pushed open the study door to find Maharaja Yashwant Rao Holkar and his prime minister, Horton, bent over a table, deep in discussion with the nawab's advisers.

'The Congress party will be happy to leave no trace of the royals,' Prime Minister Horton was saying as the nawab entered. 'We cannot let them bully us.'

'Yashwant,' the nawab cut in, 'the maharajas of Baroda, Gwalior, Kolhapur, Sandur, Dhar and Dewas Junior are all at your palace, waiting for you with a message from the viceroy.'

'All six of them? At my palace?' Maharaja Yashwant Rao Holkar stood up with a start. 'With a message from the viceroy?'

Prime Minister Horton thumped the table. 'This is Sardar Patel's work! He's trying to intimidate everyone into submission.'

'Look, whatever they tell you,' the nawab said, drawing Yashwant Rao aside, 'do not commit to acceding to India.'

DO NOT COMMIT TO ACCEDING TO INDIA...

Taking a seat, the maharaja of Indore began cracking his knuckles apprehensively. *Why had the viceroy sent him a personal message? Why was there such a large princely delegation to deliver this message?*

'Promise that you will consult me before you make a decision,' the nawab pressed him, clutching at straws in a desperate bid to keep his dream from falling apart.

Yashwant Rao turned to his friend. 'I promise you, my brother,' he said, taking the nawab's hand in his. 'I pledge myself to the unity of our cause. I shall not come to a decision without consulting you – you have my word.'

❋ Try Everything ❋

Sardar emerged from the room, exhausted and craving fresh air, having spent the last few hours with his namesake, H.M. Patel,

From army to armoury, telegraph to railways, factories to stationery – everything had to be divided between India and Pakistan after the decision of Partition was taken. A Partition Council had been established to carry out this work, in which Sardar Patel represented the Congress. 'There should be no loss to India; nor should Pakistan suffer needlessly,' were Sardar's instructions to the secretaries of the Partition Council as they took on the enormous task at hand.

and Chaudhari Muhammad Ali, the two-man steering committee charged with working out the nitty-gritty of Partition. From the stores of the public works department to the naval ships of the military – all assets and liabilities needed to be taken stock of and divided in fair measure between India and Pakistan – yet another responsibility resting on Sardar's shoulders as a member of the Partition Council – and yet another gigantic exercise that needed to be completed in a matter of weeks.

'Pandit Nehru informed me about a letter he received from the maharaja of Indore,' said Menon, as soon as Sardar emerged from his meeting. 'The Holkar wants to see the terms Pakistan is offering.'

'Why does he want to see Pakistan's terms?' asked Sardar, clasping his hands behind his back. 'What has that got to do with anything?' The delaying tactics used by some of the rulers incensed him.

'The Holkar claims the states should know the terms offered by both nations before making an informed decision.' Menon passed a nervous hand over his thinning hair. 'He also declares that he and the nawab of Bhopal will follow a common policy, calling their friendship a practical demonstration of Hindu-Muslim cooperation.'

'Hah!' Patel chuckled, amused that the maharaja was stamping his stonewalling with the secular label of Hindu-Muslim unity.

'The Holkar has tried every trick in the book,' Menon continued. 'He has written to Nehru. His deputy prime minister had a meeting with me. His prime minister has met with the viceroy's private secretary, George Abell. He sent Zafarullah Khan, the nawab's adviser, to intercede on his behalf and meet the viceroy's chief of staff, Hastings Ismay. He is...'

'Excuse me, Sardar...' Shankar interrupted, entering with files awaiting Sardar's signatures, 'the raja of Bharatpur just called. He says he received a telegram from the maharaja of Indore asking him to refrain from signing the accession papers.'

'You see?' Menon threw up his hands. 'The Holkar has gone to town with these telegrams! Jodhpur...Nawanagar...now Bharatpur. God knows whom else he has approached.'

Sardar stood ruminating by the window, gazing at the evening sky. Bhopal had clearly joined forces with Indore to convince the others to hold off signing the accession papers until the last possible moment in order to increase their bargaining power. He simply could not allow them to dictate terms to the Government of India.

'The viceroy,' said Menon, 'had sent the rulers of Baroda, Gwalior, Kolhapur and some others to meet the Holkar in Indore and bring him in. But the Holkar was away in Bhopal at the time, and it took the diwan of Kolhapur over four hours to persuade him to return to Indore and meet with the viceroy's royal delegates. When he eventually returned late that evening, after having kept the other rulers waiting all day,' Menon exclaimed incredulously, 'it seems he went straight to his room and had them all summarily dismissed. He hasn't responded to any of our calls. We have no idea what he has in mind.'

Sardar walked to the bookshelf and ran his fingers over the *Arthashastra*, the classic Indian treatise on political science. *Sama. Dama. Danda. Bheda.* Persuasion. Offering. Punishment. Division. The four tried-and-tested means to achieve one's ends had been passed down from ancient times. He pursed his lips. *If one approach failed, it was time to shift gears and try another.*

❋ Endgame ❋

Maharaja Yashwant Rao Holkar sat frozen, facing the large desk in the viceroy's study that overlooked the Mughal Gardens below, his frame frail, his face pale. His long, pointed nose accentuated his bony face and the withered lips betrayed the anxiety within. An uneasy Nawab Hamidullah sat to his left, wiping his brow. Viceroy Mountbatten looked at the two rulers seated across the table, much like a headmaster glaring at errant pupils.

'When I sent the Gaekwad of Baroda with the maharajas of Gwalior and Kolhapur and some others to meet you, I believe you refused to see them?' the viceroy said bluntly, his expression cold, his tone accusing.

The maharaja shifted uneasily in his chair but made no reply.

'And I am told, when you returned to your palace late at night,' the viceroy went on, his glare reflecting his indignation, 'knowing that the six of them had been waiting for you all day, you walked straight past them and into your bedroom, and then had them all kicked out unceremoniously. They are appalled at the way you treated them, as am I.'

'Your Excellency, I did not intend to be in any way discourteous,' the maharaja tried to mollify the furious viceroy, wishing he had sent Prime Minister Horton in his place for this meeting.

'All the states have been in close touch with us in Delhi to resolve the problem of accession,' said the viceroy, casting a sidelong glance at Nawab Hamidullah, seated beside the Holkar. 'It is only Indore that has not bothered to communicate with Delhi. And when I send a delegation to meet you, you refuse to see them?'

'I am sorry, Your Excellency...you see, I–'

'I have spent the better part of last month trying to untangle the states problem,' the viceroy cut in. 'I had invited all the princes to Delhi for a meeting on 25 July. Every state sent a representative or a response – except Indore. Do you have any explanation for this?'

'Your Excellency'—the maharaja cleared his throat—'I was in London. My ministers were unable to decide in my absence. I assure you we meant no disrespect.'

'Does nobody even reply to invitations in your absence?' the viceroy demanded. 'Anyway...when did you return to India?'

'Uh...on 29 July,' the maharaja mumbled.

The viceroy raised his eyebrows. 'I have good reason to believe you were back on 24 July.'

The maharaja exchanged a nervous glance with Nawab Hamidullah by his side and sheepishly lowered his gaze.

'What makes matters worse,' the viceroy went on, making no attempt to hide his displeasure, 'is that your prime minister has been going about claiming that I threatened you.'

The maharaja gulped in dismay. 'Your Excellency, the truth is I had promised the nawab here that I would not take any decision without consulting him. That, I assure you, is the only reason for the delay.'

'But surely you both see that my letter contains no hint of a threat,' fumed the viceroy. 'And, as I have said repeatedly, there is no coercion whatsoever. You are free to do as you like.

But you need to inform us about your decision. I resent these deliberate misrepresentations.'

'I am sorry Your Excellency is so annoyed,' the maharaja offered a meek apology.

'This is a lamentable lack of responsibility on your part, not to mention the discourtesy shown to the representative of the British Crown.'

'Your Excellency, I was ill after my return from London... in fact, I continue to be unwell,' the maharaja said, looking remorseful. 'And ever since I came back, I have been asking for the revised Instrument of Accession. I have not yet received the document.'

'The Instrument of Accession has been available for many days now,' the viceroy corrected the Holkar, gesturing to his conference secretary to make a detailed note of the discussion. 'It appears to me that you are making lame excuses.'

Feeling the heat, the maharaja pulled out a silk handkerchief from the pocket of his waistcoat and wiped the sweat beading his brow.

'But, Your Excellency, in all honesty,' the maharaja came clean, 'I did not attend the meeting because I thought the states have a free hand in deciding their future. I would like the bond my ancestors shared with Great Britain to continue. I wish that states like mine, which do not wish to become a part of India or Pakistan, are granted dominion status by His Majesty's government.'

'This has been debated and discussed several times over,' the viceroy replied, irked by the number of times he'd had to repeat himself. It seemed plain to him that the nawab of Bhopal had coached and encouraged the Holkar to drag his heels in this manner. 'The states will *not* be given dominion status by the British government,' he said emphatically, 'so do not pin your hopes on that.'

MAHARAJA YASHWANT RAO: I WOULD LIKE OUR BOND WITH BRITAIN TO CONTINUE...

The maharaja exhaled sharply, as did the nawab. The viceroy had sounded the death knell to their plans. If Britain did not grant them recognition and entry into the Commonwealth, holding out seemed like a futile effort. After all that the princes had done for Great Britain over the last two centuries, this seemed like a huge betrayal.

'Besides, let me tell you what I really think...' added the viceroy tersely. 'If Indore doesn't join India, I predict that your people will kick you off your *gaddi* within the next month. Let's not live under any illusions; you won't be able to stand twenty-four hours against your subjects when paramountcy is lifted. It is in your interest, more than anyone else's, that you get on friendly terms with India.'

The words struck the maharaja like a whiplash. He swallowed hard, and began lacing and unlacing his long, bony fingers. British paramountcy, everyone knew, had over the years resulted in the weakening of Indian kingdoms. While the princes had retained their prestige and pageantry, they stood bereft of power and authority. Moreover, the *praja mandal* organizations, which represented the people in the princely states, were stirring up trouble everywhere. In Travancore, the diwan had been attacked. In Kashmir, they had launched a movement to get the maharaja to abdicate. There was really no saying what they would do in Indore.

'See...' said the viceroy, edging closer to the maharaja, 'I am not putting any undue pressure on you. But I must point out that most of the states surrounding you have joined India. If you don't follow suit, you must be prepared for your people rising in rebellion against you. If that were to happen, the Indian Army will not be able to help you restore peace and order.'

The maharaja nodded slightly, looking intently at his shoes, the truth of those words sinking in. Without help from the British and without the Indian Army, putting down any popular uprising would be nearly impossible for his state forces.

'And furthermore, remember that my role as Crown Representative ends on 15 August,' added the viceroy. 'Thereafter I can play no part in helping you broker this bond. You will be on your own.'

'I...I...need some more time,' the maharaja mumbled. The viceroy, he knew, was a smooth operator, cleverly veiling his threats as concern.

'You have ten days,' said Mountbatten, looking up at the special calendar pinned on his wall with a countdown to Independence Day. 'If you think waiting beyond that is going to fetch you better terms, well...go ahead and wait. But, if you want my honest opinion'—the viceroy shrugged—'Sardar is not going to have a conciliatory approach after 15 August.'

Yashwant Rao Holkar locked eyes with the viceroy. And, in that moment, he realized exactly what he was up against.

Negotiating with Sardar Patel after 15 August was going to be very nearly impossible. Right here. Right now. This was the best deal Indore was going to get.

❋ An Anonymous Arrival ❋

Independence Day had come and gone, and it was a usual morning at the States Department in New Delhi.

V.P. Menon had finished his routine morning briefing with Sardar Patel and was surveying the mountain of correspondence on his table, when the clerk dropped a large plain envelope into the in-tray.

Menon picked it up, reached for the letter knife and carefully sliced it open. A set of documents emerged. Documents created by him. Documents he had seen over and over again. Documents he could recognize in his sleep.

The Instrument of Accession. And the Standstill Agreement.

Dated, stamped and signed.

And yet, Menon was perplexed. Who had sent them? They had been sent in an ordinary postal envelope and contained no covering letter.

Browsing through the fine print of the document, Menon exhaled in relief. Rising from the desk, he walked over to the door of the adjoining room and knocked.

'Sardar...' He popped his head around the door and waved the envelope in his hand. 'Looks like Indore is in.'

Patel was at his desk, writing a letter to Gandhi to apprise him of the latest refugee situation. While they were in the midst of Independence Day celebrations in Delhi, the man who had led them to the threshold of freedom had decided to stay away from it all, stationing himself instead in Calcutta. A one-man army holding the city's peace. 'Indore has missed the bus,' said Sardar, without looking up. 'Tell the Holkar he's too late.'

'The Holkar has backdated his signature and marked it 14 August,' Menon pointed out with a wry smile.

Sardar stopped writing, not sure whether the Holkar ought to be allowed that indiscretion. Each instance of accommodation and adjustment sent dissenters the wrong signal. Each concession he allowed made the Government of India appear weaker. 'Summon the Holkar to Delhi – tell him I want to meet him,' he said sternly, after a thoughtful pause.

'What about the accession for now?' asked Menon, his fingers crossed. 'Shall I tell him we accept?'

'Hmm...inform the viceroy,' Sardar nodded glumly and returned to his letter. 'Tell him that the basket of apples he promised me – it's very nearly full.'

♦♦♦♦♦♦♦♦♦♦♦♦♦♦♦♦♦♦♦

Postscript

♦♦♦♦♦♦♦♦♦♦♦♦♦♦♦♦♦♦♦

The city of Indore gained power and fame during the reign of Maharani Ahilyabai Holkar in the eighteenth century. She was the daughter-in-law of Malhar Rao Holkar, the founder of the Holkar dynasty, one among the Maratha Confederacy. She shifted the capital of the kingdom from Maheshwar to Indore.

Maharaja Yashwant Rao Holkar was noted for his progressive views and had, in fact, written to the president of the United States during the Second World War, supporting India's nationalistic demands. Yet, in later years, he shifted loyalties to the idea of a third front of princely states and did not sign the Instrument of Accession until the last minute.

However, it is said that as soon as he agreed to come in, he cooperated with the Government of India in every way. The princely kingdoms of the region were joined together thereafter with other areas to form Madhya Bharat in May 1948. Both Indore and Gwalior pressed to be declared the capital of the state. As a temporary truce, Indore was made the summer capital and Gwalior the winter capital. The state was later recast as Madhya Pradesh and Bhopal was made its capital.

After the integration of Indore, the maharaja asked that his only daughter, Ushadevi, be recognized as his heir.

♦♦♦♦♦♦♦♦♦♦♦♦♦♦♦♦♦♦♦

Did It Really Happen This Way?

♦♦♦♦♦♦♦♦♦♦♦♦♦♦♦♦♦♦♦

Sardar Patel's speech in the opening scene is taken from the text of his statement of 5 July 1947 to the princes, partly paraphrased and compressed.

The episode describing the trip made by the six Maratha rulers to Indore at the viceroy's behest, including their getting the cold shoulder from Maharaja Yashwant Rao Holkar, is based on the viceroy's report found in The Transfer of Power 1942–7, Vol. XII.

The telegrams alluded to, as having been sent by the Holkar to the other princes, and the letter sent by the maharaja to Nehru are also documented in the viceroy's report found in The Transfer of Power 1942–7, Vol. XII.

The meeting in the viceroy's study between the Holkar, Nawab Hamidullah and Lord Mountbatten took place as mentioned, and the actual discussion has been reproduced nearly verbatim from the minutes of the meeting recorded in The Transfer of Power 1942–7, Vol. XII. *It was followed up by a similar meeting between the maharaja of* Indore *and Sardar Patel.*

The surprise receipt of Indore's accession in an ordinary envelope, with no covering letter, has been recorded by Menon *in his account of the events in his book* Integration of the Indian States.

5

Breakwaters in the Storm

THE STORY OF BIKANER

PRINCELY STATE OF BIKANER IN 1947:
in present-day Rajasthan
AREA: 23,181 square miles (60,038 square kilometres) approx.
POPULATION: 12,92,938
RULER: Lieutenant General Maharaja Sir Sadul Singh
DIWAN: K.M. Panikkar
17-gun-salute state

❋ Co-Builders of India ❋

Excited spectators emerged from the visitors' gallery of the Council House, one of the most splendid sandstone structures in New Delhi, gushing about the remarkable speeches they had heard inside those hallowed halls. Congressmen in homespun khadi kurtas and white Nehru caps strode alongside maharajas in shimmering silk suits topped with elaborate turbans, their diwans and ministers in tow. Reporters and cameramen hustled about, trying to record a comment, capture a quote and grab a lasting shot of the historic moment for the next day's newspapers.

'Let the princes rise to the occasion and be hailed as the co-architects of India's independence and greatness,' declared Maharaja Sadul Singh of Bikaner, speaking to a newsperson outside the colonnaded corridors of what would later become India's Parliament House. It was a momentous occasion. The princely states were joining the Indian Constituent Assembly where, after centuries of foreign rule, Indians would draft themselves a constitution, a historic document that would form the backbone of the country.

'The princely states must work in tandem with India to create a strong centre,' said the tall and handsome maharaja of Bikaner, dressed resplendently for the occasion in an ivory-coloured suit and elegant *pagri*, his prime minister, K.M. Panikkar, by his side, 'so that the individual states and India as a whole are safeguarded in the vacuum created by the exit of the British.'

Panikkar nodded, proud of the maharaja for having resisted the advances of the nawab of Bhopal, who had done his best to persuade rulers to stay out of India and hold out against the Congress. Having been a journalist, Panikkar knew the ripple effect that such press statements could have and hoped more princes would join the handful who had decided to be in the Indian Constituent Assembly.

'What would you say to the statement of the Muslim League?' asked the press reporter as dozens of flashbulbs popped, lighting up the maharaja's face. 'Mr Liaquat Ali Khan says the princes are succumbing to pressure from the Congress.'

The maharaja heaved a sigh, aware that the League, with Jinnah and Liaquat Ali at its helm, had opted out of joining the Constituent Assembly. 'As far as my state, Bikaner, is concerned,' he replied decisively, holding up his bejewelled hands to emphasize the point, 'we were not pressurized into joining the Constituent Assembly. We are here because we consider it in our own – and India's – interests.'

Emerging from the majestic circular building through its colonnaded veranda just then, Pandit Nehru paused and nodded appreciatively at Maharaja Sadul Singh before a slew of reporters and photographers engulfed him. Liaquat Ali Khan was the finance minister in the Interim Cabinet – a colleague in the government. It did not behove him, thought Nehru, to make such a statement in public. The maharaja's reply pleased him greatly.

Acknowledging Nehru, the maharaja smiled back as he walked towards his waiting car. His decision to join India had been sealed a few days ago when Nehru had honoured him with a visit to Bikaner House, his residence in Delhi, to assure him and his brother princes that the Congress would do nothing to undermine the rulers or injure their interests. Committed to the cause of India's unity, Maharaja Sadul Singh felt confident he had made the right call.

MAHARAJA SADUL SINGH: WE JOINED THE INDIAN CONSTITUENT ASSEMBLY IN BIKANER'S – AND INDIA'S – INTERESTS...

Yet, in less than three months, events beyond his imagination and control would force Maharaja Sadul Singh to think again.

❋ Troubled Waters ❋

'Partition may hit our water supply, Your Highness,' reported Rai Bahadur Kanwar Sain, the chief engineer of Bikaner, worry lines furrowing his forehead. 'The headworks of our canal are in Ferozepur *tehsil* in Punjab...and it is strongly rumoured that the Boundary Commission, which will decide the border line, may award Ferozepur to Pakistan, because it has a Muslim majority.

Back then, the Legislative Council and Legislative Assembly, as also the Chamber of Princes, were located in a circular sandstone building known as Council House in New Delhi. The impressive structure containing 144 tall columns, was surrounded by green lawns and flowering trees. The building functioned as India's Constituent Assembly between 1947 and 1950; this was where the Constitution of India was discussed, debated and drafted. From 1950 onwards, it was India's Parliament House, the seat of both its Rajya Sabha (Upper House) and Lok Sabha (Lower House), until the new Parliament complex was constructed in 2023.

Maharaja Sadul Singh ran his fingers over the cool pink stone of Lallgarh Palace as he strolled into its lush gardens. He gazed at the swathes of green around him – the result of his father's lifelong efforts. Moved by the plight of his people dying like flies during the great famine of 1890, his father, Maharaja Ganga Singh, had vowed to ensure such a scourge would never be repeated. His dream to bring water into the desert of Rajputana from neighbouring Punjab had taken almost twenty years to fulfil. Surmounting opposition from Punjab, securing the support of neighbouring rulers and lobbying with the British by contributing to their war efforts – leaving no stone unturned in his efforts to turn the tide – Maharaja Ganga Singh had prevailed in constructing a colossal canal that brought in water from the River Sutlej into Bikaner, irrigating thousands of acres of desert land and transforming it completely. Kanwar Sain's words made Sadul Singh swallow hard.

All his life, Sadul Singh had lived in the shadow of his illustrious father and was consumed by a burning desire to surpass him. Nine irrigation projects, two railway lines, three roads, dozens of public works, personally touring remote desert villages on horseback for famine relief, representing Indian princes at the Round Table Conference in London, leading as a general in the British Army in the First World War, recipient of the Kaiser-i-Hind medal from Queen Victoria, signatory to the historic Treaty of Versailles – Maharaja Ganga Singh had been a man of indefatigable energy and unparalleled accomplishments.

Reversing the good his father had done was the last thing Sadul Singh wished to do. Bikaner had already taken its seat in the Indian Constituent Assembly, committing itself in a way to India. And yet, the choice to formally join India was still his to make.

'I believe the Indian Independence Act has a clause under which all prior agreements between states will stand abrogated,' said Kanwar Sain. 'If Ferozepur goes to Pakistan, and Pakistan gets control of the Sutlej Canal headworks, Your Highness—' his voice trailed off, the implication quite apparent.

Turning his gaze from the vast lawns to the magnificent hanging balconies and lattice carvings of the palace, Maharaja Sadul Singh straightened his shoulders, feeling the immense weight of his father's legacy.

There were no two ways about it. The Ganga Canal was Bikaner's lifeline. The fortunes of his desert kingdom and people rested on it.

For Bikaner to stay in India, Ferozepur had to stay in India.

❋ The Blessed Line ❋

Sweating profusely in the heat of midsummer Delhi, Sir Cyril Radcliffe navigated the obstacle course created by the reams of documents and reports piled haphazardly on the floor and walked over to the large map of Punjab pinned on the wall of his office room.

Destiny, if there were such a thing, had played a cruel joke on him. Entrusted with the unenviable task of drawing the line to divide India into two parts, he now desperately wished he were back in his law chambers in Lincoln's Inn in London.

Radcliffe had never been to India before, knew virtually nothing about it. And, strangely enough, *those* had been the very reasons he had been picked for the job.

Standing before the map, Radcliffe rolled up his sleeves. One stroke of his pen would affect the lives of 80 million people. Separate brother from brother, daughter from father, friend from friend, farmer from field, pilgrim from temple, people from their rivers, workers from their factories. No matter where he drew that godforsaken line, he would be cursed and despised. This, Radcliffe was certain, was as close as it got to Hell.

'The demographic data for Ferozepur, sir,' his aide, Christopher Beaumont, handed him a chart containing population-related details about the district he had been studying that morning. While the western districts of Punjab were predominantly Muslim, and the eastern parts largely non-Muslim, the central areas had a mixed population. Here communities intermingled, and wherever Radcliffe drew the line, millions of Hindus, Muslims and Sikhs would find themselves on the wrong side of the border. Ferozepur was one such area that presented a unique problem.

Radcliffe adjusted his glasses over his nose and turned his attention to the census charts. Hardly any of the records made available to him were up to date, but that was all he had.

'Ferozepur appears to have a marginal Muslim majority,' he mumbled as he browsed through the data, before turning back to the map on the wall.

'Sir, may I remind you of the representations made by Bikaner and Bahawalpur,' said Rao Sahib V.D. Ayer, assistant secretary to the Boundary Commission, whose job it was to assist the boundary commissioner in drawing a borderline that was fair and reasonable. 'Both states are interested in the water canals whose headworks from the Sutlej are located in Punjab.'

'But the census data shows that Ferozepur has a Muslim majority,' pressed Justice Din Muhammad who, along with Justice Mohammed Munir, represented the Muslim League on the Punjab Boundary Commission, 'and has the only major arsenal in the region to supply Pakistan's Army with ammunition.'

Radcliffe sighed. He wished the commission members could be more objective. Yes, he was aware of the waterworks and he was aware of the arsenal. They were both, no doubt, matters of critical importance. As was just about everything else. If he catered to the whims, fancies and views of every party and petitioner, the boundary line would never take shape. The delayed rains and scorching heat weren't helping either. And as if all of this wasn't enough, the viceroy was pressing him every day to hand in the Boundary Award – marking the dividing line – as quickly as possible.

'I'd like to believe that whichever government gets control of the river will be reasonable in working out water-sharing agreements,' said Radcliffe to the others, hopeful that India and Pakistan would come to a mutually beneficial and amicable arrangement after the Partition came through.

Justices Din Muhammad and Mohammed Munir exchanged glum glances, as did Justice Mehr Chand Mahajan and Justice Teja Singh, the Indian National Congress nominees on the commission. The members of the Punjab Boundary Commission knew better than their chairman. Given the

RADCLIFFE: MARKING THE BOUNDARY LINE DIVIDING INDIA AND PAKISTAN

devastating violence on the streets of Punjab, goodwill and sharing were the last things on anybody's mind.

'Well'—Radcliffe shrugged, pouring himself a glass of ice water—'I've been thinking that we recommend that the canal systems be administered jointly by India and Pakistan.'

'So...what about Ferozepur, sir?' asked Ayer anxiously.

'From the demographic data we have,' Radcliffe scribbled in his notebook, 'it looks like Ferozepur ought to go to Pakistan.'

❋ Leaks and Fixes ❋

'Excuse me, Panditji...Khosla here...chairman of the Central Waterways...' A well-dressed, middle-aged man broke through the crowd of people waiting to meet Nehru at the gate of his residence on York Road (present-day Motilal Nehru Marg) in New Delhi. Nehru was on his way for his daily meeting with Sardar at Patel's home on Aurangzeb Road at the end of the street. 'From the Irrigation and Navigation Commission, sir. I have an important matter to discuss...'

'Come...walk with me,' Nehru invited him, fending off the rest of the crowd.

'Sir, I am here to see you about the joint control of our waterways,' explained Khosla.

'What do you mean?' Despite the crisply tailored achkan and fresh red rose in his buttonhole, the dark circles around his weary eyes betrayed Nehru's deep predicament. 'Joint control of our waterways?' he asked, cupping his ear to eliminate the din of the throng of petitioners around them.

'We have heard,' Ajudhiya Nath Khosla leaned close to Nehru and spoke in a low voice, 'that in certain areas, the Boundary Commission may recommend joint control by India and Pakistan of common waterways and electricity.'

Nehru slowed his brisk pace and turned to Khosla with alarmed eyes.

'Sir, whatever the decision about the area west of the Sutlej,' said Khosla solemnly, 'on no account should any area east of the river go to Pakistan.'

'I have no say in the demarcation of the boundary line, my dear fellow,' Nehru reasoned. 'As you know, Sir Cyril Radcliffe heads the Boundary Commission that will demarcate the boundaries in Punjab and Bengal, between India and Pakistan.

The commission is hearing petitions from all interested parties. It is not in my hands.'

'I know, sir,' Khosla replied, whipping out a map from his briefcase as Nehru resumed walking, 'but I urge you to do something about this. It is of critical importance.'

Nehru slowed his pace and peered at the map.

'The Sutlej valley canals take water from the rivers Beas and Sutlej over here,' Khosla explained, pointing to an area in East Punjab. 'The first headworks of this system are in Ferozepur, from where irrigation water is taken to Bikaner. The entire desert region of Rajputana gets its water from here.'

Nehru stopped walking again and examined the map closely. Bikaner was one of the largest of the Rajputana states and it would border Pakistan.

'Ferozepur and Zira *tehsils* have a small Muslim majority,' Khosla whispered. 'Sir, according to the notional division laid down in the Indian Independence Act, both these fall within the purview of East Punjab, so they should go to India, but I have heard that the Boundary Commission might allocate this area in the final award to Pakistan...'

Nehru looked at Khosla, puzzled. The deliberations of the Boundary Commission were not public information. *Was someone in the commission deliberately disclosing details so they could reach him? Could they be acted upon? How much of it could be believed? How much of it was being leaked to the Muslim League?*

'It will be disastrous for us, sir,' Khosla cut into Nehru's rumination, 'if Pakistan is given control of our water and electricity. This recommendation should not be accepted under any circumstances. It will kill all hope of irrigation development in the region.'

Nehru's face turned solemn. It was an open secret that Jinnah was making overtures to the rulers of the border states such as Jodhpur and Jaisalmer, despite their having a Hindu majority. Bikaner was another border state, and Jinnah would no doubt be eager to lure Sadul Singh into the trap. It was crucial to hold on to Bikaner.

'I understand,' mumbled Nehru, the thought of sharing control of water – that most basic and critical of all resources – with Jinnah's administration sending a chill down his spine. 'I'm glad you came to me about this.'

'Also,' Khosla continued, 'it would be disastrous for India from the strategic point of view...'

'What do you mean?'

'The Sutlej is the last line of defence, sir. Beyond the bridge over the river at Ferozepur, there is no natural barrier between Pakistan and Delhi.'

'Thank you, Mr Khosla.' Nehru patted the man's shoulder. 'I shall see what I can do about this.' Nehru walked on. At the proceedings of the Partition Council, the Congress had agreed to abide by the decision of the Boundary Commission under Sir Cyril, whatever the award might be. It would be improper to interfere.

And yet, some things, however inappropriate, he reasoned with himself as he entered the gates of Sardar's house, simply had to be done!

❋ All or Nothing ❋

'Our life depends on the Sutlej, Your Excellency,' Kanwar Sain said to the viceroy, peering curiously at the rumbling air conditioner in the window of the green wall, one of the few such machines anywhere in the country.

'The Ganga Canal that feeds Bikaner begins in Ferozepur,' added Diwan K.M. Panikkar, rolling out a map on the table before the viceroy.

'I am aware of that'—the viceroy nodded solemnly, having already received a letter about the matter from Nehru—'but I cannot discuss the Boundary Award with you. It is not within my domain.'

'Your Excellency will please appreciate that if control of our water is handed over to Pakistan, it will cause us grave harm,' explained Panikkar, running a nervous hand over his goatee. 'Bikaner's entire economy depends on this canal.'

'I understand,' the viceroy reiterated, 'but I'm sorry. I have nothing to do with the Boundary Award.'

'We are not party to the boundary agreement,' protested Panikkar, raising the petition and his pitch by a notch. 'We were not consulted about it. It would be unfair to have us bear the consequences. Bikaner state has never hesitated to come to the aid of the Crown whenever called upon. The late maharaja, Ganga Singhji, was the very first to send troops to aid Britain in the First World War. Our maharaja was one of the first to join the Indian Constituent Assembly. Bikaner has—'

'Look, I sympathize with you,' interrupted the viceroy, putting up his hands, 'but I cannot be of any help.'

Panikkar sighed. A graduate of Oxford, Sorbonne and the Middle Temple, the diwan of Bikaner could have been anywhere in the world that he wished to be, but he had chosen to return to India to serve his nation and be with his family. Serving first as adviser to the maharaja of Kashmir, followed by the same position in the court of Patiala and then taking up the post of diwan in Bikaner, he had always tried brokering a closer relationship between the princes and the Congress to forge a united India. He was not going to give up that easily.

'Then, I'm afraid Bikaner has no choice.' Panikkar pursed his lips, exchanging rueful glances with Sain. For a diehard, straight-talking nationalist, this was going to be a tricky and difficult negotiation; and yet, it was a chance he was willing to take.

'No choice about what?' asked the viceroy, his eyes narrowing suspiciously.

'The maharaja has made it quite clear.' Panikkar drummed his fingers on the desk, hoping that the viceroy would fall for the bluff.

'Made what clear?' The viceroy cocked his head.

'That if Ferozepur goes to Pakistan,' Panikkar said, his face deadpan, 'Bikaner will join Pakistan.'

PANIKKAR: IF FEROZEPUR GOES TO PAKISTAN, BIKANER WILL JOIN PAKISTAN...

❋ An Intriguing Invitation ❋

A flash of lightning illuminated the dark night and thunder rumbled. A dim light glowed in the green-shuttered bungalow within the viceroy's vast residential complex.

Perhaps the long-awaited monsoon had finally arrived, Cyril Radcliffe thought to himself, looking forward to the reprieve. He poured himself a glass of gin and tonic, and pored over yet another district map of the Punjab heartland. The maps made of rice paper stuck to his sweating arms. He peeled them off, wishing he could step out for a break, but there was no time for such a luxury. And besides, whenever he ventured out, people thronged him, pleading and beseeching, telling him why he ought to draw the boundary line this way or that. Fed up, he couldn't wait for this ordeal to end.

There was a knock on the door.

'Mr Menon is here to see you, sir,' the housekeeper informed Sir Radcliffe.

'At this hour?' Radcliffe exclaimed, turning to the wall clock. 'It's almost midnight!'

'I'll get it,' said his assistant, Beaumont, pushing aside the papers on the table and ambling to the living room.

Just then a thunderclap tore through the skies and filled him with foreboding. What could have possibly brought V.P. Menon to the chairman of the Boundary Commission at midnight, two days before the award was to be handed in, Beaumont wondered.

'Good evening, Christopher,' Menon greeted Beaumont at the door.

'Won't you come in?' invited Beaumont.

'I'm in a bit of a hurry,' Menon replied. 'Just here to convey a message from the viceroy.'

A LIGHTNING VISIT

'Sure, what's it about?'

'Sir Cyril is invited to have lunch with the viceroy tomorrow.'

'Lunch with the viceroy tomorrow?' Beaumont repeated. 'Why the suddenness?'

'He is requested to be there by noon,' Menon ignored Beaumont's question.

'But, pray, since when did you become the viceroy's messenger?' Beaumont sniggered.

'But *you* are not to go,' Menon made the instruction clear, ignoring Beaumont's query again.

'I beg your pardon?'

'The invitation is for Sir Cyril,' Menon's tone was stern and crisp, 'and for him alone.'

A bewildered Beaumont goggled at Menon on the doorstep, the trees behind him lit up eerily in a flash of lightning.

'Good night, Christopher.' Menon vanished almost as quickly as he had appeared.

As Menon faded into a sheet of rain, Beaumont pinched himself. *Had this really happened? Or had he seen a ghost?*

❋ A Heated Lunch ❋

'The Boundary Commission was set up on 30 June – I have had less than two months,' Sir Cyril Radcliffe protested, wiping the sweat beading his brow, his discomfort made worse by his double-breasted black suit.

'I understand how difficult this might be for you, Sir Cyril,' Edwina Mountbatten said with a small smile, offering her guest a glass of his favourite white Alsace wine. She appeared more sympathetic than her husband, the viceroy, with whom the chairman of the Boundary Commission had never quite got along.

'We are all working under pressure, Sir Cyril,' huffed the viceroy, helping himself to another slice of luncheon meat. 'Everyone is pressed for time.'

'Your Excellency,' Radcliffe said, clearing his throat, 'as you are no doubt aware, the task of marking a boundary is a difficult one—' With less than three days to go until the ambitious D-Day, unilaterally and thoughtlessly decided by Mountbatten, Radcliffe would have preferred to be at his desk, completing his job, rather than engaging in this pointless lunch.

'The terms of reference of the commission require you to take into account other factors as well, not just whether the population is Muslim or non-Muslim,' Mountbatten cut Radcliffe short, making no effort to mask his dislike for the dull and unemotional man seated before him.

'I am quite aware of the terms—'

'Then you will agree with me,' snapped the viceroy, 'that recommending joint control of waterworks and irrigation is beyond the scope of the Boundary Commission. That is not what it has been set up for!'

Radcliffe put down his fork and stared at the viceroy. The boundary report was not out yet. *How in heaven's name did the viceroy know what he was going to recommend?*

'Your responsibility, Cyril, is to demarcate the boundary line, not suggest how India and Pakistan control their water!' the viceroy thundered on.

Radcliffe reddened. He had grown tired of this mosquito-ridden land with its furnace-like weather. Precious lives were being extinguished because of a line that would rip a country and the lives of its people asunder, and he would have to carry the crushing weight of that on his conscience to his grave. He had even decided not to take the fee he was to be paid for this dreadful assignment. The last thing he wanted was a lecture from the viceroy about how he ought to do this thankless job.

'Leave that be,' said the viceroy, adopting a more conciliatory approach. 'You must try and ensure that the waterworks are not cut off from the lands they irrigate. That is, after all, the meaning of the words "other factors" in your terms of reference, making it quite clear that you must take other relevant factors into consideration. It would be fine to make the necessary adjustments. You see, the Sikhs in Punjab are already getting the short end of the stick.'

Radcliffe knew exactly what the viceroy was driving at. Many in England had been questioning the viceroy's open support of Nehru and Patel in getting the princely states to join India; it was simply not his job. If making recommendations on waterworks was beyond Radcliffe's brief, batting for the royal states to join India was beyond the viceroy's. But Radcliffe said nothing. The sooner he could get away from this unpleasant luncheon and back to his desk, the sooner he could finish this unpleasant task and return to England.

Stony-faced, he ate on, breaking the silence only to exchange pleasantries with Lady Mountbatten every now and then, mighty glad for her presence in the room.

'I take it,' said the viceroy, delicately dipping his hands in a finger bowl at the end of the meal, 'that I've made myself quite clear.'

Radcliffe realized only then why he had been invited alone, and why Menon had come at midnight, bearing such an urgent summons from the viceroy.

Still, who was leaking information about the boundary? And how exactly? Was it Ayer? Ayer to Menon? Menon to Sardar? Sardar to Nehru? And Nehru to the Viceroy? There were too many machinations at play here, and Sir Radcliffe had little time to ponder on them.

'There's something else,' said the viceroy, not quite finished, 'make sure you send me the Boundary Award on the afternoon of 13 August – uh...that's tomorrow afternoon; not earlier.'

Radcliffe turned to the viceroy in dismay, aware that Mountbatten was scheduled to leave the next day for Karachi to be present for Pakistan's Independence Day celebrations on 14 August; he would return for India's Independence Day celebrations the following day at midnight, between 14 and 15 August. In other words, despite asking Radcliffe to rush through the award and submit it on 13 August, the viceroy wasn't going to see it until 16 August.

Nonetheless, offering no more than a perfunctory nod, Radcliffe left without another word. There was nothing left to be said.

***

The Boundary Award, known popularly as the Radcliffe Award, was published five days later – on 17 August 1947 – after India's independence.

Ferozepur was awarded to India; Bikaner stayed in India.

♦♦♦♦♦♦♦♦♦♦♦♦♦♦♦♦♦♦♦

Postscript

♦♦♦♦♦♦♦♦♦♦♦♦♦♦♦♦♦♦♦

The Ganga Canal, which was inaugurated in 1927, carried water to Bikaner from the River Sutlej in Punjab, turning about 1,000 square miles (over 2,500 square kilometres) of the desert scrubland into lush green fields. It had taken Maharaja Ganga

Singh twenty-eight long years and twenty schemes to raise money and obtain permissions for it.

The headworks of this canal were on the southern bank of the Sutlej in Punjab's Ferozepur district, which had a population of about half a million people. It was expected that, owing to its narrow Muslim majority, Ferozepur would be awarded to Pakistan by the Punjab Boundary Commission.

Sir Cyril Radcliffe, chosen to preside over the Boundary Commission, had never been to India before and knew virtually nothing about it. He had just about six weeks to draw up the boundary line dividing India and Pakistan, in both Punjab and Bengal.

On 14 and 15 August, when Pakistan and India celebrated their independence, neither nation knew where its exact boundary lay. Several people living along the notional boundary in Punjab and Bengal had no idea which country they belonged to. Lord Mountbatten had chosen to delay the publication of the award (to 17 August) as he did not want it to dampen the spirit of the celebrations. Pakistan claimed it was a ruse by the viceroy to tamper with the award in order to favour India.

The Radcliffe Line, as the boundary came to be known, zigzagged across agricultural land, railway lines, water sources, forests and industrial plants, cutting off entire communities from one another. Both India and Pakistan were unhappy with it. Radcliffe returned to England on 17 August 1947 and never came back to India, hardly ever speaking about his days as boundary commissioner, and even burning his personal records.

Whether the Boundary Award was modified, under pressure from the viceroy, to award Ferozepur district to India has been a debated issue. Pakistan claimed that the boundary line was altered at the last minute to favour India by awarding the Muslim-majority districts of both Ferozepur and Gurdaspur to India for crucial reasons. Mountbatten repeatedly denied any intervention. Just as the award of Ferozepur to India tilted the scales in the case of Bikaner, the granting of most of Gurdaspur to India was a game changer for India in the case of Kashmir (as you will see in the chapter on Jammu and Kashmir).

What really transpired?

The answers lie shrouded in mystery.

♦♦♦♦♦♦♦♦♦♦♦♦♦♦♦♦♦♦♦

Did It Really Happen This Way?

♦♦♦♦♦♦♦♦♦♦♦♦♦♦♦♦♦♦♦

The words of Maharaja Sadul Singh in the opening scene are part of a statement made by him at the inauguration of the Constituent Assembly in April 1947. That the likely water problem caused by the Boundary Award was making the maharaja anxious is evident from his correspondence with the viceroy, found in The Transfer of Power 1942–7, Vol. XII.

The communication from Khosla to Nehru and Nehru to the viceroy regarding the River Sutlej headworks in Ferozepur carrying water to Bikaner can be found in Jawaharlal Nehru's correspondence.

Sir Radcliffe hardly ever spoke about his days in India and left no diary of his time as boundary commissioner.

Reference to the midnight summons by Menon, and the lunch between Sir Cyril Radcliffe and the viceroy can be found in Disastrous Twilight: A Personal Record of the Partition of India *by Major General Shahid Hamid. The book also mentions a second invitation from Hastings Ismay the next morning.*

Discussions at the meeting between Kanwar Sain, Bikaner's chief irrigation engineer, Diwan K.M. Panikkar and Mountbatten are mentioned in a publication by Kanwar Sain and some other sources. However, neither K.M. Panikkar's biography nor Mountbatten's detailed minutes contain any record of such a meeting.

6

At Gunpoint

THE STORY OF JODHPUR

PRINCELY STATE OF JODHPUR (ALSO CALLED KINGDOM OF MARWAR) IN 1947: in present-day Rajasthan

AREA: 36,120 square miles (93,550 square kilometres) approx.

POPULATION: 2,555,904

RULER: Maharaja Hanwant Singh

DIWAN: C.S. Venkatachar

17-gun-salute state

❋ A Clandestine Visit ❋

The broad-shouldered, six-foot-tall maharaja of Jodhpur stepped nervously out of his Rolls-Royce on to the driveway of the imposing bungalow at 10 Aurangzeb Road. The secret nature of the meeting made the newly crowned Hanwant Singh uneasy. He nodded at the *yuvraj*, the prince of Jaisalmer, who was accompanying him, and threw an anxious glance at the nawab of Bhopal who had arranged the meeting. Jinnah, he had heard, was a difficult man.

'It is important,' the maharaja whispered to Syed Ahsan, Jinnah's aide-de-camp, who received them at the portico, 'that this meeting remains strictly confidential.'

'Don't worry,' Zafarullah Khan, Jinnah's close confidant, assured him as he stepped forward to greet the maharaja. 'Jinnah Sa'ab understands your position. This will remain between us.'

Sardar Patel lived a few houses away. The last thing the young maharaja wanted was for Sardar to get wind of this clandestine visit to Jinnah. The mere thought of it made him break out in a cold sweat.

'You should be glad you managed to get an appointment with Jinnah Sa'ab,' Nawab Hamidullah Khan of Bhopal reminded Hanwant Singh as they walked down the corridor, followed by their aides. 'He will be leaving for Karachi soon. These are his very last days in Delhi.'

The maharaja paused by the mantelpiece at the foot of the staircase, staring hard at the strange-looking map of India in the frame. It took him a few moments to realize that it was not actually the map of India, but a map of Pakistan as Jinnah had envisaged it, encompassing most of the northern half of the subcontinent. It sent a chill down his spine.

'Um...yes...I am grateful,' he replied distractedly as he followed the others up the stairs, 'to...um...Jinnah Sa'ab for... agreeing to meet me and to Hamidullah Sa'ab for arranging the meeting at such short notice. As you perhaps know, Jodhpur has been going through very difficult times...and...I...um... wanted to find out what Pakistan could offer us.'

Nawab Hamidullah smiled; he was thankful too, for the uncertainty and inexperience of young rulers like Hanwant Singh, who were the last hope for his dream of a Union of Princes – a dream that was getting buried deeper each day under the masterfully crafted scheme of Sardar and V.P. Menon, which was luring ruler after ruler to join India. And yet, if some states such as Jodhpur, Jaisalmer and Udaipur in Rajputana, and a few more like Indore and Gwalior, could be wheedled away from India, Bhopal could even gain a natural land link with Pakistan.

'It's good that you contacted Hamidullah Sa'ab,' remarked Zafarullah Khan. 'Jodhpur will lie on the border between the two countries. And Pakistan will be delighted to have you join us.'

'As Jaisalmer is in a similar position,' the maharaja added, 'I took the liberty of asking Maharawal Jawahir Singh Bahadur to join me. However, he was busy and has sent Prince Girdhar Singh in his place.' This was, of course, a half-truth. Apprehensive about meeting Jinnah alone, Maharaja Hanwant Singh had reached out to rulers of other Rajputana states to accompany him. The maharaja of Bikaner had flatly refused. The maharaja of Jaisalmer had sent his son on his behalf.

'You did the right thing,' Zafarullah Khan assured him, acknowledging the *yuvraj* of Jaisalmer walking behind them, as he ushered the visitors into Jinnah's study. 'You see, unlike Mr Nehru, Jinnah Sa'ab is most keen to uphold the honour of the princes. Trust me, you won't regret this!'

❋ An Irresistible Offer ❋

Hard to please, harder to persuade and yet, impossible to ignore – Jinnah's bony face and stony glare reminded Maharaja Hanwant Singh of everything he had heard about the head of the Muslim League, whose steely determination had helped him carve out a nation.

'Maharaja Hanwant Singh of Jodhpur and Yuvraj Girdhar Singh of Jaisalmer,' ADC Syed Ahsan introduced the two guests as they stepped into the tastefully decorated study.

Immaculate in a brown double-breasted suit, Jinnah stood up to shake hands with the visitors. He did not smile; he seldom did.

'Honoured to be in the presence of a dashing king and a prince this morning,' began Jinnah, making an immediate attempt to woo his guests. 'I'm told Your Highness is a great horseman, *shikari* and pilot all in one!'

'And Hanwant is quite a magician too,' added Nawab Hamidullah with a smile.

The young maharaja grinned sheepishly, flattered by the unexpected praise from the forbidding figure before him. Nearly a six-footer like him, Jinnah appeared intimidating with his silver-grey hair and cut-glass English accent, even though his frame was frail, and his face emaciated and pale.

As a Rajput leading a conservative state, Maharaja Hanwant Singh had deep reservations about accession to India. It would lead to the democratization of his state and to the loss of monarchical power, privilege and prestige. Jinnah was crafty enough to capitalize on those very fears in a bid to make up for the loss of half of Punjab and Bengal from the Pakistan of his dreams – a loss that had been a bitter pill to swallow.

'So...Hamidullah tells me you are looking to join Pakistan.' Jinnah didn't beat about the bush, gesturing to his guests to take a seat.

'I...I...was...um...' The maharaja was taken unawares by the blunt directness.

'Let us speak frankly...' began Jinnah, looking straight at Hanwant Singh. 'In India you will be a small fish in a big pond; and by all indications, you will get less priority than the important ones. But I assure you, in Pakistan you will be treated well and given your due recognition.'

JINNAH: IN PAKISTAN, YOU WILL BE GIVEN YOUR DUE RECOGNITION...

Maharaja Hanwant Singh and Yuvraj Girdhar Singh nodded in agreement. Honour meant a great deal to the Rajputs; and the royals were very conscious of position, prestige and pride. From neighbouring kingdoms and border principalities, they were also related by marriage – Hanwant Singh's brother was married to Girdhar Singh's daughter. Their status and outlook, their interests and priorities, were all aligned.

'Should you join Pakistan,' Jinnah continued, eager to swing the two border states over to his side, 'I promise to allow you to maintain your army and arsenal. You will be allowed the free import of arms, something India will never agree to grant you.'

The two rulers exchanged surprised glances. The conditions laid down by Sardar Patel for the states to join India were clear: they would have to forfeit their rights in the areas of communication, external affairs and defence; there was no question of kings maintaining private armies and arsenals. Jinnah's offer was plainly much more to their liking.

'I am also prepared to transfer all the border districts with Rajput populations currently in Sind into your charge,' Jinnah continued to pile on the perks. 'You will also be given tax concessions, and complete freedom in matters of import and export in Pakistan. I will make you the ruler of all of Rajputana.'

Maharaja Hanwant Singh couldn't believe his ears. This was far more than he had expected; so much more than the Indian side was even prepared to offer. His tense shoulders relaxed. 'Jinnah Sa'ab...we do not have access to a seaport. For trade we require...' he began with a newly gained confidence.

Jinnah nodded, looking piously earnest. 'I'm glad you are laying your cards on the table. And I understand completely. Pakistan will give you free access to Karachi port. And jurisdiction over Sind railways,' he added magnanimously. 'You can control it...use it to transport your goods.'

Hanwant Singh's eyes lit up. Up until the middle of the nineteenth century, Amarkot in eastern Sind had been under his forefathers, who had ruled a vast territory stretching up to the Indus. This was a chance to reclaim their lost glory.

'I hope the *yuvraj* is also willing for Jaisalmer to join Pakistan...' Jinnah remarked, ending with a pregnant pause.

'Jinnah Sa'ab...uh...if...if we joined Pakistan,' the prince of Jaisalmer began hesitantly, 'and if there is trouble between the Hindus and the Muslims in our states, can we be assured that you and the Pakistani government will remain strictly neutral?'

Maharaja Hanwant Singh leaned forward anxiously. This was a vital concern. While the majority of his people were Hindus, a large number were Muslims, and he wanted nothing but peace between the two communities. Although Girdhar Singh was the prince, he was about twenty years Hanwant Singh's senior in age. The young maharaja was glad for his presence at this negotiating table.

Jinnah stared hard at the *yuvraj*, making no reply. His cold, blank stare made the maharaja uneasy.

'So...' Zafarullah Khan smiled after an awkward silence. 'I take it you've consulted your astrologers and it's an auspicious day to join Pakistan,' he said, trying to make light of the moment, as he placed the accession papers before the maharaja and offered him a pen.

The maharaja gulped. While the terms were enticing, he just could not bring himself to sign on the dotted line yet.

'Here,' said Jinnah, signing a blank sheet of paper, noticing the maharaja's hesitation. 'As long as the central government in India is weak, we are both strong, Your Highness. I sign on the dotted line; you insert all the stipulations and conditions you want...'

Stupefied, the young Hanwant Singh gaped at Jinnah. A bead of sweat trickled down the side of the maharaja's face. Plagued by a seven-year drought, Jodhpur was in desperate need of relief funds. And here he was, being offered a blank cheque!

'Perhaps Your Highness should consult the local chiefs and Ba Sahib before taking a final decision?' Colonel Thakur Kesari Singh, the maharaja's ADC, clearly alarmed by the haste and speed of the talks, whispered into the young maharaja's ears.

Hanwant Singh mopped his brow and sat back. The crown had been on his head for only two months now and he knew that this was a huge call to make by himself. *Yes...he liked his ADC's suggestion. He ought to consult his chieftains and his mother before making such a crucial decision.*

'Thank you, Mr Jinnah, for your kind offer,' the maharaja replied meekly. 'I shall consider it and revert soon.'

'Do you need to think it over?' asked Zafarullah Khan, throwing open his hands in surprise. 'What's left to think about?'

'Jinnah Sa'ab, although I am the maharaja,' Hanwant Singh shook his head politely, 'this cannot be my decision alone. As you will no doubt understand, I must consult others – my ministers, my mother, the Sardars of my kingdom.'

Jinnah ground his teeth, his disappointment and frustration evident. He snatched the sheet from the maharaja's hand.

The young Hanwant Singh smiled awkwardly and stood up. As he made for the door, one thing was clear beyond all doubt: the offer he had received from Pakistan could not be bettered by India.

It was simply too good to refuse.

❋ SOS ❋

An exhausted Cadambi Seshachar Venkatachar returned to his desk in his office at the Umaid Bhawan Palace in Jodhpur, after assuring yet another throng of harrowed petitioners that they needn't panic about the impending Partition. A little less than a year ago he had accepted the post of prime minister of the largest state in Rajputana. Within months, Maharaja Umaid Singh had passed away, leaving the crown to his twenty-four-year-old son. Audacious yet endearing, Hanwant Singh was in dire need of a guiding hand – precisely what Venkatachar was hoping to be. But whispers floating about the palace circles seemed to indicate that the maharaja had turned to others like Conrad Corfield of the political department for advice, and everyone was getting understandably anxious.

What exactly did the maharaja discuss with Corfield during those late-night meetings? The question worried Venkatachar. *Corfield was known to champion the cause of the princes, taken up in earnest by the nawab of Bhopal. Together they had been urging the rulers to keep out of India and retain their independence. The Rana of Dholpur had been cosying up to the Bhopal group. As was the maharaja of Indore. Was Hanwant Singh also enamoured of those ideas?*

The people of Jodhpur had bestowed the title of 'Darbar Baapji' upon their young maharaja, for he cut a paternal figure in their eyes. He was their *anna data* – their provider and protector. In all honesty, the young maharaja was a wonderful, progressive-minded and reasonable man. He had not coerced his young bride to hide her face behind a veil and had, in fact, coaxed her to give up purdah. Teaching her English, he encouraged her to walk alongside him into the modern era. As a young lad, he had roamed the city under cover of night, putting up anti-British posters, despite his family's official allegiance to the Raj. He often said that his Hindu and Muslim subjects were like his two eyes, and never discriminated between the communities. Venkatachar knew the maharaja had his heart in the right place. But was that enough to help him meet the challenges of these testing times?

There was a knock on the door. 'A cable for you, sir.' the diwan's secretary stepped into the office and handed a telegram to Venkatachar.

Venkatachar tore it open. It was from Delhi. Sent by Thakur Kesari Singh, the maharaja's ADC. It contained five words – words that made him leap out of his seat.

MAHARAJA SAHIB MET JINNAH TODAY STOP

Pressing his eyes shut, C.S. Venkatachar placed the telegram beneath a paperweight on this desk. A meeting with Jinnah could only mean one thing – that Maharaja Hanwant Singh was open to the possibility of joining Pakistan. His worst fears had been realized. Heart pounding, palms sweating, he picked up the phone.

DIWAN OF JODHPUR: C.S. VENKATACHAR

Jodhpur, Udaipur, Jaipur and Bikaner were the key states of the two dozen princely kingdoms of Rajputana. By a strange coincidence, the diwans of all four states were men from the south, with close personal ties to each other. T. Vijayaraghavachari was the prime minister of Udaipur; V.T. Krishnamachari held the equivalent post in Jaipur; K.M. Panikkar served as diwan in Bikaner; and C.S. Venkatachar was diwan of Jodhpur. They were good friends who trusted one another implicitly. When a guide was needed at a crucial moment like this, sound and reliable counsel was only a phone call away.

'I wanted to discuss something important with you,' said Venkatachar as soon as Panikkar answered the telephone.

Jodhpur had an overwhelming majority of Hindus. If the maharaja made a rash decision and joined Pakistan, it could lead to disturbance and turmoil. 'I have just received a disturbing telegram from Delhi.'

'What's wrong?' Panikkar was a veteran of the princely states. He had served the maharajas of Kashmir and Patiala in the past and was now with Bikaner. Devoted to the nationalist cause, he was a master at manoeuvring through royal obstacles.

'The maharaja's ADC informs me that...' Venkatachar paused, drumming his fingers nervously on the table.

'Yes...? Go on...'

'Maharaja Hanwant Singh had a meeting with Mr Jinnah today,' Venkatachar let the cat out of the bag, his voice so gloomy and sombre, he may as well have been announcing someone's demise. 'You know what this could mean...'

Panikkar fell silent. Bikaner shared borders with Jodhpur. This was a matter of mutual concern.

'Hello...are you there?' Venkatachar pressed the receiver to his ear. 'This is of utmost gravity, affecting the very stability of India.'

'Yes, I hear you...' Panikkar replied haltingly.

'What...what do you suggest I do?'

'Sardar...' Panikkar said after a pause, proposing the only solution that came to mind, 'we've got to take this to Sardar.'

❋ Chasing Shadows ❋

It was a heartbreaking sight. A mass of people, pleading, begging, beseeching, grovelling – the poor and the well-to-do, men, women and children, the aged, the sick and the infirm – driven from their home and hearth into makeshift tents, reeking of disease and death – recounting episodes of the horrors of Partition that they had lived through.

Winding his way out of the severely crammed and cholera-infested refugee camp at the Purana Qila, once the seat of Mughal power, Sardar was shaken.

He stopped by the desk at the gate of the refugee camp, where a hapless official struggled to cope with wave after wave of the weary and the wounded, the homeless and the hopeless, streaming in from western Punjab. Entering and cross-checking names in enormous lists, pacifying wailing mothers searching for lost offspring, helping desperate children locate their missing parents, making continuous announcements over loudspeakers...

Exhausted and emotionally drained, Sardar squeezed the official's shoulder in encouragement and patted his back before making his way out.

Lady Mountbatten had told him she wanted his help to find a psychiatrist for a trauma centre – someone who could talk to the devastated women who had been raped and mutilated; counsel the distraught children who had witnessed the cold-blooded slaughter of their parents. The enormity of the task of feeding, clothing, rehabilitating and resettling this sea of humanity weighed on Sardar's mind as his car slowly drove out of the depressing scene.

Was this to be the fruit of their life's labours? Sardar rested his head on the backrest and closed his eyes, seeking some peace and quiet amid the din and chaos. *Had they toiled* so *hard only to witness this bloodthirsty madness*? But the harsh times denied him the chance to reflect and introspect. As his car pulled into the driveway of his home, he noticed Menon waiting at the door, his face and body language screaming doom.

'Hanwant Singh had a secret meeting with Jinnah,' Menon broke the news to Patel as he emerged from the car.

Placing an arm on Menon's shoulder to steady himself, Sardar sighed deeply. Soul-searching was for saints like Gandhi. Foot soldiers like him could only hold their heads up, keep the faith and march on.

❋ Mirrored Irony ❋

'*Khamma ghani*, Maharaja Sahib,' a gathering of Rajput chiefs in colourful turbans offered the traditional greeting, bowing before Maharaja Hanwant Singh, who was seated cross-legged on a crimson-cushioned *gaddi* in the audience hall of the Umaid Bhawan Palace in Jodhpur. The tinted glass on the windows reduced the intensity of the light streaming into the room, and the delicate *jali* work let in a slight breeze, keeping the palace cool even on a sweltering day. One by one, the men filed into the room and paid their obeisance.

Hanwant Singh stiffened. He knew exactly why the representatives from Amarkot were here to see him. It broke his heart to tell them, yet again, that he had neither the ability nor the influence to fulfil their wishes. He nodded in acknowledgement and bade the delegation be seated.

'Baapji,' the chieftain began with politely folded hands, 'as you know, our Rana has rejected Panditji's offer to be associated with the Congress. He has gone ahead and joined the Muslim League. We are Hindus – proud Rajputs of this land,' he said. 'We know we have no future in Sind. Please allow us to become a part of Jodhpur. We are most willing to accept your rule.'

The men hailed from Amarkot, later named Umerkot, an area in Sind that was soon going to be part of Pakistan. Their ruler, Rana Arjun Singh Sodha, a Hindu, had pledged his support to Jinnah. His people were understandably alarmed.

'Please, Maharaja Sahib,' pleaded another clansman, anxiety deepening the wrinkles on his sunburnt face, 'please understand our plight. We will be surrounded by Pakistan on all sides after Partition. Please help us.'

'Our traditions, our language, our culture...everything is connected with Marwar,' the chieftain explained the predicament of his people. 'Our bonds are with you, Maharaja Sahib. Our girls marry into Rajput families in Jodhpur and Jaisalmer. Our trade, our places of worship...we are bound by blood ties with Jodhpur. We are Hindu Rajputs, just like your people. We will have no future in Pakistan.'

The words struck Hanwant Singh like a whiplash. A wave of guilt washed over him. *Was the future that apparent to this unassuming old man? What would they say were they to discover that he himself had been considering throwing in his lot with Pakistan?* 'I'm afraid there is little I can do in this matter,' he said, shaking his head despondently.

'Maharaja Sahib, you are all-powerful,' the chieftain pleaded. 'Surely you can merge our Tharparkar district into Jodhpur? The Sodha Rajputs of Tharparkar will be eternally grateful to you, Maharaja Sahib.'

'As you know, Amarkot was under the rule of my forefathers once,' the maharaja replied matter-of-factly, 'and believe me, I will be only too pleased to regain those territories. I have spoken with the viceroy,' he assured them, wishing his late father were by his side to guide him at moments like these, 'but he says nothing can be done about altering the boundaries.'

Living on the fringe of the Thar, Hanwant Singh was accustomed to weathered faces, hardened by the unforgiving terrain, and yet it broke his heart to see the sorrow his words brought upon the people standing before him. They had trudged over vast distances across the desert in the scorching heat with so much hope in their hearts. It pained him to turn them away and he was filled with remorse for having met with Jinnah. Just twenty-four hours ago he had been negotiating the accession of Marwar to Pakistan and had very nearly signed on the dotted line.

He felt a cold shiver. *What had he been thinking?*

❋ Mission Mode ❋

As Sardar flopped down into an armchair in his living room, Menon filled him in with the disturbing piece of news coming in from Jodhpur. 'Note from Iyengar...' he said, handing Patel the urgent letter from the home secretary. 'It seems Venkatachar, the diwan of Jodhpur, informed Panikkar, the diwan of Bikaner, who then brought it to the home secretary's notice. It appears that Venkatachar alerted them that Maharaja Hanwant Singh was approached by Mr Jinnah and has been persuaded to stay out of the Indian dominion. We do not have all the details yet, but the meeting was arranged by you-know-who.'

'Nawab Hamidullah?' Sardar named the first person who came to mind after reading the missive.

'Who else?' Menon quipped, as Maniben brought out a cool wet towel and a glass of water for her father. It was a blisteringly hot day and Sardar had been out all morning surveying the refugee camps. Maniben was anxious about her father's health, worried sometimes that he might collapse with a heatstroke.

Sardar grimaced. They had already lost large chunks of India to Pakistan. He was not prepared to cede an inch more. 'The nawab of Bhopal is exceeding all limits now,' he said. 'Not joining India is one thing, but enticing Hindu-majority states to go over to Pakistan is quite another. I will not tolerate this. And besides, it is in complete breach of Jinnah's two-nation theory. He is making a mockery of it.'

Menon looked on, feeling utterly helpless. *The Jinnah he had known, the Jinnah who had befriended him over a decade ago, the Jinnah who had stood up against Gandhi in support of upholding constitutional values, rather than mixing religion with politics, the Jinnah who had treated a junior officer like him with respect despite being a national star himself – where had that man disappeared?* One could scarcely believe what Jinnah had turned into. Menon could no longer recognize him.

'This is most likely a result of Sir Conrad's meetings with the maharaja,' Menon grumbled, referring to the head of the political department who had been encouraging the princes to form an alliance. 'I hear they've been visiting each other and having long meetings.'

'Sardar, if Jodhpur decides to join Pakistan, other border states like Jaisalmer, Bikaner and Barmer might follow suit,' said Chandulal Chunilal Desai, the additional secretary of the States Department, emerging from Sardar's office room with a pile of files in his hands, 'and the border of Pakistan could extend up to Ajmer.'

'Panikkar has the same worry...apparently the *yuvraj* of Jaisalmer was also present at this meeting with Jinnah,' Menon added.

'This could escalate into a civil war–like situation in Rajputana,' remarked Sardar, getting to his feet. 'There is not a moment to lose, Menon. Call Hanwant Singh to Delhi for a meeting immediately.'

'Right away.'

'Alert the Jodhpur wing of the Congress party,' Sardar said to Desai. The AISPC had been agitating for years for a responsible government in the princely states and the local Congress leader, Jai Narayan Vyas, had initiated the movement in Jodhpur. He would have to be contacted. 'Send a telegram to Vyas. Tell him they must begin a mass movement there.'

'Will do...' Desai nodded, tagging behind Sardar. 'Involving the public will help. The maharaja is popular among his subjects, and he will certainly be influenced by the voice of his people.'

Bypassing his waiting daughter, Sardar walked past the dining table and went straight to his study to get to work. 'Menon, it's time to get into mission mode.'

❋ Dodging Games ❋

Located on Queensway, not far from Sardar's home, was Delhi's grand Art Deco–style Imperial Hotel, where the city's elite met and mingled, dined and danced. Diplomats and dignitaries, journalists and royalty, sat about on its open-air terrace or converged in the ornate gold-scrolled ballroom, to catch up, to converse, to contemplate.

Overlooking the green lawns, framed by a colonnade of royal palms as the sun prepared to set in the distance, was a distraught nawab of Bhopal, bent over his cup of Darjeeling tea in the terrace café, anxious about how the days ahead would unfold.

'What's the status of Jodhpur? Has Hanwant come to a decision?' the impatient nawab asked Maharaj-Rana Uday Bhan Singh of Dholpur, his ally in drawing Hanwant Singh towards the nawab's camp.

'Not yet,' replied the Rana, who was closely monitoring the bigger states of Rajputana such as Jodhpur. His state was not far from Jodhpur, and he too was in the same dilemma. Acceding to India would break an alliance his ancestors had established with the Crown. The departure of the British and the sudden winds of change towards divesting the rulers of crown and kingdom saddened him deeply. For the Rana was firmly of the belief that kings had a divine right to rule.

'When is he likely to return to Delhi with his decision?'

'I'm told he will be here tomorrow morning,' the Rana replied.

'Do you know his schedule?'

'I believe he is meeting the viceroy. And Sardar Patel too.'

'Hmm...' Nawab Hamidullah began planning his next move. Having made overtures to some states in the region, he believed Dholpur and – hopefully – Gwalior, Indore and some others were in his camp. If only he could persuade Hanwant, he mused. If Jodhpur defected, it would open up the chances for other contiguous states like Jaipur and Udaipur. And together, they'd become a force to reckon with.

'Where will he be landing? Palam or Willingdon?'

'No idea.'

'Have a car sent to both airports for Maharaja Hanwant Singh tomorrow,' the nawab instructed his aide-de-camp.

The Maharaj-Rana of Dholpur looked enquiringly at the nawab. 'What are you planning?'

'I want to meet Hanwant,' said the nawab, 'before he meets Sardar.'

***

'Wasn't the maharaja of Jodhpur supposed to come and see me this morning?' asked Patel, looking up at the clock and then at his secretary. 'Has he rescheduled the meeting?'

'No, Sardar,' replied Shankar, his private secretary. 'He has not kept his appointment.'

'No call from his secretary or diwan?'

'No.'

'What are we to make of that?

'I'm afraid I don't know, Sardar.'

'Has he come to Delhi at all?

'Err...yes...he appears to have arrived...'

'Where is he then?' asked Sardar impatiently. 'Surely we know?'

'At...uh...' Shankar hesitated. 'At Nawab Hamidullah's home.'

'What is he doing with the nawab when he has an appointment with me?' Sardar demanded.

That, of course, was only a rhetorical question. Sardar expected no reply.

The answer was as plain as the nose on his face.

***

'I went to meet the Gaekwad of Baroda...' Maharaja Hanwant Singh reported to Nawab Hamidullah. 'I told him about your idea of a third front - of us princes joining together and holding out. Of not submitting to pressure from Sardar and the Indian side. I told him...'

'And what does he have to say?' the nawab asked, leaning forward eagerly.

'He is ambivalent...hasn't made up his mind.'

'I don't have much hope from the Gaekwad,' the nawab said, shaking his head glumly, increasingly frustrated to see his fantasy of a union of princely states dying a slow death. Just the previous day he had tried winning over the rulers of Jaipur and Cochin; they seemed uninterested. Every state joining forces with India was a nail hammered into the coffin of the royal alliance. The nawab could even hear the nails being pounded in, one by one.

'Pratap Singh Gaekwad declared that he would be the first to sign the Instrument of Accession and he was the first to join the Indian Constituent Assembly,' the nawab lamented.

'The Gaekwad intends to stipulate certain terms and conditions,' said Maharaja Hanwant Singh, feeling embarrassed by this melodrama; he too had joined the Indian Constituent Assembly, but the decision to accede was another issue altogether, 'and hopes to get Sardar to agree to them'.

'Sardar will not make special concessions for anyone,' the nawab dismissed the naïve thought harboured by his brother princes. 'Do you think Nehru cares about the rulers? His agenda is to wipe us out. I have no faith in the Congress. It is appalling how it has managed to pull the wool over the eyes of all the rulers!'

The maharaja sat back. Jinnah's terms were indeed lucrative, but the decision was complicated by the fact that the majority of his people were Hindu. *If he chose Pakistan, would they accept his decision? Could he remain independent as the nawab was pressing him to do? Did he have the ability to hold out?*

'And you? What have you decided?' the nawab interrupted the maharaja's thoughts. 'You've heard Jinnah Sa'ab's offer...'

'I...um...frankly...I am unable to come to a decision.'

'Well...at least, unlike me, you are near the Pakistan border. Bhopal is landlocked and is going to be surrounded by India on all sides.'

'Hmm....' the maharaja mumbled, the desperate faces of the Sodhas from Sind flashing before him.

'One way or the other, you have to decide soon,' the nawab reminded the maharaja. 'Time is running out.'

***

❋ No Two Ways about It ❋

'How can you even think of joining Pakistan?' demanded the ochre-clad guru of the Jodhpur royal family, sitting cross-legged before the royal *gaddi* amid exotic murals in the Art Deco throne room of Jodhpur's Umaid Bhawan Palace. Jodhpur has a majority of Hindus.'

Maharaja Hanwant Singh stared moodily through the large windows at the massive ramparts of the Mehrangarh Fort in the distance, from where his forefathers had ruled for centuries. The past weighed heavily upon his young shoulders.

'If I may dare say so,' interjected Diwan Venkatachar, 'Jinnah's offer sounds too good to be true. I find it hard to believe that a newly formed nation like Pakistan will have the resources to honour all these tall promises. The *maharana* of Udaipur thinks so too.'

'So, we have heard back from the Maharana Sahib?' asked Maharaja Hanwant Singh.

MEHRANGARH FORT: A LEGACY IN STONE

'Yes, the *maharana* of Udaipur has replied.' Diwan Venkatachar nodded.

'...And?'

'He says his choice is guided by his ancestors, such as Rana Sangha and Rana Pratap,' the diwan replied, extracting the Udaipur *maharana*'s letter from a folder in his hand. 'He says, had they so wished, his ancestors could have left him a kingdom as large as Hyderabad, but they upheld the righteous path. They did not falter, and neither will he. He says he disdainfully rejects the unpatriotic idea of joining Pakistan and has affirmed that he, most certainly, will be joining India.' Venkatachar folded the letter and put it back without making eye contact with the maharaja.

Maharaja Hanwant Singh crossed his hands behind him. The *maharana* of Udaipur was the senior-most of all the rulers in Rajputana. His clarity was reassuring.

The door opened. A demure figure clad in a white saree entered. Everyone rose to greet her.

'*Khamma ghani*, Mataji-Sa.' Maharaja Hanwant Singh stooped to touch his mother's feet.

'*Khamma ghani*.' The others bowed before their former queen as she took a seat, her face reflecting a quiet dignity. In her youth, she had enjoyed travelling, horse riding and pig-sticking heats; but those days were behind her. She was now the widowed mother of the new king, a position that demanded poise and restraint.

'Hanwant...' the dowager queen got straight to the point, 'whatever it is that Jinnah has offered you, I don't want to hear about it. Joining Pakistan is simply out of the question.'

Maharaja Hanwant Singh turned to face his mother. Many years ago, Marwar had struggled with drought for several years at a stretch. His father had commissioned the construction of the grand Umaid Bhavan Palace to keep his people gainfully employed and help them to sustain themselves. He knew he was but a shadow of the great Umaid Singhji, but the urge to rise to the occasion and do his best to help his people survive the drought was just as strong.

'Ba Sahib, do you realize what that blank cheque would mean for Jodhpur?' Hanwant Singh said respectfully, sitting down at her feet. 'It could put an end to all our woes. An end to the misery and suffering of our people.'

'Go and ask Sardar Patel what he has to offer you,' said the dowager maharani stoically, knowing her words would exert a profound influence upon her son. 'I'm certain he will help us.'

The maharaja sighed. The nawab of Bhopal, who had been the chancellor of the Chamber of Princes, had repeatedly told the maharaja that he did not trust the Congress. Surely his opinion was a considered and well-informed one.

'Our people will revolt if you join Pakistan, Your Highness,' warned Venkatachar. 'We have an overwhelming Hindu majority. Under no circumstances will the Rathores accept such a decision.'

'Don't forget there have been popular demonstrations in support of Pakistan too,' the maharaja reminded them.

'Your Highness,' said the diwan, 'following your orders, we had arranged a consultation with our council of elders and Sardars. I did relay Mr Jinnah's offer to them.'

'And...what did they say?'

'An emphatic *no*. None of the chiefs are convinced by Jinnah's proposals and assurances.'

'Hanwant,' the dowager maharani placed a gentle hand on her son's shoulder. The world saw him for the carefree and flamboyant young prince he was on the outside, but she knew the simple and magnanimous man within that towering frame. 'I know you are young and can be fearless. Your dangerous stunts when you fly a plane frighten me. But just bear in mind – this decision is perhaps the most important one you will ever make.'

The maharaja stood up and paced across the room, then stopped at the window. The setting sun cast a golden hue on the rows upon rows of houses outside, all painted a signature blue, dotting the landscape of Jodhpur.

'This concerns our kingdom, our people, our legacy,' the maharani said, joining him by the window, where they together gazed at Mehrangarh's magnificent, sun-drenched ramparts. 'I will not permit you to gamble with Jodhpur's future.'

The maharaja nodded, like a young child admonished by his mother.

'You will go to Delhi and sign the accession papers...Jodhpur will join India,' Ba Sahib declared, 'and that is final.'

❋ All Cards on the Table ❋

The plaintive notes of the *koel* and the sweet song of the *bulbul*, announcing the dawn of a new day in the luxurious Mughal Gardens outside the window, did little to soothe the nerves of Maharaja Hanwant Singh as he reached for a glass of water. The sandwiches, stacked neatly on the silver salver before him, did not whet his appetite as he sat stiffly, mopping his brow in the viceroy's waiting room. *Why had Menon hauled him out of his suite at the Imperial Hotel at this ungodly hour in the morning and accompanied him personally to Government House? Why had the viceroy summoned him* so *urgently*? Hanwant Singh could hear his heart pounding.

The door swung open, and the viceroy walked in, "All right, Hanwant – what's all this I've been hearing?'

The maharaja put down his tumbler and stood up with such a start that he nearly choked. Baffled, he eyed Menon, who was standing behind the viceroy.

'Come on! Come clean now,' the viceroy prompted him. 'Have you been meeting Jinnah?'

'Uh...I just...wanted to...' the maharaja stuttered, dabbing his lips with a lace-edged damask napkin, throwing another enquiring glance at Menon. *Had the viceroy invited him on his own, or had Menon engineered this?*

'I believe Mr Jinnah made you various offers to entice you to join Pakistan – is that correct?' asked the viceroy, gesturing to his guest to be seated.

The maharaja stiffened. *How had news of his meeting with Jinnah leaked*? He was speechless.

'You do realize what your defection to Pakistan could lead to,' the viceroy demanded testily. 'Do you not see that it would expose other states like Udaipur and Jaipur, which are further inside India, to the boundary of Pakistan?'

'Those rulers have also been approached by Mr Jinnah,' the maharaja admitted in a low voice. There was no point in putting up a charade. Mountbatten and Menon clearly knew all there was to know. 'They had been invited to the same meeting with Jinnah Sa'ab. They refused to join me.'

The viceroy relaxed slightly. 'I believe you were to meet Sardar Patel as well, but didn't go?'

'I...um...I meant to go...but was indisposed that morning...'

'Indisposed or imprisoned?' The viceroy raised a sceptical eyebrow at the maharaja.

Picking up a glass of orange juice from the coffee table, the maharaja took a nervous sip.

'I believe Nawab Hamidullah detained you?' The viceroy rephrased his question.

'I wouldn't say that...' The maharaja put down the glass. 'I paid him a visit...'

'Look, you may not realize it, but Sardar knows exactly what's going on,' said Menon.

The maharaja threw Menon a cold glare. *Didn't he always?*

'I...um...was only keen to understand'—the maharaja glanced uncomfortably at the viceroy—'what Pakistan could offer us.'

'When I met you last month along with the diwan of Baroda, you specifically told me that your state would accede to India,' the viceroy exclaimed, his hands spread out in puzzlement.

'Anyway, now that you're finally here,' said Menon, taking a seat beside the maharaja, 'tell me exactly what Jinnah has offered you.'

Hanwant Singh goggled in disbelief at Menon and Mountbatten, aghast at their unabashed interrogation, almost as if he had been charged with a crime. Reluctantly, he drew a sheet of paper from the pocket of his coat. 'Pakistan has agreed to give me all this,' he said quietly, handing the note to Menon.

Menon and Mountbatten perused the list, pausing now and then to look at the maharaja in amazement.

'Yes...Jinnah has given me a blank cheque,' said the maharaja a trifle smugly. 'He says I can ask for any amount I desire for my privy purse.'

'I would caution you against falling prey to Jinnah's promises,' Mountbatten warned. 'Have you thought of the consequences of Jinnah reneging on his word?'

'Well, let me ask you: what guarantee do I have that India will honour its promises?' the maharaja demanded, his voice gaining in confidence at seeing the dumbfounded faces of the two men before him.

'Look,' said Mountbatten, leaning forward, 'at least in India, your territory will be contiguous with the other Rajputana states. You will be among your own people. You will have better bargaining power.'

'Your Highness, this is not even worth the paper it is written on.' Menon returned the list to the maharaja scornfully. 'Let me make it abundantly clear what India can and cannot offer you: India will provide you with relief provisions to help you overcome the severe drought Jodhpur has been facing; Sardar has agreed to give the matter top priority, even if it means diverting food from other parts of the country.'

The maharaja slipped Jinnah's list back into his pocket, certain that Menon would now try to match it. Nevertheless, India's offer did surprise him. The food situation in the country was dire and the refugee crisis was making it worse. The promise could only mean that Sardar was going all out to hold on to Jodhpur. His spirits began to lift.

'And,' Menon counted off the points on his fingers, 'Sardar has agreed that the Government of India will give the highest priority to build a railway line from Jodhpur to Kutch, so as to open up a port for you. Also,' Menon continued, 'to allow the Rajputs to carry and import arms without any restrictions.'

The maharaja's jaw dropped in astonishment. 'What about the privy purse?' he asked. 'Jinnah said I was at liberty to fill in any figure I want.'

'The amount India will pay you will be the same as for your peers,' Menon replied firmly. 'We shall make no false assurances and offer you no blank cheques. If you want to sign on false hopes, as you seem so willing to do with Jinnah, then we too will agree to all your demands most readily.'

'Frankly, this is a great offer, and you should appreciate that Sardar is making concessions for you,' said the viceroy. 'And, although legally you are free to join Pakistan if you so desire, given that the principle underlying Partition is the separation of Muslim- and non-Muslim-majority areas, it would be advisable for you to join India.'

The young maharaja nodded slightly.

'Hanwant'—the viceroy stood up—'I know you well. You are a reasonable man and a good ruler. I know you have nothing but the best interests of your people at heart. Let that be your guiding light. Now, if you will excuse me, I need to pop inside for a meeting with a delegation from Hyderabad. I am juggling several balls at the moment, so I have to go. Sorry...but do take your time. Menon will be ready with the accession documents whenever you decide to sign.'

The maharaja nodded non-committally, rising slowly as the viceroy prepared to leave.

'Hanwant, I have been a friend of your father for a long time,' the viceroy turned around at the door to play his final trump card. An infallible memory was one of Mountbatten's uncanny strengths, as was his deep understanding of human nature. Coupled with his connections, his charisma and charm, he had been able to win over the most obstinate of opponents. Aware that the young maharaja missed his father acutely, Mountbatten played his ace. 'If Umaid Singhji were alive today, I know he would have wanted Jodhpur to join India.'

❋ The Target ❋

'Your Highness, are you ready to sign?' Menon enquired. For well over half an hour now, the maharaja had been pacing the carpeted floor of the room, downing several glasses of water.

'Your Highness?' Menon called out, a little louder this time.

The maharaja was immersed in his thoughts. Deeply disturbing news came in daily – of riots, murder and mayhem. People were dying like flies, villages had been reduced to graveyards. Hindus and Muslims across British India were at each other's throats. Hanwant Singh did not want his people to meet such a fate.

'Your Highness,' Menon repeated, edging closer to the maharaja, 'you've seen our terms. Are you ready to sign the accession documents now?'

A PISTOL IN DISGUISE!

The maharaja spun around and whipped out a pen from his pocket in a flash. Instantly, the pen transformed into a .22 calibre revolver. He pointed it at Menon's temple.

'I refuse to accept your terms,' the red-faced maharaja fumed. He was breathing hard and perspiring heavily. His hand trembled.

Menon took two steps back. Life had taught him to craft complex documents and push past political tangles, not to dodge bullets and get out of gunfights. He took a deep breath and put his hands up in the air.

'Your Highness,' he said, trying to keep calm, 'if you think your problems will disappear by killing me, you are seriously mistaken.'

The maharaja kept his gun pointed at Menon's head. 'If you ever go back on your word, I will kill you,' he thundered. 'Kill you – do you understand?'

'Stop indulging in juvenile theatrics, Your Highness,' Menon advised the maharaja, outwardly unruffled but trembling like a leaf on the inside. 'You know as well as I do that you are not going to shoot.'

'Promise me, promise me,' the maharaja shouted, his hand shaking, 'that you will not betray me.'

'I promise,' said Menon, looking straight into the maharaja's eyes. 'You can be assured that Sardar Patel will keep his word.'

The door opened. The viceroy entered. And froze.

'Good gracious! What in heaven's name is going on here?' exclaimed Lord Mountbatten, while walking straight towards the maharaja. 'Hanwant! What do you think you're doing?'

Exhaling hard, the maharaja put down the gun. Menon sighed in relief, the colour returning to his face.

'I...uh...I am sorry,' apologized the maharaja sheepishly. 'The last few days have been extremely stressful. My decision is going to impact over a million of my people. I'm...I'm terribly sorry,' he said. 'I completely lost my composure.'

The intriguing pen-revolver had been crafted in the maharaja's metals workshop in the Mehrangarh Fort. Hanwant Singh, who was a member of the Magic Circle (a British organization, founded in 1905, for promoting magic), had a keen interest in technology and had designed a variety of experimental firearms including swords, *khukuris* and walking-stick guns. When Lord Mountbatten developed a fascination for the pen-revolver, the maharaja gifted it to the viceroy later. The device is displayed at the Royal Armouries Museum in Leeds, UK.

'We are all labouring under extremely trying circumstances,' the viceroy admonished the maharaja, 'but we must not allow the times to overwhelm us.'

'I cannot tell you how ashamed I am,' the maharaja repeated, taking Menon's hand, the enormity of his momentary madness finally hitting him. 'I deeply regret my behaviour.'

'I understand, Your Highness,' Menon replied evenly. 'I won't hold it against you.'

'What an intriguing device this is,' the viceroy remarked, watching the maharaja flip the revolver back into a pen. 'Anyway, now tell me...have you come to a decision?'

'I am ready,' the maharaja sighed and sat back down, 'ready to sign...' Glad to finally hear those words, Menon placed the accession papers on the table.

'And this is your final decision?' asked the viceroy, keen to avoid further twists and turns.

'Yes,' nodded the maharaja, gripping the pen tightly. 'Jodhpur will join India.'

♦♦♦♦♦♦♦♦♦♦♦♦♦♦♦♦♦♦♦

Postscript

♦♦♦♦♦♦♦♦♦♦♦♦♦♦♦♦♦♦♦

The twenty-four-year-old maharaja, Hanwant Singh, had succeeded to the *raj gaddi* of Jodhpur state only two months before India's independence and was almost lured by the promises made by Jinnah to join Pakistan. The location of his kingdom at the border of the two dominions was, indeed, a crucially strategic one. But for the timely intervention of everyone involved, the Jodhpur pendulum may easily have swung the other way.

The pen-into-gun episode actually took place in the viceroy's waiting room before the maharaja signed the accession papers. However, the maharaja apologized profusely to Menon immediately thereafter and the incident became a joke between them in later years, with the maharaja even inviting Menon to stand for elections from Jodhpur.

Diwan Venkatachar later became secretary of the States Ministry and subsequently secretary to India's first president, Rajendra Prasad.

After two controversial marriages in quick succession, the young maharaja, known to be a daredevil pilot, died in a crash while piloting a plane in 1952 at the young age of twenty-nine.

The Bollywood movie *Zubeidaa* is said to be based on the life of Maharaja Hanwant Singh's second wife, Zubeida, whom he married in 1948, a little after the episodes covered in this chapter. His ancestral home, the Umaid Bhawan Palace in Jodhpur, is one of the largest residences in the world, with 347 rooms. The erstwhile royal family still lives in one wing of the palace, and a part of it is now a luxury hotel. The splendid Mehrangarh Fort in Jodhpur remains one of the finest and best-preserved forts of India.

♦♦♦♦♦♦♦♦♦♦♦♦♦♦♦♦♦♦♦

Did It Really Happen This Way?

♦♦♦♦♦♦♦♦♦♦♦♦♦♦♦♦♦♦♦

The secret meeting between the maharaja of Jodhpur and Jinnah, which opens this chapter, is mentioned in several sources, including in V.P. Menon's book Integration of the Indian States.

The urgent SOS *from the maharaja's* ADC, *Colonel Thakur Kesari Singh, to Diwan Venkatachar and further from the diwan to Delhi (via either K.M. Panikkar, the diwan of Bikaner, or Home Secretary H.V.R. Iyengar, or perhaps both), alerting Sardar about the maharaja's meeting with Jinnah, has been referred to in the book* India's Bismarck: Sardar Vallabhbhai Patel *by Balraj Krishna, among others. The camaraderie between the diwans of Rajputana, and several of the other events described in this chapter find mention in K.M. Panikkar's autobiography (originally in Malayalam).*

Nawab Hamidullah's hand in discouraging Maharaja Hanwant Singh from meeting Sardar Patel is disputed. The nawab denied it and even offered an elaborate explanation to the viceroy for his actions. The record of this is to be found in The Transfer of Power 1942–7, Vol. XII.

The episode of the Rajputs of Amarkot (now Umerkot) in Sind, which today falls within Pakistan, requesting Hanwant Singh to help them, is based on stray references. Although the raja of Amarkot was a Hindu Rajput, he was a member of the Muslim League and acceded to Pakistan.

The climax scene is based on the events recorded by both V.P. Menon and Mountbatten respectively in Integration of the Indian States *and* The Transfer of Power 1942–7, Vol. XII. *The key dialogues between the parties are representative of actual conversations with certain creative liberties.*

7

Indian First

THE STORY OF RAMPUR

PRINCELY STATE OF RAMPUR IN 1947:
in present-day Uttar Pradesh
AREA: 894 square miles (2,315 square kilometres)
POPULATION: 477,042
RULER: Nawab Sir Raza Ali Khan Bahadur
DIWAN: Bashir Hussain Zaidi
15-gun-salute state

❋ Rifts Within ❋

'After Partition...I will be moving to Pakistan,' Sahabzada Yaqub Khan whispered into Nawab Raza Ali's ear as they stood side by side, admiring artefacts in the Italian sculpture gallery of the grand Raza Library.

The nawab of Rampur, leaning forward to examine a particularly spectacular piece kept within a niche, froze momentarily. *Hindu or Muslim. India or Pakistan. Stay or leave. The moment of reckoning was upon them all.* And yet... his nephew's decision surprised him. Yaqub was a fine young lad with a bright, promising future. 'Have you given it proper thought, my boy?' the nawab turned to face him.

'Yes...I have,' Yaqub replied, lowering his gaze.

'You are a respected officer in the Indian Army,' the nawab whispered, glancing at Yaqub's mother and brother a few paces away. 'Your family is here...as is your ancestral home...'

'Hmm,' Yaqub nodded slightly.

'Does your mother know?' asked the nawab softly.

'Yes...I have told her,' Yaqub replied, his voice even softer.

'And?' the nawab raised his eyebrows. 'What did she say?' The nawab's brother had served as prime minister of Rampur for many long years. Why his son would even think of leaving his privileged and comfortable home, and adopting an alien land, was beyond him.

Yaqub shook his head, unable to speak, his eyes welling up.

'Yaqub, this is the land of our people, this is your home... this – all this – it is yours,' the nawab raised his hands to the canopied ceiling above, at a loss for words. 'This, my child, is

THE RAZA LIBRARY

all part of your heritage, your legacy.' He gaped at his nephew, unable to wrap his head around the boy's decision. 'Why should you leave?' the nawab remonstrated, throwing up his hands in disbelief. 'Why would you leave? How can you leave?'

The outburst caught the attention of the others in the gallery. Yaqub's mother, his brother Yunus and Diwan Bashir Hussain Zaidi all turned towards them.

'*Beta*...our ancestors fought for this land. Your great-grandfathers died for it. How can you make any other place your home?' The nawab cajoled his nephew.

Swallowing a lump in his throat, Yaqub made no reply.

The Rampur Raza Library, where this scene is set, is a grand building in Rampur containing about 17,000 manuscripts in Hindi, Sanskrit, Arabic, Persian, Urdu and Turkish, including paintings and ancient palm-leaf manuscripts in various Indian languages, and a collection of over 60,000 books.

The nawabs of Rampur were great patrons of learning, and the library was founded by Nawab Faizullah Khan, the first nawab of Rampur, in 1774.

Several rulers of the princely states were patrons of the arts. Due to their support to artistes and musicians, various nuanced traditions emerged from the princely states, which were then given the name of the kingdom where they originated. So we have the Patiala *gharana*, Gwalior *gharana*, Rampur *gharana* and so on, which are the various schools of Hindustani classical music shaped by musicians who belonged to those kingdoms. The Rampur *gharana* of music flourished during the reign of Nawab Hamid Ali Khan who ruled Rampur between 1889 and 1930. Famous *ghazal* singers like Begum Akhtar and court singer Jaddanbai (Hindi cinema actor Nargis Dutt's mother) were from Rampur.

'Did you hear Yaqub?' the nawab asked Yunus, who had sidled closer to his brother, along with the rest.

Yaqub's mother nodded slightly, drawing the gold laced *pallu* of her saree over her head. Diwan Zaidi looked on curiously.

'And what is your decision?' the nawab asked.

'India is my home, and this is where I belong,' replied Yaqub's mother stoically, turning away from her son. 'India is where I have lived. And India is where I shall die.'

❋ Rifts Without ❋

Named after a Hindu deity, ruled by a Muslim nawab, the 15 gun-salute state of Rampur, situated about 130 miles (220 km) from Delhi and within the United Provinces, had an overwhelmingly Hindu majority. Upon Independence, the tiny kingdom, covering just over 2,000 square kilometres, would be surrounded by Indian territory – reason enough to ward off even the most persistent petitioner for Pakistan perhaps. But Liaquat Ali Khan, Jinnah's right-hand man in the Muslim League, and the man slated to become Pakistan's first prime minister, was no ordinary crusader.

Standing before the imposing oil painting of Queen Victoria outside the Great Banquet Hall of the splendid Khasbagh Palace (or Kothi Khas Bagh) of Rampur, Khan threw a glance around the imposing building – the first air-conditioned palace in all of India, complete with a heated swimming pool and a luxurious movie theatre. Its *shahi khazana* – the treasure vault – was the stuff of legends, known to be bursting at the seams with sparkling rubies, rare emeralds, priceless gemstones and brilliant diamonds.

'His Highness and Diwan Zaidi are ready to see you, sir.' The nawab's ADC motioned Liaquat Ali towards a door leading into the nawab's study.

Liaquat Ali glanced at a portrait of the nawab, posing beside his gold throne, wearing his Golconda-diamond-studded crown and the portrait of Zamani Begum in her diamond tiara and necklace. He adjusted the Astrakhan 'Jinnah' cap on his head and followed the aide, playing out the strategy in his mind. Rampur was a wealthy and industrialized state with an annual income of over 100 lakh rupees. Should he succeed in winning over Rampur to his side, Khan mused, Pakistan could gain a very crucial advantage – a profitable, pocket-sized base in the very heart of India.

'As-*salaam-alaikum*, Nawab Sa'ab,' Liaquat Ali greeted his host warmly.

'*Wa-alaikum-salaam*,' Liaquat Sa'ab!' the nawab responded with a friendly hug. 'To what do I owe the honour of hosting the soon-to-be prime minister of Pakistan?'

'I come bearing an important request,' Liaquat Ali got straight to the point as he took a seat, 'and I hope you won't disappoint me.'

Diwan Zaidi stiffened. He harboured no illusions about the purpose of a visit from a senior leader of the Muslim League at such a critical moment.

'We would like Rampur,' began Liaquat Ali without beating around the bush, 'to join Pakistan.'

The nawab exhaled gustily and sat back. In all their years of existence, the Muslim League had done nothing, nothing at all, for the princely states, completely ignoring the rulers and the people there. Now that Pakistan was about to take shape, they were feverishly scurrying hither and thither, making overtures to rajas and nawabs to strengthen Pakistan and weaken India. *Opportunistic* and *loathsome* were the words that sprang to the nawab's mind. Yet, he maintained a poker face and turned to Liaquat Ali. 'I do not see matters as you do,' he replied after a brief silence. 'My people are mostly Hindu. There is no question of joining Pakistan.'

'But you are a Shi'a Muslim,' Liaquat Ali pointed out, the warmth vanishing from his voice, 'and the decision, as you know, is to be taken by the ruler.'

'Liaquat Sa'ab, my state will be surrounded by Indian territory. And if that's not an obvious enough reason for you, then let me tell you that I am quite secure with the idea of being in India.'

'What a tragedy,' Liaquat Ali clicked his tongue in disapproval. 'What a tragedy that, after all that we've been through, Muslims like you should still back the Congress party.'

The grandfather clock in the study chimed ten times as the two men stared at each other in awkward silence.

'Look...it is not too late,' Liaquat Ali resumed his pitch. 'As a well-wisher...I urge you to join forces with Pakistan.'

'I'm afraid that is just not possible,' replied Diwan Zaidi, in support of the nawab. 'Rampur sits in the United Provinces... in the very heart of India. It will be surrounded by India on all sides.'

'How is that of any consequence?' Liaquat Ali shot back, throwing up his hands. 'Have you forgotten the criterion of the two-nation theory? It has nothing to do with geography.'

The nawab and his diwan exchanged glances. Liaquat Ali, they had heard, was mild-mannered – supposedly a contrast to the joyless Jinnah. The outburst surprised them.

'The two-nation theory, Liaquat Sa'ab, was based on the religion of the people, wasn't it?' argued Zaidi, maintaining a dignified tone. 'And the people of Rampur are overwhelmingly Hindu. How can we join Pakistan?'

Cracking his knuckles furiously, Liaquat Ali looked away.

'Let's say we join Pakistan...' continued the nawab, leaning forward, 'how will Pakistan aid Rampur if we were in trouble? We have no land link at all with Pakistan. Neither West nor East Pakistan is even remotely near us.' As it was, Pakistan was going to take birth in a peculiarly unusual form, with its western and eastern halves separated by over a thousand kilometres of Indian territory. Wasn't that complicated enough?

'Have faith in us, Nawab Sa'ab, we will provide you with complete moral support,' replied Liaquat Ali.

Moral support? Zaidi rolled his eyes. *Was that all the League had to offer?*

'Look...we have a plan,' Liaquat Ali also leaned forward in his seat.

'What plan?' enquired the nawab, only half interested.

'A land corridor between East and West Pakistan,' Liaquat Ali Khan smiled slightly as he visualized the prospect. 'It will cut through India. Rampur will be connected to Pakistan via this corridor.'

'Excuse me? Do you really think Pakistan will have a corridor cutting across India?' Zaidi suppressed a disbelieving chuckle. 'You've got to be joking.'

'I am appalled by your attitude, Zaidi Sa'ab,' Liaquat Ali Khan chided the diwan. 'As a fellow Muslim, you ought to be supportive and advise the nawab to accede to Pakistan. Instead, you mock our efforts.'

DIWAN ZAIDI: YOU REALLY THINK PAKISTAN CAN HAVE A LAND CORRIDOR THROUGH INDIA?

'Well,' smiled Zaidi cheekily, 'if you can have Rampur flown magically to Pakistan's borders, I might ask the nawab to accede to Pakistan. Else, I'm afraid we have no choice in the matter but to join India.'

Deeply offended by the impudent barb, Liaquat Ali got to his feet in a flash. 'You might find yourself in grave trouble,' he warned, waving a finger at the nawab, 'if you do not accede to Pakistan.'

'And what is that supposed to mean? Are you threatening me?' The nawab stood up to face him, unperturbed.

'You are free to take it as you like,' said Liaquat Ali, straightening his suit and topi. Threatening and shouting were not in his nature. Why, he himself was of the same *nawabi* stock, an aristocrat from the same region, and had been raised with the same impeccable cultural refinement as the man who stood before him. However, the meeting was clearly not proceeding according to plan and his temper was beginning to fray. 'If you desert Pakistan,' Liaquat Ali said, his face red, his jaw quivering, 'you can be sure of trouble!'

❋ To Caesar and to God ❋

'A Pakistani corridor through India?' Jawaharlal Nehru scoffed, walking out from the viceregal study after a meeting. 'Has Jinnah completely lost his mind?'

'And notice how carefully Jinnah plants the story in the London newspapers through British correspondents in Delhi to influence opinion in England,' V.P. Menon pointed out.

'No one asked Pakistan to secede,' Sardar said. 'Jinnah has got what he wanted. Let him leave us to our devices now.'

Mountbatten shrugged, pausing for a moment as they reached the vicereine's room—'I'm only conveying his request.'

Dressed in a crisp St. John uniform, Edwina Mountbatten was in her study, in the middle of a meeting with her Red Cross team – men and women who had volunteered to join her relentless efforts in comforting the sick and the destitute, languishing in the dozens of refugee camps across the capital. Even the spaces and kitchens within the viceroy's house had been thrown open to provide help to them upon her initiative and insistence.

EDWINA MOUNTBATTEN: SPEARHEADING RED CROSS EFFORTS TO HELP PARTITION REFUGEES

'You know, I have often joked that Dickie could charm a vulture off a carcass,' joked Hastings Ismay. 'He is blessed with the knack of persuading anyone, about just about anything. Only, when he first met Jinnah this March did I discover the limit to Dickie's charm.'

'Jinnah and his fantasies,' Sardar Patel laughed, linking his hands behind his back, as two guards held open the large, teak doors and ushered the men into the foyer. The idea amused him. 'What else would Mr Jinnah like? An army base within Indian territory? A naval base in our waters?'

'I hear you, and I shall convey to Mr Jinnah that the corridor is not on the table,' Lord Mountbatten winked.

'No question at all about it,' Nehru concurred, as they proceeded towards the grand stairway. 'Liaquat Ali, I hear, has approached the nawab of Rampur. In Sind, the League's Feroz Khan Noon is bending over backwards to convince the Hindu ruler of Radhanpur to join Pakistan. Jodhpur and Jaisalmer too find themselves in Jinnah's net...'

'Jhara...Diodar...Suigam...Tharad...' Menon rattled off more names, adding to the list of Hindu states being approached by Pakistan. 'Are we interfering with Bahawalpur or Khairpur or Kalat?' he demanded, referring to the Muslim princely states geographically contiguous with Pakistan, making no mention of India's interest in the Muslim-dominated North-West Frontier Province where the Congress was pushing for a plebiscite. 'If only we could render unto Caesar that which is Caesar's, and render unto God that which is God's.'

The men agreed, with a shrug of their shoulders and a nod of their heads, as the orange ball in the sky painted the Parade Grounds below in ruddy shades. Fair play was no longer the name of the game.

NEHRU: I CAN'T BELIEVE JINNAH EXPECTS US TO GRANT HIM A LAND CORRIDOR CUTTING THROUGH INDIA!

'Pakistan appears to want to cut a neat wedge through the Rann of Kutch,' said Sardar, gazing into the distance. 'A slice of Pakistan cutting through Gujarat and Rajputana, straight into India's heart.'

'This corridor business has got to be the most absurd thing I've ever heard,' scoffed Nehru, unable to take his mind off Jinnah's audacious demand as they descended the flight of stairs towards their waiting cars. 'I can't believe Jinnah expects us to grant Pakistan an 800-mile land corridor stretching across India,' he threw his hands up in disbelief. 'How does such a thought even occur to that man?'

'Let's not forget,' grunted Sardar, 'this is exactly how most of us reacted when he first demanded Pakistan.' Sardar hadn't forgotten how, not too long ago, he himself had dismissed the idea of Pakistan as Jinnah's mad dream.

Who would have thought, they mused, gazing at the setting sun in the distant horizon, that Jinnah's mad dream would one day become a raging nightmare. And that, some day, they would all get sucked into playing a deliberate, definitive and decisive role in making that nightmare come true.

❋ Indian Army: Split into Two ❋

There was not a dry eye in the house that evening as the army band played the old Scottish tune 'Auld Lang Syne', and all gathered on the lawns of the Imperial Delhi Gymkhana Club raised their glasses to toast the ballad about old friendships and shared memories. Comrades-in-arms, who had lived and served together all their lives in the famed British Indian Army would soon be separated to serve either India or Pakistan. But, for one last time, they stood arm in arm, shoulder to shoulder, singing like brothers.

Beneath a large neem tree towards the end of the lawn, General Cariappa mounted a wooden platform and presented a silver trophy to Brigadier Agha Mohammad Raza, a token of his friendship and affection, as the band fell silent. Wiping moist eyes, Cariappa moved to the microphone on the stage. 'I say *au revoir* deliberately and with it I associate the honest and sincere wishes of every one of us here...' he began slowly, swallowing a lump in his throat.

GENERAL CARIAPPA: THE ARMIES OF INDIA AND PAKISTAN SHALL MEET EACH OTHER AS THE BEST OF FRIENDS...

Field Marshall Claude Auchinleck, or The Auk as he was known, sniffled, empathizing with the man on the stage. The Auk would soon be the joint supreme commander of the armies of India and Pakistan. He had dedicated his entire life to the Indian Army and knew no home other than India. It broke his heart to even think of going back to England – a place where he would find himself a complete stranger. It grieved him to have to rip apart the Indian Army – an institution he loved more than anything else. He had fought in both World Wars, led dangerous military campaigns and had even served in hostile terrain, but nothing had pained him as much as having to preside over the division of his beloved army. He wiped away a tear.

'We shall meet each other frequently as the best of friends,' General Cariappa continued, 'in the same spirit of good comradeship that we have had the good fortune to enjoy all these years. We have been together for so long on the same team'—Cariappa's eyes welled with tears again—'lived together, worked together, played together, fought together... May this spirit continue even after we are separated.'

There was a round of applause as the men in uniform hugged each other, vowing undying friendship and wishing each other well. Their wives exchanged tearful notes of farewell, promising to stay in touch.

Sitting a few chairs away with a deathly pale face, Jinnah was dressed in a black sherwani - a change from the crisply cut English suits he usually sported - adopting a dress code more suited to his new home in Karachi. The Indian Army was being partitioned in haste upon his insistence, despite considerable objection from The Auk. Pakistan simply had to have its own army by 14 August, he had argued. It was non-negotiable.

Only a few tables away, Nehru nodded and smiled at familiar faces, keen to have every British soldier out of the country as soon as possible; their mere presence was a stark reminder of India's colonial subjugation.

On stage, Brigadier Raza accepted the memento from General Cariappa and took the microphone, 'I am deeply touched by this true spirit of comradeship and genuine feelings of brotherhood...' Raza's voice quivered, his eyes moist as well. 'The armed forces of Pakistan will always uphold their traditions under which they served shoulder to shoulder with the Indian armed forces and will continue to do so whenever required not only for our own people but also for the inhabitants of this subcontinent and universal security.'

Brotherhood. Friendship. Camaraderie. The evening was filled with happy promises.

And yet, in the months and years to come, the love and the memories would all be forgotten. In less than three months, they would all be at each other's throats.

***

Just over 220 kilometres from Delhi, in the kingdom of Rampur, another tear-filled parting was taking place.

'Just imagine that I'm stationed in Karachi instead of Delhi, Ammi, that's all.' The nawab's nephew, Yaqub, tried to cheer up his weeping mother as she held the Holy Quran above his head. He passed beneath it, took it in his hands and kissed it.

'You will be enlisted in the Pakistani Army as soon as you get there,' Zaidi reminded Yaqub. 'And your brother Yunus is in the Indian Army...'

Yaqub remained silent, trying hard to maintain his composure. However, his bloodshot eyes gave him away – clearly he had spent the night tossing and turning in anguish.

Zaidi sighed, greatly perplexed by the irony of it all. The cherished goal of freedom had arrived at India's doorstep at long last, but celebration was the last thing on anybody's mind.

'In case of war between India and Pakistan, you will be fighting as enemies,' said Zaidi, hoping that Yaqub could somehow, even now, be persuaded to stay.

'Why must we think of such inauspicious things?' Yaqub smiled, putting an arm around his brother. 'After Partition, India and Pakistan will be friends. There will be no war. And I will return often to meet you all.'

Yunus's eyes filled with tears. He knew his brother was leaving reluctantly. The Auk had pressed Yaqub to take over command of the bodyguards for Pakistan's governor general, as no one else in Karachi had the suitable training for such a challenging post. Particularly with rumours of death threats and assassination plots against Jinnah surfacing every now and then, Yaqub was laying himself on the sacrificial altar of Jinnah's mad dream. Leaving his mother and brother, his home and hearth, his land and his people – to guard the father of Pakistan and keep him safe. He hugged his brother tight, swallowing a lump in his throat.

'Inshallah!' Zaidi exclaimed, as they recited verses from the Holy Quran together, invoking Allah's blessings for the departing Yaqub.

Bidding goodbye to the well-wishers gathered to see him off, Yaqub sat in the car that was to take him to the railway station. He turned back to take one last look at his childhood home. 'I'll be back soon, Ammi,' Yaqub squeezed his mother's hand as the car began to pull away. 'I'll see you in a few months.'

Sahabzada Yaqub could not have been more wrong.

For, in a matter of months, India and Pakistan would be at war, and brother would battle brother. Yaqub Khan would fight for the Pakistani forces, and Yunus Khan for the Indian Army. And despite his heart's deepest desire, Yaqub Khan would never return to see his mother or his home ever again.

❋ The Price of Principles ❋

Zaidi stood at the gate of the whitewashed colonial-style bungalow, watching Yaqub's car disappear in a cloud of dust even as the others from his farewell party dispersed. One man's ambition was ripping families apart; tearing up a nation;

turning brother against brother, friend into foe. It seemed unreal and yet...here he was, witnessing the madness.

'Zaidi Sa'ab,' an orderly rushed over to the diwan as he stood there, lost in his thoughts. Blood dripped from a gash on the man's forehead, his nose was broken, his right arm hung limp on his side, and his clothes were torn and soiled.

'*Ya Khuda!*' exclaimed Zaidi, turning towards the man. 'Whatever happened to you?'

The orderly stopped short of the diwan and fell to the floor, gasping.

'*Da...dan...!*' he rasped.

'What?' Zaidi bent down, his voice laced with panic.

'*Danga!* Riots!'

'Where?'

'Everywhere,' the man mumbled and passed out.

'Help me get him inside,' Zaidi yelled to an attendant and dashed to the spiral wrought-iron stairway at the corner of the bungalow. He raced to the terrace, taking two steps at a time, ran to the balustrade at the edge and then froze.

Rampur was ablaze!

❋ Murder and Mayhem ❋

'Oh dear!' exclaimed the viceroy, shaking hands with the nawab and his diwan who had hurried from Rampur to Delhi. 'You both look unwell. Is everything all right?' he enquired, pushing aside the huge piles of paper on the table, documents over which he had been labouring for days to recreate his family tree that connected him to half a dozen members of royalty across the world – from the tsar of Russia to the kaiser of Germany. But even as he took pride in the royal blood that pulsed through his veins, in his ancestry from Queen Victoria, his kinship with King George VI, he was pressing the rajas and nawabs of India to renounce their royal status and merge into the melting pot of democracy.

'I'm afraid, not at all,' the nawab sank into the couch. 'The situation in Rampur is spiralling out of control even as we speak!'

'Riots have broken out all across the state...' Zaidi explained hurriedly. 'We have driven through the chaos to get here.'

'Government buildings are being set on fire,' the nawab said, anxiously.

'Police stations too,' Zaidi added. 'Even policemen are being attacked.'

'And murdered.'

'There's rioting and looting on the streets.'

'A staff member who worked under the inspector general of police was burnt alive!'

The viceroy listened in dismay as the nawab and Zaidi took turns to recount the horrors that had been unleashed in Rampur over the last few days.

Mountbatten reached out to the nawab whose son, Murtaza Ali Khan, had been the viceroy's ADC. Having known the nawab and his family well, he had been one of the few visitors to have ever been given a personal tour of the fabulous treasure vault of the Rampur palace.

He knew the nawab was an unbiased ruler – neither partial to Muslims, nor prejudiced against Hindus. Rampur had, in fact, been one of the first states to announce its accession to India and the nawab was the first Muslim ruler of a large state to do so.

'Whom do you suspect is instigating the riots?' The viceroy leaned forward.

'There's no doubt it is the Muslim League,' said the nawab softly as a bearer entered the room with a large silver tea tray.

'Jinnah has been bringing every possible pressure to bear on me to prevent me from acceding to India,' the nawab continued after the bearer had left the room.

'Undoubtedly the goondas of the Muslim League...' the diwan agreed, checking to see if the door was closed – these days even walls had ears and one could never be too careful – '...to bully the nawab and coerce him into reversing his decision.'

'Liaquat Ali Khan and a few other Muslim League members came to see us a few days ago,' explained the nawab. 'They made serious threats if Rampur did not join Pakistan.'

'Your Excellency,' said Zaidi, 'Rampur needs help. And urgently.'

The viceroy leaned forward to pour out the tea into the exquisite cups of fine china, glancing up at the countdown calendar he had had pinned in every room, to remind one and all of the number of days that remained until the transfer of power. The number ten in bold, black digits stared back at him.

Ten days left, the viceroy thought to himself, as he handed his guests their tea. For ten more days, the burden to stem the rising turmoil rested upon his shoulders. 'Sardar Patel has taken control of the entire contingent of the viceroy's police force,' he said to his haggard guests after a pause. 'It is now a part of the federal police force, and Sardar will loan the forces to any ruler who requires help.'

Zaidi heaved a sigh of relief. The lightly spiced tea and the news lifted his spirits.

'May I request that the forces be dispatched immediately to Rampur to control the situation?' the nawab asked Mountbatten, his pleading eyes conveying his urgency and desperation.

'Undoubtedly! We will provide you with every help you need,' the viceroy nodded reassuringly as he sipped his tea. 'Don't you worry. Rampur will be saved.'

❋ Making the Choice ❋

Nawab Raza Ali Khan linked his hands on his lap, unfazed by the threats of the member of the Muslim League in the room.

Three hundred men of the Crown's representative police had arrived in Rampur. Another half a battalion of troops was on its way.

The riots had been quelled. Cases of looting and arson had reduced substantially. Miscreants had fled the area. The presence of the soldiers had brought life in Rampur back to normal.

'What is your final answer, then?' the visitor from the Muslim League asked the nawab.

'I have only one answer,' replied the nawab, looking straight at his guest.

'And what is that?'

'I have already conveyed it,' said the nawab, mildly irritated.

'So you do not intend to change your mind?'

'Tell your higher-ups,' Zaidi said, smiling, 'that these pressure tactics of the Muslim League will not work. The nawab's decision is final.'

Miffed, the representative of the Muslim League glared at the nawab.

'Don't waste your time,' the nawab replied without flinching, gesturing to the door to show his unwelcome guest the way out. 'I am an Indian first and a Muslim only after that. So go and tell your political bosses'—Nawab Raza Ali Khan stood up decisively—'Rampur stays with India.'

♦♦♦♦♦♦♦♦♦♦♦♦♦♦♦♦♦♦♦

Postscript

♦♦♦♦♦♦♦♦♦♦♦♦♦♦♦♦♦♦♦

Rampur was a 15 gun-salute state, now part of present-day Uttar Pradesh; its nawab was one of the earliest rulers, and the first Muslim ruler of a large state, to accede to India. Although the state did not have geographical contiguity with East or West Pakistan and was a Hindu-majority kingdom, the Muslim League put enormous pressure on the nawab to join Pakistan.

The nawab's nephew, Yaqub Khan, was the only member of Rampur's royal family to migrate to Pakistan and, in the 1980s, he became Pakistan's minister for foreign affairs. He was, like several others, simply wrong about his assumption that India and Pakistan would be friends after Partition. The two countries went to war over Kashmir merely months after Independence. Yaqub Khan fought in the war for the Pakistani Army, and his brother Yunus Khan for the Indian Army.

General Cariappa (later Field Marshal Cariappa) went on to become the first Indian commander-in-chief of the Indian Army.

Field Marshal Claude Auchinleck, who professed great love for the Indian Army and was loved by his soldiers (with whom he spoke fluently in their own languages), was perceived as pro-Pakistan in later times by many of the Indian leaders. He is said to have disapproved of Mountbatten's haste in dividing the Indian Army, a task for which he said he would have needed three years. He would return reluctantly to England after his services ended and be delighted every time he discovered an Indian restaurant in London. Finding himself a stranger in England, he settled down in Italy and died at the ripe old age of ninety.

As a royal family, the Rampur rulers had patronized several classical musicians and helped keep alive the rich tradition of Hindustani classical music, especially the *khayal* style of singing.

♦♦♦♦♦♦♦♦♦♦♦♦♦♦♦♦♦♦♦

Did It Really Happen This Way?

♦♦♦♦♦♦♦♦♦♦♦♦♦♦♦♦♦♦♦

The opening scene in the Raza Library has been imagined to introduce the reader to the principal characters of the story and the situation facing them.

The scene describing Liaquat Ali Khan's visit to Rampur, his threatening the nawab to coerce him to join Pakistan and the reference to the Pakistani land corridor cutting across India is based on the account in Once a Prince of Sarila: Of Palaces and Tiger Hunts, of Nehrus and Mountbattens, *written by Narendra Singh Sarila. The fact that the League approached several kingdoms to join Pakistan is mentioned by Ian Copland in* State, Community and Neighbourhood in Princely North India, c. 1900–1950.

Details about the splitting of the Indian Army are based on accounts in Disastrous Twilight: A Personal Record of the Partition of India *by Major General Shahid Hamid and* The Great Divide: Britain – India – Pakistan *by H.V. Hodson.*

While based on references, some creative liberty has been taken to describe the reaction of Indian leaders to the corridor proposal, Yaqub's departure for Pakistan and the riots in Rampur.

Details of the visit by the nawab of Rampur and the diwan Zaidi to the viceroy seeking help to quell League-sponsored trouble in Rampur can be found in a confidential report of Mountbatten in The Transfer of Power 1942–7, Vol. XII.

8

Western Disturbances

THE STORIES OF BARODA AND NAWANAGAR

PRINCELY STATE OF BARODA IN 1947:
in present-day Gujarat
AREA: 8,235 square miles (21,328 square kilometres)
POPULATION: 2,855,010
RULER: Maharaja Sir Pratap Singh Rao Gaekwad
DIWAN: B.L. Mitter
21-gun–salute state

PRINCELY STATE OF NAWANAGAR IN 1947:
in present-day Gujarat
AREA: 3,791 square miles (9,819 square kilometres)
POPULATION: 504,006
RULER: Jam Sahib Sir Digvijaysinhji Jadeja
13-gun–salute state

❋ Trouble Brewing ❋

'Mitter Sa'ab! Mitter Sa'ab!' the tense chief of the princely state of Vadia called out, rattling the garden gate.

Senior lawyer Sir Brojendra Lal Mitter, former law member of the Governor General's Executive Council, and present diwan of Baroda, was browsing the newspaper in his front lawn, humming his favourite tune. The morning news had pleased him immensely: British prime minister Clement Attlee had announced that Britain would withdraw from India by next year. It was music to the ears of every diehard nationalist who had been working tirelessly to see this day. Putting down the paper, Mitter rose to open the gate, a spring in his step.

'*Shun thayoo, bhai*? Where's the fire?' he smilingly asked his troubled visitor.

'It's being lit even as we speak, Mitter Sa'ab,' replied his tense counterpart of Vadia state, clutching the pleats of his dhoti, his flushed face matching his pink turban.

'What's going on?' Mitter took off his reading glasses and led his guest in, signalling to his staff to bring out refreshments. 'Calm down and tell me what happened.'

'Junagadh is importing arms and ammunition from Sind...' the chief whispered, casting a fearful glance over his shoulder, as if expecting to be spied upon.

'Is that so?' The diwan's genial smile vanished instantly. Junagadh, a key princely state in Kathiawar, the peninsular region of Gujarat, was ruled by an eccentric nawab, who had declared a state holiday for the wedding of his favourite dog. *What could the unpredictable Nawab Mahabat Khanji be planning now*? 'How do you know?' he asked.

'The consignment of weapons is being channelled through our port in Vadia,' replied his visitor, dropping into the cane chair in the garden.

'And what do you think is the purpose?' asked Mitter. 'Have you any details?'

'I hear the nawab has plans to...' the chief trailed off as the tea trolley was wheeled out. 'I hear...' he continued as soon as the bearer turned away, 'that he plans to conquer Kathiawar when the British withdraw from India next year.' He gingerly poured out the piping-hot tea from his cup into his saucer.

'Surely you are imagining things.' Mitter dismissed the chief's fears as paranoid delusions, although he was aware that, if the nawab really wanted to become overlord of Kathiawar, nothing could prevent him from creating mischief. The region was a scattering of about 200 kingdoms and estates, ruled by various chiefs – many feudal and antiquated – held together only by their pledged allegiance to the British monarch. Once the British left, that fragile link would be broken. *And then, what would become of them all? Would Britain's withdrawal result in utter chaos?* Suddenly, Mitter didn't feel quite so jubilant anymore.

'Even the Jam Sahib of Nawanagar is strengthening his armed forces.' The chief paused to slurp his tea noisily. 'I hear...' he lowered his voice conspiratorially and drew his chair closer to Mitter, 'that the Jam Sahib too dreams of being overlord of Kathiawar after the British exit.'

Mitter's face fell. Nawanagar was an important state, and its ruler held some sway in the region.

'What do you want from me?' he asked sombrely. 'I mean... what do you want from Baroda?'

'Mitter Sa'ab, Baroda is a powerful state,' said the chief matter-of-factly, 'Vadia is small and cannot hold its own against Junagadh or Nawanagar if either of them decides to invade us. I would like to know whether Baroda will stand by us should we find ourselves in trouble.'

'Most certainly,' Mitter assured the chief without hesitation. Baroda was after all the largest and most important state in the region.

By the time the chief of Vadia left, feeling somewhat confident, Brojendra Lal Mitter had forgotten the upbeat tune he had been humming in celebration of the morning news. He no longer felt like a blithe songbird released from its cage; instead, like a hostage trapped atop a volcano.

❋ Kashmir to Kanyakumari ❋

Even as Mitter agonized over the days to come, Viceroy Mountbatten was busy formulating plans for the future of India with Nehru and Menon in the grand Viceroy Lodge in Simla.

Meanwhile, Sardar Patel stole a few minutes of solitude under a blossoming laburnum at the Lodhi Gardens in Delhi – rare moments of calm before the city awoke and his overwhelmingly onerous duties robbed him of any chance of quiet contemplation.

Linking his hands behind his back, Sardar reflected upon the months ahead that would mark the end of their long struggle for freedom. While everyone speculated about the transfer of power, the new constitution, Partition and Pakistan, he knew that the single biggest problem was going to be the princely states. Over 500 states scattered across the subcontinent – each with its own peculiar problems. *Where was he to begin?*

Pausing at the Athpula, the eight-pillared stone bridge built by Mughal emperor Akbar, Patel reflected upon the many powers that had attempted to unify this vast land from the rugged mountains in the north to the mighty seas in the south. Illustrious kings; powerful dynasties; giant corporations – they had all tried, and failed. *Would destiny bestow upon him the good fortune of uniting this nation as one, and achieve what none before him had managed to pull off?*

***

'Good morning, Shankar,' Sardar greeted his private secretary as he walked into his home. 'Send out invitations to the rulers of Jodhpur and Patiala for lunch next week.'

'The maharajas?' Shankar turned to Sardar curiously. 'Here at home?'

Sardar nodded, stopping by the spinning wheel in the living room. Following Gandhi's example, he too had taken to spinning many years ago, and all his clothes were hand-spun by his daughter Maniben, who also doubled up as systematic

SARDAR PATEL: THE FRUIT OF ONE'S LABOUR IS NOT IN ONE'S HANDS...

secretary and meticulous housekeeper. 'Invite the Jam Sahib too,' added Sardar, as he examined the fine yarn spun by Maniben, before sitting cross-legged at the *charkha* to spin for a short while.

'Jam Sahib Digvijaysinhji of Nawanagar?' Shankar asked in surprise.

'Here for lunch?' Maniben looked up from her papers in alarm.

'Yes...' Sardar nodded, his eyes on the yarn. Shankar and Maniben exchanged speculative glances, the Rajkot episode from a few years ago flashing through their minds. The ruler of Nawanagar had plotted and schemed against Gandhi and Patel. Sardar had nearly lost his life; Maniben had been jailed. *And now Sardar wanted to have the Jam Sahib over for lunch?*

'Do you think that's a good idea?' Maniben asked, filled with misgivings.

'And will the Jam Sahib accept?' added Shankar sceptically.

Sardar sighed deeply, aware of the wide gulf of mistrust between him and the Jam Sahib. *How could a man go out of his way to befriend another, knowing the latter had tried to take his life?* But this was no time to hold on to old hostilities. He would have to let go of personal grudges, break down walls and build bridges instead. For the sake of India's unity and future, he too would have to stay focused solely on the target, much like Arjuna who had kept his gaze pinned on the eye of the bird, ignoring all else.

'The Jam Sahib's brother...he is a colonel in the Indian Army...' Sardar paused spinning and closed his eyes as he tried to recollect the name. 'Himmatsinhji...' He snapped his fingers as the name sprang to mind. 'Call Colonel Himmatsinhji. Perhaps he can be a bridge between us. Let's give this a try.'

'This is going to be very interesting...you in this hand-spun khadi'—Maniben gently pulled her father's leg—'having lunch with Mr Diamond Buttons—' she laughed, referring to the moniker Nehru had given Jam Sahib Digvijaysinhji, who was reputed to have the most exquisite collection of gems and diamonds, his famed Nawanagar necklace being the stuff of legend.

Sardar Patel half-smiled, although his mind was clouded with apprehensions. It was going to take a monumental effort to bring in nearly 600 princes; to convince them to step out of their autocratic, feudal worlds and embrace an egalitarian, democratic India. However, he could only do his duty and be diligent in performing his dharma, he thought to himself, recalling Lord Krishna's wise words of counsel in the *Bhagavat Gita* – the fruit of the labour was not in one's hands.

'Why not chronicle all this?' Maniben suggested, turning in earnest to her father. Gandhi and Nehru spent hours writing, leaving a record of their lives and thoughts for future generations. Her father had lived a life no less eventful, but hardly ever preserved

You may have heard of the Ranji Trophy in the context of domestic Indian cricket. Ranji is short for Ranjitsinhji, a famous cricketer and ruler of Nawanagar. Digvijaysinhji, the ruler of Nawanagar in the story, was the nephew and successor of Ranjitsinhji.

Ranjitsinhji also loved to dazzle in an assortment of gems; he was a collector of rare jewels. Jacques Cartier, the jeweller who designed some of Ranjitsinhji's jewellery, described the Jam Sahib's collection as 'unsurpassed in the world, not perhaps in quantity, but certainly in quality'.

The fabulous necklace around which the plot of the Hollywood movie *Ocean's Eight* is set, is a replica of the famous Nawanagar necklace that was commissioned by Maharaja Ranjitsinhji and made by Cartier.

his letters or penned his thoughts. 'Why not write an autobiography? Note down all this history for posterity?'

Rising from the *charkha* and walking into his study, Sardar pointed to the files awaiting his attention on his desk. 'I'd much rather create history...' he retorted, as he sat down and picked up the first folder carefully marked for him by Shankar, 'much rather create history, my dear, than waste precious time writing it.'

❋ An Exalted Legacy ❋

As Srimant Maharaja Sir Pratap Singh Rao Gaekwad of Baroda walked out of the royal stables, he patted the mane of his favourite colt as he passed by its stall, and then turned around to gaze at the vast and fabulous edifice of the Lakshmi Vilas Palace behind him.

LAKSHMI VILAS PALACE: LARGEST PRIVATE RESIDENCE IN INDIA

Four times the size of Buckingham Palace in London and spread across 700 acres, the Indo-Saracenic structure was by far India's biggest private residence and perhaps one of the largest in the world. Marble verandas with scalloped arches; impressive façades topped by tear-shaped domes; carpeted corridors leading to tastefully appointed rooms – the palace was quite simply breathtaking. The Gaekwad was proud of his spectacular inheritance, comprising not just the grand palaces and staggering wealth, but also the legacy he carried as the grandson of the great Sayajirao Gaekwad III, one of the most able and enlightened rulers in all of India.

From banning child marriage to eradicating the scourge of untouchability, the maharaja's grandfather had been a torchbearer of reform. Sayajirao III's progressive outlook and magnanimity had helped a genius like Babasaheb Ambedkar to break free of the social stigma of untouchability that held back many a Dalit child. A patron of the arts, Sayajirao III had nurtured the fine talent of the pioneering artist Raja Ravi Varma – building him a studio and rewarding him well for his masterful work. So great was the maharaja's reputation that it was said that when he visited England, Queen Victoria sent her personal carriage to receive him – an honour not extended to many.

Considered neither as capable nor as illustrious as his grandfather, the present maharaja of Baroda was nonetheless one of only five princes to be extended a 21-gun salute by the British, a privilege taken most seriously in royal circles where pageantry and spectacle were the order of the day. As he saddled his horse and put on his breeches to ride out that sunny morning, gazing up pensively at the Tudor-inspired princely flag of Baroda, emblazoned with crown and scimitar, his mind was clouded by doubt.

From private trains to personal jets, the royal family of Baroda, with a revenue of crores, lacked for nothing.

However, times were changing. Mass movements had begun all across India for a democratic government. In Baroda too, Congress supporters like Raj Mehta and his coterie had been spearheading the demand to end monarchy. *Would his kingdom be engulfed by this crusade too? Or would the flag of Baroda continue to fly high?*

***

Gin ghar, gin takht. Diwan Mitter recalled that old adage one heard around Baroda, as he looked out of his study and spotted the maharaja riding in the palace gardens. *The saddle was his home, the saddle was his throne.*

With a sigh, he turned back to the pile of palace accounts on his desk and to the maharaja's financial affairs, which had been giving him increasing headaches. A few years ago, the Gaekwad had doubled his own annual privy purse, raising it arbitrarily to rupees fifty lakh. He drew heavily from state funds for his jaunts abroad and extravagant purchases. He had recently married again; his second wife, Sita Devi, had been married before, had a child and had re-converted to Hinduism from Islam. It had raised many an eyebrow for the Gaekwad had brazenly broken the law against bigamy enacted by his revered grandfather.

With a heavy heart, Mitter began scrutinizing the accounts. No doubt the Gaekwad had inherited an immense fortune, a splendid legacy and an incredible amount of goodwill, but in a matter of just a few years he had squandered most of it away. The big day was approaching, Mitter knew, and the princes would have to choose – India, or independence. *Could the Gaekwad be counted on to take the right decision?*

❋ A Bridge Too Far ❋

'Sahibji, thank you for coming...' Sardar walked down the steps of his house to greet the Jam Sahib and his wife on a blazing summer day. 'I must thank Himmatsinhji for pulling off this miracle,' he smiled, his hands folded politely in greeting.

'Thank you for inviting us,' the Jam Sahib replied as he emerged from his Rolls-Royce. Decked in a silken suit, diamond rings glittering on his fingers, he stood out in stark contrast to Sardar in his simple hand-spun dhoti and kurta.

'We are most honoured by your invitation,' said the maharani formally, returning Sardar's warm smile, before enquiring about his health.

'There are good days and bad days,' Maniben said, leading the royal couple and Himmatsinhji into their frugal home. Her father had been having intestinal troubles for many years now, but his work left him little time to worry about himself. Sardar made a wry joke about his condition, making light of the matter, as he always did. The Jam Sahib relaxed a little, feeling somewhat at ease.

They settled into the living room, exchanging pleasantries and making small talk. Several years ago, when he had given up a successful legal career and shed his 'Western' persona, Sardar had been inspired by Gandhi to speak in his own language. As he laughed and joked in Gujarati with the Jam Sahib and the maharani, it felt like they had established an instant rapport.

Lunch was brought out. 'We are both sons of Gujarat,' Sardar said to the Jam Sahib as they moved to the dining table, 'bound together by her soil. We belong to the land of Mahatma Gandhi. Let us not falter in our duty to the nation.'

The Jam Sahib sipped his cool buttermilk.

'Look...the princes need to realize that they can survive only as trustees of the people,' Sardar steered the conversation towards the agenda of this lunch meeting, as he tore into a fluffy *phulka*. 'Don't heed the advice of those in pursuit of selfish ends,' he warned the Jam Sahib, referring indirectly to the nawab of Bhopal who was trying to entice the princes to keep out of India. 'The princes, the people...we are all one big family,' he made an earnest appeal to his guest, setting all personal differences aside.

The Jam Sahib said nothing as thoughts of his illustrious predecessor flashed through his mind. Known as 'the prince of a small state, but king of a great game', Maharaja Ranjitsinhji had been a flamboyant cricketer, no doubt, but he had also been an able administrator, multiplying the revenues of his state many times over, apart from leading the princely cause as chancellor of the Chamber of Princes. *Would the great Ranji have concurred? Would he have handed over his state on a platter to India?*

RANJI: PRINCE OF A SMALL STATE, KING OF A GREAT GAME

Sardar pressed on. It was time to change, he said; time to let bygones be bygones. The past was but a memory; it was the future that mattered.

At a nod from the maharaja's brother, Sardar remembered Himmatsinhji's advice – if you can bring the maharani around, he had told Sardar, the Jam Sahib can be persuaded. 'I am willing to forget the past and look ahead,' said Sardar, turning to the maharani. 'I hope the Jam Sahib will see things the same way.'

Chewing his food in silence, the Jam Sahib exchanged uncomfortable glances with the maharani. She appeared to be deeply moved by Sardar's words, touched by his warmth, nodding every now and then to indicate her agreement with his line of thought. Perhaps Sardar did have a point after all.

As they finished their meal and rose from the table, the Jam Sahib appeared to have been won over. 'You have my word,' he said, taking Sardar's hand in a warm clasp. 'I am committed to a united India, and I will certainly help bring the princes around to that cause.'

'I appreciate your noble gesture...' said Sardar, greatly relieved to hear these words. The effort appeared to have borne fruit at the end of the day.

'You have a daunting task ahead,' said the Jam Sahib as they prepared to leave. 'My plane is available to you should you wish to travel,' he made an earnest offer. 'And, please, don't hesitate to let me know if I can be of any assistance to you.'

'I cannot tell you how grateful I am for your support...' Sardar thanked the Jam Sahib, having got much more than he had expected. The Jam Sahib was a respected figure in Kathiawar, having been the chancellor of the Chamber of Princes until a few years ago. Winning him over, Sardar hoped, would have a ripple effect on the other princes.

As the guests got into their car that warm afternoon of 11 May, Maniben and Shankar admitted sheepishly that perhaps they had been wrong, after all, about the whole Jam Sahib affair. Rarely, if ever, did Sardar err in his judgement.

Waving the guests goodbye as their car pulled out of the driveway, neither Shankar, nor Maniben, not even Sardar himself, suspected anything amiss.

But this was one of those rare instances when Sardar had completely misread his man!

❋ An Unholy Gathering ❋

'If Travancore can declare its independence, so can the states of Kathiawar,' Jam Sahib Digvijaysinhji Jadeja thundered into the microphone, addressing the small audience gathered in the Durbar Hall of Nawanagar Palace and showcasing his undeniable flair for politicking – a battlefield where promises were made to be broken. *And why not! Weren't the British doing just that, by unilaterally withdrawing the arrangement of paramountcy with the princes?*

The Kathiawari chiefs nodded along enthusiastically. Travancore's recent decision to stay out of India had emboldened them, given flight to their dreams, their ambitions further fanned by the Jam Sahib's infectious energy. Jamnagar, Bhavnagar, Gondal, Porbandar, Morvi, Dhrangadhra, Nawanagar and Junagadh – all coastal states of Gujarat – were filled with new hope. For, like Travancore, their peninsula too had access to the sea; and they too could dream of consolidating themselves into an independent sovereign nation.

'Quite right – you are all maritime states – nothing can stop you from doing likewise,' Major Healy, the political agent seated beside the Jam Sahib, expressed his wholehearted concurrence. Healy's superior, Conrad Corfield in the political department was championing the cause of the princes, reminding them that the only way they could stand up against the risk of being wiped out was by banding together and staying out of India. 'You can keep all the earnings from your ports without sharing the revenue with Delhi,' suggested Healy, pushing forward Corfield's position.

'The advantage in creating a Union of Kathiawar and staying independent is manifestly clear', the Jam Sahib said, nodding at the political agent. 'We can carry on our business without any interference from Delhi. We retain the rights and power over

LET'S CREATE AN INDEPENDENT UNION OF KATHIAWAR!

our kingdoms. We shall be our own masters.' He made clear what they collectively stood to gain by sticking together.

'We should create a federation of states in Kathiawar,' Anantrai Pattani, the diwan of Bhavnagar, mooted an idea, 'and declare our sovereign independence as the Union of Kathiawar.'

'I shall bless this union with a gift of one crore rupees,' declared the Jam Sahib, holding his hand to his heart and bowing humbly, the rock-like diamond pinned to his turban glinting in the light of the magnificent chandeliers. His announcement was received with rapturous applause.

'And we must resist Baroda,' Pattani suggested. 'The Gaekwad cannot impose his will upon us. He has made his intentions clear by joining the Indian Constituent Assembly... We shall not be bullied.'

'Absolutely,' Healy agreed. 'The tribute you states pay to Baroda is more than a hundred years old. The times are changing – paramountcy is coming to an end. There's no reason why you must continue to accept Baroda's suzerainty over the region.'

'I propose we constitute a council to govern our Union,' suggested the diwan of Dhrangadhra.

'And I propose the Jam Sahib be elected president of this Union,' the diwan of Bhavnagar held up the Jam Sahib's hand.

The suggestion was hailed enthusiastically with thumping of tables, signatures of allegiance and pledges of support. The Jam Sahib was felicitated; laddus were distributed; and money promised.

The volcano that Mitter had dreaded some months ago was about to erupt.

❋ Turban Turns ❋

'The Jam Sahib?' Sardar's forehead furrowed.

Mitter nodded, closing the door behind them.

'And the political agent is helping them, you say?' Sardar held Mitter's arm for support, shocked, betrayed, and at a complete loss for words.

The diwan of Baroda drew up a chair for Sardar and threw open the windows of the cubicle to let in some fresh air. Outside, members of the various drafting committees of India's Constitution could be seen, sitting or strolling about the gardens of Council House, discussing the day's progress.

'The Jam Sahib visited me a month ago and promised to do his best to keep Kathiawar united...and even...' Sardar swallowed hard, unable to complete the sentence. Setting aside the bitter past, he had naïvely placed his faith in the Jam Sahib. *How had he allowed himself to be misled so easily?*

'Well, he is keeping Kathiawar united no doubt,' Mitter said, grimacing, 'only perhaps not as a part of India.'

'Bapu has often warned me,' Sardar lamented, holding his head in his hands, recalling Gandhiji's advice, 'about being wary of people like the Jam Sahib...whose words, despite being honeyed, have more twists and turns than their turbans. I should have remembered his sage advice...'

Sardar reached for a glass of water. Dominion status for India under the British Commonwealth had not been acceptable. Partition and Pakistan had been a bitter pill to swallow; nevertheless, they had borne the heartbreak for the greater goal of independence. *But how much more could one compromise?*

'You were the first state to join the Constituent Assembly...' whispered Sardar, his voice barely audible. 'What is Baroda's position, Mitter?'

'I'd advise you to grant the princes some time,' Mitter drew up a chair opposite Sardar. 'They are not accustomed to dealing with such radical changes and at such speed. The princely states have a long history and are firmly rooted in tradition. Any major change will take time.'

Sardar rubbed his tired eyes, bracing himself mentally for more shocks and disappointments.

'Sardar, I appeal to you to exercise a little patience,' pleaded Mitter earnestly. 'Many princes want to march in tandem with the rest of India; however, they operate at a different pace.'

'I understand,' Patel sighed deeply. 'Unfortunately, none of us has the luxury of time.'

'I too am trying my best...but...' Mitter hesitated, averting his gaze. Sardar waited, his eyes narrowing. 'The Gaekwad... he...' Mitter broke off, reluctant to add to Sardar's troubles. 'The Gaekwad no longer heeds me.'

'What do you mean?'

'The Gaekwad...I'm afraid...has now turned to others for advice.'

❋ The Final Hurrah ❋

It was the last of the glitzy events of colonial Delhi. The viceroy in his full naval regalia; maharajas in their shimmering silk tunics; their diwans in crisp formal suits. A grand reception beneath glittering chandeliers; the walls covered with full-length portraits of past viceroys striking valiant poses; the clink of fine china; the fragrance of fresh roses.

But today the light and lustre only served to underscore the melancholy of the men inside the room. Rulers of princely states across India were seated around the triumvirate of Mountbatten, Patel and Menon in a semicircle, waiting to sign up for their annihilation, or, as a later historian would put it, lined up like sheep being led to the slaughterhouse.

The slaughter, as it turned out, would be a seemingly gentle affair – no blood, no gore. The dashing viceroy would use his inimitable charm to coax them in; the senatorial Sardar would preside over the extinction of their ilk; and the sagacious V.P. Menon would conduct the grand orchestra before the princes took their final bow.

'After 15 August, I can no longer guarantee that you will be offered the same terms and conditions,' the viceroy addressed the gathering with his usual flair, up to date with the ambitious plans the princes were hatching behind his back. 'Nor will I be able to mediate on your behalf as the Crown representative. You are being given a one-time-only offer by the Congress; an offer that is not likely to be repeated.'

Beneath the whirring of the ceiling fans, murmurs broke out among the princes.

'I'm not waiting to find out what happens after 15 August,' whispered someone. 'I'm signing tomorrow.'

'I might do the same,' sighed another, playing straight into the viceroy's hands.

The rulers used titles such as maharaja, *maharana*, *maharao*, *maharawal* and *sawai*, among others, before their name. Muslim rulers used nawab; the ruler of Hyderabad was called the nizam. They also had honorifics granted to them by the British. Sample this title used by Maharaja Yadavindra Singh of Patiala: 'Lieutenant General His Highness Farzand-e-Khas-e-Daulat-Inglishia Mansur-e-Zaman Amir-al-Umra Maharajadhiraja Rajeswar Sri Maharaja Sir Yadavindra Singh Mahindar Bahadur, G.C.S.I., G.C.I.E., G.C.V.O., G.B.E., LL.D., A.D.C., the Maharaja of Patiala'. The nizam of Hyderabad was the only ruler permitted to use the term 'exalted' before his title and was therefore addressed as 'His Exalted Highness'.

These titles, honorifics and other privileges like the seating order they had to follow, carried great weight for the royal class as a mark of position and prestige.

The Gaekwad, seated in the front row as stipulated by protocol, cast a skittish look at his diwan. Undoubtedly, events were moving too fast for anybody's liking, accelerated curiously enough by the viceroy. The princes were baffled, blindsided and unable to keep pace. On the other hand, Sardar, as ingeniously advised by Menon, was playing his cards superbly – turning disadvantage into advantage and using the paucity of time to race to the finish line.

'Those of you trying to stockpile arms would do well to remember,' warned the viceroy, 'that the weapons you get are likely to be obsolete against those of the Indian Army.'

The Jam Sahib, sitting a few seats away from the Gaekwad, stole an uneasy glance at Patel. *Had Sardar got wind of their gathering?* His gaze turned to his brother princes. Each one eyeing the other anxiously, each worried about his own peculiar problems. *Did he stand a chance, holding out with such an edgy bunch of allies?*

'I have been assured that you can keep your titles,' announced the viceroy, turning to Patel to indicate that the promise had Sardar's blessings. 'If you accept this offer, the Government of India will not interfere in your internal affairs. Your succession rights will remain secure. And you will be allowed to keep all the honours bestowed on you by the king of England.'

Patel nodded slightly. He had nothing but contempt for pompous royal titles, but he knew that their knighthoods and gun salutes meant the world to the maharajas. They could keep their pointless privileges, he mused, folding his arms – as long as they handed in their key powers to the Government of India.

'I would like to hear from you now,' the viceroy told the princes, honouring his pact with Sardar to bring in 565 apples into his basket. 'We wish to know your thoughts on the question of accession.'

As the viceroy ended his speech, V.P. Menon cast a quick glance around the room and knew instinctively that he had done the right thing by suggesting to Sardar and Nehru that they bring Lord Mountbatten into their team. The rajas and nawabs had undoubtedly been floored by Mountbatten's charisma and charm, and bowled over by his wit and words. He was, after all, the great-grandson of Queen Victoria and cousin to the king of England. The princes considered him one of their own: blue-blooded and therefore deserving of their allegiance. Mountbatten appeared to have cast a spell upon them, which he hoped would draw them out of their coop and herd them into the Indian pen.

'Whom do you think His Excellency is going to call first?' whispered one of the diwans in the back row as the viceroy's staff bustled around, making arrangements for the one-on-ones scheduled next. With the nawab of Bhopal having resigned as chancellor of the Chamber of Princes, the plan of floating a third front of princes was now floundering like a ship without a captain. The rulers, left to their own personal ambitions and dynastic differences, were rudderless and divided.

'There's no need to work on us,' another replied, his voice more confident. 'We are signing tomorrow.'

'Our maharaja, too...in fact, he has already given the viceroy his word,' remarked a third.

The Jam Sahib loosened the top button of his brocaded silk tunic. *Would he get the short end of the stick if he didn't sign up now?* The viceroy's words played on his mind. He tried to read the expressions of his brother rulers from Kathiawar. *What were they planning to do?*

'Look at the faces of the rulers,' whispered one of the diwans in the back row, as the rajas and nawabs were ushered by the ADCs to meet the viceroy first, then Menon and finally Sardar. 'They look lost. Wandering about like letters without a postage stamp.'

'Baroda will be the first to sign,' the Gaekwad declared all of a sudden, eager to be seen in the lead.

All eyes turned towards him. They were, all of them, in the same boat, drifting from the safe shores of certainty into the choppy seas of ambiguity. But they were trying, nevertheless, to put up a brave front, even vying with one another to impress the viceroy.

'Nah!' the Jam Sahib elbowed the Gaekwad out of his way, not wanting to be outdone, surprising even himself. 'That privilege will go to Nawanagar,' he smiled. 'We will be the first to join India.'

Seated stoically like a majestic sculpture, Sardar Patel watched as they lined up before him, pledging their loyalty one by one, to him, to the Congress and to the new India. But Patel had burnt his fingers and was not one to forget his lessons so quickly. He knew it was never quite over until it was over.

❋ Not So Fast ❋

Far away from Delhi, in his sprawling sea-facing apartment in Bombay, Maharaja Pratap Singh Gaekwad watched the white-crested waves lapping at the shoreline, a copy of the Instrument of Accession in hand. He enjoyed spending time here, far from the heat and political atmosphere of Delhi. More so now after the recent high-tension durbar hosted by the viceroy.

'Have you had a look at this?' he asked Hanwant Singh, the maharaja of Jodhpur, who had flown in to meet him.

'Yes...I...I have,' nodded Hanwant Singh. 'I...uh...had a word with...Hamidullah a few days ago,' the young maharaja said, referring to the nawab of Bhopal. 'He is still hopeful that the union of princes can come through...if we just stick together.'

'Hmm...' The Gaekwad exhaled deeply. He knew that the nawab of Bhopal had been floating the idea of a third front. But Baroda had taken its place in the Indian Constituent Assembly, and he wasn't convinced by Hamidullah's arguments. And yet, his son was soon to marry Hanwant Singh's sister. They were going to be family. It was only appropriate that he lend Hanwant a patient ear.

'I've had a look at the draft of the Instrument of Accession, Your Highness...' the Gaekwad's lawyer emerged from the adjoining room, where he had been studying the document and taking stock of the maharaja's assets. Palaces in Baroda, properties in Bombay, fine jewels, exquisite paintings – his assets ran into crores.

'And? What do you think?' the Gaekwad prompted, reaching out to catch the raindrops outside the window.

'Well...you mustn't concede to India's conditions so readily,' the advocate said, shrugging – he was the new adviser, about whom Mitter had warned Sardar. 'You must hold out for more.'

Hanwant Singh nodded in agreement. Nawab Hamidullah had arranged a meeting between him and Jinnah to find out what terms Pakistan could offer Jodhpur; there was always scope to bargain for more.

'Your Highness, Baroda is a premier state – a 21-gun-salute one at that,' the lawyer explained. 'Surely it deserves more than the other states.'

'I had promised the viceroy that I would be the first to accede,' the Gaekwad mumbled.

'That promise is not legally binding,' the lawyer retorted.

Watching a *tonga* trot along the seaside promenade below, the Gaekwad weighed his options. Horse races were won with speed, he mused, but political races – they were a whole different ball game. *Political races were won with time.*

❃ Dinner Update ❃

The phone rang in V.P. Menon's house.

'All quiet on the states' front?' Sardar checked in with Menon in his routine late-night phone briefing before he called it a day.

'Some more states have signed,' Menon updated Sardar.

'Good...good...what about Nawanagar?' asked Sardar, still reeling from the unexpected stab in the back by Digvijaysinhji.

'The Jam Sahib has signed,' Menon replied. 'We have received Nawanagar's accession.'

Sardar heaved a deep sigh of relief.

'But the Gaekwad of Baroda'—Menon gripped the receiver between his ear and shoulder, as he shuffled through some documents—'he has requested to meet you. He wants an appointment.'

'Why can't you discuss this in the morning?' Menon's wife called out to him from behind. Sardar's late-evening calls almost always interfered with his meal. 'Your dinner is going cold again.'

'Meet me about what?' asked Sardar.

'You will be back with Sardar at sunrise anyway - can't this wait?' Mrs Menon fretted.

'The Gaekwad wants to discuss the accession,' Menon waved his wife away.

'What's left to discuss?' asked Sardar. 'When he met us at the viceroy's reception, the Gaekwad said that he would sign the document. And I've spoken to Mitter. He didn't mention anything.'

'Sardar...' Menon paused, 'the Gaekwad has fired Mitter.'

There was a long silence at the other end. Mitter was an able and efficient diwan, favouring Baroda's accession to India. But he had warned Sardar that the Gaekwad had turned elsewhere for advice. Sardar knew this could only mean trouble.

'The Gaekwad says he met his lawyer in Bombay, who has advised him to add some clauses,' said Menon.

'What clauses?' There was less than a week left to independence. Sardar's patience was wearing thin.

'Additional conditions - a list of special reservations for Baroda...' replied Menon.

'Out of the question.'

'Shall I...should I call the Gaekwad for a meeting?'

'Forget it,' said Sardar, exhausted with princely somersaults and royal tantrums. 'I have no interest in seeing the Gaekwad.'

❋ When the Stars Align ❋

'You have put me in a rather awkward position,' the viceroy looked the Gaekwad in the eye. 'When we met last, you assured me that you would be the very first state to accede to India. Accordingly, in all publicity arrangements, Baroda was placed first. But then you leave Delhi without signing?'

The Gaekwad tried to smile and began offering a lame explanation, but the viceroy hadn't finished yet.

'What's more, I'm told you are proposing new conditions?'

The Gaekwad shifted uncomfortably in his seat. As it was, Sardar and Menon were a handful to deal with, but with the viceroy's backing now, they were an impossible triumvirate.

'There can really be no explanation for this sort of behaviour,' the viceroy admonished him.

'Your Excellency,' the Gaekwad mumbled, 'we...the states...had been given to understand that we could remain independent if we so desired,' he said wistfully, '... and I...I was only...waiting...'

'Waiting for what?'

'Uh...my royal astrologers...'

'Astrologers?' the viceroy threw up his hands in frustration.

'Yes, for the astrologers to select an auspicious day...'

'For what?'

'For signing the accession papers, Your Excellency,' the Gaekwad's face reddened. 'I wished to sign on the right day. When the stars were aligned.'

PRATAP SINGH RAO, THE GAEKWAD: I WISHED TO SIGN ON THE RIGHT DAY.

The viceroy rolled his eyes. He'd had just about enough

contending with astrologers and auspicious dates! After he had announced the day for the transfer of power, a whole host of pandits had raised a huge hue and cry about 15 August being an inauspicious day. To the viceroy's chagrin, the Indian leaders had sided with them, forcing the transfer ceremonies to take place at the stroke of midnight on 14 August instead, even compelling him to create a special post in his office titled 'Astrologer to the Governor General'.

'All right,' he sighed. 'What do your astrologers say? Is it the right time to sign now? Are the stars aligned?' he asked sardonically.

'Um...yes...yes, Your Excellency,' the Gaekwad smiled sheepishly. 'I'll sign the papers immediately. I'll go straight to meet Menon, and I hope...to...uh...take part in the Independence Day celebrations on 15 August.'

Hoping the Gaekwad would keep his word this time, the viceroy stood up and shook his hand. As he watched the ruler of Baroda depart, the viceroy cast an apprehensive glance at the calendar on the wall. One more apple tossed into Patel's basket, and in the nick of time; but there were some more to go.

The volcano of Kathiawar had not erupted.

Not just yet...

♦♦♦♦♦♦♦♦♦♦♦♦♦♦♦♦♦♦♦

Postscript

♦♦♦♦♦♦♦♦♦♦♦♦♦♦♦♦♦♦♦

One among the five major states entitled to a 21-gun-salute, Baroda in Gujarat was one of the remaining portions of the erstwhile Maratha Empire. The maharaja adopted the title of

Gaekwar/Gaekwad and ruled over one of India's richest and most progressive kingdoms.

Later, when Junagadh in Kathiawar acceded to Pakistan (which you will read about in the chapter on Junagadh), the Gaekwad offered to help the Indian government on the condition that they would make him the king of Gujarat and also agree to his other stipulations. To which Sardar had tersely replied, 'We don't need your help.'

After Sardar's death in 1950, the Gaekwad began to question the Instrument of Accession and refused to abide by its terms, claiming that he had been coerced into signing it. In 1951, the president of India ordered the removal of the maharaja of Baroda for fraud because he was caught embezzling from the coffers of the state treasury – making him the only ruler to be dethroned by the Government of India.

The Jam Sahib and the other rulers of the region, on the other hand, eventually fell in line. Since Kathiawar was a maze of about 200 small states, the States Department pressed for uniting them into one administrative unit. In January 1948, Nawanagar and certain other states were combined to set up a United State of Kathiawar. The following year, more states were merged into this confederation and the resulting union was renamed Saurashtra. The Jam Sahib was bestowed the title of *rajpramukh*, or head, of this new coalition.

While this story may paint a certain kind of picture of the Jam Sahib of Nawanagar, it is worth noting that in 1942, during the Second World War, the Jam Sahib of Nawanagar played a key role in rescuing over 1,000 Jewish children from Poland and granting them refuge in his kingdom when no other nation was willing to provide them sanctuary.

B.L. Mitter, the diwan of Baroda, was a member of the drafting committee of the Constitution of India.

Nawanagar state is now known as Jamnagar.

◆◆◆◆◆◆◆◆◆◆◆◆◆◆◆◆◆◆◆

Did It Really Happen This Way?

◆◆◆◆◆◆◆◆◆◆◆◆◆◆◆◆◆◆◆

News that arms were being imported by Junagadh and rumours about the Jam Sahib of Nawanagar, as relayed by the chief of Vadia to the diwan of Baroda, find mention in Sardar's Letters – Mostly Unknown, The Year 1949, Post-Centenary Volume II, *as does the information about the meeting of Kathiawari rulers.*

Sardar's decision to start working on the princes is borne out by Maniben's diary, which recorded lunch meetings with various princes even before the establishment of the States Department. Sardar's specific conversation with the Jam Sahib is creative liberty.

The reception at Viceroy House with the princes in attendance took place more or less as described in several sources, the primary source being Viceroy Mountbatten's report found in The Transfer of Power 1942–7, Vol. XII. *The same source also records the meetings of the maharaja of Baroda in Bombay, his negotiations for better terms, the mention of astrologers and his eventual consent to sign the accession document a few days before 15 August. On his part, the nawab of Bhopal denied asking the maharaja of Jodhpur to reach out to the maharaja of Baroda. In* Integration of the Indian States, *V.P. Menon states that Baroda was one of the first to sign the Instrument of Accession.*

9

Crushed at the Crossroads

THE STORY OF PATIALA

PRINCELY STATE OF PATIALA IN 1947:
in present-day Punjab
AREA: 5,942 square miles (15,390 square kilometres)
POPULATION: 1,936,159 (approx.)
RULER: Maharaja Yadavindra Singh
17-gun-salute state

❋ Ominous Rumblings ❋

'My ancestors won the state by the sword, and I plan to keep it by the sword!' thundered Maharaja Yadavindra Singh, warning those backing the Congress. 'I am the sole representative of Patiala and do not recognize any organization such as the Praja Mandal to represent my people. If you want to do Congress work, get out of the state.'

The towering frame of the six-foot-four-inch maharaja was enough to intimidate anybody, his immaculate gem-studded Patiala-style turban, the bejewelled kirpan tucked into his sash and rolled beard only adding to his majesty. Exuding charm and confidence, the charismatic Yadavindra Singh had just ascended the *gaddi* after the death of his flamboyant father, Maharaja Bhupinder Singh, whose exploits were the stuff of legend. The young king had an exalted legacy to live up to.

'The Congress can bully the British government, but if it ever tries to interfere in my state,' he roared, wagging a threatening index finger, 'it will find in me a force to contend with.'

Punjab was a vast area comprising both British India and Princely India, with the princely states consisting of Sikh states like Patiala, Faridkot and Kapurthala, Muslim states such as Malerkotla and Bahawalpur, and the Jat states of Nabha and Jind – with Patiala being the most prominent of them all. Maharaja Yadavindra Singh's ancestors had pledged allegiance to their British overlords and he was making it abundantly clear that he would not take kindly to the Congress encroaching into his territory through the Praja Mandal, also called the All

India States Peoples' Conference (AISPC), by pushing for democracy and clamouring for reform.

'Stop your Praja Mandal activities,' the maharaja warned. 'Stop your agitations, otherwise I shall use strong measures. Remember, I am a military man. My talk is blunt and my bullet straight!'

YADAVINDRA SINGH: THE CHARISMATIC MAHARAJA OF PATIALA

It was 1939 when these tough words left the maharaja's lips, a time when the world beyond was changing. A fascist power was on the rise in Germany, a war of epic proportions was on the verge of breaking out in Europe and the sun was threatening to set on Britain's empire. Events that would become a springboard for the rise of a political party called the Muslim League that had so far been on the fringes of Indian politics. Events that would make Maharaja Yadavindra Singh eat his words.

❋ Secret 'Sandooq' ❋

Not too far away from Patiala lay the princely state of Mamdot. Its ruler, Nawab Iftikhar Hussain Khan – wealthy landlord, close confidant of Jinnah and head of the Punjab Muslim League – was a busy man in the summer of 1946, hatching conspiracies, spearheading propaganda and preparing for war.

'We have seen what happened in Calcutta and Bihar,' the nawab addressed those gathered for the secret meeting at his residence, Mamdot Villa, in Lahore. Both areas had witnessed gruesome bloodbaths after Jinnah had flagged

In 1927, the AISPC, also called the Praja Mandal, came into existence to represent the interests of the people of the princely kingdoms. Their aim was to secure people's representation in the administration of the princely states. The British only accepted the rajas and nawabs as the true representatives of these states and refused to recognize their subjects. The princes too were against the Praja Mandal and many reacted harshly to their protests and agitations.

Although the Indian National Congress supported the AISPC in the early days, it refused to intervene directly in the internal matters of the princely states. This was called a policy of *benevolent neutrality*. But, over time, this policy began to change and, by 1947, Congress leader Jawaharlal Nehru was also heading the Praja Mandal.

off Direct Action Day, which had been the clarion call to Muslims across the nation to step up the Muslim League's demand for Pakistan. 'We must be ready,' stated the nawab.

Eyes riveted on the framed picture of Mecca on the wall, Muslim Leaguer Mian Abdul Bari's thoughts wandered. After the war had broken out in Europe and the Congress leaders put behind bars for launching the Quit India movement, the Muslim League had gone from strength to strength. From the holy *pirs* in Sufi *dargahs* to the mullahs sermonizing in mosques, from the weather-beaten Muslim peasant to the wealthy Punjabi landlord – the League had slowly drawn them all in. Even influential Punjabi families like the Hayats and the Noons had shifted loyalties to the League.

'As long as premier Malik Khizar Hayat Tiwana and his Unionist Party hold the reins in Punjab,' the nawab lamented, referring to the coalition government in power in the Punjab Assembly that administered the part of Punjab that lay in British India, 'Pakistan will not become a reality. We need to ramp up the pressure.'

Despite winning more seats than any other party in the provincial elections, the Muslim League had not been able to form the government in the British-India-administered province of Punjab. Its place had been usurped by an alliance of the Unionists, the Akalis and the Congress – all opposed to Partition. It infuriated the nawab that, in spite of being the single largest party, the League was helpless to influence the tide of events.

An attendant brought out cups of fragrant *kahwa* as Choudhary Mohammed Hassan, another League member, distributed bundles of pamphlets to the handful of journalists present. The leaflets had a picture of Jinnah in his black fez on the cover, with the green flag featuring crescent and star flying overhead, verses from the Quran in neat calligraphy below. Inside were reminders of the alleged suffering of Muslims.

'This is good,' remarked the nawab, perusing the flyers through his thick-rimmed spectacles, 'but we need to do more,' he said emphatically, 'much more.'

'The work requires funds, Nawab Sa'ab,' interjected Begum Jehanara Shahnawaz, the daughter of a prominent Leaguer and the party's first female member, who had spearheaded efforts for the emancipation of Muslim women. Following the Congress model, the League too had opened its membership for as little as two annas (16 annas made a rupee). As a result, its grassroots membership had increased phenomenally, with several thousand members across Punjab. Even so, an operation as large as what they had in mind required deep pockets.

'That is precisely the agenda of our meeting today,' the nawab noted pensively. 'We will need jeeps...trucks...weapons...

iron jackets,' he began listing out the requirements. 'I propose we start a Secret Sandooq.'

'Only the inner circle will be in on this,' whispered Muslim League member Ranarullah Khan.

'*Janaab*, I've informed Zafar that we require 100 iron jackets,' said party member Abdul Bari, referring to a colleague.

'And we have ordered 7,000 steel helmets from the military stores,' chipped in Choudhary Mohammed Hassan.

'Mumtaz will take care of the hand grenades,' said Begum Shahnawaz, speaking of her daughter. Arrangements for purchasing arms from the frontier province that bordered Afghanistan were being worked out by her sons-in-law, Rashid and Mohammed.

'Excellent,' exclaimed the nawab. 'Have our boys distribute them quickly as soon as the consignment gets here. We must...'

'*Allahu Akbar*...'

The evening air was pierced by the fluty voice of the muezzin from the minaret of the Badshahi mosque behind them. Built by Mughal emperor Shah Jahan, the mosque was the very place where, six years earlier, Muhammad Ali Jinnah had moved the historical resolution making the demand for Pakistan.

As the sun dipped behind the splendid Shalimar Gardens, the pride of the city of Lahore, the nawab and his coterie stepped on to the veranda and spread out the *janamaz* mats; the begum drew a dupatta over her head and disappeared into the prayer room inside. Each one of them had only one prayer on their lips – Pakistan!

❋ A Troubled Forecast ❋

Even as the Leaguers in Lahore conspired to topple the government of Punjab province, Congress leaders in New

NEHRU: PRINCELY STATES ARE OBSOLETE IN MODERN INDIA...

Delhi were locked in an exhausting battle with the rulers to get them to shed their monarchical past and embrace a democratic future, while labouring tirelessly over creating a fitting constitution for India. The League had stayed out while the princes played a dangerous game of wait-and-watch. Meanwhile, critics were predicting doom because, if all other parties kept out, the Constituent Assembly would be reduced to a Congress party exercise.

Nerves frayed and patience worn thin by the unending debates, Jawaharlal Nehru and the other Congressmen soldiered on nevertheless in their exercise to woo the rajas and the nawabs.

'If the states do not join the Constituent Assembly, the gap between us will only increase,' Nehru appealed to the rulers and their diwans who had formed a Negotiating Committee on behalf of the princes. 'I am free, I think, to say,' he declared, 'that princely states are obsolete in modern India.'

Not one to buckle under Nehru's eloquence, C.P. Ramaswami, the diwan of Travancore, stood up to speak, making no secret of his dislike for the Congress triumvirate. 'By that yardstick,' he sniggered, looking Nehru in the eye, 'I think I am free to say that some political parties in India are totalitarian.'

There was a hushed gasp in the hall. Sardar Patel looked grimly towards N. Gopalaswami Ayyangar, former diwan of Jammu and Kashmir, who had been studying the states' situation closely. Patel was beginning to see first-hand that

Ayyangar's assessment of the princes had been dead right: the Congress would have to lock horns with the princely states in a long-drawn tussle.

Watching Nehru and CP sparring, Maharaja Yadavindra Singh felt a nervous tingle in his fingers. He was keen to do the right thing, but worried about his frontiers, his autonomy and his sovereignty.

Breaking the awkward silence, Nawab Hamidullah of Bhopal, the chancellor of the Chamber of Princes, stood up to speak next. 'Before we can consider joining the Indian Constituent Assembly, the princes would like satisfactory assurances on the scope of the subjects you seek to discuss in the constitution,' he said, reflecting the concerns of several rulers, 'and perhaps postpone the discussion meanwhile?'

'India has no intention of forcing anyone to join us,' responded Patel gruffly, bolstering Nehru's passionate appeal with his no-nonsense approach.

Nawab Hamidullah's lips curved into a slight smile. He had been encouraging rulers to steer clear of the Assembly and form a third front. So...*had Sardar finally given in?*

But Patel was not done yet. He paused, looking each state representative in the eye. The Jam Sahib of Nawanagar; the nawab of Bhopal; CP from Travancore; Maharaja Yadavindra Singh of Patiala. *His talk too would be straight and his words blunt.* 'We have no intention of forcing you to join India,' he reiterated, his voice firm, 'but events may force you to.'

For Maharaja Yadavindra Singh, who had warned the Congress to get out of his state only a few years ago, Patel's threat, couched strategically as a concession, could not have been more ominous. For even as they deliberated in Delhi, a storm had begun brewing in Punjab. A storm so fierce, so unforgiving, so ruthless, that neither Yadavindra Singh's blunt talk nor his straight bullet would help rein it in.

❋ The Match Is Lit ❋

Spring was unfolding its magic across Punjab, that abundant land of five rivers. Fruit trees were beginning to blossom, the *rabi* crop was about to ripen, and farmers were gearing up for the harvest. Yellow fields of mustard, tall patches of sugarcane, babbling canals, chirping songbirds, women humming folk songs as they worked in the fields – Punjab was a picture of rural bliss.

But the bounties of the season were the last thing on Malik Khizar Hayat Tiwana's mind, that March of 1947. Standing before the mirror, adjusting his *turre-wali pagri*, the premier of Punjab province cut a tense figure. Although a Muslim, Khizar did not see eye to eye with the Muslim League or support the demand for Pakistan – a stand for which the nawab of Mamdot and his followers were giving him hell. His coalition ministry comprising Sikhs, Hindus and Muslims had governed British-India-administered Punjab for a while, and Khizar wanted nothing more than peace and unity.

And yet, the ship he captained was veering into a tempest. League workers supporting Pakistan had been rabble-rousing across Punjab, turning

While *Punjab* is the name of a state in present-day India, it is also the name of a very large region in the north-west of the Indian sub-continent. Some parts of this vast region called *Punjab* consisted of princely states (like Patiala). Other parts of *Punjab* lay in British India, where it was called the *Punjab Province*. Under the Government of India Act, 1935, provinces (administrative units) of British India were given greater autonomy, and elections were held in these provinces. In 1947, Unionist Party Leader, Malik Khizar Hayat Tiwana, was the premier of the province of Punjab.

MALIK KHIZAR HAYAT TIWANA: HOW COULD ONE MAN HOLD BACK A STORM?

Muslims against Hindus and Sikhs, and inciting the people against his government. For months he had resisted the League agenda and had done his utmost to block their divisive politics – going so far as to ban the Muslim League guards. But they had harassed him and hounded him, branding him a traitor and a betrayer. They had whipped up public sentiment through sustained propaganda, claiming that the Muslim League alone could represent the Muslims of India, and portraying him as the chief obstacle on their road to Pakistan.

Things had come to a head now. Agitators stampeded through cities and villages, beating their chests and sloganeering: '*Mar gaya Khizar* [Khizar is dead]!' They pasted his pictures on parading donkeys, maligned and slandered him. On the streets, in the bazaars, in the administration, his own staff and even little children – they loathed him, ridiculed him, derided him.

After months, the Muslim League's sustained mud-slinging campaign and intimidation seemed to be on the verge of drowning out the one spark of hope that remained. As Khizar sat down at his desk and picked up his pen that spring, he was a demoralized and defeated man.

After all, how long could one withstand the onslaught? How could one man hold back a storm?

Coerced into abandoning ship, Malik Khizar Hayat Tiwana brought down pen to paper and signed his letter of resignation, stepping down as the premier of the province.

The very next day, Punjab went up in flames.

❋ Pakistan Murdabad! ❋

News of Khizar's resignation spread like wildfire, a spark dropped in a dry haystack.

Sir Evan Jenkins imposed governor's rule in the province as the coalition government tottered. An emergency meeting of legislative members was called at the Assembly Chamber in Lahore to save the situation from spiralling out of control.

As Akali leaders emerged from the building, a vast crowd of Muslim youth greeted them with banners and green flags. '*Hans ke liya Pakistan; lad ke lenge Hindustan* [We have taken Pakistan with a smile; we will take Hindustan by force]!' they chanted as they gheraoed Charing Cross (now Faisal Chowk) in Lahore.

'*Pakistan zindabad* [Long live Pakistan]!' was their battle cry.

Shoulders stiff and straight, in a towering rage, senior Akali leader Master Tara Singh took two steps forward, undeterred by the mob. Six-footer Udham Singh Nagoke and twenty-three other fierce-looking Akali leaders in turbans ranged behind him. They were the Akalis – the Immortal Ones – the fighting force of the Sikhs. If the Muslims wanted their Pakistan in the holy land of the Sikhs, they weren't going to get it without a fight.

'*Pakistan...murdabad* [Death to Pakistan],' hollered the sixty-one-year-old Tara Singh, as he unsheathed his kirpan.

The frenzied crowd edged closer. '*Khoon ke dariya bahenge, Pakistan leke rahenge* [Streams of blood may flow, but we will take our Pakistan],' screamed a young lad at the front of the mob, raising the green flag of the All-India Muslim League. The crescent moon tattooed on his arm bore testimony to his dedication to the cause.

'*Leke rahenge...Pakistan*,' the mammoth mob repeated after him, pumping their fists in the air. '*Leke rahenge...Pakistan*,' they repeated, the sloganeering reaching a crescendo.

Outraged, Tara Singh charged forward. '*Jo bole, so nihal*,' he raised a counter slogan.

Shoulder to shoulder by their leader, the Akalis raised their kirpans. '*Sat Sri Akal*,' they called out. The Sikhs may have been a minority in Punjab, but they would not give in easily.

Blood rushing to his face, Master Tara Singh sprang forward. Leaping upon the raised platform, he gripped the green Pakistani flag hoisted there. '*Pakistan murdabad*,' he roared, ripping the flag with his strong hands. 'We may be cut to pieces,' he thundered through clenched teeth, 'but we shall never...never...NEVER...concede Pakistan!'

❋ Rawalpindi Ravaged ❋

As those in positions of power started to light the match, powerless ordinary people across Punjab began to feel the heat. Young Bir Bahadur watched his father, Sant Raja Singh, pace up and down on the roof of the haveli in their village of Thoa Khalsa, distraught by the distant wails and shrieks that pierced the tense night air.

'Tauji...Gurdwara Dukh Bhanjani Sahib has been attacked...' –' Bir Bahadur's cousin burst through the door. 'They are armed with spears and axes. Some even have firearms. They have descended on the village with buckets of gasoline. And they...they're...dragging out women...setting houses on fire!'

Residents of the area had made a pact with the Muslim gangs roaming the countryside of Rawalpindi, permitting them to loot whatever they wished, on the condition that those taking refuge in the gurdwara would not be harmed. But the mobsters had broken their promise. With the silencing of Khizar's voice, every value the premier had stood for – reason, peace, balance – had all gone up in smoke. Extremists took centre stage now, turning the cradle of Indian civilization into a lawless jungle.

'The women and girls...' panted the panic-stricken boy, 'some of them...they're...jumping into the wells, Tauji.'

'*Leke rahenge Pakistan*,' the muffled roar in the distance got louder and clearer. '*Pakistan zindabad*.'

Sant Raja Singh rushed down into the courtyard, Bir Bahadur hard at his father's heels, to find the women of their extended family gathered in the little room below the staircase, their heads covered, muttering the *ardas* around the holy Guru Granth Sahib.

Sant Raja Singh ran towards the door.

'*Pakistan...zindabad*,' the slogan echoed like a death knell from beyond the walls.

He ran to the storehouse at the back – two gunny bags of wheat and maize lay in a corner; *no place to hide!*

He dashed to the cattle shed – a cow and its calf peered at him curiously.

'*Zinda jala dalo* [Burn them alive],' the screaming mob had entered the *mohalla*.

There was no time!

'*Waheguru...*' He ran back into the house, looking up at the framed picture of Guru Nanak Dev, the first Sikh guru who had preached the message of brotherhood and equality. *Hadn't he lived his whole life by those tenets*? His moist eyes moved to the dusty frame below. Pictures of two young boys wearing *patkas* on their heads smiled back – nine-year-old Zorawar and six-year-old Fateh, sons of Guru Gobind Singh, ruthlessly bricked alive in a wall on the orders of the Mughal governor of Sirhind.

A wave of fear washed over him.

'*Ya Ali, ya Ali!*' The walls reverberated with slogans in support of Pakistan.

Clenching his fists, Sant Raja Singh advanced towards the weeping women, took down the double-edged sword – the *khanda* – pinned to the wall and unsheathed it. '*Sachche Padshah...*' his lips quivered as he spoke the *ardas*, 'we will not allow your *sikki* to be stained.' Saying a silent prayer, his bloodshot eyes glowering in the dull light of the lantern, he charged towards his daughter, Maan Kaur, and pulled her out into the courtyard. Bir Bahadur clung to his mother's kurta, aware that something terrible was about to happen, even as his sixteen-year-old sister stood facing her father fearlessly.

Singh looked at his daughter's moonlike face for a moment and swallowed the lump in his throat. The next instant, he swung the sword over her head and brought it down in a flash.

'Tauji,' his horrified nephew screamed as a lifeless Maan slumped to the floor. '*Tauji, ae tussi ki kitta* [Uncle, what have you done]?'

Emitting a blood-curdling scream, fourteen-year-old Bir Bahadur squeezed his eyes shut and crept behind a charpoy.

His face quivering and hands trembling, Sant Raja Singh staggered unsteadily.

'*Naara-e-taqbeer, Allahu Akbar*,' the frenzied mob was nearly at their door. No time to weep and mourn.

Raising his bloodstained sword again and again, Singh decapitated twenty-six women and girls of his family that night. Death was preferable to dishonour.

'*Allahu Akbar*,' the hysterical mob kicked open the front door, lanterns and lathis in hand.

'*Pakistan zindabad*.'

But they would find not a single lady to abduct or kill or rape inside that home. Only a river of blood.

❋ Sacred Land of Wisdom ❋

'*Ek Onkar Satnam...*' the words of the Gurbani echoed down the sacred pool in the *granthi*'s soulful voice. *There is but one God; His name is truth.*

Yet, words of wisdom would cut no ice with Master Tara Singh today as he circled the marble pavement and completed the *parikrama* at the Golden Temple in Amritsar. The lump in his throat would remind him every moment of his family, his home, his people – massacred mercilessly in Rawalpindi. Until about a hundred years ago, the Sikhs had ruled all of Punjab, with the great Maharaja Ranjit Singh's

THE GOLDEN TEMPLE OR SRI HARMANDIR SAHIB GURDWARA IN AMRITSAR, PUNJAB

empire extending from Tibet to Sind. But today, his brethren stood defeated and disgraced in their own land. A pulsating rage throbbed in his temples.

Touching his head to the cool marble floor, his beard soaked with tears, the Akali leader bowed before the Akal Takht, which contained the Guru Granth Sahib, perhaps the only holy book in the world containing verses penned by those of other faiths – Muslims like Baba Farid; Hindus like Surdas; syncretic poets like Kabir. The Sikhs had absorbed their words of wisdom, reciting them with as much fervour and devotion as those of the Sikh gurus.

But today, the wisdom of Guru Nanak and Baba Farid would fall on deaf ears. No sermon or prayer, no holy book or fakir had the power to assuage Tara Singh's rage. That turmoil would be tamed with nothing less than revenge.

❋ Operation Seduction ❋

While luxuriant green fields turned crimson from the bloodbaths in Punjab, the red carpet was being rolled out in the magnificent Durbar Hall of the Viceroy House in New Delhi. Dressed immaculately in his white naval uniform, complete with row upon row of medals and an unending line of ribbons and crosses, Lord Louis Mountbatten took over as India's last viceroy from the harried Lord Wavell, whose best efforts had failed to resolve the Indian deadlock.

Britain wanted out. The viceroy's immediate task was to work out a scheme by which power could be handed over to Indians by June 1948. But hand over power to whom? The Congress? Or the Muslim League? Meanwhile, the maddened mobs were at each other's throats on the streets – in Bengal, then Bihar, now Punjab. Even before the sound of the bagpipes from the Royal Scots Fusiliers and the boom of the cannons of the Royal Horse Artillery to welcome the new viceroy had died down, Lord Mountbatten was a worried man. How was he going to shine a torch through this gloom?

As a military officer of the Royal British Navy, he knew only one way to begin – by taking soundings and getting his bearings right. He would meet the Indian leaders and the British governors, the rulers and the residents, and seek their ideas to help him break the stalemate. That, he hoped, would help him chart a course through the choppy waters ahead, shifting gears from what the previous viceroy, Wavell, had named 'Operation Madhouse' to his very own 'Operation Seduction'.

Sitting back in his study with his team of advisers, Mountbatten went over the notes carefully crafted by his conference secretary, Vernon Crum, recording the discussions he had had over the last few days.

'India is like an elephant, Your Excellency,' K.M. Panikkar, the diwan of Bikaner, had explained to the new viceroy, 'and the part Jinnah wants for Pakistan – they are the two ears. An elephant,' Panikkar had said matter-of-factly, 'can survive quite well without its ears.'

'The situation in Punjab is tense…' Governor Jenkins of Punjab had briefed the viceroy after handing in a report of casualties, in which Bir Bahadur's beloved sister, with a face like the moon, had been reduced to a mere statistic. 'More than 5,000 have lost their lives in the last month alone in Punjab,' the governor lamented. 'After the resignation of Mr Khizar, the field is clear for the troublemakers in the Muslim League. Lawlessness is rampant.'

'A few months ago, we were sitting on a bag of gunpowder,' Sir Frederick Burrows, the governor of Bengal, had warned him about the worsening conditions there, 'but now we are sitting on a whole keg of gunpowder that could detonate at any moment.'

MOUNTBATTEN: A SOLUTION SEEMS IMPOSSIBLE...

With a grimace, the viceroy turned the page of the report he was holding.

'Hand over power to Jinnah,' Gandhi had said to his utter amazement two days ago. 'If that can help avoid Partition, so be it. I will convince Jawahar and Vallabhbhai to accept a Muslim League government. I will bring in the Congress.'

Mountbatten shook his head, flabbergasted. The idea seemed implausible, impossible – in fact, preposterous. He turned to the next flagged note.

'Those who demand Partition can have it,' Nehru had stated categorically, 'but they cannot coerce unwilling parts of India to join Pakistan.' Of all the Indians he had met so far, the viceroy had related most to Nehru. He found himself nodding in agreement and turned the page.

'If the League insists on Partition,' the pragmatic Vallabhbhai Patel had indicated, 'the only alternative is the division of Punjab and Bengal.' After dismissing Pakistan as Jinnah's mad dream once upon a time, Patel appeared to have made his peace with the idea of Partition, and the division of Punjab, even if reluctantly so. Moreover, he had been the messenger chosen to take the painful news of the Congress Working Committee's decision endorsing the division of Punjab in the event of Partition, to Gandhi. 'Now... this is going to be a problem, isn't it?' The viceroy sat back, smacking the page with the back of his hand. 'This business of dividing the provinces.'

'Here's what the Sikh leader had to say,' his chief of staff, Hastings Ismay, handed him the minutes of the meeting with Akali leader Baldev Singh.

'The attacks on Khizar were intended to establish Muslim domination,' Singh had remarked. 'The League wants to bulldoze its way to achieve Pakistan, but the Sikhs will never accept Muslim rule. The only solution is the division of Punjab.'

Eyes on the clock, Mountbatten put aside the notes with a sigh and straightened his necktie, preparing to meet the last of the Indian leaders on his list. A man upon whom he would go on to bestow the choicest of expletives in the coming days – from colt and dolt, to psychopathic and hopeless, to evil genius and a one-man band – Muhammad Ali Jinnah.

❋ Son, Our Faith Is in Trouble ❋

Fed by five gurgling rivers, the breadbasket of the nation and the doorway to the subcontinent – Punjab was the land of plenty, of plurality, of prosperity – made even more bountiful by the sweat and toil of the enterprising Punjabi.

Mirroring this agrarian lifestyle of his people was Patiala's maharaja, Yadavindra Singh – *prince amongst princes; giant among men* is how writers would describe him in years to come. A first-class cricketer, the finest polo player, an athlete par excellence, a star on the hockey field and tennis court, a champion in swimming and shooting, angling and mountaineering – the maharaja dreamed of taking Indian sports on to the global stage. From district superintendent to inspector general of police; from secretary in the forest department to commander in the Indian Army – the dashing thirty-three-year-old prince had done it all. But, of all his myriad interests, his first love remained gardening and horticulture.

'Master Tara Singh is here to see Your Highness,' the maharaja's ADC came rushing into the fruit garden one morning, where Yadavindra Singh was bent over a patch of melons, instructing his young gardener, Sukhwindar, on the benefits of timely weeding and pruning.

Like a mountain rising from the ground, the towering frame of the maharaja emerged from behind the thicket – a scowl on his face, mud on his hands. 'Now?'

'He is...uh...waiting inside,' the ADC scratched his head, wondering if he had missed informing the maharaja about a scheduled appointment. 'Shall I ask him to come back some other time?'

'*Na*,' Yadavindra Singh brushed him off. 'It's all right...' he dusted his clothes, instructing Sukhwindar to complete the weeding, and headed back into the palace. Unlike his father who had had a distant relationship with the Akalis, Yadavindra was a sympathizer, embracing their teachings to adhere more strictly to Sikh traditions.

As the maharaja quickly changed and made his way to meet the Akali leader, he found Tara Singh seated on the ground, head bowed in silence before the hallowed *Hukumnama*, a letter written in the hand of Guru Gobind Singh himself, preserved and revered within a sacred sanctorum in the palace. The Guru, who often sent out letters to his followers, had signed this letter to the head of the Patiala royal house with the point of his arrow.

'*Tera ghar mera asai*,' Tara Singh read the last words of the letter out loud. *Your home is like my own.*

He turned around to face Yadavindra Singh, his fiery, red eyes brimming with tears. '*Puttar*...it is a matter of pride that your family has been bestowed with such an honour by our last Guru,' he said, holding the maharaja by his shoulders. 'Our faith is in trouble, son...' His voice was low but determined. 'It is time to destroy our enemies.'

❋ Rose between Thorns ❋

'A rose between two thorns!' Jinnah remarked with a guffaw as he posed between the viceroy and vicereine for a photograph. The photographer grimaced, certain that Jinnah had rehearsed those lines assuming Edwina Mountbatten would be placed in the centre of the picture. The Mountbattens smiled awkwardly before Jinnah and the viceroy made their way into the study for a tête-à-tête.

'India has never been a true nation, Your Excellency,' Jinnah began. 'It only looks so on the map,' he explained, putting down his cup of tea. 'You see...the Muslim and the Hindu – they have very different concepts of life, different heroes. Islamic culture is based on the Arabic and Persian way. The Hindus look to Sanskrit origins. Our social customs, our way of life – they are not alike. You see...both groups have their own distinctive culture and civilization. They are entirely different nations.'

'Mr Jinnah, I have also met Maulana Azad...' the viceroy interjected, referring to the scholarly and erudite Congress leader. 'He is a Muslim too, but his views differ very much from yours.'

'Azad is a poster boy for the Hindus,' Jinnah scoffed, with a dismissive wave of his hand. Making Azad the Congress president, Jinnah believed, was a clever manoeuvre by Gandhi, a cunning strategy to woo India's Muslims. 'You mustn't make too much of his views.'

'Assuming for a moment that you're right, Mr Jinnah,' the viceroy continued, 'I'm concerned that any Partition

JINNAH: I ASSURE YOU – INDIA AND PAKISTAN WILL LIVE IN HARMONY.

plan could lead to bloodshed. There is already so much of it in Punjab.'

'To harness together two nations in a single yoke, Your Excellency, will only lead to even more strife,' Jinnah pressed on. 'Let me tell you about a case I once handled between two warring brothers,' he recalled, leaning back casually. 'They fought bitterly over the property left to them under their father's will, but two years after the case was decided, they became the greatest of friends. I assure you'—Jinnah sounded dead earnest—'all these troubles will cease after Partition. India and Pakistan will live in harmony.'

'I certainly want nothing more than peace and harmony,' the viceroy sighed. 'Anyway...do tell me more. Where exactly will your Pakistan lie?'

Jinnah leaned forward. It had been seven years since the League had first demanded a sovereign state, but no clear map had emerged yet. 'The Frontier, Punjab, Sind, Baluchistan, Bengal, Assam–' Jinnah listed out the areas comprising the Pakistan of his dreams.

'At the outset, may I point out,' the viceroy interjected, 'that the Frontier has a Congress government. Nor is the League in power in Punjab.'

'But the Muslims are an overwhelming majority in the Frontier and in Punjab,' Jinnah exclaimed. 'The Muslims have been living under Hindu domination for far too long.'

'Let me get this right, Mr Jinnah,' said the viceroy, 'your argument is that India's Muslim minority cannot be forced to live under a Hindu majority...am I correct?'

'Quite right. It is unacceptable,' replied Jinnah.

'By your own logic then, the Hindu minority in Bengal and Punjab cannot be made to live under a Muslim majority.'

Jinnah cocked his head, taken aback. 'No...no...that is not so,' he protested, realizing the implication of the viceroy's words.

'Partitioning Bengal and Punjab then is the only way out,' stated the viceroy matter-of-factly.

'The Muslim League cannot agree to the partitioning of either Bengal or Punjab,' argued Jinnah. 'Whether you look at it historically, or economically, or geographically – or even politically, or morally – it just cannot be justified.' He threw up his hands in exasperation. 'It will sow the seeds of discord... the results will be disastrous for everyone. The Muslims, Your Excellency,' Jinnah stressed, 'are a majority in Punjab.'

'And the Hindus are a majority in India,' the viceroy shot back.

'Pakistan must be viable,' Jinnah turned to practicality, realizing his own argument was being used against him. 'Without the whole of Punjab and Bengal,' Jinnah muttered, 'it will be a...a...' he stammered as he searched for the appropriate expression, 'a mutilated...moth-eaten Pakistan.'

'It is not just Hindus,' pointed out the viceroy. 'Punjab has a large number of Sikhs too, and I understand they do not wish to live under Muslim rule.'

'The Sikhs...' Jinnah growled, 'comprise only four million of the 28 million people in Punjab.'

'Precisely, Mr Jinnah,' countered the viceroy, baffled by Jinnah's intractable stance. 'Just as you don't desire Congress rule foisted upon the Muslim minority of India...on the very same principle, League rule cannot be foisted upon the Hindu and Sikh minorities of Punjab and Bengal.' Sauce for the goose simply had to be sauce for the gander.

Jinnah drew back and exhaled deeply, examining his long bony fingers in silence.

'The Congress is willing to agree to Partition,' continued the viceroy after a pause, 'but they support the Sikh demand for the partition of Punjab. Their argument is that no non-Muslim areas should go to Pakistan.'

'This is a sinister move...a vile move!' Jinnah fired up, enraged, the vision of Pakistan suddenly floundering. *What good was a divided Punjab?*

Having played his gamble, Mountbatten observed Jinnah's expressions closely. *If the prospect of a truncated Pakistan was unviable, would Jinnah drop his demand altogether?*

Jinnah gritted his teeth. Having come this far, he wasn't going to back down. 'Even if you give me a Pakistan of this size,' he muttered, pulling out a matchbox from his pocket, 'I will take it.'

Feeling defeated, Mountbatten sat back with a sigh. Usually, his charisma and oratory were enough to persuade even the most stubborn of opponents, prompting Hastings Ismay to joke that he had the ability to charm a vulture off a carcass! But the head of the Muslim League was clearly made of another mettle, leaving the exhausted viceroy to fret later in exasperation, 'The only man Jinnah listens to... is Jinnah himself!'

❋ Azad Punjab ❋

'The partition of India can only mean one of two things for us,' Master Tara Singh sounded out his royal audience assembled under glittering chandeliers in the splendid Moti Bagh Palace at Patiala. 'Either we will live as minorities in their Pakistan; or we will see our beloved Punjab cleaved into two halves.'

'We Sikhs stand to lose the most by Partition,' remarked senior Akali leader Gyani Kartar Singh. 'Our people will be browbeaten in West Punjab by the Muslims, and overpowered by the Hindus in the east.'

Maharaja Harinder Singh Brar of Faridkot shook his head glumly, horrified at both prospects.

Staring out of the window, Maharaja Yadavindra Singh watched his daughters playing in the garden below. *What was their future to be?*

Dressed in his sparkling topaz turban, Maharaja Jagatjit Singh of Kapurthala fidgeted restlessly with the *kara* around his strong wrist, itching to avenge the dishonour to the Sikhs.

Other Sikh rulers too sat in stony silence, their stern visages reflecting their deep misgivings.

'We have all seen the carnage they unleashed in Pindi,' Tara Singh reminded them, a shiver running down his spine. 'They will soon overrun the whole of Punjab...it is a question of Sikh honour,' he stated, stroking his flowing white beard. 'Either we settle with the Muslims...or we prepare for war!'

'What is it you propose, Masterji?' asked the raja of Faridkot. 'What do you have in mind?'

'My view is simple. Why must we bow before Jinnah?' asked Tara Singh. 'Everywhere we find people pressing for their own home. The Muslims want Pakistan; the Jews want Palestine. We too must have a home of our own. We too must be the masters of our own destiny,' he urged the rulers. 'Instead of relying upon the *angrez*, or being at the mercy of the blessed Congress,' he proposed, 'I say why not seize Punjab for ourselves and have our own nation? *Sadda apna mulak hona chahida hai.*'

The maharajas exchanged glances. The proposal had been mooted before, but nobody had taken it seriously. Perhaps now, in view of the changed circumstances, it would merit more consideration.

'We must organize ourselves to match the Muslim threat with our own Akal Fauj,' declared Master Tara Singh. 'If the League wants Pakistan, let them ford an ocean of Sikh blood.'

Kingdoms like Patiala, Faridkot, Kapurthala and Jind had their own British-trained armies, and were equipped with the latest weapons – mortars, armoured vehicles and even aircraft. If the Sikhs stood any chance of putting up a fight for Punjab, the maharajas would undoubtedly have to play their part.

MASTER TARA SINGH: THIS IS OUR SACRED LAND.

'This is our sacred land...the land of our Gurus. How can we let the Muslims have it?' Tara Singh implored. 'The Hindus have their India,' he said, 'the Muslims are going to get their Pakistan...' he paused to look each of the princes in the eye, 'instead of getting ground to dust between them, I say...let us have our Sikhistan!'

Maharaja Yadavindra Singh exhaled hard, reminded of the prophecy of his royal astrologer who had predicted that the Sikhs were destined to rule Punjab. He had even foreseen the man who would lead the Sikhs to that goal – a towering personality whose description matched the maharaja of Patiala.

Taking Tara Singh's hand in his own to signify his support, Maharaja Yadavindra Singh's chest swelled with pride. Cometh the hour, cometh the man!

❋ Brokering a Compromise ❋

As the hot winds of April blew across the wheat and corn fields of Punjab, the province's governor, Evan Jenkins, was a worried man. With every passing day, control was slipping out of his hands. The spark in Rawalpindi had spread to Multan, then Lahore, then Amritsar, turning into a raging inferno. Muslims had started the butchery; Hindus and Sikhs were now retaliating. *Was there no end to this cycle of violence?*

'Look...I think the Sikhs are kicking up an unreasonable fuss,' said Jenkins to the delegation of senior Akali leaders he had called for a meeting. 'Mr Jinnah guarantees freedom of worship and personal freedom to minorities in Pakistan. There is no reason why you must fear for the Sikhs and their gurdwaras in Pakistan.'

'I have seen a good deal of Mr Jinnah,' Kartar Singh snorted disdainfully. 'Far more than you, Mr Jenkins. I do not trust his words.'

Delegation members Mohan Singh and Harnam Singh, usually jovial men, sat behind their leaders with long faces, nodding along. While Jinnah had been crying hoarse all along about Muslims being a separate nation, he was now saying his Pakistan would be a secular home to people of all faiths and communities. They found this hard to believe.

'And even if I am wrong now,' Kartar Singh continued, 'Mr Jinnah is not immortal. I tell you, the Sikhs will be in great danger in Pakistan after he is gone.'

Jenkins rolled his eyes, exhausted with trying to work out a rational solution. He had hoped that all concerned could discuss the problem like grown men and settle the dispute. But trust had eroded completely between the communities.

And yet, if the madness and violence were not stopped now, the situation was only going to escalate. All kinds of reports reached his ears. Of the impulsive maharaja of Faridkot supplying the Akali militia with grenades and guns. Of Sikh *jathas* being given refuge and vehicles in his palace. Of the maharaja of Patiala mobilizing for a military showdown; producing rifles and procuring weapons through his British employee, Mr Hutton. Of Bren guns and machine guns being distributed to young men across Punjab.

'You Britishers don't seem to understand the importance of the integrity of the Sikh community,' Kartar Singh explained candidly, 'or the significance of our holy shrines. We will not let go of Amritsar or Lahore. Or Nankana Sahib and other historical gurdwaras. We Sikhs have turned Punjab verdant and fertile with our sweat, toil and blood,' he fumed, worried that the newly developed canal colony of Lyallpur, to which he belonged, would be given to Pakistan. 'How can we just abandon it all and hand it over to *them*?'

'So, what is it you have in mind?' Jenkins demanded impatiently. *Surely they could see that the problem could not be solved by beating each other to death!*

'We will form a Sikh state,' declared Kartar Singh. 'It will form a buffer between Pakistan and India...'

'The Muslims got rid of the Sikhs in Rawalpindi, didn't they?' added an infuriated Mohan Singh. 'They grabbed all the land and property of our Sikh brothers. We will do the same.'

'Sir, you are responsible for ensuring justice for the Sikhs,' said Jathedar Mohan Singh, lending urgency to his leader's vision. 'We must have a substantial exchange of population. The Muslims move west, and the Sikhs move east. Else, we will have no choice but to drive out the Muslims.'

Jenkins's eyes narrowed. A *population exchange*?

'The Sikhs are being ridiculed, sir,' argued Kartar Singh. 'They're calling us cowards. We have no choice but to fight,' he expostulated.

'Mr Kartar Singh,' said Jenkins tersely, glancing furtively at Master Tara Singh sitting quietly in the corner, 'the government will not allow lawlessness and disorder. How are you going to fight against trained troops?'

'We know we are at a disadvantage,' Kartar Singh admitted despondently, 'but we will not give in. We shall fight as revolutionaries if need be,' he said, his voice lifting valiantly. They would cut railway tracks, damage telegraph lines, destroy canal headworks, if they had to. 'By God, we will fight till the end for our Punjab.'

'This is a foolish idea, Mr Singh,' Jenkins shook his head. 'Please listen to me—'

'Tell me, Mr Jenkins,' Kartar Singh cut in, 'if Britain were invaded today, would you just sit around doing nothing? Or would you stand up and fight?'

'Look...I understand your sentiments.' Jenkins interlaced his fingers on the desk. Having served in Punjab for so many years, he hated to see the province destroying itself. 'The viceroy has suggested the Sikh leaders talk this out with the League,' he said, hoping a peaceful settlement could still be brokered. 'Jinnah is willing to meet you. Why don't you talk and settle this?'

'No.' Master Tara Singh, who had been sitting silently thus far, stood up with a start. 'No,' he shook his head vehemently.

'I shall not kiss the hand besmirched with the blood of innocent Sikhs.'

❋ Dinner with Jinnah ❋

While the Akali leaders were determined to stay away from Jinnah and anything he had to offer them, the ruler of Patiala decided to give the leader of the Muslim League a patient ear, before coming to a decision. 'A Patiala peg for Your Highness.' Maharaja Yadavindra Singh felt a nervous tingle in his fingers as he took the glass from Jinnah's bony hand. Out there in Punjab, Muslims and Sikhs were at each other's throats, while here he was, in Jinnah's stately Delhi villa, sipping whisky with the man responsible for the carnage. A wave of guilt washed over him.

'Cheers!' Jinnah raised his glass in a toast with the viceroy, thanking him for bringing the maharaja to meet him. The portly Liaquat Ali Khan stood by his elegant wife, Begum Ra'ana, and Jinnah's sister, Fatima, playing perfect hostesses on a sweltering evening.

It is said when a team of Englishmen arrived in Patiala for a game of cricket during the reign of Maharaja Bhupinder Singh (father of Yadavindra Singh), the home team was worried about losing the match. To boost their chances of winning, on the evening before the game they poured out double measures (pegs) of whisky for their guests. Their hangover the next day caused the English to lose the match to the maharaja's team. When an angry political agent confronted the maharaja about this, the king is said to have replied: 'Yes, in Patiala, our pegs are larger!' Ever since, a larger measure of whisky – calculated as the distance between the little finger and the index finger – is called a Patiala peg!

'I'm anxious for the Sikhs to join Pakistan,' Jinnah broached his agenda earnestly, 'and I am prepared to give you anything in return,' he told the maharaja. 'Anything!'

Eyes riveted on a silver map of India on an oak-plaque on the mantel showing regions forming Pakistan marked in green, Yadavindra Singh whirled around, startled by Jinnah's statement.

'Even an entire state in Pakistan under your control,' Jinnah mooted his grandiose plan, leading his guests into the little garden outside. 'Very nearly an Azad Punjab, eh?' he smiled.

'Absolutely,' agreed Liaquat Ali, seconding his leader's notion, as they seated themselves around a coffee table beside a neatly pruned row of rose bushes. 'Pakistan is willing to offer Your Highness the position he rightly deserves.'

'Your Highness, the maths is simple,' said Jinnah, putting down his glass and lighting a cigarette. 'If Punjab remains united and joins us, its five million Sikhs will be a large and influential minority in Pakistan. But if Punjab were to be divided as the Congress want, the Sikh population will be reduced by half and become a minority in both countries,' Jinnah explained. 'That seems rather foolish to me.'

The maharaja leaned forward and dropped a cube of ice into his whisky. Of course, he knew the numbers. In West Punjab, Muslims outnumbered them by far, and in the east, the Hindus.

You shall be the leader of the Sikh state within Pakistan, Your Highness,' said Liaquat Ali Khan, sugar-coating Jinnah's offer. 'You can retain all your property and privileges, even command your own army.'

The maharaja of Patiala pursed his lips. *Would the carnage in Punjab end if he accepted their offer?*

'You know as well as I do that the Sikhs are so distributed in Punjab that any partition of the province will invariably divide them,' remarked Liaquat Ali Khan, dabbing his mouth with a napkin. 'I'd urge you to consider this offer seriously.'

Placing a plate of roasted chicken breast on the glass table, Begum Ra'ana Liaquat Ali pulled up a chair beside the maharaja. 'Your Highness,' she said, her face radiant, 'let me tell you something about myself. My ancestors are Hindu, and I was brought up a Christian. Before marrying Liaquat Sa'ab, I converted to Islam. I think I'm better placed than most to say that the League does not discriminate when it comes to people of other faiths. Trust me'—she drew her chair closer—'Pakistan will be an inclusive state. The Sikhs will be most welcome and safe in Pakistan. You have nothing to fear.'

Yadavindra Singh smiled uncomfortably, his eyes on the rapidly melting cube swirling in his glass. After the massacre in Rawalpindi, nothing anyone said about an inclusive Pakistan cut any ice with him.

'So...what do you say?' Jinnah rose from his chair. 'Fatima dear, bring His Highness another drink.'

'No, that's quite all right,' Yadavindra Singh excused himself, looking uneasily at his watch. 'It's late...I should get going now,' he rose to shake hands with his hosts. 'Thank you, Mr Jinnah. I shall get back to you about your kind offer.'

Yet, no matter which way Yadavindra Singh looked at the proposal, he simply could not silence that persistent voice whispering menacingly inside his head, '*Could Jinnah be trusted?*'

❋ Lunch with Sardar ❋

If Jinnah had wooed the maharaja over chicken and whisky over dinner, Sardar would try his hand with *dhokla* and *chhaas* over lunch.

'Thank you for accepting my invitation,' Sardar greeted Maharaja Yadavindra Singh at the door with one of his most charming smiles. Dressed in a simple hand-spun saree, his daughter Maniben stood beside him, welcoming the royal visitor with folded hands.

'Honoured to meet you, Your Highness,' V.P. Menon shook hands with the towering maharaja, hopeful that if Sardar managed to convince the new chancellor of the Chamber of Princes, perhaps he would be able to carry the rest of the princes into the fold as well.

'I am happy that Patiala has joined the Constituent Assembly,' Patel noted as they took their seats in the living room. 'And I look forward to your cooperation in the matter of accession also.'

Yadavindra Singh drew in a deep breath. His meeting with Jinnah had yielded little. The Sikhs seemed unwilling to settle with the League and plans for Sikhistan looked much too tenuous to take off. *Was brokering long-term peace with India the best option?*

'Your place is with us in India...' Sardar told the maharaja in his straightforward manner, 'and you know that as well as I do. States that have joined the Indian Constituent Assembly must forthwith accede to India on the three subjects of defence, external affairs and communications. And, as a member of the Constituent Assembly, you will be participating in framing India's Constitution. You will have a direct voice in the shaping of government policy.'

Maniben placed a tray of chilled water on the low coffee table; the maharaja grabbed a glass. May could be unforgiving in Delhi.

'I won't hide it from you, Sardar,' he said after a gulp of the cold water, 'Jinnah has been offering me everything under the sun to join Pakistan...'

'Your Highness, we know the princes have also been in talks with Sir Corfield,' Menon confessed to the maharaja. 'We know that he has been encouraging the states to stay out of India. But let me tell you frankly that the Government of India does not see eye to eye with the political department, and by conferring with them or Jinnah, you are being misled.'

'Mr Menon,' the maharaja turned to the states secretary for whom he had the highest regard, 'it is true that Nawab Hamidullah of Bhopal has been asking the princes to stay out. However, a number of the rulers, including myself, have broken away from him.'

Sardar nodded, feeling somewhat reassured.

'I understand from the maharaja of Bilaspur,' said Menon, 'that all the Punjab states have decided to take a common stand that would best safeguard their interests. We would like to know what you have in mind.'

'Sardar, while we appreciate the logic of all your suggestions, the matter requires a careful and cautious approach.'

Menon, like his boss, was not a man to mince words. 'Your Highness, sooner or later, the princes must realize this,' he said matter-of-factly as they moved to the lunch table. 'independent of India, you cannot exist.'

❋ Won't Be Betrayed Again! ❋

'Kafirs!' thundered Master Tara Singh, flinging a copy of *The Tribune*, dated 18 May 1947, on the table. 'The Muslims call us infidels! And you went to meet their leader?' He glared at the newspaper report of the maharaja's meeting with Jinnah.

'His followers are out there,' Tara Singh whirled around, his eyes spitting fire, 'hacking down our people. How,' he demanded, 'how can we even consider talking to this man?'

Maharaja Yadavindra Singh heaved a sigh and turned to the other Sikh leaders. 'Look...all I'm suggesting is that we hear him out and listen to his proposal once.'

'Do you know how a *shikari* behaves when he is out on a hunt?' Kartar Singh held up his index finger as if teaching the young maharaja a lesson. 'He is careful not to disturb the birds that he intends to shoot!' He paused for the import of his words to sink in. 'Jinnah is doing just that – lulling us Sikhs into a false sense of security before mowing us down.'

'Look...I went to meet Jinnah upon the viceroy's insistence,' Maharaja Yadavindra Singh cut in. 'The British are leaving, and we need to seriously think of our future...'

'The British have created this goddamned mess...' – Master Tara Singh sprang forward like a panther. 'Have they given any thought to us? Who fought shoulder to shoulder for the *angrez* in their wars? Who sacrificed their lives to defend these *firangis*? It was us.' He thumped his chest. 'The Sikhs! We fought their bloody wars! We – the children of Punjab! Our fathers. Our brothers. Our sons. They died for these ungrateful British. And this is what we get?'

'If we don't join Pakistan, the alternative is the division of Punjab...' pointed out Yadavindra Singh. 'Are we prepared for that?'

'He claims that Muslims will not be treated well in India,' Kartar Singh fumed, 'but wants us to believe that Sikhs will be treated well in Pakistan. Can you believe that even for a second?'

Maharaja Yadavindra Singh turned to his former prime minister, Hardit Singh Malik. 'What do you think?'

'By all means, have a meeting with him.' Hardit Singh shrugged thoughtfully. 'But let *him* come to see you. He has something to ask of you...'

'No! No! No!' Tara Singh threw up his hands vehemently. 'There is no question of compromising with Jinnah. We cannot live under a Muslim majority. Are we cowards to fear death? Guru Gobind Singh prayed for death on the battlefield by the sword of the enemy. I too prefer the death of a warrior.'

Having served on the front lines in wartime, Yadavindra Singh was the last man in need of a sermon about battles, bravery and sacrifice. What worried him, was something entirely different. 'We have more than a million of our people in West Punjab...over 700 shrines,' he reminded the furious Tara Singh. 'Scores of gurdwaras...the most sacred sites like Nankana Sahib. Can we run the risk of having all that cut off from us?' he demanded, acutely aware of the strong public sentiment among Sikhs about the holy shrines.

'On our past rests our present and future...and the future of our children,' said Tara Singh firmly. 'No, Your Highness,' he shook his head grimly, rejecting the maharaja's every plea for consideration and negotiation. 'We shall not be betrayed again.'

❋ Jinnah Tries Yet Again ❋

Anxious for a solution, thirsting for peace, following the suggestion of his former diwan, Yadavindra Singh extended an invitation to Jinnah, despite opposition from Master Tara Singh. *Why not meet at a neutral place*? Jinnah had responded cleverly, astutely aware of the nuanced craft of negotiation. And so it was that former diwan Hardit Singh Malik's brother had been selected to play host for the get-together at 4 Bhagwan Das Road in New Delhi, with an irate Master Tara Singh and an incensed Kartar Singh joining in most reluctantly.

'Look...' Jinnah began with sincerity, 'I assure you that everyone – no matter of what colour, caste or creed, no matter what our relationship in the past – will first, second and last, be a citizen of Pakistan with equal rights, privileges and obligations.'

'Hmph,' scoffed Tara Singh under his breath. In the wake of the butchery in Punjab, Jinnah's eagerness to win over the Sikhs sickened him.

'Mr Jinnah, you're being very generous,' said Hardit Singh, 'but we would like to know exactly what we can expect. Pakistan will have a government, a parliament, defence forces...what part will the Sikhs play in all this?'

'Mr Malik, are you familiar with what happened in Egypt?' Jinnah began his answer with a question. 'I shall deal with the Sikhs as Zaghloul Pasha dealt with the Copts when Egypt became independent.'

The Sikh leaders looked at one another.

'Well...let me explain...' Jinnah said, crossing one leg over the other. 'You see...the Copts were the Christian minority in Egypt. Like you, they too were apprehensive. After listening to their concerns, Pasha advised them to come back with specific demands. When they returned a few days later, Pasha took the list from them and without reading it, he wrote, "I agree". This,...' Jinnah said emphatically, adjusting the monocle clamped to his eye, 'this is exactly what I will do with your demands.'

Hardit Singh exchanged uneasy glances with the maharaja. The Akalis were determined that they would not accept Pakistan. And, here, the League leader was offering the Sikhs everything they possibly desired. 'Mr Jinnah...supposing, God forbid'—he hesitated—'supposing you are no longer there when the time comes to fulfilling your promises. I...I mean—'

'What he means is...' an agitated Kartar Singh stepped in to clarify, 'would you put down your promises on paper? Would you be willing to incorporate these commitments into Pakistan's Constitution?'

Jinnah seldom laughed, but the question made him throw back his head in mirth, like he had been told a hilarious joke. 'I've given you my word...' he dismissed the idea with a wave of his hand. 'In Pakistan, nobody will renege on my promise.'

Tara Singh locked his fiery eyes with the maharaja's, glowering with an *I-told-you-so* look.

'Worry not, my friends,' Jinnah reiterated, studying his Sikh guests with his penetrating glance, 'in Pakistan...my word will be like the word of God!'

❋ Pakistan's in the Bag! ❋

From Kashmir to Kanyakumari, anxious listeners switched on their radio sets for the historic broadcast of 3 June. In Patiala and Rawalpindi, in Amritsar and Lahore, people gathered in tea shops, in shops, in homes. The streets went quiet, the plundering paused, even if momentarily, as everyone waited with bated breath for the big revelation. *Would India march into the dawn of freedom in one piece; or would she be severed into two?*

'This is All India Radio,' the familiar baritone of the broadcaster crackled through the transistor at 6 p.m. sharp. The viceroy was to address the people first, followed by Congress leader Jawaharlal Nehru. Akali leader Baldev Singh would go next and, finally, the head of the Muslim League, Muhammad Ali Jinnah. A brief pause followed the announcer's lines.

Viceroy Mountbatten's British-accented voice came through first. 'For more than a hundred years, 400 million of you have lived together and this country has been administered as a single entity. This has resulted in unified communications, defence, postal services and currency. My great hope is that communal differences do not destroy this.'

Somewhere in Punjab, crouching over the radio, Tara Singh felt his pulse quicken.

'To my great regret,' the viceroy went on, 'it has been impossible to obtain concurrence either on the Cabinet

Mission Plan or on any other plan that would preserve the unity of India... The only alternative to coercion is Partition.'

The bomb had been dropped; the dreaded verdict pronounced; the final decision was out. Partition it was going to be.

The words echoed like a death knell in Tara Singh's head. A tear crept down his cheek.

'We have given careful consideration to the position of the Sikhs.' The viceroy got to the point that all of Punjab was waiting for.

Huddled by a static-filled radio connection along with his followers, at the gurdwara in Nankana Sahib, Kartar Singh cupped his ear.

'This valiant community forms about an eighth of the population of Punjab,' the viceroy read from his prepared speech, 'but they are so evenly distributed that any partition of this province would inevitably divide them. All of us who have the good of the Sikh community at heart are very sorry to think that the partition of Punjab, which they themselves desire, cannot avoid splitting them to a greater or lesser extent.'

Clutching his head in dismay, Kartar Singh gazed at the white dome of Gurdwara Janam Asthan glowing in the light of the setting sun. Nankana Sahib, as they called it, was the revered birthplace of Nanakdev, their first Guru. *Could the holiest of their shrines now fall into Pakistan's hands?*

'I want to make it clear that the ultimate boundaries will be settled by a boundary commission,' the viceroy said next, as if in response to Kartar Singh's fears, 'and will almost certainly not be identical with those that have been provisionally adopted.'

A notional boundary had been laid down in the Indian Independence Act, much like the one set down by the previous viceroy, Lord Wavell. But the finalized border was still an uncertainty, a factor that would add greatly to the woes of those living around what would soon become an international boundary.

'I have made no mention of the Indian states...' the viceroy got to the question of the princely states next. 'If the transfer of power is to be effected in a peaceful and orderly manner, every single one of us must bend all his efforts to the task,' he said. 'This is no time for bickering. We cannot afford any toleration of violence – all of us are agreed on that. I have faith in the future of India and am proud to be with you all at this momentous time. May your decisions be wisely guided.'

Turning up the volume of the radio in the elegantly furnished study of Moti Bagh Palace in Patiala, Maharaja Yadavindra Singh pursed his lips. So, Punjab was to be divided, and the states were being asked to commit to the task and play their part in India's future. That was how the British would repay the Sikhs and the princes for their blood and sweat in the wars! His thoughts wandered back to his meeting with Jinnah and Liaquat Ali Khan. They had been most charming and had gone out of their way to offer him everything conceivable – from promising to make him head of a Sikh state within Pakistan, to allowing the Sikhs their own army. It sounded most attractive. And yet, he knew deep down, that it was an impossible offer to trust or accept.

Seated stoically by the maharaja's side, Maharani Mehtab Kaur was already thinking of the road ahead. Thousands had begun pouring into the kingdom from West Punjab with their tales of woe, in the hope that they would be safe in Patiala. The maharani had opened round-the-clock community kitchens and medical camps across the state for the sick and hungry. This announcement only meant that she would need to ramp up her efforts.

'It is with no joy in my heart,' Nehru took over from the viceroy, his voice soft yet firm, 'that I commend these proposals, although I have no doubt in my mind that this is the right course of action. For generations we have dreamt and struggled for a free, independent and united India. The proposals to allow certain parts to secede is painful for us to contemplate'—Nehru paused, his anguish perceptible in his voice—'nevertheless, I am persuaded that our present decision is the right one even from the larger point of view. The united India that we laboured for was not one of compulsion or coercion, but a free and willing association of a free people.'

Squatting in the staff quarters of Moti Bagh Palace, gardener Sukhwindar stared disbelievingly at the radio. After resisting the idea of Partition for so long, the Congress had given in. His eyes welled with tears, his thoughts shifting to his married sister in Multan and to his beloved in Sialkot. *Would he ever see them again*? Remembering Gandhi's assurances, he was consumed by a wave of pure rage. Partition, Bapu had assured the people, would only take place over his dead body!

'We stand on a watershed,' Nehru continued, '...dividing past from future. Let us bury the past...forget all bitterness... let there be moderation in speech and writing...'

The words fell upon young Bir Bahadur's ears as hollow meaningless soundwaves as he sat reeling with trauma, leaning into a radio set far away from where the speeches were being read.

'There has been violence - shameful, degrading and revolting violence...' Nehru went on in earnest. 'This must end. Political ends are not to be achieved by means of violence...'

Bir Bahadur could make little sense of any of these happenings. Back in his village, he had grown up under the loving care of his neighbour, Ma Hussaini, a wrinkled old

Muslim woman whom he had lovingly called Dadi. In school, his best friend was Aslam; Sargat Ali, his favourite teacher. Village elders like Chacha Zaman and Masi Noor Jehan had been like extended family. He remembered Arif Bhai, the young man who had given up his own life to save him from a snakebite. A teardrop trickled down his cheek. The world seemed to have gone mad, and nothing, absolutely nothing, seemed to make any sense any more.

'Neighbour has risen against neighbour,' lamented Akali leader Baldev Singh, taking the microphone after Nehru. 'Thousands of innocent lives have been lost. Men, women and children roam from one place to another, homeless and destitute...'

As the Akali leader implored Sikhs to accept this unpleasant settlement, Bir Bahadur covered his face with his hands and wept. He missed the sweet taste of the waters of the Dhella Dhulla stream in his village, of Chacha Sarwar's guavas, aunt Barkat's melons. The people he loved, the sights and sounds he cherished, the smells and flavours he enjoyed – would now only live on as a painful memory.

On the radio, it was finally the turn of Muhammad Ali Jinnah – the man of the moment whom his followers lovingly called the Quaid: 'The world has no parallel for the most onerous and difficult task which we have to perform,' he reminded the people of India as he stood poised upon the threshold of his dreams. 'I most earnestly appeal to every community and particularly to Muslim India to maintain peace and order...'

Even as Jinnah spoke and Bir Bahadur mourned and Sukhwindar wept, the streets of Punjab were engulfed in a sea of euphoria. Muslim Leaguers rushed about exultantly, distributing sweets, beating drums and waving the green flag of Pakistan. Their dream was finally going to come true.

'*Pakistan zindabad*,' Jinnah ended his short address, the first and last he would ever make on All India Radio. Delivered in his crisp, anglicized Urdu, the phrase would puzzle most listeners, who were left wondering why the Quaid had proclaimed '*Pakistan's in the bag!*'

❋ An Unenviable Task ❋

Sweating profusely in a green-shuttered bungalow by the viceroy's house in Delhi, Sir Cyril Radcliffe – brilliant barrister from England – sat with his head buried in his hands, a glass of gin and tonic by his side. Never before in his illustrious legal career had he held a brief as exhausting or faced a challenge as unforgiving as the one he grappled with now – to draw a line dividing India into three parts on the basis of obsolete and unreliable census records and statistics.

Punjab was home to sixteen million Muslims, constituting a little over half the state's population, concentrated in the west; fifteen million Hindus, living mostly in the east; and around five million Sikhs, forming about 15 per cent of the population, who were distributed all over the region. Drawing this line would have been hard even if all the parties had been on amicable terms; but to do so in a climate of violence and hostility was a thankless task.

He could mark the boundaries along rivers; but what would become of the fields irrigated by the rivers? He could consider population as the guiding factor; but what about districts where Muslims and non-Muslims were in equal proportion? He could mark the border by religious contiguity; but what about a community's sacred shrines?

Lahore had a large number of Hindus; but if he gave it to India, Pakistan would be left with no big city other than

Karachi. Gurdaspur had a Muslim majority, but its economic life was tied to the Sikhs. Nankana Sahib was most sacred for the Sikhs, but it was in West Punjab which had a larger Muslim population than Sikh. The stroke of his pen had the power of severing workers from their jobs; farmers from their lands; factories from their resources; and the devout from their places of worship. Villages and farms, rivers and canals, factories and banks...the list was endless. What all could he possibly factor in?

Staring gloomily at the outdated records and expansive maps spread out on the table, Radcliffe refilled his glass. Evan Jenkins, governor of the province, a man who knew Punjab like the back of his hand, had told Viceroy Mountbatten that he would require about four years to divide Punjab peaceably.

Cyril Radcliffe – a man who knew nothing about the place and had never set foot in India before – had about forty days!

❃ Rise of the Jathas ❃

The 3 June announcement shook everyone – from those in the corridors of power to those on the fringes of society. But accompanying the Partition bombshell was a much bigger time bomb. Pulling off a rabbit-out-of-the-hat act, Viceroy Mountbatten had suddenly announced that power would be transferred not in June 1948, as first envisaged, but on 15 August 1947.

In ten weeks!

The announcement had triggered a mad scramble. Army to factories, books to chairs – everything was listed, evaluated and divided. Table lamps to typewriters; ink pots to chamber pots; umbrella racks to hat pegs – Pakistan would take 20 per cent of all movables; 17.5 per cent of the cash balances;

the rest would remain with India. People were added to the list – commanders, civil servants, clerks, secretaries, station masters, sweepers – they all had to make a life-altering decision – India or Pakistan?

As a mass of humanity rose in a huge swirl – panicking, packing, selling, moving – demands from the obvious to the bizarre poured in. Some Hindu sadhus wanted the River Indus retained in India as the Vedas had been composed on its banks. Muslim fanatics demanded that the Taj Mahal be dismantled and shifted to Pakistan as it was a Mughal monument. The Sikhs raised a clamour for the Golden Temple and Nankana Sahib.

Following the 3 June announcement, the Punjab Legislative Assembly had met and voted formally to divide Punjab, and Master Tara Singh took up the reins of the Sikh cause.

'O Sikhs! O Hindus!' he appealed to the sword-wielding Akal Fauj volunteers. 'Our brethren are threatened by those who call us infidels. Our lands are about to be overrun. Rise now, my friends,' he exhorted his followers. 'If we can snatch the government from the *firangis*, none can stop us from protecting our lands from the Muslims.'

"*Waheguruji Ka Khalsa*,' screamed enraged crowds. They had all lost a friend, a relative, a loved one – in Rawalpindi, in Multan, in Lahore. They would not let their blood go unavenged. '*Waheguruji Ki Fateh*.'

'Should we just stand by and watch as they drag us out of our homes?' Tara Singh whipped up the gatherings he addressed into an emotional frenzy. 'Are we to sit idly by while they butcher our children and snatch our land?' he roared. 'Is the Khalsa sleeping?'

'*Pakistan murdabad*,' the *jathas* supported his call to action.

'Be ready,' Tara Singh implored his followers. 'Let us rise as one. Our motherland is calling for our blood!'

❋ Face-Off ❋

Even as Radcliffe sweated it out in his little office, those on the ground who would bear the brunt of his ruthless scalpel, were busy making their own plans – plans that had reached the viceroy's ears.

'May I ask what this means?' demanded Mountbatten, placing the Akali resolution of 8 July on the table before the Sikh leaders. It proclaimed quite proudly that the Sikhs would not accept any award that did not suit them. It read:

> The Sikhs declare in unequivocal terms that the partition of the Punjab should be effected in a manner whereby their integrity and solidarity is maintained and they get an adequate share in the canals and canal colonies and their sacred shrines are included in Eastern Punjab. Any partition which does not secure this for the Sikhs will be unacceptable to them.

Baldev Singh stared at the document in blank astonishment. Maharaja Yadavindra Singh said nothing.

Jenkins had been sending the viceroy regular updates from Punjab. Daily news of raids and riots; fighting and fires; stabbings and bombings. In just three days, between 19 and 22 July, there had been six serious bomb explosions in Lahore. Non-Muslims were nervous about residing or serving in West Punjab; Muslims were equally apprehensive about jobs in East Punjab. The refugee problem was becoming unmanageable, prompting the Partition Council to form a Punjab Boundary Force under Major General Rees. But with fires raging from Amritsar to Lahore and Sheikhupura to Sialkot, the demands on the force were far too many.

'The Sikhs are jittery, Your Excellency,' Baldev Singh explained. 'They only want to safeguard their position. We hope the Boundary Commission will be fair to Sikh demands and give its decision by 15 August.'

'I believe you said in a speech that if the decision is against the Sikhs, you will resist it,' Mountbatten glared at Baldev Singh. 'Look...it was *you* who asked for Punjab to be partitioned,' he exclaimed, his hands spread open in exasperation. 'I told you to settle with Jinnah, and he was prepared to concede an autonomous homeland to the Sikhs within Pakistan. But you wanted Punjab divided. And you told me the Sikhs would accept the decision of the Boundary Commission. I want you to know,' the viceroy was beside himself with rage, 'that I will not hesitate to use aircraft or machine guns to restore sanity if required.'

'Your Excellency,' Maharaja Yadavindra Singh protested, 'the Sikhs are only anxious that the boundary line should meet their just claims. It is not just a matter of population. For instance'—he leaned forward—'may I mention the special claim of the Okara tract, in which I am particularly interested because it is inhabited by Sikh soldiers who fought in the World Wars. Patiala took interest in recruiting these soldiers for Britain in the war. These people cannot be left to their own devices now.'

'The boundary line is not in my hands...' the viceroy responded with his oft-repeated refrain. A few days ago, the maharaja had brought along an entire delegation of retired Sikh officers to meet him about the boundary, and he had had to fend them off. 'As you know, the Boundary Commission, under Sir Radcliffe, has been appointed to look into all claims.'

'There's also the question of Nankana Sahib, Your Excellency,' the maharaja went on, 'the birthplace of Guru Nanak, the founder of our faith. The Sikh community considers it sacrosanct. Under no circumstances will the Sikhs agree to allow this to go into foreign territory. I urge you to ensure that this area is given to India,' he pleaded, Jinnah's offers to have the Sikhs join Pakistan now firmly dead and buried as far as he was concerned.

'Look,' the viceroy said, sighing, tired of being asked time and again to tinker with the boundary line, 'there appears to be a widespread belief that the boundary line will be approved by me, but nothing can be further from the truth,' he enunciated emphatically. 'So, I'm afraid that it is quite impossible for me to consider your representations...however, it is my responsibility to keep law and order,' he added sternly.

'Very well, then,' the maharaja drew in a deep breath, infuriated that the British who had created this almighty mess, and for whom the Sikh people had sacrificed so much, could walk away so nonchalantly. 'The Sikhs,' he said, looking the viceroy in the eye, 'have no other option but to fight.'

❋ The Great Exodus ❋

It began as a trickle; but soon turned into a raging flood.

A pen-stroke on a map was about to turn citizen into refugee; friend into foe; neighbour into rival.

Neither the Congress, nor the League, and certainly not the British, had anticipated this kind of a mass migration. Had they been naïve or just negligent to have imagined that they would have a line drawn on a map and *that* would be the end of all their problems? Even Gandhi was saying that people should not leave their homes.

Nevertheless, regardless of what the leaders said, Punjab was on the move, in an exodus of staggering proportions. Hindus and Sikhs going east; Muslims moving west. Droves and droves of them. Dozens left by bullock carts, hundreds by lorries, thousands by train and millions on foot, clutching their few possessions. Tense families emptied their bank lockers; some buried their jewellery in their homes; others left behind their house keys with neighbours, hoping to return after the dust had settled. Women and children were sent to the safer side, the men of the house promising to follow soon. Anxious students dropped out of university. Columns and columns of refugees marched, first in the scorching sun, then in the unrelenting rains, their homes and their farms dissolving into aching memories.

Flying over the chaotic and heart-wrenching sight in a special silver DC-3 aeroplane, was Muhammad Ali Jinnah – the man at the root of all that suffering. As endless rows of people trudged along below, unending lines of *kafilas* on the move; vultures circling above them to feast on decomposing corpses; putrefying bodies abandoned in canals; rivers running red with blood; burnt shells of houses; thick palls of smoke hanging over charred villages, Jinnah – the founder and father of Pakistan – dressed for his grand arrival in Karachi in a close-fitting knee-length sherwani and ankle-hugging churidar, clothes he had not worn for decades, pored over newspaper after newspaper on board the flight, greatly pleased with the laudatory reports about his historic achievement.

Meanwhile, rumours of a Sikh–Hindu plan for war spread like wildfire. All kinds of stories flashed across the grapevine.

That the maharaja of Faridkot had distributed over 1,000 firearms and was mobilizing a Khalistan army.

That the maharaja of Patiala was supplying explosives, providing training and troops for the effort and that he planned to take over half of Punjab.

That Nabha was pitching in with arms and Kapurthala with funds.

That the princely states of Alwar, Dholpur, Bikaner and Bharatpur were aiding the sinister effort with ammunition.

It was being said that the Sikhs would oppose the boundary line come what may; that the Akalis had declared a

Sikh state with Simla as its capital. That the Sikhs planned to march to Lahore and take the city by force. That large-scale trouble would be sparked if Nankana Sahib was not included in East Punjab.

In West Punjab, Muslim mobs threatened Sikhs and Hindus, forcing them to convert to Islam, gunning down thousands and grabbing their property. Retaliating in the east were Sikh Akal Fauj and Shahidi *jathas* in red-and-orange bandanas and turbans, supported by the RSS cadres in khaki uniforms, marching across the countryside with clubs and crowbars, attacking and evicting Muslims.

Newspaper correspondents would report never having seen anything even remotely as horrendous as the sights they had witnessed during the partition of India. Appeals by leaders for communal harmony would fall upon deaf ears. Punjab was in the hold of a hysterical wave of insanity; gripped by a thirst that would be satiated with nothing less than blood.

❋ August Adventure ❋

As Punjab imploded, India was poised on a historic threshold; in two weeks, she would march into the dawn of independence. But even as Delhi geared up for the grand day – setting up visitor galleries and bandstands – the viceroy was busy plucking the apples he had promised to drop into Patel's basket, hosting a lavish lunch for the royals to woo them with his charisma and eloquence.

Red carpet below, sparkling chandeliers above, clink of silver and fine china, razzle-dazzle of resplendent *pagris* and sashes, soft music, low murmurs, tense faces and busy staff. The viceroy's speech over, the final drill was all set to begin.

'So, this is it.' Maharaja Yadavindra Singh sighed, exchanging notes with his friend Maharaja Sadul Singh of Bikaner, as they listened to the viceroy's staff explain the plan and procedure.

'Lining us up like lambs outside the slaughterhouse, aren't they?' joked one of the princes, pointing to the placards the viceroy's ADCs were placing at the two ends of the Banquet Hall.

'AYE' on the right; for those who intended to join India.

'NAY' on the left for those who intended to keep out.

The drill was simple. Like schoolmasters taking the roll call, the ADCs would call the princes one by one. And like schoolchildren, the rulers would walk into one of the two sections, depending on what they had decided. Watching over the drill, like hawk-eyed headmasters, were the master of ceremonies, Lord Mountbatten, the senatorial Sardar, and the architect and discreet conductor of this grand orchestra, V.P. Menon.

The ceremony, it was announced, would begin with the chancellor of the Chamber of Princes. The band fell silent. The bearers stood at attention.

'Lieutenant General His Highness Farzand-e-Khas-e-Daulat-Inglishia...Mansur-e-Zaman...Amir-al-Umra Maharajadhiraja Rajeswar Sri Maharaja Sir Yadavindra Singh Mahindar Bahadur, G.C.S.I., G.C.I.E., G.C.V.O., G.B.E., LL.D., A.D.C., the Maharaja of Patiala,' the aide took half a minute to read out the complete title of the maharaja of Patiala.

There was a hush in the hall; everyone was silent and still. Even the wind outside appeared to have died and not a leaf stirred on the trees in the garden. All eyes were on the resplendently dressed Maharaja Yadavindra Singh in his majestic Patiala-*shahi* turban, with his bejewelled kirpan tucked into his silk sash. Sardar took a deep breath;

Mountbatten pursed his lips; Menon adjusted his glasses nervously over his nose. Maharajas and nawabs watched with bated breath. Diwans and ADCs sat at the edge of their seats. As head of the Chamber of Princes, Patiala's decision would have a ripple effect.

Aye or nay? What was it going to be?

Maharaja Yadavindra Singh rose from his seat, ramrod straight, chin up, eyes looking straight ahead. As he stepped forward, one could have heard a pin drop. Turning sharply to his left, he walked straight towards the placard with three bold letters.

NAY.

A collective gasp echoed through the hall. Sardar's heart skipped a beat, Mountbatten held his breath, Menon mopped his brow.

One glance at the stunned onlookers and Maharaja Yadavindra Singh could keep up the ruse no more. Bold and boisterous, he threw up his hands and marched past the first placard – into the AYE lobby, filling the shock and silence in the room with his infectious laughter.

'Phew!' Menon exhaled as Sardar and the viceroy exchanged uneasy glances.

The maharaja's little prank lightened the sombre atmosphere and the room soon filled with peals of laughter. Despite all that Punjab had been through, the large-hearted Punjabi hadn't lost his sense of humour and ability to laugh.

A few days later, eight rulers of Punjab would meet in the banquet hall of the Moti Bagh Palace in Patiala for a solemn ceremony that would forever tie their destinies together with that of India. Maharaja Yadavindra Singh and other Sikh princes would sign away their right to defend their own kingdoms and hand it over to the Government of India by signing the Instrument of Accession.

As the days wore on, Punjab would edge closer to the precipice and fall deeper into the abyss. Thousands would wake up on 17 August to find themselves on the wrong side of Radcliffe's accursed line. Another mass of humanity would move; over a million would lose their lives; rivers would run red with blood.

It would take months; but spring would eventually return to Punjab once more. Vultures would make way for songbirds; festival music would replace cries of anguish; and fields strewn with corpses would bloom once again with mustard and corn. And, just like its babbling rivers and ripening fields, the enterprising, high-spirited, brave and resilient Punjabis would try to put the scars of Partition behind them, rebuild their lives, and move on.

◆◆◆◆◆◆◆◆◆◆◆◆◆◆◆◆◆◆◆

Postscript

◆◆◆◆◆◆◆◆◆◆◆◆◆◆◆◆◆◆◆

It is widely accepted that over a million people lost their lives during the partition of India. Between 4.5 million Hindus and Sikhs moved from Pakistan to India; about six million migrated in the reverse direction. While this story ends with the accession of Patiala, violence continued to rack Punjab and, in fact, some of the most heinous incidents took place after 15 August.

Before 1947, Master Tara Singh had insisted Sikhs were in danger from Muslims and the League. After 1947, he began to say that Sikhs were under threat from Hindus and the Congress. He was arrested along with hundreds of his followers several times after Independence for defying bans and making inflammatory speeches.

Sir Cyril Radcliffe left India the day after handing in his award and seldom spoke about his days as boundary commissioner.

Bir Bahadur Singh returned to Pakistan as an old man in 2000 and met some of the friends he had grown up with. Almost his entire village turned up to welcome him for his emotional homecoming. Survivors of Thoa Khalsa and Rawalpindi would meet every year in March at a gurdwara in Delhi to honour the memories of those who had suffered the brutalities of March 1947.

Diwan Khizar Hayat Tiwana left politics after his resignation and settled in Simla for a few years, before moving to Pakistan.

After accession, the states of Punjab were reorganized as Patiala and the East Punjab States Union (PEPSU), and Maharaja Yadavindra Singh was made *rajpramukh* of the Union. He later became the Indian ambassador to Italy. His son Captain Amarinder Singh became a Congress leader, and chief minister of Punjab several times.

♦♦♦♦♦♦♦♦♦♦♦♦♦♦♦♦♦♦♦

Did It Really Happen This Way?

♦♦♦♦♦♦♦♦♦♦♦♦♦♦♦♦♦♦♦

The maharaja's words in the opening scene are drawn verbatim from his speech of 1939, quoted in Hindol Sengupta's book, The Man Who Saved India: Sardar Patel and His Idea of India.

References to the 'Secret Sandooq' have been taken from Khushwant Singh's book The Sikhs.

The Constituent Assembly discussion scene is a compression of multiple meetings, the source material for which are Towards the Integration of Indian States 1919–1947 *by Urmila Phadnis and Narayani Basu's book* V.P. Menon: The Unsung Architect of Modern India.

All events related to Partition mentioned in the chapter are drawn from records: Partition: The Story of Indian Independence and the Creation of Pakistan in 1947 *by Barney White-Spunner;* Midnight's Furies: The Deadly Legacy of India's Partition *by Nisid Hajari;* The Great Partition *by Yasmin Khan; and* Indian Summer: The Secret History of the End of an Empire *by Alex von Tunzelmann are some of the source materials.*

Disastrous Twilight: A Personal Record of the Partition of India *by Major General Shahid Hamid and* Once a Prince of Sarila: Of Palaces and Tiger Hunts of Nehrus and Mountbattens *by Narendra Singh Sarila also throw light on the events, personalities and locations mentioned in the chapter.*

The story of Bir Bahadur Singh's family has been mentioned in Urvashi Butalia's The Other Side of Silence *and in more detail in Butalia's essay titled* 'A Necessary Journey: A Story of Friendship and Reconciliation', *which recounts inter alia Bir Bahadur's journey back to Pakistan as an old man.*

Some parts of the chapter are drawn from imagination such as the incident set in the Golden Temple, in order to throw light on the cultural and political background of Punjab. The character of Sukhwindar is also based on imagination to throw some light on the worries of ordinary people. Creative liberties have been taken with adding/editing dialogues.

The Sikh Sanksar's *special issue on the maharaja of Patiala published in December 1974; 'Master Tara Singh Souvenir (1981)' of the* Sant Sipahi *magazine;* The Akali Movement *by Mohinder Singh;* The Idea of the Sikh State *by Gurbachan Singh and Lal Singh;* and Amritsar: Mrs Gandhi's Last Battle *by Mark Tully and Satish Jacob are some of the sources for the background material on the Sikh leaders, the Sikh state demand and other Sikh matters.*

Records of discussions between Lord Mountbatten and the Indian leaders are to be found in the Transfer of Power *volumes;*

some of the leaders' quotes are taken from their public speeches to provide a gist of their position.

The Master and the Maharajas: The Sikh Princes and the East Punjab Massacres of 1947 *by Ian Copland has been the author's main source detailing the association between Tara Singh and the Sikh princes, including Maharaja Yadavindra Singh. Other books such as* The Punjab: Bloodied, Partitioned and Cleansed *by* Ishtiaq Ahmed *also refer to these meetings, as also to the meetings between Jinnah and the Sikh leaders. Some of Jinnah's statements in those scenes are drawn from his inaugural address to the Pakistan Constituent Assembly; the conversation between them has been imagined based on these sources.*

The lunch scene between Sardar and the maharaja is actually a compression of multiple meetings; reference to the lunch can be found in Rajmohan Gandhi's Patel: A Life, *while the general discussions are to be found in* V.P. Menon's Integration of the Indian States. V. *Shankar's* My Reminiscences of Sardar Patel *also throws light on several events mentioned in the chapter.*

The AIR announcement of 3 June is an extract of the speeches of the leaders; reactions of specific listeners have been imagined, while the general response is based on recorded material.

10

A Woman Takes Charge

THE STORY OF TRIPURA

PRINCELY STATE OF TRIPURA IN 1947:
present-day Tripura
AREA: 4,116 square miles (10,660 square kilometres)
POPULATION: 512,010
RULER: Maharani Kanchan Prava (ruling as regent on behalf of her minor son, after the sudden death of Maharaja Bir Bikram Kishore Debbarma)
DIWAN: Satya Vrata Mukherjee
13-gun-salute state

❋ A Dying Wish ❋

'The days ahead are going to be difficult,' Maharaja Bir Bikram Kishore Manikya Debbarma Bahadur struggled to speak, as an attendant propped up the king of Tripura on satin pillows. The late evening sun dancing into the room through the lace curtains and the fragrance of the summer blooms wafting in from the splendid gardens outside did little to uplift the sagging spirits of those in the palace's main bedchamber. 'You...must...you...' he gasped, the rest of his words morphing into a breathless whisper.

'Please...' Maharani Kanchan Prava pleaded with her husband, wringing a scarf dipped in cologne-scented water and placing it on his fevered brow, 'don't strain yourself.' She looked up worriedly at the doctor standing by the foot of the bed.

'I don't have much time, Prava...' the maharaja mustered up all his strength to speak. Their son Prince Kirit was only fourteen – too young to take over from him just yet. 'You have to take charge...'

Struck down in the prime of life by a deadly bout of pneumonia, Maharaja Bir Bikram Kishore of the ancient Manikya dynasty, which had ruled Tripura for centuries, knew his time was up. In a few months, British paramountcy would come to an end, heralding the dawn of a new era – a phase he had eagerly and enthusiastically anticipated; but destiny seemed to have other plans.

The maharani dabbed her eye with the edge of her *pallu*. The despondence in the doctor's eyes conveyed more than words could. Only thirty-nine years old, Bir Bikram had a long, promising reign ahead of him. In his short span as the ruler, he had infused new life into the kingdom – restructuring education, introducing land reforms and planning for a bright future for his people. *Was all that energy and goodness going to fall by the wayside?*

The maharaja gestured to his diwan to step closer. Satya Vrata Mukherjee leaned over the intricately carved four-poster bed.

'It is my wish,' whispered the maharaja, his eyes half closed, his speech slurred, '...that Tripura...' He paused, overcome by another harsh bout of coughing.

The maharani massaged his back; the doctor dashed forward; an attendant held out a spittoon. The maharaja waved them all away.

LAST WISH: MAHARAJA BIR BIKRAM KISHORE MANIKYA DEBBARMA

'I wish...that Tripura...accedes... to India...' the maharaja gasped, severely short of breath. 'That...' he continued, his chest heaving violently with the effort it took to speak, 'would be...the...the...right thing...to do...'

Stooping over the bed, head lowered, voice mellow, Diwan Mukherjee nodded obligingly, 'Yes, Your Highness. It shall be as you wish.'

Reciting the Lord's name over and over, the maharani massaged her husband's hand. The road ahead suddenly appeared longer, darker, bleaker. The times were turbulent and the palace abuzz with intrigues.

How would Tripura pull through?

❋ Plots in the Palace ❋

Strolling along the tree-lined walkway leading to the magnificent Ujjayanta Palace, Prince Durjoy Kishore Debbarma, younger brother of the late Maharaja Bir Bikram Kishore, linked his hands behind him, his mind a riot of plots and plans after the death of the maharaja.

'We will support your bid for the crown,' repeated Abdul Barik in earnest, his gaze darting furtively. Known to most as Gedu Mian, Barik's meteoric rise from being the royal family's elephant-keeper to the leading contractor of Agartala had taken most people by surprise. With close connections to the Muslim Leaguers through the local political party, Anjuman-e-Islamia on the one hand, and links with some members of the royal family on the other, he had smoothly manoeuvred his way around. 'In return, we only ask that you sign the accession papers in favour of Pakistan...' he whispered to the prince.

Pausing by a flowerbed overlooking a pond, Durjoy Kishore scratched his chin thoughtfully. With Dada Maharaja gone, the throne of Tripura had been rendered vacant at a crucial time. Paramountcy was about to end; Partition was around the corner. Every ruler would soon be asked to make a choice – India or Pakistan? Gedu Mian's offer intrigued him.

'Prince Kirit,' continued the Muslim Leaguer, speaking of the late maharaja's son, 'is only fourteen...still a minor'—planting the seed of rebellion in Durjoy Kishore's mind. 'If you agree, the Government of Pakistan will support your bid for the crown, and I assure you that the debt will never be forgotten by the people. You can count on that.'

As fountains danced in the centre of the pond, Durjoy Kishore's heart skipped a beat. The kingdom of Tripura comprised hills and plains. While the hilly region, belonging to the royal family, had a largely Hindu and tribal population, the

Chakla Roshanabad area of the plains, which was controlled by the British, had a large Muslim population. *Would Gedu Mian's proposal work?*

'We must act before Maharani Kanchan Prava or her supporters seize control,' urged Gedu Mian. 'There's a rumour afoot that she may take over as regent in her son's name. We... er...you...need to act soon.'

Eyes fixed upon the spire of the Jagannath Temple across the pond, Durjoy Kishore pursed his lips. As the deceased maharaja's younger brother, he was as much a contender for the throne as anybody else. His forefathers had ruled the kingdom for over a hundred years from the Ivory Throne of the Tripuris, which was said to have been a gift from the legendary Pandavas.

He nodded, locking eyes with Abdul Barik, his mind drawn in by the man's proposal.

Barik bowed to the prince in respectful deference, a crafty smile pinned to his face. The seed had been planted; all he needed to do now was wait for his effort to bear fruit.

❋ Shillong Alert ❋

Drawing the *pallu* of her saree over her head, shock and worry writ large over her delicate features, Maharani Kanchan Prava stared in dismay at the delegation of messengers bearing the urgent summons from Agartala.

She had moved to Shillong a few weeks ago, to tear herself away from the memories that now loomed like dark shadows in every room of Ujjayanta Palace. Every framed portrait, every piece of furniture, every nook and corner was a stark reminder of Bir Bikram's absence. Time and distance away from Agartala, she had hoped, would help her come to terms with her husband's untimely death. But as news of the conspiracy being hatched behind her back reached her, she realized she would have to put aside her grief for the sake of the kingdom and its people.

'Your Highness,' Thakur Prabhat Chandra Roy, a freedom fighter and staunch advocate of reform in Tripura, addressed the maharani, his voice betraying his anxiety. Over the years, Roy had worked diligently to arouse a national spirit among the people of Tripura, from braving imprisonment for opposing the British Raj to encouraging education and industrialization. 'The Muslims may be in a majority in the plains, but they are a small minority in the state. Under these circumstances, a decision to join Pakistan will be resisted by our people. Prince Durjoy Debbarma's plans will only sow discord and drive a wedge between the Tripuri people.'

The maharani sighed. 'The maharaja had conveyed his desire to join India when he uttered his last words on his deathbed,' she said softly. 'Mr Mukherjee was present...'

'Mukherjee is supporting Prince Durjoy and Gedu Mian,' cut in Prafulla Ray, another member of the delegation.

The maharani caught her breath, her anxious eyes conveying her disappointment and disbelief. *Could this be true?* 'But...' she whispered, unable to make sense of Mukherjee's sudden and inexplicable change of heart. *Had Mukherjee not promised her husband that his final wishes would be respected?*

'The area of Chakla Roshanabad in the plains is also a part of Tripura, according to the treaty between the British and Tripura signed over a century ago during the time of Krishna Manikya...' said Joysingh Debbarma, yet another member of the delegation from Agartala.

'But after the Muslim League's Direct Action Day last year, the area was forcibly taken over by the League,' Roy interrupted. 'We cannot let it fall into Pakistan's hands.'

Thakur Roy approached the maharani. As a reformer who had vociferously urged women to break free of their shackles, it now fell upon him to bolster young Kanchan Prava's confidence. 'Maharani, it is time you took matters into your own hands.'

Rising from the chair, the maharani walked to the window, inhaling the sweet scent of the rose garden below. The cool mountain air of Shillong, its lush green valleys, sweet birdsong and quiet walks had somehow helped her children cope with the sudden loss of their father. But there appeared no alternative now but to return to the heat of the fire. Watching her daughter with her riding instructor in the royal stables outside, Maharani Kanchan Prava straightened her back. If Durjoy Kishore assumed he could get away with his schemes because she was an outsider to Tripura with no political experience, he was forgetting the rich legacy of the magnificent maharanis of the Manikya dynasty.

'All right,' she said, turning to her ADC, her voice crisp and confident. 'We return to Agartala tomorrow.'

❋ Stirring up Trouble ❋

'*Naraa-e-Takbir. Pakistan zindabad!*' The slogan echoed down the narrow streets of Agartala.

Abdul Barik Khan Chaudhuri looked on in approval. His party, the Anjuman-e-Islamia, had allied with the Muslim League and together they would wrest Tripura for Pakistan.

'*Allahu Akbar!*' rose the deafening cry as hundreds, toting League flags, stormed into the city centre. '*Ladh ke lenge Hindustan* [We will take India by force]!'

'The slogans must reverberate across Tripura,' said Muslim League leader Tofazzal Ali, buoyed by the success of the League's agitations in the Chittagong Hill Tracts of Assam. There too, the League was campaigning for the region to be given to

East Pakistan. 'We must scale up. Organize demonstrations in Sonamura, in Udaipur...' he instructed the League supporters. Udaipur by the River Gomti had once been the ancient capital of Tripura before Agartala, and Sonamura was the site of the maharaja's fabulous Lake Palace.

'It will be done,' replied Gedu Mian over the shouting crowds. 'Prince Durjoy Kishore is with us. So is Mukherjee. We needn't worry.'

'Are you certain we can trust the prince?' asked the leader of the Muslim League, leaning towards Gedu Mian. 'Is there going to be a coup in the palace?'

'*Pakistan zindabad! Pakistan zindabad!*' The procession marched on.

'Trust me, brother,' Gedu Mian assured the Muslim League leader, taking his hand in his own, 'Tripura will soon belong to Pakistan.'

❋ Tripura of the Fourteen Gods ❋

On the banks of Rudrasagar Lake, the maharani's wistful eyes rested on the reflection of the dome-shaped minarets of the marble-and-sandstone Neermahal Palace, sparkling and dancing in the waters.

Two decades ago, Maharaja Bir Bikram had commissioned the spectacular royal residence, instructing his architects to build a unique water palace, along the lines of the Lake Palace in Udaipur. The Neermahal was a treasure of Tripura – a legacy of her late husband, a joy to behold. And yet, here she was, firming up talks to sell the royal properties. Looking up at the grand balconies and pavilions, Maharani Kanchan Prava felt a twinge of sadness.

'Have you heard of the *Rajmala*, young prince?' the high priest of the royal family asked young Prince Kirit. 'Do you know it traces the story of your great dynasty all the way back to the ancient days of the Mahabharata?'

Prince Kirit's eyes widened in awe as he turned to his mother. Sitting down by his side, the priest began recounting the fifteenth-century chronicle of the kings of Tripura to the boy.

'Many hundred years ago, King Tripur ascended the throne of the kingdom,' the old man started narrating the legend behind the Kharchi Puja, Tripura's grandest festival, 'but slowly, he grew arrogant towards his subjects. He began to believe that he was God himself, rather than God's earthly representative. Tired of his oppression, the people began to pray to Lord Shiva for respite from his cruel ways.'

The royal audience listened in rapt attention; the maharani stared into the shimmering waters of the lake with the palace lights mirrored in its soothing waters.

'Lord Shiva warned the king to mend his wayward ways...' the priest continued the tale, 'but when the king did not heed his ultimatum, Shiva struck King Tripur down with his mighty *trishul*. The raja's death was followed by utter chaos, disorder and lawlessness. The people, tired and hopeless, turned to Lord Shiva once more for help.'

The maharani's thoughts drifted to the daily chaos playing out on the streets of every town and city in the kingdom. Processions and

The Ujjayanta Palace is a splendid Indo-Saracenic-style building, surrounded by lakes and gardens, in the centre of Agartala. It is said that Rabindranath Tagore, a great friend to the erstwhile maharaja, named the palace. It now houses a government museum. The Neermahal Palace is also another spectacular palace situated by a lake in Tripura.

demonstrations by Muslim League supporters, and arson and looting had become commonplace, leaving the kingdom paralysed.

'This time the Lord spoke to the widow, Maharani Hiravati,' the holy man continued his story, switching to a deeper voice. "Re-establish the temple of the fourteen gods once again," Lord Shiva commanded her, "and pray every day. Celebrate the festival of Kharchi from the eighth lunar day of the month of Shravan for seven days and you will be blessed with a son who will rule over the kingdom justly."'

Prince Kirit sat up straight, drawing himself closer to his mother. The priest looked at the dowager maharani, addressing her through the boy.

THE SPECTACULAR UJJAYANTA PALACE IN AGARTALA, TRIPURA

'The queen did as she was told...and was very soon blessed with a little boy, who grew up to become King Trilochana, the best and the bravest raja of Tripura,' he said, blowing the conch as he said those words.

As the powerful, lilting note of the conch shell echoed around the stunning lake palace, to Maharani Kanchan Prava's troubled mind, the message of the legend was abundantly clear.

Kharchi Puja is a popular festival of Tripura during which the fourteen deities of the dynasty are worshipped. Hence, it is also called the Festival of the Fourteen Gods. It is celebrated over a week in Agartala, the capital of the state, during the month of July and attended by thousands.

When the kingdom is kingless and turmoil reigns, it is time for the queen to take charge.

❋ To Delhi, to Delhi ❋

Maharani Kanchan Prava sat demurely beside her father, Maharaja Yadvendra Singh Judeo of Panna, and Thakur Roy, in the office of the states minister, having journeyed all the way to Delhi to alert Sardar about the worsening problem in the north-east.

'My grandson, Prince Kirit Bikram, is a mere boy,' said Maharaja Yadvendra Singh Judeo, curling his bejewelled fingers around his wooden staff. 'My daughter, Kanchan Prava, as you know, is ruling as regent on his behalf until he attains majority.'

Sardar turned to the maharani, who was as young as his own daughter. He noticed her downcast eyes, the shadow of bereavement on her face, tense fingers resting on her knee. She had lost her husband just two months ago, but here she was, holding her own in a room full of men used to wielding authority. 'I appreciate your decision to come straight to Delhi and meet me,' he said, acknowledging her courage.

'Sir...' Maharani Kanchan Prava spoke softly, 'it was my late husband's desire that Tripura should accede to India...' she paused, her face impassive but her voice strained, 'but...the Muslim League's national guards are creating a lot of trouble in the state.'

Sardar listened attentively. Tripura had joined the Indian Constituent Assembly before the maharaja's death. Its representative, Girija Shankar Guha, had taken his place as the state's representative in the proceedings underway to determine independent India's future. It seemed but natural, therefore, that the state would align with India. But circumstances had changed suddenly, almost everywhere, after Viceroy Mountbatten's announcement of 3 June – with some states declaring independence and others aligning with Pakistan. Tripura fell on the border – the line demarcating East Pakistan would run not too far from its boundary. It was, undoubtedly, a matter of concern.

'Not a single day goes by, sir, without communal conflict or strife of some kind,' the maharani expressed her anguish. 'The League guards are carrying out extensive propaganda, pressing for Tripura to join East Pakistan. My late husband had provided shelter to over 10,000 Bengali refugees after the Dhaka riots of 1941, and then again, after Jinnah's Direct Action Day last year. But the influx now is beginning to scare the local people.'

Sardar sighed. Maharaja Bir Bikram had been a strong king. He had participated in the war for the British when the Japanese had come to Agartala's gates, and had even been honoured with the Knight Grand Cross of the Order of the British Empire. He had pushed for reform and had helped all refugees impartially after the riots. Destructive groups were now taking advantage of his demise.

THE MAHARANI TAKES MATTERS INTO HER HANDS

'You see, Tripura is bordered by Chittagong...Noakhali... Sylhet...' the maharani's father, the maharaja of Panna, explained, 'and there is a very real fear among the people that all these areas may be given to Pakistan in the final Boundary Award. Some Muslims in the state have been emboldened by this to demand that Tripura too join Pakistan. They're distributing all sorts of pamphlets and inciting trouble...'

Sardar exchanged glances with V.P. Menon. A delegation from Assam had met him only recently over the question of Sylhet in their state, expressing exactly the same fears. The geography was indeed the crux. As things stood, Tripura was accessible to India only through a narrow strip of railway route that traversed through Bengal; and there was every possibility that the boundary line being drawn up by Sir Cyril Radcliffe might circle around the north, west and south of the kingdom.

To the maharani too, the Chittagong Hill Tracts in Assam were a cause for deep worry. There was talk that the area might be given to East Pakistan despite its non-Muslim majority in order to compensate Pakistan for the loss of Calcutta. If indeed Radcliffe decided to hand over the Hill Tracts to Pakistan, it would box in Tripura, leaving the state surrounded by Pakistan on the north, west and south, with only a small territory contiguous with India through Assam on its east. Even that was blocked by a range of hills. *What if Tripura acceded to India and was then left with no land contact with India?*

'League leaders are stirring up tensions in Agartala,' the maharani pressed on. 'Rallies are being held across the state to pressurize me to accede to Pakistan...and'—she stopped, hesitating for a moment to wash the family's dirty linen in public, but left without a choice—'I am ashamed to say my brother-in-law and our diwan...are...uh...are leaning towards the Muslim League.'

'And the referendum in Sylhet,' added Thakur Roy, 'has been forcibly captured by the League after tremendous rigging.' The Sylhet province of Assam had been given the right to vote on whether to join India or Pakistan. The vote had gone against India, with thousands of Muslim League members resorting to atrocities and hooliganism to intimidate people into voting for Pakistan. 'Having taken Sylhet by force, the League threatens to capture Tripura now,' he explained, 'and fearing the Boundary Award, thousands of refugees are flocking to our borders. It has become very hard to handle.'

'I appreciate your concerns,' said Sardar, still seething over the Sylhet debacle. Nearly three-quarters of Tripura's periphery was likely to become an international border with Pakistan. He could not let Tripura turn into another Sylhet. 'India will provide military help to Tripura should anything untoward happen there,' he promised his guests.

'My people are very anxious about the boundary situation,' the maharani beseeched Sardar for his immediate attention, 'as am I.' He undoubtedly had to put out many fires across the country, but she needed him to prioritize the volcano threatening to erupt in the north-east.

MAHARANI KANCHAN PRAVA

Having grown weary of the incessant battles with the Muslim League, the Congress had agreed to Partition. However, even after the Congress had given in to so many of their demands, the Muslim League was unwilling to give peace a chance. Equally unwilling to compromise with India's security and be terrorized by League violence, Sardar turned to the maharani. 'We will keep vigilant watch in Tripura and you can rest assured...' he told her firmly, 'India will protect Tripura. You have my word.'

❋ 15 August 1947 ❋

For most people across India, it was a day of jubilation. For many, it was also a day of immense sorrow.

As caravan after caravan of battered refugees poured into Tripura from what was no longer India, but East Pakistan, Maharani Kanchan Prava prepared to deliver a message to her anxious people.

'Our state is released from British paramountcy today,' she declared triumphantly. 'As such, Tripura is to march on a new path, free from interference,' she said, trying to make her subjects see the silver lining in their suffering.

'You know the council of regency has been formed to perform the administrative functions of the state under my presidentship,' she announced her decision to appoint a council of ministers, in which she had included two Hindus and one Muslim, to ensure fair representation of both communities. 'The council of regency will assist me in administering the state until my son attains majority.'

The message was meant to make it absolutely clear and send out a strong signal to all within and outside the palace – that she, the maharani, was in charge – and end the machinations of those who wished to topple the crown.

'Late Maharaja Bikram Kishore Manikya Bahadur granted administrative reforms for his beloved subjects,' the maharani reminded the people of the legacy to which her son was the rightful heir, and went on to list the various progressive measures planned for the people. 'It will be my first duty to carry on with those initiatives and, in accordance with the wishes of the maharaja, Tripura will have a full democratic constitution. The interests of the people of Tripura and their economic welfare are our foremost concerns,' she said, assuring the Tripuris of a return to normalcy and a brighter future.

And, finally, Maharani Kanchan Prava announced the crucial decision, leaving no scope for ambiguity. 'According to the will of all classes of people, I accept the title of regent or representative of the ruler from today on behalf of my beloved son, Shri Srijuta Maharaja Kirit Bikram Kishore Debbarma Manikya Bahadur,' she declared boldly. 'And I would like to announce today that, as regent and representative of the state, I have signed the accession papers in favour of India...' she continued, driven by the desire to fulfil her late husband's wishes and reassured by Sardar's promise. 'Tripura has acceded to India.'

As the maharani's gentle voice carried her firm message to her people, the clouds cleared and the sun peeped out from behind grey skies, shining over the troubled kingdom of Tripura. The days ahead would witness more violence; League workers would resist; the communists would join the fray. But Sardar Patel would keep his promise, and take swift and bold measures to save Tripura, ending yet another frightful tussle between India and Pakistan, over yet another princely state.

♦♦♦♦♦♦♦♦♦♦♦♦♦♦♦♦♦♦♦

Postscript

♦♦♦♦♦♦♦♦♦♦♦♦♦♦♦♦♦♦♦

Tripura, a 13 gun-salute state, was one of only three kingdoms of the north-east to be bestowed with a gun salute. Events in the kingdom had an important bearing upon the entire region.

Even after accession, Tripura continued to face problems. There was much propaganda in East Pakistan by the Muslim League that Tripura belonged to East Pakistan, including news of preparations to invade Tripura and impose an economic blockade. The home ministry received this intelligence and Sardar Patel dispatched Akbar Hydari, the governor of Assam, to keep an eye on Tripura, and took timely action, including having minister S.V. Mukherjee and Prince Durjoy Kishore Debbarma removed and exiled from the state.

The state was subsequently integrated into India in 1949 as a part-C state administered by a chief commissioner. Initially a Union Territory, Tripura was granted full statehood in 1972.

Tripura faced a mounting refugee crisis after Partition with thousands coming in from East Pakistan, which led to several years of ethnic conflict between the people in the state.

♦♦♦♦♦♦♦♦♦♦♦♦♦♦♦♦♦♦♦

Did It Really Happen This Way?

♦♦♦♦♦♦♦♦♦♦♦♦♦♦♦♦♦♦♦

The maharaja's death just before Independence and the subsequent events regarding the conspiracy are based on records drawn mostly from references in A Constitutional History of Tripura *by Dr Jagdish Gan-Chaudhuri. Passages in Anindita Ghoshal's book* Refugees, Borders and Identities: Rights and Habitat in East and Northeast India *also mention these episodes.*

The scene at the Neermahal Palace has been imagined to provide a glimpse into the history and legends of the state.

All dialogues have been imagined based on historical events, as there is no record of what exactly was said during these meetings and exchanges.

An invaluable source of information about Tripura is a Facebook group called Triveg, where its group administrator, Dr Sourish Deb Barma, regularly puts out thoroughly researched and footnoted posts on the history of Tripura. An additional source of information for this chapter was Bikash Chaudhuri from Tripura, who shared his first-hand knowledge of some of the personalities and events featuring in the story.

11

Twist in the Tale

THE STORY OF JUNAGADH

PRINCELY STATE OF JUNAGADH IN 1947:

in present-day Gujarat

AREA: 3,337 square miles (8,642 square kilometres)

POPULATION: 670,719

RULER: Nawab Sir Mahabat Khan Rasul Khanji III

DIWAN: Shah Nawaz Bhutto

13-gun-salute state

❋ In League with the League ❋

Lighting up a Craven "A" cigarette, Jinnah examined the map of Junagadh before him. The 13-gun-salute state was a seafaring kingdom in Kathiawar but shared no land connectivity with Pakistan. And yet, as he waited in his new study in Karachi for a phone call from the diwan of Junagadh, he couldn't help but wonder how that little princely state could become a key player in his masterstroke.

Junagadh was a political oddity. It had a Hindu majority in population and an eccentric nawab who was Muslim. Parts of other princely states that had acceded to India were interspersed in Junagadh; and fragments of Junagadh were enclosed within the boundaries of its neighbouring states. It had the holiest of Hindu and Jain temples, and a staunch Muslim Leaguer named Shah Nawaz Bhutto as diwan.

'Mr Bhutto on the line, sir,' Jinnah's ADC said, interrupting his musings.

Jinnah cleared his throat and picked up the receiver, 'Good morning, Shah Nawaz. What's the news?'

'Uh...not good, I'm afraid...' sighed Bhutto, the Sindhi Muslim Leaguer from Karachi, who had taken over only recently from his ailing predecessor as Junagadh's prime minister. 'The nawab's constitutional adviser, Mr Nabi Baksh, has advised him to join India...' Bhutto apprised Jinnah. 'And the nawab himself appears to favour participating in an association of Kathiawari states.'

'Hmm...' Jinnah threw his head back to gaze at the ceiling. 'Well, that can change.'

'Quaid-e-Azam, the nawab has just returned from a holiday in Europe,' said Bhutto through the crackling line. 'I am doing my best to convince him.'

'Good...' Jinnah released a puff of smoke. 'You must keep at it.'

'But there are other voices...' added Bhutto, 'regional voices, urging the nawab to join India.'

SHAH NAWAZ BHUTTO: I'M TRYING MY BEST TO CONVINCE THE NAWAB TO JOIN PAKISTAN...

'Junagadh must not fear Indian threats,' Jinnah reassured him. 'You are not far from Karachi by sea. Pakistan will not allow Junagadh to be stormed...'

'Right, sir...' Bhutto pursed his lips, amused at the jolt Junagadh's accession to Pakistan would give the Congress high command.

'But remember...' added Jinnah, lightly touching the little green flag of Pakistan on his desk, astutely aware that the timing of a strike was almost as critical as the blow itself. 'Keep out under all circumstances until 15 August'.

❋ Gut-Wrenching Blow ❋

Sardar's heart sank as he caught sight of the screaming headline. His mouth dry, his mind numb, he bent down and picked up the newspaper. He had just returned from his morning walk in Lodi Gardens, past euphoric crowds waving the tricolour, celebrating India's dawn of independence; and here, already, was the first stab in her back. His eyes scanned the article:

JUNAGADH ACCEDES TO PAKISTAN!

The government of Junagadh has been faced with the problem of making its choice: accession to India or Pakistan...After anxious consideration and careful balancing of factors, the Government of Junagadh has decided to accede to Pakistan...

SARDAR: A PART OF PAKISTAN INSIDE INDIA!

Sinking into a chair, Sardar squeezed his eyes shut.

It was 17 August 1947, only days since they had all taken their first breath as citizens of a free nation. Partition had been a bitter pill to swallow, but they had forced it down with a heavy heart in the hope that it would settle all disputes – like two warring brothers parting in the interest of long-term peace. But even before the bloody wounds and shameful scars of that colossal separation had had a chance to heal, Pakistan had chosen to deal India a deceitful and devious blow.

Sardar exhaled deeply. Junagadh was in Kathiawar, surrounded by Indian territory and the nerve centre of trade in Gujarat. Now, in Pakistan's hands. As an Indian, he was affronted. As a Gujarati, he felt pained.

Freedom for India had been a lifelong dream.

Freedom had come.

Yet India remained an elusive dream.

❋ We Are Not Sleeping! ❋

'Sardar, have you heard?' V.P. Menon burst through the door, his wavy hair dishevelled, his eyes heavy with dark circles.

'Hmm...' nodded Patel, deep in thought, sitting across from his secretary Shankar and C.C. Desai, the additional secretary of the States Department.

'After all our courtesies and telegrams, we are left to find out from newspapers,' Menon threw up his hands. 'The nawab did not even have the decency to inform us himself!'

Sardar swallowed hard, shocked and distressed in equal measure as he reflected on the rumblings that were reaching his ears – about Junagadh recruiting Baluchis and Hurs from Pakistan in its state forces; of Muslims flooding the state in huge numbers and buying up property; about Hindus fleeing the state; of the local Bahauddin College being affiliated with Sind University in Karachi. As much as he hated to admit it, the truth was that Jinnah had dealt India a devastating blow.

'Only last week the nawab held meetings with his people,' Menon paced up and down the office room. 'Most were in favour of joining India and the nawab had indicated he would go along with them. Clearly, it was all just eyewash!'

'A farce,' Sardar nodded. 'The nawab and Bhutto must have been in cahoots with Mr Jinnah all along.'

'The Jam Sahib of Nawanagar had mentioned to me the likelihood of Junagadh joining Pakistan,' Menon went on. 'But Nabi Baksh, the nawab's constitutional adviser, met me in Delhi and told me that he had advised the nawab to accede to India.'

'But Pakistan is not even connected to Junagadh,' exclaimed Sardar's daughter Maniben, placing cups of tea and a plate of fruit on her father's desk.

'Nobody is going to be happy about this.' Sardar stood up, disturbed that the sacred pilgrimage site of Somnath, revered by millions of Hindus, was now within the territory of Pakistan.

'Everyone has criticized the nawab,' Patel's secretary Shankar pointed out reports in the vernacular newspapers. 'Citizens, political groups, leaders in Kathiawar and outside—'

'This could set a precedent,' interrupted Menon. 'The nizam of Hyderabad will be emboldened to follow suit. Can you imagine what will happen then?'

'We will have pockets of Pakistan within India.' Sardar read the writing on the wall, linking his hands behind his back.

Desai felt a chill down his spine. It was a terrifying thought.

'All right, let's approach this constitutionally,' Sardar got down to practicalities. 'First, write to the high commissioner of Pakistan, pointing out that this accession is invalid on the grounds of the areas being geographically incontiguous.'

'Right away.' Menon pulled up a chair and flipped open his diary.

'Sardar,' Desai interjected, 'the Indian government should consider drastic measures in Junagadh...perhaps...perhaps cut off food supplies,' he suggested. 'Perhaps dispatch armed troops to Rajkot as a show of our strength...or get smaller districts within Junagadh to accede to India – get an entry point into the area.'

Sardar nodded. This was a question of India's prestige, a time for bold steps. 'Write to the railway board,' said Sardar. 'Ask them to stop the supply of coal and petrol to Junagadh.'

Shankar scribbled hurriedly.

'Contact the communications department,' Sardar continued with his instructions, eyes closed in concentration. 'All calls in and out of Junagadh with Pakistan to be tapped and intercepted with immediate effect. Menon, you will leave for Junagadh immediately to meet the nawab.'

Menon nodded, his back straight, his mood lifting.

'And put a call through to Defence Minister Baldev Singh,' Sardar added. 'A company of the mobile military of the state armed police must be kept in readiness to go to Rajkot immediately. Tell the Jam Sahib in neighbouring Nawanagar to have his troops ready to move in.'

Shankar hurried off as Sardar picked up his cup and put it back down. Cold tea and cold feet – neither held any appeal for him.

Hyderabad had not acceded to India. And Sardar had granted the nizam an extension.

Kashmir had not decided one way or the other. Sardar was willing to see why.

But Junagadh, deep within Gujarat, had gone and joined Pakistan. And he was not going to sit by and allow the grass to grow under his feet.

❋ Dodgeball with Cricket ❋

The nawab of Junagadh, Sir Mahabat Khan Rasul Khanji III, was known to be quite an eccentric character, and stories about his colourful lifestyle had not escaped Menon's ears.

'So, tell me,' Menon asked, turning to Nilkanthrai Mohanlal Buch, the soon-to-be regional commissioner, who was accompanying him by car from Rajkot to Junagadh, 'how many dogs does the nawab have?'

'Can't say exactly...' laughed Buch. 'Last I heard...more than eight hundred.'

'You can't be serious,' Menon gasped. He was no stranger to the flamboyant lifestyle and quirks of the princely order, yet the nawab's dog count astounded him.

'A few years ago...' the driver jumped at the opportunity for some friendly banter, 'Nawab Sa'ab declared a state holiday for the wedding of his favourite dog, Roshanara, with Bobby. He even invited the viceroy to the event.'

Forgetting his pressing anxieties for just a moment, Menon laughed heartily.

'Sa'ab...the bride was decked up in diamonds and carried in a silver *palki* to the Durbar Hall,' the driver went on. 'The groom was dressed in brocade and gold, and led by a military band. They say the nawab spent 300,000 rupees on it.'

'For a wedding of dogs?' Menon exclaimed, amused and outraged in equal measure as he gazed out at the countryside. Mahatma Gandhi, Father of the Nation, was a son of Kathiawar; as was Muhammad Ali Jinnah, the founder of Pakistan. The great cricketer Ranjitsinhji Jadeja, the erstwhile Jam Sahib of Nawanagar, was a royal scion of this land; as was this oddball nawab he was about to meet. What diversity in the offspring of this land, he thought to himself as the car came to a halt. 'What's the matter?' he enquired.

'Another border crossing,' Buch shrugged.

They had stopped for the fifth time in less than an hour at one crossing after another along their short journey. Kathiawar, Menon reckoned, a patchwork quilt of about 200 kingdoms and fiefdoms, simply had to be united into one region in the future.

And yet, it was the presence of these very tiny estates that he was counting on now. As Desai had pointed out, Mangrol,

THE ANIMAL-LOVING NAWAB OF JUNAGADH ONCE ARRANGED A GRAND WEDDING FOR HIS FAVOURITE DOGS

Manavadar and Babariawad – three seemingly insignificant estates held by chieftains were under the nawab of Junagadh. If Menon could somehow persuade them to throw off Junagadh's yoke and ally with India – perhaps the tide could change in India's favour?

***

'Here we are,' said Buch, as the car drew up outside a cosy guest house. 'I can see Mr Bhutto is waiting for you.'

'Hope your journey was pleasant,' the diwan of Junagadh came forward to greet Menon as soon as he stepped out of the car.

'Quite eventful, really,' Menon shook hands with Bhutto, then followed him up the stairs, as Buch took his leave and left. 'Especially the aggressive toll collection every few miles! Anyway, I have come bearing an important message for the nawab from the Indian Cabinet'—he got to work without wasting a moment. 'I must meet him immediately.'

'I...I'm afraid that won't be possible,' replied the diwan, scratching his toothbrush moustache as they seated themselves in the shaded porch.

'What do you mean?' demanded Menon, thirstily gulping down a glass of cool lemon juice served to him.

'The nawab is unwell.'

'But this is urgent,' Menon put down the empty glass.

'Mr Menon,' said Bhutto, looking helpless, 'he has been in bed for ten days.'

Menon stared at Bhutto, certain that this was a ruse. 'I have to deliver this message personally to the nawab.'

'The doctor has advised the nawab to rest,' the diwan shrugged, looking apologetic.

'Please, Mr Bhutto,' pleaded Menon, 'I will only be a few minutes...'

'Sir, I myself have not met him for the last four days.'

Menon heaved a sigh. That the nawab would evade a discussion on the matter of accession had certainly crossed his mind; but that the diwan would be so brazen as to block any chances of a meeting was unsettling.

'All right,' he nodded, realizing there was little point in pressing the matter. 'I'll meet Prince Muhammad Dilawar,' he said, referring to the nawab's heir apparent.

'I'm afraid, that is not possible either,' Bhutto shook his head.

'Why?' Menon remarked sarcastically. 'Is he sick too?'

'Er...no,' replied the diwan matter-of-factly. 'The prince is away playing cricket!'

❋ Leaving No Stone Unturned ❋

Frustrated by his failed attempts to meet the nawab and his son, Menon headed back to Rajkot. Aware that if the problem of Junagadh were not resolved quickly, the whole of Kathiawar

OTHER TERRITORIES INSIDE JUNAGADH: ROUGH MAP TO SHOW THE UNIQUE CONDITION IN JUNAGADH STATE

could disintegrate into a battleground, he was reminded of an adage he had learnt in Delhi: *ghee seedhi ungli se na nikle, toh ungli tedi karni padti hai* (when the straight path bears no fruit, give the crooked way a try).

As things stood, Junagadh was territorially in India, but legally in Pakistan. But all was not lost - at least not yet. The whole of Kathiawar was a patchwork of kingdoms - some embedded within others, like a box inside a box. Among them, Mangrol, Manavadar and Babariawad - three feudatory states that had been under the control of Junagadh - could prove to be the game changers, if Menon played his cards right.

Sipping his tea in the luxurious, high-ceilinged reception of the Rajkot Residency, Menon glanced at his watch. The chief of Mangrol, whom he was scheduled to meet first, was over an hour late. Mangrol, a semi-independent Hindu-majority kingdom, sandwiched between Porbandar and Junagadh, was ruled by a Muslim Sheikh. Would the Sheikh go against the nawab?

A car pulled up in the driveway and spluttered to a halt. Menon stood up.

A rotund man in a bright turban emerged, hurried up the stairs and into the foyer of the building where Menon was waiting. 'I am sorry the Sheikh could not come to see you'— he pressed his hands together conveying both salutation and apology at once.

'I wanted to meet the Sheikh directly,' said Menon, annoyed that far from resolving the conflict, even speaking with anyone of consequence was proving impossible. 'I had made it clear in my telegram that I wanted to meet the Sheikh and his constitutional adviser.'

'The constitutional adviser is away in Delhi...' the emissary lowered his voice, 'and the Sheikh...he is also anxious to meet you...but...uh...worried that his car will be stopped...'

'Stopped? By whom?'

'The Junagadh authorities,' whispered the emissary. 'He will have to pass through Junagadh to get here.'

Menon clicked his tongue, enraged to be thwarted by trivial hurdles.

'I will send a car for him with a special number plate,' he said. 'He will not be stopped.'

***

'The Khan is suffering from boils,' the diwan of Manavadar came to meet Menon the next day, singing a similar song about his chief.

Menon rolled his eyes. Manavadar was a tiny state with a Hindu majority, surrounded by Junagadh on three sides and ruled by a Muslim Khan. The state's allegiance could prove critical.

'I wish the Khan could have come himself,' Menon sat back, his shoulders slumped.

'Sir, Manavadar has already entered into a standstill agreement with Pakistan,' the diwan said firmly.

'Do you understand what this means?' Menon leaned forward. 'The economic interests of your state are bound to the rest of Kathiawar! Is it not obvious that you will be isolated? An island of Pakistan surrounded by India on all sides?'

The diwan slurped his tea noisily, unnerved by Menon's fierce glare and stern tone. Karachi had warned him to take a tough stand and not give in under any circumstances. 'Uh...I am only conveying the Khan's position,' he mumbled.

'The Khan's position is unacceptable,' Menon thundered. 'Go back and tell him that! And come back tomorrow with your final decision.'

'I...I...will be back tomorrow morning,' the diwan put down his cup and made a hurried exit. Menon exhaled hard as he watched the man leave. He knew the fellow was never coming back.

***

'Thank you for sending a special car for me,' smiled the Sheikh of Mangrol.

Menon offered him a seat, glad that at least one of the rulers he had wished to meet had finally shown up.

'My constitutional adviser,' the Sheikh got straight to the point, 'has advised me to accede to India.'

'Excellent advice,' Menon drummed his fingers on his knees. 'And what is your view?'

'I agree with him...' nodded the Sheikh.

Menon's spirits lifted.

'I...uh...am willing to join India...' the Sheikh said hesitantly, '...but I have...uh...one condition'.

'Yes?'

'The Indian government should recognize Mangrol as an independent state.'

'Look...with the lapse of paramountcy, every state has become independent,' Menon explained, relieved to discover the Sheikh's moderate expectation. 'We are all starting with a clean slate.'

The Sheikh beamed, glad to know that Mangrol's long years of subservience to Junagadh would finally come to an end.

Menon eyed the smiling Sheikh and handed him the documents. 'The Instrument of Accession to India and the Standstill Agreement...for your signature.'

The Sheikh flipped through the pages; he had seen the draft already. He nodded, then placed them on the table and pulled out his pen.

Menon sat back, looking on with quiet contentment as the Sheikh signed the papers.

Junagadh inside India's territory was legally in Pakistan.

Mangrol inside Junagadh's territory was legally in India.

Swords drawn. Horns locked. Game on.

India? Or Pakistan? Who was going to blink first?

❋ The Trap ❋

Jinnah poured himself some whisky as his sister, Fatima, unpacked a chest of photographs and books in their new home in Karachi. It was not quite like the stately home they had lived in on Aurangzeb Road in Delhi or the palatial mansion on posh Malabar Hill in Bombay, but this one was special, because it was in the land of his dreams.

'Look at this,' Fatima smiled, pointing to a picture of Jinnah standing outside the high court in Bombay. 'How young you look!'

Dina, Jinnah's only child, was born in London in 1919 to Jinnah and his wife Rattanbai Petit. After her mother's death at a very young age, Dina was raised by Jinnah's sister, Fatima, who moved into their home to help. It is said that Dina later developed strained relations with her father as he did not approve of her marriage to Neville Wadia, who came from a wealthy Parsi industrial family. After Partition, while Fatima accompanied Jinnah to Karachi, Dina opted to stay back in India. The Wadia family that she married into owns many businesses in India, including Bombay Dyeing and Britannia Industries, and is co-owner (among three others) of the Punjab Kings team in the IPL.

Giving up her career as a dentist, Fatima had devoted herself to look after her brother and his young daughter, Dina, after the death of Jinnah's wife, Rattanbai (or Ruttie), had left Jinnah distraught. Now, Fatima was all the family he had left – his own daughter having chosen to remain in India after Partition.

Smiling slightly, Jinnah looked at himself in the framed mirror on the wall. His youth spent, an ailing man stared back – his emaciated frame, sunken eyes and protruding cheekbones nearly giving the secret away. His lips, darkened from years of heavy smoking, whispered death – a daily dose of fifty cigarettes and Cuban cigars awaiting its inevitable toll. The doctors had given him less than two years. He was determined to make every day count.

'And look at this,' chuckled Fatima, holding up a large volume of *The Complete Works of Shakespeare* she had unpacked from the box. Jinnah smiled at the memory that flashed before his eyes – of his youthful student days in England, when he had dreamed of becoming a theatre actor, enthralled by *Romeo and Juliet* and all of Shakespeare's masterpieces.

Still, it was Junagadh more than Juliet that occupied his thoughts that evening, as he lit up a cigarette despite strict advisories from his doctors. Now, in the December of his life, his dream had finally come true. And yet, it was incomplete. Kashmir, that gorgeous crown of India, had still not fallen into Pakistan's lap. Old or dying, he would fight to the bitter end, and Junagadh was, indeed, turning out to be a game changer. Any attempt India made to escape the situation there, Jinnah reckoned, was going to work to Pakistan's advantage.

If the Indian government gave in to the nawab's decision, it would mean that India accepted the right of a Muslim ruler to take a Hindu-majority state into Pakistan, regardless of geography and religion. Pakistan could then turn that argument around to claim the greater prize – Hyderabad – which was also a Hindu-majority state ruled by a Muslim.

If, on the other hand, the Indian government decided to challenge the nawab's decision on the basis that a Hindu-majority state could not join Pakistan, and contest it with force, that too would serve him well. On the one hand, he could present Pakistan as a victim – a small fledgling nation, bullied by its large, aggressive neighbour. But, more importantly, it would set a precedent and give Pakistan an excuse to intervene in Kashmir, a Muslim-majority state with a Hindu ruler, where the maharaja was still vacillating.

Alternatively, if India did neither and demanded a plebiscite instead, claiming that the people of Junagadh had the right to decide the future of their state, Pakistan could press for the same principle to be applied in Jammu and Kashmir. And a plebiscite in Muslim-majority Kashmir, Jinnah was certain, would go against India.

No matter which way the wind blew, only good fortune awaited Pakistan, mused Jinnah, as he rifled through more photographs from Fatima's trunk. He caught sight of his picture with Gandhi, standing outside Jinnah's palatial Malabar Hill house in Bombay. What Gandhi had become for India, was what he had once aspired to be. *Why, hadn't Sarojini Naidu even called him the harbinger of Hindu-Muslim unity! But the Congress had insulted him, spurned him and rejected every offer of friendship. Gandhi's two apostles – that impetuous Nehru and shrewd Vallabhbhai – had never given him the respect or recognition he deserved.* The Hindu press had hounded him, labelled him a traitor, ignored his contribution to India's freedom. Bitterness rose like bile within him.

Tapping his cigarette on his jade ashtray, he mulled over the meeting scheduled the next day with Lord Mountbatten, who had travelled from New Delhi to Karachi. No...*the story was far from over yet; for the old fox still had some tricks up his sleeve. The pendulum had swung; it was about to be game, set and match for Muhammad Ali Jinnah.*

❋ Arzi Hukumat ❋

'We declare,' proclaimed Samaldas Gandhi, Congress leader of Kathiawar, 'that from this day forward, we are the Arzi Hukumat – the provincial government of Junagadh.'

A triumphant cry rose from the massive crowd – a sea of Gujaratis residing in Bombay gathered in large numbers for the rally. Their life and their faith, their travel and their trade were inextricably linked with Junagadh, and they simply couldn't allow the nawab to turn it over to Pakistan.

A PARALLEL GOVERNMENT IN JUNAGADH: ARZI HUKUMAT ZINDABAD!

'*Bharat Mata ki jai! Arzi Hukumat zindabad!*' they hollered with gusto, determined to do whatever it took to take back Junagadh – even support a parallel government, if need be, with money and volunteers.

'For now, we will set up our headquarters in Rajkot, within Indian territory,' announced the towering U.N. Dhebar, another of the many Congress leaders who, inspired by Gandhi, had given up an illustrious legal career to serve in the freedom struggle. Dressed in khadi, Dhebar was a simple Gandhian, unaccustomed to rallying crowds. But these were unusual times. 'The capital will be moved to Junagadh as soon as the situation eases,' he added.

'Samaldas Gandhi will be our president,' Dhebar continued, holding up the hand of Mahatma Gandhi's nephew.

'*Samaldas Gandhi zindabad. Bharat Mata ki jai*,' the swelling crowd in Congress caps responded.

'We issue this proclamation on behalf of the people of Junagadh,' Samaldas Gandhi went on. 'The nawab has forfeited his right to claim the allegiance of his subjects.'

'Down with the nawab!' The clamour rose louder.

'We hereby announce the constitution of the provisional government comprising six members, with all power, authority and jurisdiction vested in the nawab of Junagadh,' declared Samaldas Gandhi. 'The people are very angry, but we must remember at all times that we are followers of Gandhiji. All protests will be carried out peacefully. And we urge the Indian government,' he continued, 'to take note of the crisis and initiate immediate action.'

'*Arzi Hukumat zindabad!*'

'*Samaldas Gandhi zindabad!*'

'Down with the nawab!'

'Down with the nawab!'

❋ Checkmate ❋

'How can the Sheikh retract his accession?' an agitated Menon, now back in Delhi, drew up a chair in Sardar's living room. 'This is unbelievable!'

Sardar rose slowly from the small breakfast table.

'Please'—Maniben came in, holding a glass of water along with some pills—'it's time for your medicines.' Sardar had been unwell for nearly five years now, waking up each morning to intense pain in his bowels. And yet he went about his day like an active sixteen year old.

'The Sheikh now claims he signed it under duress.' Sardar gulped down his pills. 'Or, as he puts it'—he pointed towards the telegram on the table—'under extraordinary circumstances.'

'What "extraordinary circumstances"?' Menon threw up his hands. 'The Sheikh signed the Instrument of Accession most willingly in front of me. He even asked that the Government of India recognize Mangrol as an independent state.'

'The Sheikh says here that,' said Sardar, handing the telegram to Menon, '*if Mr Menon had been here for an hour longer, I would have retracted the accession before he left.*'

'What a bunch of lies,' Menon bristled.

Sardar walked towards the coffee table at the end of the room upon which sat a neatly laid out rosewood chess set. 'We have reasoned with them, warned them, requested them,' he said, pulling up a chair, 'but they remain obdurate. We cannot be blind to the consequences.'

'On my way back, I met Morarji Desai,' Menon scratched his receding hairline. 'As home minister of Bombay, he assured me he can keep things under control there. But he has requested that you take a firm line about Junagadh. He has also asked for more ammunition for the police. I also met Samaldas Gandhi,

Dhebar and the rest. They have set up a parallel government after a huge rally in Bombay—'

'I understand their frustration,' Patel cut him short, looking at the pieces on the chessboard, 'but a hasty step could invite disaster. It's not as if we need another cause for conflict with Pakistan.'

'Sardar, there is a lot of anger in Kathiawar against the nawab,' Menon sat across from Sardar. 'I'm afraid it will soon turn into rage against the Indian government if we don't act. The Jam Sahib of Nawanagar told me categorically – if Delhi doesn't take action, the people will see it as a sign of weakness.'

'Look...this situation needs to be handled delicately,' said Sardar, eyeing the chessboard. 'Hyderabad is still sitting on the fence. We do not want the nizam to go the Junagadh way. News coming in from Kashmir is not encouraging. A misstep in Junagadh could backfire.'

'No doubt Jinnah is using Junagadh,' Menon leaned forward. 'To him, Junagadh is merely a pawn.'

'Of course.' Sardar placed his fingers thoughtfully upon a black pawn on the chessboard. 'Jinnah is playing the pawn so that Pakistan can have the queen.'

'Kashmir...' Menon picked the piece off the board.

'Hmm...' nodded Sardar, moving his pawn forward, 'and I do not mind playing along as long as India wins the king.'

Menon locked eyes with Sardar.

Pawn. Queen. King.

Junagadh. Kashmir. Hyderabad.

How would this stalemate end?

❋ Veiled Threats ❋

A dashingly handsome man with a keen eye on the future, Lord Louis Mountbatten wanted history to remember him kindly. But presiding over the vivisection of India, and the horrors of Partition that it entailed, had blotted and blotched the glory he wished to have associated with his name. And yet, as Governor General of India now, life had given him another chance – to set right his legacy, to create a unified India and to leave behind a subcontinent in peace. Many a fire still blazed between India and Pakistan, but he hoped to put them all out before the end of his term.

'Can we speak about Junagadh?' he broached the issue, festering for three months now, with the prime minister of Pakistan as they came out of the conference room after a round of meetings in Karachi.

'Frankly,' began the Pakistani premier, Liaquat Ali, adjusting his glasses over his round face, 'the Government of Pakistan spent nearly a fortnight discussing the difficulties involved in Junagadh's accession. But as Veraval in Junagadh is not far by sea from Karachi, we decided to accept the nawab's offer to join Pakistan.'

Leaning against a wall behind him, Mountbatten gazed out at the makeshift tents that formed the offices of the Government of Pakistan. Furniture and stationery were in short supply; files dispatched from Delhi had arrived in a damaged condition, or not at all; staff was insufficient. The Government of India, on the other hand, had continued to function ceaselessly from its seat of power in New Delhi, even acting uncharacteristically churlishly at times in accommodating its new neighbour – India, for instance, had six printing presses, but Sardar had refused to send even one over to Pakistan. 'Legally, your action may be right...' he conceded, willing to see why Liaquat Ali seemed disgruntled, 'but it is indefensible both morally and ethically.'

'Even from a practical point of view,' pitched in Hastings Ismay, who had accompanied Mountbatten to Pakistan,

'Veraval port is nearly 300 miles from Karachi and closed during the monsoon months.'

'The decision to join India or Pakistan was left to the rulers,' said Liaquat Ali, as if to suggest that there was little in it for them to question, 'wasn't it?'

'Look, Pandit Nehru is suggesting a referendum to allow the people of Junagadh to decide,' Mountbatten offered an alternative, knowing Liaquat Ali to be the more reasonable of the two men at the helm of affairs in Pakistan. He had put the matter to Jinnah just the previous day, only to have it brushed aside. And, in Pakistan, where nobody dared to contradict Jinnah, if there was any chance at all of a dialogue about Junagadh, it rested with Liaquat Ali. 'Nehru seeks to invite the Government of Pakistan to submit the matter to the people of the state. Why not settle this amicably?'

'Well, the rulers had been told that they had the right to decide,' the Pakistani premier shrugged, aware that a referendum in the Hindu-majority state of Junagadh would go against Pakistan. 'And the nawab has decided, of his own free will. What have the people got to do with it? And, pray, tell me,' he added casually, 'if a referendum can be held in Junagadh, why not in Kashmir?'

'Just look at the map, Liaquat,' Mountbatten placed his hand on the prime minister's shoulder, making one more attempt to try to make the man see reason, 'it is not a viable solution for Junagadh to be in Pakistan. Liaquat, you know that as well as I do—'

'Why not?' Liaquat Ali grinned mischievously, using the same line as Jinnah. 'What will India do about it? Go to war with Pakistan?'

The deceitful trap dawning upon him, Lord Mountbatten stared aghast at the premier of Pakistan.

'Go ahead, then,' Liaquat Ali suppressed a slight smile, acutely aware that the outcome was well and truly in Pakistan's bag. 'Let India commit an act of war in Junagadh, and then we'll see what happens.'

❋ Setting a Precedent ❋

Meanwhile, Junagadh was also on the minds of those in New Delhi, taking centre stage in a series of frenzied meetings. 'Over a hundred thousand Hindus have fled from Junagadh, sir,' Menon flagged up the ground realities. 'Junagadh has sent troops into Babariawad. People are losing faith in the Indian government. We need to act – and act fast.'

'Any aggressive military action in Kathiawar,' warned General Rob Lockhart, chief commanding officer of the Indian Army, 'may lead to war between India and Pakistan. And with the bulk of our forces involved with internal security, the army is in no position to wage war.'

'Yes, I understand,' Nehru nodded glumly. Drained by colonial rule, bleeding from Partition, scarred by weeks of the most horrendous violence, India had neither the will nor the resources to fight a war. 'It would impair our international standing.'

'But Pakistan has committed an act of war,' Sardar thumped his palms on the table. 'They committed the first act of aggression. Junagadh has sent its troops into Babariawad. And Babariawad, like Mangrol, had also acceded to India.'

'A Pakistani sloop has reached Veraval even as Junagadh's forces entered Babariawad,' Menon pressed on. 'Pakistan is not responding to any of our telegrams and letters...'

Distressed by the dilemma, Nehru bit his lip. For his entire life, he had devoted himself to the call of ahimsa by Gandhi; and he wished to avoid war at all costs. *Hadn't India seen enough violence over the last few months*?

'I have just returned from Karachi,' said Lord Mountbatten. 'I know that Pakistan is in no position to declare war. They have barely been able to set up their government there. Their military commanders have put it to me in writing. Pakistan will not fight. We mustn't do anything that would show India in a poor light.'

'Just think about it,' Patel threw up his hands, 'a state with more than 80 per cent Hindus is being forcibly dragged into a Muslim nation. This wholly contradicts Jinnah's two-nation theory. A head-on challenge to India. An act of perfidy.' He paused to stare at Mountbatten, then at Nehru. 'If Junagadh is allowed to rebel, it would embolden the others. Already, that Razvi has been inciting his followers in Hyderabad, mocking the Indian government for not being able to rein in a small state like Junagadh.'

'The nizam has assured me that Hyderabad will sign the Instrument of Accession,' said Lord Mountbatten.

'Hadn't Junagadh assured us? Not once, but twice?' Sardar shot back, deeply suspicious of the pro-Pakistan bias in many a British officer, including Claude Auchinleck, the joint commander of the Indian and Pakistani armies. It appeared that the British wanted to keep Pakistan in their good books so their government could count on a friendly partner among the Islamic nations whenever required, and to cultivate a base in the region to counter any Soviet threats in the future. 'This is an act of war...plain and simple,' Patel said, pounding the table with his fist. 'India. Must. Respond.'

'I'm afraid the British officers in the Indian Army would not be able to engage in a war between the two dominions,' said General Lockhart.

'This is unacceptable,' Patel objected vehemently, his eyes turning to Nehru.

Circumspect and cautious, Nehru took a deep breath. Lately, differences had driven a wedge between Sardar and him. Nehru abhorred conflict, preferring a path of conciliation;

Sardar's approach was blunt and straightforward. Nehru obsessed about the world's perception of India; Sardar cared more about what mattered to Indians. Nehru spoke of lofty ideas; Sardar stayed focused on ground realities.

Yet, despite their differences, they were bound to each other by their love for India and their desire to serve her. Nehru nodded slightly, alert to Sardar's cue. They could not let the military chiefs disobey the Cabinet. 'I protest at this stand taken by the military'—Nehru swung around, pointing an accusing finger at the army chiefs. 'I agree with Sardar. This is a political decision.'

'We are only doing our duty'—shrugged General Lockhart, taken aback by the abrupt swing in the prime minister's mood —'in,' uh, drawing the Cabinet's attention to the facts...'

'What you are saying, in effect,' Nehru fixed General Lockhart with a fierce stare, 'is that if the Indian government decides to deploy the army, you will not obey.'

General Lockhart exchanged glances with the naval chief who had accompanied him. Clearly, the political leaders of India were not going to be bulldozed by India's military.

'This is not only disloyal,' said Nehru, turning to face Mountbatten, 'it is also highly improper!'

The generals looked at Mountbatten warily, then backed down without further protest. In India, the military would adhere to the political heads, and not the other way around. In reconciling their differences at the key hour of reckoning, Nehru and Patel had set a crucial precedent.

'We are prepared,' said Sardar definitively, 'to give Pakistan one more chance to withdraw its troops from Babariawad, which has acceded to India. One. Last. Chance!'

***

'Junagadh has not withdrawn its troops from Babariawad. And, now, they have marched into Mangrol,' Prime Minister Nehru apprised the gathering at their next meeting. 'Now this, you will all agree, is an attack by Pakistan on Indian territory.'

'Let us not forget,' said Lord Mountbatten, 'that the Sheikh of Mangrol has withdrawn his decision to join India.'

'But the Sheikh signed the document right in front of Menon,' argued Nehru. 'He had the chance to consider it for nearly three hours. How can he claim that he signed it under pressure?'

'One may contest it, but as things stand today,' Mountbatten continued playing devil's advocate, 'legally there is no accession to India.'

'On the other hand,' Nehru put on his lawyer's hat, 'it could well be said that the retraction was made under pressure from Pakistan.'

'Quite right,' agreed Sardar,

'And his accession was accepted by the Government of India,' added N. Gopalaswami Ayyangar, senior statesman and former diwan of Jammu and Kashmir, who had been working on the states' matter closely.

'As I see it, there can be no objection to Indian troops being deployed in Mangrol,' Nehru tapped the table with his index finger. 'It is a part of India and has been attacked by Pakistan. We can't wait any more.'

'And besides,' added Patel, 'there is no dispute at all about Babariawad.'

'Junagadh too claims Babariawad as a part of its territory,' Mountbatten pointed out. 'It claims that the chief of Babariawad had no right to accede to India independently.'

'Last week, the nawab avoided meeting me,' Menon said, 'but the diwan indicated he is open to a joint meeting with Pakistan to sort this out.'

'There is simply no question of negotiation,' Sardar brushed off the notion with a wave of his hand. 'Junagadh's troops must be withdrawn from Mangrol and Babariawad. Only then can we think of talking to Pakistan.'

'Menon,' said Nehru, 'shoot off a telegram to the diwan, pointing out the constitutional position of Babariawad and Mangrol. In the meantime, our armed forces must be prepared to occupy Babariawad and go to the assistance of Mangrol.'

'Why not refer the matter to a neutral third party like the United Nations?' suggested Mountbatten, conscious of the buzz from London, which had reached his ears, that Winston Churchill had been led to believe by Pakistan that Mountbatten was biased in favour of India. His reputation was at stake here.

'Absolutely not,' Patel brushed aside the very idea.

'We have accepted the accession of Mangrol and it is Pakistan that has a problem with it,' Nehru shot back. 'Let Pakistan go and seek arbitration if it must, not us.'

'Well, this has created other problems,' pointed out N. Gopalaswami Ayyangar. 'Other states in the region that have acceded to India are now asking for protection, else they say they will withdraw their accession.'

'There is simply no other way out,' Patel shook his head. 'We have to send in our military...'

'The Kathiawari defence forces will be posted on Junagadh's borders,' Nehru cut middle ground. 'Inside Indian territory,' he stressed. 'They will cross into Junagadh if – and only if – Junagadh takes offensive action.'

'But let it be clear,' added Sardar with steely determination, 'that, if needed, India shall be prepared to occupy Junagadh by force.'

❋ Taking Flight ❋

'Hurry up,' Nawab Mahabat Khan hovered over the treasurer by the *toshakhana*. 'Pack it all up.'

'*Ji, huzoor!* It's done,' the treasurer placed silk bags containing gold coins and precious jewels into a large metal case. Two attendants stood by to carry the heavy box to waiting cars.

'Your Highness, the pilots are ready,' an attendant hurried in to inform the nawab.

'Good...good...' the nawab mumbled incoherently. 'Come... come on, now...on the double! Roshanara, Bobby, Shamsher, Rubaina, Roxana – time to go,' he hollered.

Dogs in diamond-studded collars ran up to their master, sensing the alarm in his voice. German shepherds and bull terriers, border collies and scotties, dogs of every colour and size, a retinue of their trainers and attendants in tow, barked incessantly to get his attention.

'Shhh...shhh...it's all right, my beauties...it's going to be fine,' the nawab petted them. 'Get them all into the cars,' he told the kennel keepers.

'Where are we going?' Munawar Jahan Begum, the nawab's senior-most wife, hurried out.

'To Karachi.'

'Now? Why?'

'Get ready, Begum Sahiba,' he said to an astonished Munawar Jahan. 'And inform the other begums. Pack up everything. We're all leaving.'

'The jewels and the cash are stowed in the cars, Nawab Sa'ab,' the treasurer informed the nawab.

'What about the shares and securities? I told you I want everything. Pack it all!'

The treasurer rushed away once again.

'Ask the doctor to get ready,' the nawab ordered another bewildered member of his staff. 'We cannot possibly travel without a veterinarian.'

'But...why...why are we leaving?' Munawar Jahan demanded. 'That too in such a hurry?'

'Don't you understand?' the nawab cried. 'The Indian Army is at our gates. They have already taken over Babariawad. It is only a matter of time before they finish us off. Get moving now!'

'*Ya Allah!*' Munawar Jahan hurried away, calling out to the nawab's other wives.

'Don't forget to gather the children!' the nawab called after her as an afterthought, as she disappeared into the *zenana*, and he hobbled off to check on the dogs.

Half an hour later, when the royal family, complete with staff, vet, dogs and all, were accommodated into the waiting cars, the nawab turned to look back at his palace, lit up in golden hues under the late afternoon sun. Passing his mother Ainabibi's palace, he was filled with anguish; and, by the time the car sped off towards the Chowk, he was nearly in tears.

THE GIR FOREST: THE LAST HOME OF THE ASIATIC LION

As the muezzin's fluty call to *azan* from the marbled courtyard of the Jama Masjid filled the evening air, a disheartened nawab stepped into the Dakota and looked back at the silhouette of the Girnar mountains that cradled his kingdom.

'Where's Sadiq?' Dadiba Begum, the nawab's fifth wife, suddenly shrieked in horror, looking all over the little plane for her son. 'Sadiq! I've forgotten Sadiq.'

'Tch!' the nawab clicked his tongue impatiently. 'Go back and get him,' he said to his wife, annoyed. 'And come to Karachi later. We can't wait.'

As a weeping Dadiba Begum disembarked, the nawab threw one last longing glance at the densely forested hills in the

The story about the nawab's love for dogs and the lavish state marriage for his favourite dogs reflect the famously quirky lifestyle of Indian royals. It is said that while he took his dogs carefully to Karachi, he forgot to take one of his children. His wife had to get off the plane and go to Pakistan later with the child. It is also said the nawab spent much time dressed as a woman, putting up pantomimes for his family and guests, raising many eyebrows. Due to all this, despite being known as a kind and fair ruler, he had the reputation of an eccentric.

In its heyday, the Asiatic lion inhabited a large territory stretching all across the continent. Today, it is found only in the Gir National Park near Junagadh. The reason for this is attributed to the nawab's love for animals and the special care he took to preserve forests, particularly the dwindling lion population around Junagadh. His kindness towards animals also extended to his banning cow slaughter, promoting the famed Gir cow and the Kathiawari stallion.

distance, where Asia's last remaining lions roared, wondering if he would ever see those magnificent beasts again.

Teary-eyed, he mumbled, 'Who will look after my lions now?'

❋ A Call for Help ❋

'The nawab and his family have left for Karachi,' a frantic Bhutto updated a fuming Jinnah over the telephone. 'The Secret Service had warned us of a serious security threat to his family.'

'Damn!' Jinnah swore under his breath. 'Why did you allow him to leave?'

'Quaid-e-Azam, after joining Pakistan, we received hundreds of messages from our Muslim subjects congratulating us. But today the Muslims of Kathiawar seem to have lost all enthusiasm for Pakistan...' Bhutto sounded dejected, defeated.

'I'm sure the Congress is trying its best to create trouble there,' Jinnah grumbled. 'Any encroachment on Junagadh is a hostile act by India on Pakistan.'

'Samaldas Gandhi and his followers have set up a parallel government, the Arzi Hukumat,' Bhutto's voice was laced with panic. 'They are on their way from Bombay to Rajkot, bringing village after village under their control. They've reached as far as Kuntyana. And...and...the Indian officials are threatening to attack Junagadh from both inside and outside. We are surrounded by Hindu rulers on all sides. Pakistan must come to our defence,' Bhutto pleaded.

Jinnah clicked his tongue impatiently. The nawab's hasty decision to fly the coop was going to foil his carefully laid plans.

'Jinnah Sa'ab, our revenue, our railways, our customs have all hit rock bottom. The food situation is dire...' Bhutto pressed on. 'It's like...we're being devoured by wolves!'

Bhutto had good reason to be alarmed. Conditions in Junagadh were volatile and unstable, and only worsening by the day. Alarmed Hindus were leaving the state in droves. Businesses were shutting down. The state earnings were in a shambles.

'Pakistan will come to your aid, Shah Nawaz,' Jinnah assured the diwan. 'Have patience. A generous allotment of foodgrains has been sanctioned for Junagadh.'

'Sir, Muslims here are being subjected to all kinds of hardship and humiliation. People are completely disheartened. They want the matter settled at the earliest.'

'Look...seven companies of the Crown police are being deployed to Junagadh,' Jinnah's voice was tense.

'If Pakistan is unable to come to our rescue at this critical moment, we are finished,' Bhutto predicted the worst.

'We are doing the best we can, Shah Nawaz. What else do you suggest?'

'Perhaps a joint meeting with India?' Bhutto said meekly. The sending in of troops, Bhutto knew, would lead to needless violence. 'I want to avoid bloodshed at all costs,' Bhutto pleaded. Partition had left them all stunned. Nobody had anticipated the kind of monstrosities and depravities it had unleashed and continued to unleash in Punjab and Bengal. He wanted none of that in Junagadh.

'Let India withdraw its troops from Junagadh's borders first,' Jinnah said curtly, the little state in Kathiawar now no more than a sacrificial lamb in his game for power and prestige; a mere pawn that could be let go, for the greater prize. 'Pakistan will back off in Junagadh,' Jinnah ended the conversation, 'if India will let go of Kashmir!'

❋ Entrapped! ❋

'Pakistan must withdraw its troops from Babariawad first,' Nehru pressed Pakistan's prime minister who was visiting

Delhi for a meeting of the joint defence council. 'The chiefs of Babariawad have declared their right to accede to India.'

'Babariawad is a part of Junagadh...and Junagadh is a part of Pakistan,' retorted Liaquat Ali. 'In fact, it is India that needs to call off its troops from the Junagadh border.'

'They will stay there and not go beyond, provided the Junagadh troops are withdrawn from Babariawad and Mangrol,' Nehru shot back. 'In any event, not until the legal positions of both are established.'

'Very well, then. Let's obtain an independent legal opinion about the claims of Babariawad and Mangrol.'

'But that does not help us decide the question of Junagadh,' Nehru was exasperated.

Sitting between the premiers of India and Pakistan, Lord Mountbatten watched them argue like schoolboys.

'The people of Junagadh are up in arms...they are against the nawab's decision,' Nehru continued.

'The ruler has the absolute right to decide without reference to the people,' Liaquat Ali Khan stood firm.

'Would India be willing to hold a referendum in Junagadh to know the will of the people there?' Lord Mountbatten intervened with a question. 'And will both of you agree to abide by its result?'

'India objects to the nawab's decision to join Pakistan...' Nehru's reply was measured. He paused, acutely aware of the conundrum into which India had been thrown by Jinnah. On the one hand, a referendum in Hindu-majority Junagadh would undoubtedly go India's way; but on the other, its repercussions could cost India dearly in Kashmir. '...And...is...willing to abide by a referendum in Junagadh.'

Liaquat Ali's lips curved into a slight smile.

If India could challenge the decision of the ruler of Junagadh, Pakistan could do the same in Kashmir.

If India could take the matter to the people for a referendum in Junagadh, Pakistan could do the same in Kashmir.

If India could argue that Hindu-majority Junagadh ought to remain in India, Pakistan could do the same with Muslim-majority Kashmir.

What went for Junagadh, would have to go for Kashmir.

'I would assume India will follow the same principle in other states as well...' Lord Mountbatten added, 'if such a need does arise.'

Drumming his fingers on the table, Liaquat Ali waited, like a hunter by a snare.

Nehru heaved a sigh, remembering his letter some months ago to Bakshi Ghulam Mohammad, the Muslim Conference leader in Kashmir. *Circumstances have conspired against us, and we have been caught in a net*, he had penned to describe India's predicament. Looking up at Liaquat Ali's smug smile, Nehru knew those words had rung true. The destiny of Kashmir would be determined by the twist of fate in Junagadh.

Jinnah had checkmated India and trapped them all in a vicious net!

❋ Throwing in the Towel ❋

The room was filled with gloom: tense faces, drooping shoulders and grim eyes as half a dozen members of the Junagadh state council filed sombrely into the assembly hall. Larger-than-life oil paintings of golden retrievers and labradors attired in silken brocades and jewel-encrusted collars gazed down at the glum gathering.

Diwan Shah Nawaz Bhutto watched the members take their seats, wondering if this would be their last meeting. The nawab had fled Junagadh, leaving his council in charge of the state.

'The situation arising from the economic blockade is very disturbing,' began Captain Harvey Jones, senior member of the council. 'Law and order has broken down. The Arzi Hukumat have taken over Navagadh and Kuntyana. This requires a complete reorientation...' Jones remarked, looking around at the other members for their reactions.

The council members nodded wordlessly.

'...which might involve a reversal of the earlier decision to accede to Pakistan,' suggested Jones, spelling out the writing on the wall.

'I understand,' mumbled Bhutto, resigned to the fate that Junagadh might, after all, slip out of Pakistan's grasp. 'I am prepared to hand over the government...' he said, his voice barely audible, 'to Samaldas Gandhi and the Arzi Hukumat.'

'But have you heard from the nawab?' asked an elderly member of the council, a tad perturbed. 'How can one just hand over power like this?'

'Yes, the nawab has been in touch,' replied the diwan, extracting a sheet of paper from the file before him. 'In his last message from Karachi, the nawab has asked me'—Bhutto read from the telegram—'to use judicious discrimination, as the situation demands, to resolve the issue.'

'Any such arrangement will only be temporary and pending honourable settlement, of course,' said Jones. 'So...shall we speak to Samaldas Gandhi?'

'The Muslim Jamaat of Junagadh is apprehensive about that,' said the elderly member. 'If at all such a move is made, they wish that power be handed over to the Government of India and not the Arzi Hukumat.'

'Fair enough,' Jones shrugged.

'I will wire all the concerned parties immediately,' said Diwan Bhutto. 'I hope we are able to resolve this at the earliest.'

❋ Midnight Matters ❋

It was past midnight when Menon pulled up in his car outside 1 Aurangzeb Road. Walking to the porch, he peeped in through a window. Everything was ominously dark and silent. He walked over to the door and rang the bell.

A light flickered on inside, followed by shuffling footsteps. The door opened. 'What's wrong?' asked Sardar's daughter Maniben, alarmed to see Menon at this hour.

'You must wake up Sardar...' said Menon, 'it's urgent.'

'He has only just gone to sleep, that too after much difficulty...' Maniben protested, letting Menon inside. 'Lately his pain has been excruciating.'

'I know,' Menon looked apologetic, 'but this cannot wait.'

'Is this about Junagadh?' asked Maniben.

A door opened inside. 'Menon?' Sardar appeared in the living room, tossing a light shawl over his shoulder. 'What's the matter?'

'I'm sorry to bother you so late, Sardar...' Menon began apologetically.

'Never mind...tell me,' Sardar sat down; his breathing laboured, his eyes surrounded by dark circles. Overworked, tired and unwell, Sardar had taken India to the threshold of freedom and past it. And yet, there was neither rest nor respite for the seventy-two-year-old.

'I am coming directly from Panditji's house...we just got a call from Mr Buch regarding Junagadh,' Menon explained. 'Bhutto has written to Mr Buch saying that he is willing to hand over power to the Indian government...under protest.'

'Hmm...' Sardar massaged his knees.

'I have drafted a reply from our government to the Government of Pakistan – if you could take a look...' Menon handed him the draft.

Maniben turned on a second light. Sardar drew the page closer and began to read:

> The Government of India accedes to the request of Diwan Shah Nawaz Bhutto of Junagadh to take over the administration in Junagadh with a view to avoiding disorder and chaos. We desire to find a speedy solution to the problem in accordance with the wishes of the people of Junagadh. We would like to discuss the question and other matters affecting Junagadh with Pakistan at the earliest.

'The rest of it is all right, but make no offer of a referendum,' Sardar handed the sheet back to Menon. 'There is simply no need to refer to the wishes of the people.'

'Prime Minister Nehru has approved this draft, sir...'

'Look...the nawab made a mistake under pressure from those bent upon mischief, and found support from Pakistan,' said Sardar. 'Now the nawab has fled. The administration has collapsed. The diwan himself has offered to hand over Junagadh to the Indian government. What more is required to justify stepping in?'

'The decision of the nawab to accede to Pakistan has to be reversed legally,' Menon argued. 'A referendum is the only way. And besides, it is only a matter of formality. We all know it will work to India's advantage.'

'That is not the point, Menon. The majority there are non-Muslims...' Sardar paused, a coughing spell swallowing up his words as Maniben brought him a glass of warm water. 'A referendum is unnecessary. Even uncalled for. Why do you want a millstone around your neck?' Sardar struggled to speak.

For the next half an hour, Sardar argued against taking the vote of the people of Junagadh. Menon debated it, Sardar challenged it, as Maniben and the ticking clock looked on.

'Fine! Send the telegram if you insist'—Sardar finally gave in. 'But...ensure that you say nothing in the telegram that appears friendly.'

Menon nodded, then stood up to leave, apologizing once again for the intrusion at such an ungodly hour.

'*Chalo*, another chapter comes to a close,' mumbled Sardar, rising slowly and making his way to his bedroom, knowing that sleep would elude him, as it so often did.

Would gaining Junagadh result in losing Kashmir?

Only time would tell.

♦♦♦♦♦♦♦♦♦♦♦♦♦♦♦♦♦♦♦

Postscript

♦♦♦♦♦♦♦♦♦♦♦♦♦♦♦♦♦♦♦

Early on 9 November, Indian troops entered Junagadh state and occupied its capital without resistance. The administration was taken over by the Indian regional commissioner.

Brigadier Gurdial Singh, who led the Indian troops on the mission, had been a victim of Partition. He had lost his entire family and property in the communal killings that ravaged Punjab only a few months ago. Keeping his personal suffering aside, he conducted the army operation to occupy Junagadh without any communal bitterness or hatred. Speaking of the takeover, Menon writes in his book *Integration of the Indian States*: 'A deputation of Junagadh Muslims assured me later that they had nothing to complain of either during or after the occupation. The credit for this must go to Brigadier Gurdial Singh, Samaldas Gandhi and Buch.'

Ultimately, a referendum was held in Junagadh on 20 February 1948, under an officer who was neither Hindu nor

Muslim. Of the 201,457 registered voters, 190,870 cast their vote. Of these, 190,779 (more than 99.95 per cent) of the people voted to join India. Only 91 votes went in favour of Pakistan.

U.N. Dhebar became the first chief minister of Saurashtra, later formed by merging various princely states in the region.

Pakistan claimed that India's actions were a violation of Pakistan's territory – a breach of international law and an act of hostility. For several years, Pakistan laid claim to Junagadh, even depicting it as a part of its official map.

Like the nawab of Junagadh, the Sheikh of Mangrol, the Khan of Manavadar and Diwan Shah Nawaz Bhutto all subsequently moved to Pakistan. The nawab, later regretting his hasty flight, requested the Indian government to be allowed to return to India. That never came about. Shah Nawaz Bhutto's family continued to wield power in Pakistan and his son, Zulfikar Ali, and granddaughter, Benazir, both later became prime ministers of the country.

◆◆◆◆◆◆◆◆◆◆◆◆◆◆◆◆◆◆◆

Did It Really Happen This Way?

◆◆◆◆◆◆◆◆◆◆◆◆◆◆◆◆◆◆◆

The conversation between Jinnah and Bhutto that opens the chapter, and the episodes that follow, are derived from sources, including V.P. Menon's The Story of the Integration of the Indian States.

The scene with Jinnah reminiscing has been imagined to provide the reader with a glimpse into Jinnah's life, background, his thoughts and relationships – the material for which has been drawn from biographies of him, including an account written by his sister, Fatima, titled My Brother.

The rise of the Arzi Hukumat, the flight of the nawab to Pakistan and other events narrated here, are based on books such as The Man Who Saved India: Sardar Patel and His Idea of India *by Hindol Sengupta,* India's Bismarck: Sardar Vallabhbhai Patel *by B. Krishna and* V.P. Menon: The Unsung Architect of Modern India *by Narayani Basu, among others.*

Several meetings of the Cabinet and the defence committee with Nehru, Patel, Menon, Mountbatten, Ismay and others over the Junagadh issue have been compressed into two meetings to keep the narrative crisp and pacy. Letters have been converted into conversations to keep the flow informal.

Dialogues, in some cases, are verbatim extracts of what the parties involved had said. In several cases, the language is too formal and wordy to be used directly and has been suitably modified. However, in all cases, the dialogues represent the position taken by each party in the story.

12

Sitting on the Fence

THE STORY OF JAMMU AND KASHMIR

PRINCELY STATE OF JAMMU AND KASHMIR IN 1947:
present-day Jammu and Kashmir, and Ladakh
AREA: 82,258 square miles (213,047 square kilometres)
POPULATION: 4,021,616 approx.
RULER: Lieutenant General Maharaja Sir Hari Singh
DIWANS: 1. Pandit Ram Chandra Kak;
2. Janak Singh; 3. Mehr Chand Mahajan
21-gun-salute state

❋ Fishing for Trouble ❋

'Kashmir shall not join Pakistan,' Maharaja Hari Singh declared emphatically, as his station wagon bumped along the road flanked by towering poplars and swaying willows, leaving behind fields of saffron and mustard, and headed towards the mountains dotted with ancient Hindu temples and revered Sufi shrines.

Viceroy Mountbatten tore his eyes away from the picturesque valley blooming with zinnias and dahlias, to look at his host in surprise. 'Are you sure about this?' The viceroy cocked his head.

The gurgling waters of the River Lidder splashed over pebbles and babbled around the bend as the car made a sharp turn alongside. An unbroken range of snow-capped mountains came into view. For one breathtaking moment, worldly matters were forgotten.

'Let me tell you,' the viceroy continued after a pause, 'Mr Jinnah has assured me that you will be given an honoured place in Pakistan.'

'Uh...no...' Hari Singh's manner was typically guarded. 'Not Pakistan.'

'Well, the choice is yours, of course,' the viceroy said with a shrug.

'I do not wish to join India either,' Hari Singh clarified. 'Jammu and Kashmir shall be independent.'

'I beg your pardon?' The viceroy's eyes narrowed.

'Look...' the maharaja pointed to the pine forests ahead, 'this land has everything – stunning snow-covered mountains, serene lakes, crystal-clear rivers, wildflower meadows, beautiful gardens...' He paused, inhaling the crisp spring air. 'I will turn my kingdom into the Switzerland of the East!'

'Your Excellency,' Ram Chandra Kak, the maharaja's diwan, addressed the viceroy from the rear seat. 'What do *you* think Kashmir should do?'

'You must consider your geographical location,' the viceroy replied, 'the political situation and the composition of your population.'

'Well,' Kak clicked his tongue, 'in other words you advise us to join Pakistan.'

'Either India or Pakistan...' the viceroy turned back to the maharaja. 'You can't be independent!'

'Why not?' countered Hari Singh. 'Switzerland is a neutral state in Europe, isn't it?'

MAHARAJA HARI SINGH: KASHMIR SHALL JOIN NEITHER INDIA NOR PAKISTAN!

'Your state is very large, and your people are spread thin across Ladakh, Jammu and Kashmir,' Mountbatten said, scratching his chin. 'Besides, you are landlocked and not self-sufficient.'

'Whose resources are adequate to meet all their needs, Your Excellency?' Kak asked matter-of-factly.

Mountbatten sighed; this was precisely the situation he dreaded. Kashmir was too close to Russia to be left independent. Britain would prefer the area being in strong, capable hands, to guard against the Soviets turning their ambitions southwards in Asia.

'Come, Dickie!' the maharaja said to the viceroy, pulling up at a clearing by the river beside his deodar-wood-finished fishing lodge. 'Time for some trout fishing!'

The viceroy stared at the maharaja in bewilderment. A few months later, he would promise to bring Patel a basketful of apples: in other words, rally the princely states together to ally with India. But, for the moment, seated beside the nonchalant Hari Singh, who was treating the viceroy's visit as no more than a pleasure trip, he was going to have to make do with just a handful of fish!

❃ The Caged Lion ❃

Even as the hereditary king of Jammu and Kashmir was out fishing, the man hailed by Kashmiris as the king of their hearts, was confined to a jail cell.

'Jinnah's two-nation theory is rubbish,' scoffed Sheikh Abdullah with a dismissive wave of his hand. 'I will never accept the premise that Muslims and Hindus are separate nations.'

Incarcerated by the maharaja on charges of sedition, Abdullah, the president of the National Conference, a key political party in the state, paced the visitors' room in Srinagar Central Jail.

'So, what is to become of Kashmir?' his young daughter, Suraiya, enquired. The people called her father 'Sher-e-Kashmir'. What future did the resistance against Maharaja Hari Singh have without the Lion of Kashmir?

'What about Jinnah?' asked Khalida, his other daughter.

'No...' Abdullah shook his head firmly, 'Kashmir has no future with Pakistan. Last year, when I raised the cry for the maharaja to quit Kashmir, Jinnah opposed me, declared it a movement of renegades,' he reminded his family. 'Now, suddenly, he wants to paint Pakistan as the champion of liberty of the Kashmiri people? No, Kashmir has no future with Pakistan,' he repeated.

'Well, at least that's one thing that you and the maharaja agree on,' smiled Begum Akbar Jehan, handing her husband some walnuts she had brought along.

'*Alhamdulillah*! Praise be to God, Begum. You've got to throw yourself into the movement,' Abdullah encouraged his wife. 'Lead by example – the women and the youth must work together to build the Kashmir of our dreams.'

SHEIKH ABDULLAH: KASHMIR HAS NO FUTURE WITH PAKISTAN...

Suraiya smiled. The maharaja had crushed the movement but not her father's spirit. Rising from humble origins as the son of a poor shawl maker, he had gone on to become a beacon of light for ordinary Kashmiris.

'You are witnessing history in the making,' Abdullah's voice quivered with emotion. 'We will have a liberated Kashmir where Hindus and Muslims will live together in peace and prosperity. Together we will build a Naya Kashmir!'

❋ A Flame in the Heart ❋

'I knew this would happen,' Nehru pounded the table, face wan, cheeks sunken, heart bleeding for his beloved Kashmir. 'The maharaja is the master of evasion.'

Sardar Patel sat in stoic silence. Gandhi placed his hand on Nehru's shoulder, sensing his pain.

'He simply refused to discuss the matter'—Mountbatten threw up his hands in exasperation—'and took me off on fishing trips!'

'What about Sheikh Abdullah's release from jail?' asked Nehru. 'Did you get a chance to discuss that with the maharaja?'

The viceroy shook his head. 'The maharaja promised to meet me on the last day but did not show up, claiming he was ill.'

'Unbelievable!' Nehru fumed. 'Sheikh Abdullah is the pulse of the people. We must work towards his release.' Maharaja Hari Singh's Dogra ancestors had bought the Valley from the British colonialists for 75 lakh rupees, one horse, twelve goats and three cashmere shawls. It seemed outrageous that such an arrangement could determine the future in a world embracing democracy.

Patel threw Nehru a troubled glance. While the interim prime minister was an admirer and supporter of Abdullah, Patel preferred to tread more carefully. And, yet, Kashmir was a frontier state of utmost importance for India. 'I'm sure the Muslim League will make capital out of this situation,' Patel said grimly. 'I'm certain Jinnah has approached the maharaja.'

'I met Jinnah,' said the viceroy. 'He denies it.'

'The maharaja's regime is unpopular,' Nehru continued angrily. 'His opponents are being punished and jailed, denied food, and fuel for keeping warm! The maharaja's police is firing at common people...the brutalities are endless. Kashmir cannot go on like this! I must go to Kashmir at once.'

'Your presence is needed here in Delhi, Jawahar,' the viceroy cut in, 'with only days left for the transfer of power.' Amid all the uncertainties during his trip, one thing had been crystal clear to Lord Mountbatten: Hari Singh and Kak harboured a bitter hatred for Nehru. His going to Kashmir would only exacerbate the situation.

'Between visiting Kashmir when my people need me and being prime minister, I prefer the former,' Nehru retorted crisply. 'Kashmir is like a flame in my heart! When I think of Sheikh Abdullah behind bars, I hang my head in shame...'

'Jawahar...I am prepared to go in your place,' Gandhi stepped in at a nod from the viceroy.

'Bapu, the journey will be hard on you,' Nehru protested.

'I insist on going.'

'Have you forgotten how the maharaja welcomed you on your last visit?' Patel made a snide jibe. Nehru had been detained by the maharaja's police when he had tried visiting Abdullah a year ago. 'Neither of you needs to go.'

'I agree,' added the viceroy. Wasn't he glad the pragmatic Patel was helming the States Department rather than the impetuous Nehru! 'You cannot dedicate so much of your time to a single state at this juncture.'

'All right,' Nehru relented. 'Bapu...you must meet Sheikh Abdullah, and get the maharaja to secure his release.'

'I will try my best,' Gandhiji promised, holding Nehru's hand. 'Let's leave the rest in God's hands.'

❋ Balancing Act ❋

Diwan Rai Bahadur Pandit Ram Chandra Kak ran his hands over the miniature ornamental Kashmiri houseboat on the mantelpiece outside Jinnah's study. An archaeologist by training, nothing pleased the diwan of Kashmir more than exploring ancient ruins scattered around the Kashmir Valley, digging up clay figurines and dating old antiques, piecing together the glorious history of this ancient land of great scholars and saints. Waiting outside Jinnah's office on the eve of India's independence, Kak wondered if he would ever find the time to wear his archaeologist hat again.

Glancing at the newspapers stacked on the side table, Kak was amused by the irony of his situation: the Hindu press painted him as pro-Pakistan; the Muslim media labelled him pro-independence; Delhi called him pro-maharaja – when all he wanted was a fair deal for the people of Jammu and Kashmir.

'The Quaid is ready to see you...please come in.' Jinnah's young private secretary, Khurshid, peeped into the hallway.

Kak stood up, adjusted his coat and strode into the study.

'Good afternoon, Mr Kak,' Jinnah stuck out his bony hand to greet him. 'I'm glad you agreed to meet us.'

Kak stared in disbelief at Jinnah's pale face and emaciated frame, as he exchanged polite greetings with him and Liaquat Ali Khan, who was also in the room. The leader of the Muslim League had lost much weight since Kak had last seen him.

'Kashmir has a Muslim majority, Mr Kak,' Jinnah got straight to the point, gripping his jade cigarette holder as he sat down. 'It is only right and proper that the state accedes to Pakistan.'

'Ladakh is largely Buddhist and Jammu has a large number of Hindus,' countered Kak. 'We need to factor in their wishes as well, sir.'

'The majority...' Jinnah reiterated, tapping his cigarette for emphasis on the rim of the crystal ashtray.

'...an overwhelming majority,' Liaquat Ali Khan clarified.

'An overwhelming majority...' Jinnah corrected himself, 'is Muslim; is it not, Mr Kak?'

Kak nodded slightly. There was no ambiguity on that count.

'Look...' said Jinnah, sensing Kak's discomfort, 'by immediate accession to Pakistan, you are likely to get far better terms from Pakistan than you will get later.'

'I understand,' said Kak evenly, 'but the maharaja would like Jammu and Kashmir to stay independent after 15 August.'

'I see...' Jinnah sat back in his chair, exchanging glances with Liaquat Ali Khan.

Kak shifted his gaze from Jinnah to his deputy and back, trying to read their response.

'Honestly, Mr Kak, I do not mind if Kashmir does not accede to Pakistan...' Jinnah confessed, sounding quite candid. Then, wagging his index finger at the diwan, he added, '...just as long as you don't join India.'

❋ A Milky Rebuff ❋

'Vaishnava jana to tene kahiye je peeda paraayi jaane re...'
(Those called the people of Lord Vishnu understand the pain of others...)

Gandhi's favourite hymn echoed down the waters of the Jhelum while cries of '*Mahatma Gandhi ki jai!*' reverberated through Lal Chowk, the city centre of Srinagar. Hundreds thronged the roads and bridges, many perched atop buildings and trees, and even jostled on boats and riverbanks to catch a glimpse of the Mahatma.

Adjusting her headscarf, Begum Akbar Jehan, sitting beside Gandhi on the raised wooden platform, began reciting selected verses from the Quran after the hymn. When the recitation was over, Gandhi turned to Sheikh Abdullah's wife. 'I see thousands here...and I am unable to distinguish between a

Kashmiri Hindu and a Kashmiri Muslim. You are all one people. You have one language, one culture...'

The begum pressed her palms together and bowed to the Mahatma, her eyes moist.

'Courage, my dear child,' Gandhi blessed her. 'You must not lose heart.'

'*Mahatma Gandhi ki...jai*,' the crowds shouted.

'India will be liberated on 15 August,' a man in the crowd screamed. 'What of Kashmir?'

'What can we do? What can the people do when our Sheikh is behind bars?' another voice demanded.

GANDHI: THE WILL OF THE PEOPLE IS PARAMOUNT...

'Will you not speak to the maharaja about releasing our leader?' asked a young woman.

'I am not here on a political mission or to make speeches,' Gandhi replied, eyeing Ram Chandra Kak sitting glumly in the front row. 'I am here to meet you people...that is all.'

Kak stiffened his shoulders, irked by the cloak of purity concealing the politics. Who in their right minds was going to believe there was nothing political about Gandhi's visit to Kashmir!

'I want to say this,' said Gandhi, 'if all parties involved – India, Pakistan, the maharaja, the people – can come together, it would prevent much trouble. But the will of the Kashmiri people...' he concluded, holding up his index finger, 'what you decide...that is paramount.'

'*Mahatma Gandhi ki...jai!*' the crowds chanted as Gandhi stood up to leave for the City Palace. '*Mahatma Gandhi zindabad!*'

Waving to the crowd, Gandhi hurried to the car that was waiting to take him to meet the man who held the reins of Kashmir's future in his fumbling hands.

***

Bowing respectfully before Gandhi, Maharani Tara Devi, dressed elegantly in a pink saree, held out a silver tray. 'When a great seer graces us with his presence,' she said softly, 'it is our custom to offer milk.'

'I cannot accept milk from a maharaja whose subjects are distressed,' Gandhi refused the offering, taking the colour out of the maharani's cheeks. 'Your subjects are unhappy,' he turned to the maharaja, 'this is not a good sign.'

The maharaja gritted his teeth in silence.

'I have been out touring the Valley over the last few days, meeting locals, talking to ordinary people,' Gandhi went on.

'It is clear Your Highness does not enjoy the confidence of his people. And the diwan,' Gandhi looked straight at Kak, 'appears to be a most unpopular man.'

Kak's face reddened. He was now convinced beyond doubt that Gandhi had come as a messenger for Nehru and a flagbearer for Abdullah.

'The only person the people respect is Sheikh Abdullah,' Gandhi said, making his agenda explicit. 'The people want their beloved leader released from jail.'

Swallowing the insults and insinuations, the maharaja locked eyes with Gandhi, but said nothing. After all, who could cross the Mahatma! But he knew deep down that this was not going to remain a solitary stand-off. Tremors were sure to follow.

❋ Kashmir in My Lap ❋

Adjusting the monocle on his eye, Jinnah started reading the letter among the many he received every day. It began with profound praise, waxing eloquent about his role in creating history. Sitting back at his desk, he perused its contents with great satisfaction:

> *My Quaid-e-Azam, God is my witness... What we hundred million Muslims couldn't do, your one word could do... The Muslims of Kashmir are firmly for Pakistan and are behind you... They expect much help from the Muslim League and from you. May your glory ever remain in the ascendant.*

Jinnah beamed, delighted to know that the people of Kashmir supported him. With its abundant resources, the state was destined to play a decisive role in his cherished goal of Pakistan. But between the pro-monarchy Hari Singh, and the pro-Nehru Sheikh Abdullah, he had to choose his friend wisely.

He scribbled something in the margin of the letter and dropped it into the out-tray for his secretary, before turning to the next letter. It was a lengthy one, containing a detailed report about the tribes along the North-West Frontier. It mentioned the Mohmands, the Musa Khels, the Usman Khels, the Khawazais and the Afridis – guerrilla fighters and soldiers of Islam – who together could raise a *lashkar* (a military force) of over 200,000 soldiers in case jihad was proclaimed. No wonder, Jinnah mused, putting the report down, that that part of the country was referred to as the subcontinent's Gunpowder Magazine.

'Is what I hear true?' Fatima Jinnah pushed open the study door and handed her brother his pills. Expressly forbidden by him from disclosing his illness to anybody, Fatima was the only person, apart from his doctors, who knew that Jinnah was a dying man. 'That you have bought a houseboat in Srinagar?' she asked, pouring him a glass of water. 'The *Mayflower*?'

'Well...now that we won't have the pleasure of gazing at the sunset from our balcony on Malabar Hill,' Jinnah grinned, 'I thought, what better than a houseboat on Dal Lake?' If all went well, he had plans to celebrate Eid next month at the Srinagar Mosque.

Fatima clasped her hands together. 'I suppose that means the Kashmir issue is sorted then?'

'Just like ripened fruit, my dear,' Jinnah assured his sister, 'sooner or later, Kashmir is bound to fall into my lap.'

❋ An Offer from Pakistan ❋

Sitting cross-legged on his divan, Maharaja Hari Singh eyed the three men across the carpeted floor. *Had he not made it abundantly clear that he wished for Jammu and Kashmir to remain independent*! But Pakistan, it seemed, was simply unwilling to listen.

'Your Highness,' began Khurshid, Jinnah's private secretary, also a Kashmiri, 'Pakistan extends its hand of friendship to you. Jinnah Sa'ab is keen to come and meet you.'

'I...er...would advise him not to do so for the time being...' the maharaja shifted uncomfortably on his velvet cushion. After the trouble stirred up by Gandhi, another high-power visit was the last thing he wanted.

'Jinnah Sa'ab will be disappointed...' Khurshid reached for the apricots and pistachios on the silver salver. 'Nehru supported Sheikh Abdullah's Quit Kashmir movement against you. Jinnah Sa'ab did not.'

'Pandit Nehru even prepared Sheikh Abdullah's case in court,' added Major Shah, Pakistani joint undersecretary of foreign affairs, to further instigate the maharaja against India.

'And may I remind Your Highness what Gandhi said last month?' Khurshid was young but knew how to stoke a fire. 'He said that the wish of the people – not the decision of the ruler – is paramount.' He sat back, allowing the maharaja to mull over his words.

'Your Highness, we did not support Sheikh Abdullah's movement against you either...' said Chaudhary Hamidullah, leader of the Muslim Conference that was a rival to Abdullah's National Conference party in the Valley.

The maharaja interlaced his fingers thoughtfully, staring intently at the floral design on the carpet. Kashmir shared borders with China, the Soviet Union and Afghanistan. With India to its south, it would be completely engulfed by giants. *Was he equipped to defend his territory against them all? Should he throw in his lot with Pakistan?*

'After all, Pakistan is incomplete without Kashmir,' Shah reached for the copper *samavar* and poured himself some steaming *kahwa*. 'As you no doubt know, the letter K in Pakistan's name stands for Kashmir.'

'That is the only sensible choice,' Chaudhary Hamidullah cautioned the maharaja. 'The Muslims of Kashmir will revolt and rebel if you accede to India. On behalf of the Muslim Conference, I urge Your Highness to join Pakistan.'

'Whenever you are ready, Your Highness...' Major Shah gently slid a large manila envelope on to the table.

The maharaja stared hard at the envelope. If he signed the papers, Jammu and Kashmir would become a part of Pakistan. But that went against his every instinct.

He was a Dogra Rajput, a Kashmiri Hindu. *What future did a Hindu ruler have in a theocratic nation created for Muslims?* On the other hand, India was showing no respect for royalty; Nehru wanted a *people's* government. *What future did a monarch have in a democratic nation meant to be a republic?*

The only choice, Hari Singh said to himself for the umpteenth time, the only reasonable choice open to him was to join neither, while maintaining cordial relations with both.

'I'm agreeable to sign...' the maharaja said solemnly as the men from Karachi drew closer to him, 'only the standstill agreement for the moment.'

His guests fell back, both dismayed and disgruntled. The standstill agreement merely meant that both the Pakistani government and the maharaja would maintain status quo in respect of all activities between them such as trade and transport, pending any further decision. But Jinnah's emissaries had come for the ultimate kill, not for scraps.

The maharaja sighed deeply as the words of Swami Sant Dev, his *rajguru*, echoed in his ears. The grand fantasy the royal astrologer had painted danced before his eyes: of the Dogra flag fluttering atop Lahore Fort; of reclaiming vast territories his ancestors had once controlled. He was sure it was just a matter of time. And until that day was within his grasp, he would sit it out on the fence, bide his time, and ride out the storm.

❋ Act of Treason ❋

'They are hoisting the Pakistani flag on the General Post Office, Your Highness,' Janak Singh, the newly appointed eighty-year-old diwan, alerted the maharaja.

'What temerity!' exclaimed Hari Singh, putting away the newspaper showing jubilant scenes of Independence Day celebrations in Delhi. 'Order the police to bring it down immediately.'

'I had a bad feeling that something like this would happen,' Maharani Tara Devi muttered.

'Your Highness, the Pakistani flag is being hoisted all across Poonch,' the octogenarian said softly, referring to the maharaja's largest *jagir* in western Jammu. 'In fact,' he paused, 'some Poonchis have declared independence.' He lowered his eyes. 'Uh...I am told the Muslim Conference is setting up a parallel government there, calling themselves Azad Kashmir.'

Maharaja Hari Singh's face contorted with rage. Historically, the Poonchis had never submitted willingly to Dogra rule, but setting up a parallel government was a blatant act of treason.

'There is unrest in Gilgit too, Your Highness...' Janak Singh moved on to an update from the north-west.

Blood rushed to the maharaja's face. Jammu and Kashmir had only just passed into his hands after years of British rule. And in a matter of days, things were spiralling out of control. He could not let that happen; could not allow his adversaries to take him for a pushover. The rebels would have to be taken head-on.

'Call the inspector general of police for a meeting,' Hari Singh ordered through clenched teeth. The Poonchis shared close links with the Muslims of Punjab and the Frontier. He knew that things could quickly escalate and get out of hand. 'Have an order issued: the Muslims of Poonch are to be dispossessed of their arms with immediate effect.'

For once, the dilly-dallying Maharaja Hari Singh had chosen to make a swift decision. It was a decision that would cost him dearly in the days to come.

❋ Operation Gulmarg ❋

Nearly 400 years ago, in Kalanaur village in present-day Gurdaspur district, a fourteen-year-old boy named Akbar had been crowned the *badshah* of Hindustan. Now, many years hence, Gurdaspur had become the stage for the beginning of yet another dramatic saga.

'How can Gurdaspur be given to India?' fumed Malik Ghulam Muhammad, Pakistan's finance minister, staring glumly at the newspaper on the conference table, whose bold headlines announced the line dividing India and Pakistan. 'Gurdaspur has a Muslim majority. The whole damn district should have been given to us.'

Liaquat Ali Khan, the Pakistani prime minister, sank into a chair beside the Quaid; betrayed, embittered, enraged. That most of Gurdaspur in Punjab had been awarded to India by the Boundary Commission, which had been formed to draw up the final border between the two countries through Punjab and Bengal, had come as a rude shock.

'Totally perfidious,' swore Jinnah, outraged at the seemingly unjust and perverse nature of the decision.

The loss of Gurdaspur stung them all deeply. It was much more than a fertile tract of land in Punjab; it contained, in fact, the only narrow strip of usable road connecting the rest of India to Kashmir. Had Gurdaspur been awarded to

Pakistan, Maharaja Hari Singh would have lost land access to India and sooner or later, joined Pakistan. But, by giving Gurdaspur to India, the boundary award had, in effect, kept alive India's hopes of gaining Kashmir. It was a death blow to Pakistan.

'Sabotage! It is an act of sabotage,' Ghulam Muhammad cried wildly.

'There is no doubt about it. India is out to throttle us, choke us, destroy us'—Liaquat Ali Khan snapped shut the file

Not wanting to sour the Independence Day celebrations in Pakistan and India on 14 and 15 August respectively, Lord Mountbatten had decided to keep the boundary award a secret, making it public only after Independence Day. Although it had been delivered to him on the morning of 13 August, he opened it only on 16 August, and had it published on 17 August 1947.

Hence, when both nations celebrated their independence, the people had no clear idea what the actual frontiers of their country looked like; and many spent the dawn of Independence in fear and uncertainty, unsure whether the next sunrise would find them residing in India or Pakistan.

On Independence Day, the Pakistani flag had been hoisted all across Gurdaspur, assuming it would be given to Pakistan as the district had a Muslim-majority population. Based on that, Pakistan had even appointed a deputy commissioner for the district. The man served only three days before being unceremoniously packed off on 17 August when news of the award finally broke and it became clear that most of Gurdaspur in Punjab had, in fact, been awarded to India.

containing the boundary award. 'A complete breach of faith. An eyewash.'

'I'm told the rulers of Patiala, Faridkot and Kapurthala visited Maharaja Hari Singh,' said Shaukat Hayat Khan, a former major of the British Indian Army, who had been sitting silently at the far end of the table. 'Rumour has it that the maharaja might be secretly negotiating with India.'

'Gurdaspur should have been ours by right,' Ghulam Muhammad said. 'Ferozepur should have been ours. Jammu and Kashmir ought to be ours.' He pounded the table. 'If we can't get them by right, we must seize them by force.'

'I've been receiving desperate telegrams from our people in Poonch,' Liaquat Ali Khan told Jinnah solemnly. 'Muslims there are being butchered by the maharaja's army. Their weapons have been seized. Entire villages have been set ablaze.'

'We cannot just sit by and watch our Kashmiri brothers being massacred,' Ghulam Muhammad growled, turning to the defence secretary, Iskander Mirza. 'We've simply got to set things right.'

'All is not lost, *janaab*,' Shaukat Hayat Khan said encouragingly. 'Kashmir can still be ours. But we have to act fast...' He tapped a file code-named 'Operation Gulmarg' and slid it across to Jinnah. 'The entire plan is chalked out,' he nodded at Colonel Akbar Khan, the director of weapons and equipment in the army.

'Sir,' Akbar Khan saluted the Quaid, 'our Kashmir mission will be assisted by Khurshid Anwar – our man in the Frontier region,' he said. 'And supported by Brigadier Sher Khan.'

Jinnah opened the file.

'We have two options,' Akbar Khan continued. 'Either we supply Kashmiris with arms and money to fuel an uprising that will compel the maharaja to join Pakistan,' he scanned the gloomy faces around him, 'or, we arm Pathan tribesmen and bring them into this operation, which will be led by ex-servicemen from the army. That should also keep the Frontier tribes occupied. One option is attacking through the Muzaffarabad–Srinagar axis,' he rolled out a map. 'That plan would involve...'

'Major General Akbar Khan,' intervened Prime Minister Liaquat Ali, his confidence growing, 'you will lead this operation, under the code name Tariq. You will be assisted by Brigadier Sher Khan and, as you suggest, Khurshid Anwar can be our man in the Frontier for liaising with tribes there and recruiting fighters.'

Reminded of the report he had received months ago with information about the Frontier tribes, Jinnah held up a hand, 'Go ahead...' he levered himself up from the chair, nodding slightly at his prime minister. He had once dreamed of a grand Pakistan stretching across the whole of northern India, but the Congress had short-changed him and compelled him to accept a moth-eaten and splintered Pakistan; forced him to swallow a divided Punjab, a broken Bengal. Every step of the way, he had given in – even agreeing to have a nation split into two disconnected pieces divided by a thousand miles of Indian territory in between. But the Gurdaspur betrayal bored a hole through his heart.

JINNAH: GO AHEAD, BUT DON'T TELL ME ABOUT THE OPERATION. MY CONSCIENCE MUST BE CLEAR...

'Go ahead with the operation...' said Jinnah, moving his stick-like frame slowly towards the door.

'But don't tell me,' he held up his hand, 'my conscience must be clear.'

❋ Blockade and Browbeat ❋

'Your Highness, rice and wheat supplies are being deliberately withheld by Pakistan,' Major General Janak Singh apprised the maharaja. 'Ten wagons of salt on the way to Kashmir have been waylaid and held back in Rawalpindi.'

Maharaja Hari Singh listened to the report quietly as he pushed around the *guchchhi* pulao and *haak* on his plate. Kashmiris were accustomed to adding salt to their *noon* chai; but now, not even the palace kitchen had enough to put in the food. He rose from the table. The situation was serious – petrol and kerosene were running out; sugar and salt supplies had been cut off; timber trade had ground to a halt. Business in carpets and furs had ceased; food supplies had stopped; luxury materials like pashmina to perishable ones like fruit were held up in godowns.

'The railway line from Jammu to Sialkot has also been suspended,' his old diwan continued. 'Worse, Pakistan has been arming people along the border. There is,' he dropped his voice to a whisper, 'talk of an invasion.'

Wiping his mouth with a napkin, the maharaja rose from the table. He had been fending off Jinnah's invitation for talks in Karachi, sensing a trap. News of an intended attack now confirmed his suspicions that Pakistan was trying to force his hand.

'We've signed the standstill agreement with Pakistan,' said Janak Singh, following the maharaja into his study. 'This blockade is a breach of the agreement.'

Waiting in the anteroom of the wood-panelled study, Diwan Singh, the maharaja's ADC, stood to attention as

Hari Singh entered. 'A message has just arrived from Karachi, Your Highness,' he said crisply, handing Janak Singh a leather folder.

'Read it,' ordered the maharaja, gazing at his riding and polo photographs lining the walls. He wished for a brief moment he were out at the racecourse in Bombay or at his stud farm in Nagbani. Here he was instead, entangled in a complex web of politics.

Janak Singh's face turned white as he glanced at the telegram inside the folder. 'It's...it's from the prime minister of Pakistan,' he mumbled.

'What does he say?' the maharaja demanded.

'It...uh...it is...it's a warning.'

'Read it out!' Hari Singh knitted his eyebrows.

'The Pakistani prime minister warns Your Highness...' Janak Singh said faintly, 'that if you do not accede to Pakistan, Jammu and Kashmir must be prepared for the gravest consequences!'

❋ The Lashkar Rises ❋

Within a mud-walled compound of Landi Kotal, high up in the mountains of Khyber Pakhtunkhwa, at the very north-western edge of the subcontinent, twenty-year-old Majid huddled around a fire with his cousins, Haider and Mushtaq. Sitting around them were dozens of their Pathan tribesmen, gathered for the village council meeting, sipping *kahwa* in clay cups – all young, sombre, stony-faced, listening intently to the rabble-rouser in a green Muslim League shirt addressing the *jirga*, the tribal council.

'The infidel maharaja is massacring our Muslim brothers in Poonch,' Khurshid Anwar thundered, as he began his aggressive rhetoric. Not for nothing had he been trusted by Pakistan's top brass for the task of liaising with and recruiting men from the Frontier for the operation. 'Thousands of our brethren have been butchered in Punjab! Are we going to sit idly by like shameless cowards?'

The pick of the British Indian Army had been posted in these frontiers over the years, to keep Soviet ambitions in the region in check. Neither war nor weapons were a novelty to the Pathans of these barren mountains. They thrived on battle, even settled family disputes by blood feuds. Out on

WE SHALL CELEBRATE EID IN SRINAGAR!

these rugged mountains, three ideas ruled supreme: the spirit of Islam; the call to jihad or holy war; and the idea of *shahadat* or martyrdom.

Standing beside Anwar, tribal warlord Khan Ahmad Wani Khan nodded in agreement. 'Not one infidel should be left alive,' the man in the long robe and flowing beard goaded his men, raising his rifle in the air.

'The maharaja is going to gift Kashmir to India,' Khurshid Anwar's voice reached a feverish crescendo, as his volunteers distributed League pamphlets containing anti-maharaja propaganda for the handful among them who could read. 'But I say Kashmir belongs to *us*! To Pakistan! It is our bounden duty to fight for what is ours.'

'*Pakistan zindabad*,' the chorus echoed in the mountains. Gunshots were fired into the orange sky.

'Inshallah...' Anwar exclaimed. 'If you people join us, we can take Kashmir and free our Muslim brothers from the maharaja's sinful rule. To arms until victory...'

'*Pakistan zindabad*,' the tribesmen repeated. '*Quaid-e-Azam zindabad*.'

'*Iman*! *Jihad*! *Shahadat*!' the compound reverberated.

A flutter of excitement surged through young Majid's veins. Grazing goats on the mountain slopes made for a dull life. At an age when his moustache had only just begun to sprout, the thought that he might some day chance upon the rich bazaars and plentiful orchards of Kashmir suddenly felt like a dream within reach. He offered thanks to the Almighty. Goatherd no more; he was now Allah's chosen warrior.

'You must keep ready your jeeps, trucks and weapon carriers; stock up on petrol and other essentials,' Anwar instructed them, after having successfully whipped up their emotions. 'Collect food and necessities from every *ilaaqa*, each locality. All movement must take place under cover of night and in complete secrecy. We gather at the Peshawar grounds by next Thursday and then go along the main Muzaffarabad road to cross into Kashmir. By the will of Allah, we shall celebrate Eid in Srinagar.'

'Inshallah! May Allah bless our mission and favour us with glory in the cause of Islam,' Wani wished the men success.

The evening *azan* pierced the cool dusk air.

'*Mashallah*,' Anwar looked heavenward. 'May the exalted Allah receive our prayers!'

❋ Before the Snow ❋

Meanwhile, in New Delhi, Nehru linked his hands behind his back, strolling beside Patel from his residence in York Road to Patel's home on Aurangzeb Road; a walk which they often took to discuss matters away from prying eyes and snooping ears. 'News from the Frontier is disturbing,' he sighed. 'I'm told of intense propaganda in Peshawar, of factories producing ammunition, of Swat tribes being supplied with arms. I hear that the Pakistani government and military are colluding to mount an attack.'

Sardar tossed his shawl across his shoulder. Similar intelligence reports had reached his ears.

'I understand Pakistan's strategy is to infiltrate at a time when the snow isolates Kashmir in winter...' Nehru explained haltingly. 'I doubt the maharaja's forces can meet the challenge. Only Sheikh Abdullah can save the situation because he can carry the people with him. The maharaja must be pushed to release Abdullah and urged to accede to India before winter cuts off Kashmir.'

'Let's say we convince the maharaja to release Sheikh Abdullah and they both join forces,' Sardar postulated, 'can we be certain Abdullah will push Hari Singh to accede to India?' Unlike Nehru, Sardar wasn't entirely sure of the Sheikh's leanings.

'In all manner of things...' Nehru began with his oft-repeated phrase, 'we have an asset in the National Conference, provided it is handled properly. Abdullah has repeatedly assured me of being opposed to Pakistan and of abiding by my advice.'

'All right...I will write to Mahajan,' nodded Sardar. Mehr Chand Mahajan, the newly appointed diwan of Jammu and Kashmir – the third diwan there in nearly as many months – was his trusted man. With such disturbing news from the Frontier, perhaps aligning with Abdullah was the only viable way forward, particularly considering that winter was fast approaching and heavy snowfall in the mountains would soon cut India off from Kashmir.

❋ The Lion Roars ❋

'*Sher-e-Kashmir...zindabad! Sheikh Abdullah...zindabad!*'

All of Srinagar resounded with the name of one man. Men, women and children, the young and the old, poured into the streets, cramming every nook and corner – chanting, clapping, singing, rejoicing. Their Lion was free!

Rows of *shikaras* carrying water chestnuts and lotus stems accompanied the procession as Abdullah was ferried down Dal Lake. Hundreds lined the banks, forming a long, continuous archway of clasped hands as their beloved leader stepped off the boat and made his way to the rostrum.

'*Alhamdulillah!*' Abdullah, dressed in his trademark double-breasted suit with a fez cap, raised his hands to the skies, his voice booming through the loudspeaker, 'Praise be to Allah!'

The frenzied crowd, wild with excitement, reached out to touch him. They leaned out of balconies, queued along the quaysides, balanced precariously on boats, climbed atop the *chinars*. Holding placards and banners, they showered him with rose petals, buried him in garlands, hailing him as their hero.

'I don't know why I was arrested,' Abdullah began with a shrug of his shoulders, 'and frankly...' he flashed his big smile, 'I don't know why I was released.'

'*Shukr khodayus*,' the women in the crowd raised their hands to thank the Almighty. '*Sahee salamat vot*. Thank God you have returned safely.'

'When I was imprisoned, I did not know those were to be the very last breaths I would take in an undivided India,' Abdullah continued, sounding pained. 'Today, when I walked out of prison, I see that India has been broken into two. India's dream of freedom has been fulfilled. But what about the people of Kashmir? What about us? We too must now see to it that our long-cherished desire is fulfilled.'

Jostling for space in the packed crowd, a young boy by the name of Maqbool Sherwani, punched his fists in the air in exuberance, '*Sher-e-Kashmir...zindabad!*' he cried, delighted that a year in jail had not broken his beloved leader. 'Long live the Lion of Kashmir!'

'*Sheikh Abdullah...zindabad*,' the crowds repeated after him, breaking free of the cordon and rushing towards the dais.

'We are now faced with the question of accession to either India or Pakistan,' Abdullah said sombrely into the microphone, 'but no decision is possible while we are slaves! "Freedom before Accession" must become our resounding slogan.'

'*Azadi!*' someone screamed in the distance.

'Freedom! *Azadi!* The crowd repeated.

'The decision must be in the best interests of the people of Kashmir,' Abdullah sounded out his terms. 'I assure the maharaja that we do not intend to dispossess him of his throne. All we seek is a democratic constitutional government.' He paused, choosing his next few words carefully. 'I am a friend of Pandit Nehru, and I will be going to Delhi to meet him. I have great respect for Mahatma Gandhi. But...' he paused, 'the people's will is supreme. And if the people of Jammu and Kashmir decide to accede to Pakistan...I will be the first to sign my name.'

❋ A War of Nerves ❋

Sardar scanned the reports on his desk as he waited to be connected with Mahajan, the maharaja's new diwan in Srinagar, his eyes lingering on the concluding words of Sheikh Abdullah's speech made some days ago in Srinagar. His deep misgivings about Nehru's friend resurfaced.

Could the Sheikh be trusted?

The phone rang.

'Hello, Mahajan,' his voice was firm and authoritative. 'We have little time, so I'll keep it brief.' Sardar's manner was always direct, his words seldom superfluous. 'Given the situation, I request you to reach out to Sheikh Abdullah,' he said, keeping the promise he had made to Nehru despite his own reservations, 'and make a substantial gesture to win his support.'

'Good morning, Sardar...' Mahajan's voice crackled through the tenuous connection, 'the maharaja has released Abdullah as per your wishes. What more do you want from us?'

Having just completed a stressful assignment as a member of the Radcliffe Boundary Commission, tasked with drawing the ill-fated line dividing India and Pakistan in Punjab, Mahajan had looked forward to returning to his post as a judge of the Punjab High Court. But circumstances had dropped him from the frying pan into the fire. It tested his patience to be serving an uneasy and indecisive maharaja who tended to procrastinate and postpone.

'Look, the demand for a responsible government is mounting everywhere,' Sardar said. 'Brute force is not the way to deal with external dangers nor with internal upheaval...'

'Sardar, I accept your views,' Mahajan raised his voice over the static disturbance, 'but we are working on a war footing. Practically all our Muslim military and police have deserted us... we are surrounded on all sides.' His voice was laced with panic.

'Mahajan, India is committed to give you maximum support—' Sardar began.

'Pakistan Radio has launched an intense propaganda,' Mahajan interrupted him. 'Baseless charges are being made, inciting people against the maharaja's regime. Thousands of Hindu and Sikh refugees are pouring in from Pakistan,' Mahajan began listing his woes. 'Bridges are being destroyed and we are desperately short of provisions, weapons, essentials. Delhi doesn't seem to...'

'I understand it all,' Sardar interjected, 'but in such times, you need a strong ally. You need the people's support. The maharaja is not popular'—he was compelled to repeat Nehru's refrain—'befriending Abdullah is the best chance he has.'

Mahajan paused. 'This is not the time to discuss these matters, Sardar,' he said sombrely. 'We are waiting for the help you promised. That is all I can say for now—'

The line went dead. Sardar inhaled deeply and closed his eyes.

Until a few weeks ago, Sardar had had little time or attention for Kashmir. But Junagadh's accession to Pakistan had changed everything. The two-nation theory, the foundation upon which rested the entire edifice of Pakistan, had been turned upon its head by Jinnah's belligerent claim to a Hindu-majority kingdom inside Indian territory. Jinnah's game was dangerous and dirty. And Sardar was determined to deliver a befitting reply.

Maniben popped her head into the study with a stack of letters that had arrived for her father. She worried about him. Seventy-two and dealing with illnesses, he slept at eleven at night, woke up at three in the morning. Worked too hard, rested too little, and never let on about his pain or suffering to anybody. Years ago, he had received news of his wife's death while he was in the middle of a court case. He had argued on, not allowing his emotions to derail his client's future. That was the man he was.

'I need to speak to Baldev Singh right away,' he said, jotting down points he wished to discuss with the defence minister:

– Widening of roads leading into Kashmir.

– Setting up of secret communication channels.

– Repairing telegraph lines and damaged bridges.

– Diverting civilian planes to carry troops at short notice.

– Wireless equipment for Srinagar airport.

– Additional petrol and aviation fuel...

'*Naashto*?' Maniben asked from the door.

Sardar waved her away. Food, sleep, rest – they'd all just have to wait.

❋ A Bloody Betrayal ❋

Winding through the Jhelum valley road, Majid, the young goatherd-turned-warrior from the northern mountains, ran his fingers over the cold steel barrel of the rifle in his hands. His cousin Haider tapped the cartridge belt at his waist, a jubilant smile pinned to his face. At the back of the vehicle, their companions Khwaja and Nooruddin pretended to be having a mock fight, mowing down infidels with their guns, as Mushtaq grinned through crooked teeth. Guns were no novelty for these men from the North-West Frontier Province – they had grown up with gunfire resounding in their ears. *But fighting a jihad – now wasn't that gratifying! They were now the mujahideen – holy fighters.* It made them feel all-powerful, almost superhuman.

Behind them, a convoy of 300 lorries snaked along the mountain road. Afridis and Wazirs, Mahsuds and Swatis,

OCTOBER 1947: ATTACKERS FROM PAKISTAN ENTER THE KASHMIR VALLEY

Pashtuns and Pathans. As their truck laboured up the slope, and across the mountain pass at Lohar Garhi, Majid eyed the city of Muzaffarabad below. Nestled between the rivers Jhelum and Neelum, it looked like a gleaming jewel. Raising his eyes to the starry sky, he offered thanks to Allah for bringing him to the threshold of the land of milk and honey.

Wrapping his shawl tightly around himself, Majid imagined the hero's welcome he would receive when he returned from this expedition. He would floor his friends with countless tales of his daring exploits; enthral his young wife, Amina, with stories of his bravery; delight his father with the riches he would take back home.

'Halt!' Their leader Khurshid Anwar's voice startled Majid out of his reverie. The driver Sikandar stepped on the brakes as the truck came to a stop before a bridge over the Jhelum. Behind them, the column of trucks screeched to a halt.

Sairab Khan, leader of the Muslim League's Green Shirts, got out of the Ford station wagon that led their convoy.

'We wait here,' Khurshid Anwar said to the men, pulling on a thick jacket over his shoulders. 'Wait for the sign.'

***

Up on the ridge, Anwar jumped out of the truck and joined Sairab Khan up to the edge of the bend. They stood motionless, staring into the darkness below. Majid and Mushtaq stood a few paces behind them.

'No sign yet...' Anwar stroked his long henna-dyed beard nervously.

'Don't fret,' replied Khan, opening his arms to the skies. 'Trust in *His* great design!'

Majid reached into his pocket and pulled out some tack made of chickpea and jaggery. He had survived on that for over two days. His stomach growled. He stuffed a fistful despondently into his mouth.

'Look,' Khan tugged at Anwar's arm, pointing ahead.

'*Mashallah*,' Anwar exclaimed, his eyes piercing the foggy night to catch a glimpse of a tiny flame dancing across the bridge. Gradually it turned brighter.

'No doubt about it,' Sairab Khan threw a brotherly arm around Anwar. 'That's the sign.'

'What's going on?' Majid whispered to Mushtaq.

'The Poonchis have fulfilled their promise,' Mushtaq smiled menacingly, hugging his brother Nooruddin. 'They've killed the maharaja's commander and wiped out the entire battalion. They'll soon open out the road to us into the Valley,' he rubbed his hands gleefully.

Majid's eyes widened with surprise. *Was it going to be that easy*?

'Praise be to Allah!' Sairab Khan jumped back into his vehicle, signalling to the convoy to follow. 'Muzaffarabad is ours.'

Hundreds of headlights blinked on. Engines revved up. '*Allahu Akbar*!' the hordes screamed, punching their rifles and shooting some rounds jubilantly into the air as their lorries hurtled down the embankment. The road to Srinagar was now open.

'A few more days, brother,' Anwar said to Sairab Khan, 'and Kashmir will be ours.'

❋ Off the Fence ❋

'Muzaffarabad has fallen, Your Highness.'

The maharaja dropped his soup spoon with a clang and sat back with his eyes squeezed shut.

'Lieutenant Colonel Narain Singh and his men were murdered in their barracks,' reported Brigadier Rajinder Singh,

Kashmir's chief of army staff. 'In their sleep,' he added through gritted teeth. 'Betrayed by their own soldiers.'

'Cowards!' the maharaja cursed, a vein throbbing in his forehead. 'Bloody traitors!' Only a few days ago, he had ordered Lieutenant Colonel Narain Singh to secure the Domel–Muzaffarabad route that formed the gateway into the Valley, and had asked him specifically if he could trust the Poonchi soldiers in his contingent. 'More than the Dogras, Your Highness,' Narain Singh had replied without hesitation. 'Oh, Narain'—Hari Singh sighed regretfully—'what a fatal betrayal you have suffered!'

'The rebel soldiers led the invaders into Muzaffarabad,' Brigadier Rajinder Singh continued his update. 'They have wreaked havoc in the town – looting the bazaar, killing civilians, kidnapping children, raping women...' he stopped, nauseated by the atrocities.

The maharaja pressed his fingers against his closed eyelids again, pained by the news. 'I must go...' he rose from the table impatiently. 'Bring me my uniform,' he instructed his ADC. 'I will lead the forces at the border.'

'Your Highness, please reconsider...' Brigadier Rajinder Singh pleaded. 'Allow me to lead the men.'

'No, Rajinder...as head of the state, it is my responsibility,' the maharaja insisted. 'I cannot let the Valley and my people fall into the hands of those barbarians.'

'Please, Your Highness...I must dissuade you,' pleaded the Brigadier again. 'The raiders mustn't get to you. Kashmir is safe if you are safe.'

The maharaja collapsed into a couch, the adrenalin rush ebbing. 'Very well, Rajinder'—he gave in. 'Collect as many officers and men as possible from the Badamibagh cantonment and proceed immediately towards Uri.'

'Right, sir,' replied the army chief in relief. The *lashkars* were on the Muzaffarabad–Srinagar road and would pass through Uri next. It was vital to hold them back there until help arrived.

'Tell me honestly, Rajinder...' the maharaja asked, 'how are things looking on the ground?'

'Not good, Your Highness'—Singh's reply was candid. He paused, mentally gathering his litany of woes. Their weapons were obsolete, their vehicles old and rusty. The rain would slow them down. *Where could he begin?* 'Pakistan has blocked off all our petrol supplies,' he said. 'We have very few vehicles and men.'

'How many?' the maharaja asked grimly, knowing his forces were spread thin from Jammu in the south to Ladakh in the north. And with the Muslim soldiers playing truant, his army was now suddenly down by half.

'At best I would be able to gather a platoon of 150 men.' Brigadier Rajinder Singh swallowed hard. 'The tribesmen, I believe, number about 6,000 in all!'

The maharaja paled, the import of Pakistan's dirty plan finally dawning on him. With the *lashkar* hordes descending upon his kingdom, far from the beautiful valley turning into the Switzerland of the East, Kashmir could soon transform into a mass graveyard. 'I have no choice left now,' the maharaja sat back, resigning himself to his fate in despair. 'Batra...you must go to Delhi...' he mumbled to his deputy prime minister incoherently. 'Only the Indian Army can save us now!'

❋ Alarm Bells ❋

Prime Minister Nehru's house, 17 York Road in New Delhi, resembled a war room.

A row of white official cars crowded the driveway. Civil servants in black coats trooped in and out, clutching confidential files. Secretaries scurried about bearing SOS cables and dispatching urgent telegrams. ADCs attended to three constantly buzzing telephones in the reception area. Dozens of Partition refugees gazed blankly out of tents in the rear compound where they had been accommodated.

In the living room, the trio, comprising the prime minister, the home minister and the defence minister, stared in dismay at a fidgety Mahajan seated on the sofa.

'I shall not mince words,' repeated the diwan of Jammu and Kashmir. 'Either the Indian Army flies into Kashmir immediately, or I go to Pakistan and negotiate terms with Mr Jinnah.'

One could have heard a pin drop.

Nehru leapt out of his seat, seething at the blatant ultimatum from Hari Singh. 'The maharaja has been sitting on the fence for months,' he exploded, 'and now that his tail is on fire, he wants the whole world to swing into action?'

'What is the alternative?' demanded Mahajan. 'If the army is not sent in, Kashmir will be out of India's hands. Thousands

THE PRIME MINISTER'S HOUSE IN NEW DELHI: NERVE CENTRE OF FRENZIED ACTIVITY

of *kabailis* – the tribesmen – have crossed into the state. If you do not save Srinagar now, I'm afraid there will be no Srinagar left to save.'

'Look...your deputy, Batra, came to us with the same story'—Patel tried reining in his growing annoyance—'but your maharaja has not yet acceded to India. Jammu and Kashmir is not legally a part of India. On what basis can we send in the Indian Army? And besides,' he said, exchanging a quick glance with the defence minister, 'we have hardly any time to mobilize our forces!'

Taking the cue, Baldev Singh nodded. The Indian government had, of course, been preparing steadily for a stand-off in Kashmir. Yet, it was vital to make the maharaja aware of the enormous stress his dilly-dallying was exerting on them all.

Two staff members entered the living room, bearing large trays, ushered in by Nehru's daughter, Indira. Mahajan declined the coffee and snacks. He had no appetite.

Sardar accepted a glass of water, eyeing the diwan seated opposite him. Mahajan had been the Congress' nominee on the Punjab Boundary Commission; he was their man, and he had even taken up the posting in Kashmir after consulting him. *How could he go to Pakistan?*

As the men continued their agitated discussion in the hall, seated in an inner chamber was another guest from Kashmir – Nehru's dear friend, Sheikh Abdullah. Listening keenly through a crack in the door, Abdullah tensed. Ten thousand of his party volunteers had raised their own militia against the invaders, but he knew better than anyone else that it was only a stopgap arrangement. Like Mahajan, he too had come to Delhi to plead for help from the Indian government. Deep within, he knew Mahajan was bluffing; confident that the maharaja would never approach Pakistan, aware that it was no more than a ruse to get India to rush to Kashmir's aid.

Pulling out a pen from the pocket of his waistcoat, he flipped open a notepad, deciding to place his bets on the maharaja's gamble. His heart racing, he hurriedly scribbled a note, sent it out to Nehru, and waited.

Would the Indian government take the bait?

***

Nehru's face lost colour as he read Abdullah's note. The Sheikh had written that he agreed with Mahajan. The prime minister heaved a sigh. 'This is not an ideal solution,' he mumbled, 'but time has left us with little choice. Schedule a defence committee meeting,' he instructed his private secretary, M.O. Mathai, who was minuting the proceedings attentively.

Mahajan exhaled in relief, his eyes locking briefly with Sardar's. Instantly, Sardar knew that the threats of going to Pakistan had been nothing more than idle posturing by the maharaja to pressurize the Indian government; nonetheless, he understood Mahajan's predicament.

'But you listen to me now, Mahajan'—Nehru turned around in a flash, his nostrils flaring in fury—'I have no more patience for the maharaja's histrionics. We will come to Kashmir's aid, but on three conditions.'

The prime minister listed his own ultimatum, 'One'—Nehru held up his thumb—'Jammu and Kashmir will accede to India. Two'—Nehru drew closer—'the maharaja will agree to a new constitution and democratize the administration. And three'—he continued, holding up three fingers—'he will include Sheikh Abdullah in the administration.'

'Uh...His Highness might have an objection to...uh, he...has asked me to convey...' Mahajan protested, finding himself in a spot, because he knew the maharaja despised Abdullah.

'Fulfil my three conditions, Mahajan,' Nehru snapped, 'and the Indian Army will save Kashmir.'

❋ Blow It Up! ❋

Brigadier Rajinder Singh gazed out at the dak bungalow in the distance. It was at this very location in Uri that the maharaja had ordered Nehru's arrest and detention one year ago; and now he was dispatching urgent emissaries to Delhi, begging for Nehru's help. *How the tables had turned!*

THE VALIANT BRIGADIER RAJINDER SINGH: BUYING TIME FOR THE INDIAN ARMY

'Hold the enemy at Uri at all costs and to the last man!' the maharaja's last instructions rang in his ears. But even with the reinforcements brought in by Captain Jwala Singh, his men were outnumbered by far.

'Your orders, *janaab*?' asked Nasib Singh, raising his voice to be heard over the babbling waters of the Jhelum behind them.

Brigadier Rajinder Singh turned to his deputy as he weighed his options. He had information that the Pakistanis were some distance away. If he advanced with a battalion towards Garhi to mount a surprise attack on the raiders

RAIDERS FROM PAKISTAN LEAVE A TRAIL OF PILLAGE AND PLUNDER IN KASHMIR.

there, it would give his troops time to create additional hurdles along the main road.

'Blow up the bridge,' he replied, pointing to the steep girder bridge over the stream that the raiders would have to cross to advance towards Srinagar.

'Yes, sir,' Nasib Singh saluted and hurried off. 'Gather the explosives – move them into position,' he ordered the men.

With that bridge over the river destroyed, Brigadier Rajinder Singh hoped the enemy's march to Srinagar could be momentarily delayed – buying a day, perhaps two, for the

Indian Army – if at all the maharaja managed to convince Delhi to send its forces by then.

As he prepared to advance bravely towards Garhi, Brigadier Singh did not know – he could not have known – and he would not live to find out...

The day, or two, that he would buy the Indian Army, would change everything in Kashmir. Forever.

❋ Discussions and Dilemmas ❋

'Tribesmen from the Frontier have entered Kashmir at various places between Mirpur and Muzaffarabad,' the newsreader announced staidly on All India Radio, '...leaving a trail of pillaging, looting, arson and rape in their wake as they advance into the Valley. The Pakistani government is supporting them with transport and weapons.'

Young Maqbool Sherwani, who had cheered the release of his leader Sheikh Abdullah some months ago, stiffened as he listened to the news on the radio, huddled along with other tense listeners in a tea shop in the Baramulla market. The bazaar was abuzz with hectic activity. People were hurriedly stocking up on emergency provisions, fearing the long haul ahead. Muzaffarabad had fallen. Domel had fallen. Chinari had fallen. And, after putting up a stiff resistance, Uri had fallen too.

A hand rotated the black knob on the radio, switching the frequency to Radio Pakistan. 'Sardar Mohammed Ibrahim has set up an Azad Kashmir government in Poonch with the full support of the people,' a newsreader announced in chaste Urdu. 'The Muslims have revolted against the Dogra regime. Tribesmen from the Frontier have declared jihad to support the Poonchis.'

'The British are responsible for this mess,' exclaimed a listener in a beige *pheran* seated beside Sherwani – the manager of the Mahura power station that supplied electricity to large parts of Kashmir, he was the only man who owned a car in town.

'No, this is all the maharaja's fault,' remarked a young man, in annoyance. 'He has been oppressing Muslims all along. Pakistan is a country for Muslims, and Kashmir has a Muslim majority – it should join Pakistan,' he declared emphatically, looking around to garner support. 'I say we join the raiders in liberating Kashmir.'

'Mian, have you lost your mind?' retorted Abdul Aziz, the owner of the tea stall, as he served cups of steaming-hot *kahwa* to his customers. 'Do you think these accursed *kabailis* give two hoots about us or about Islam? Muslims are being murdered along with Hindus and Sikhs. These men have no religion'—he spat in contempt.

'Kashmiri Muslims have been suffering under Dogra rule,' protested the youngster. 'The Pandits get all the jobs, all the money. Our Muslim brothers from across the border are here to help us...'

'These barbarians are no Muslims,' scowled Aziz. 'They only want our land and money. We should protect our Hindu and Sikh neighbours!'

'Aziz Mian is right...' a hunchbacked senior whom they all called Hajji Chacha advanced his two-penny worth to pacify the hot-headed youngster. 'Don't trust these self-appointed warriors of Islam.'

Unconvinced, the young boy poured himself some chai, but said nothing out of respect for the old man's advanced years and grey hair.

'Chacha, do you think these Pathans will attack Varmul?' another customer asked worriedly, his attention on more personal matters. Baramulla, or Varmul, as the locals called it, was on the Muzaffarabad-Srinagar road. 'I was thinking of going to my uncle's house in Sopore for a few days.'

'I'm heading to the *bijli-ghar*,' said the manager of the power plant at Mahura. 'If I sense the Pathans approaching, I'll shut off power to Varmul. You can all take that as a warning signal and leave town.'

'Perhaps we should send women and children away from town to the villages if that happens,' the old man said, nodding sagely. Mahura was a fair distance away. The signal would give the people enough time to leave.

'Why should anyone go anywhere?' demanded Maqbool Sherwani defiantly. 'This is our home. Our land.'

Only nineteen years of age, Sherwani was a mere cub. But he had listened in rapt attention each time the Lion had roared. With India in his heart and the words of Sher-e-Kashmir in his mind, the young boy took a vow, no less than that taken by Gandhi some years ago – for the sake of Kashmir, for the sake of his motherland – he would Do. Or he would Die.

'Let's stand up and fight,' Sherwani goaded the others, his face flushed, his temples throbbing, as he punched his fists in the air, '*Hamlavar, khabardar! Hum Kashmiri hain tayyar* [Attackers, beware! We Kashmiris are ready]!'

❋ Abandon Ship ❋

The fog-covered poplars and willows loomed like ghosts, thought V.P. Menon, peering through the windshield as he drove from the Srinagar aerodrome to the City Palace, along with Colonel Sam Manekshaw and Wing Commander H.C. Dewan. The three men had been sent to Srinagar by the Indian government to assess the situation after the maharaja's urgent plea for help to Delhi. Srinagar had greeted them with dark, empty streets, an eerie silence and dense cold air, thick with uncertainty.

'The place has a terrible little airfield,' grunted the colonel, mentally going over the many challenges a military operation in Srinagar could pose. With the Banihal Pass cut off by snow, road transport was impossible. The airstrip was rarely used, except for the maharaja's plane. The aerodrome did not have the infrastructure for sustained air operations: there were no navigational or landing aids; no crash-and-rescue facilities; no fuel dumps or refuelling.

'Hmm...the airstrip is unpaved and grassy,' nodded the wing commander, who had just flown them all in from Delhi. 'Landing and take-off raise a cloud of dust, drastically reducing visibility' – he sighed. 'And without air traffic control, a safe landing is dependent entirely on pilot vision.' Wing Commander Dewan clicked his tongue, realizing that landing several flights in quick succession was fraught with peril, as their car approached the driveway of Maharaja Hari Singh's palace, shrouded in darkness.

Diwan Mahajan, harrowed and dishevelled, rushed out as he heard the car pull up. 'I beg you, please...' Mahajan pleaded as soon as Menon and Colonel Manekshaw disembarked, 'the raiders have captured the Mahura power plant. They are very close to Srinagar...' His voice quavered. 'Please,' he begged Menon with folded hands, 'please do something.'

Menon looked at Mahajan calmly in the dim light of lanterns in the patio. 'My dear man,' he said with a straight face, 'we can't just "do something". *You* had so many days to decide, and you did nothing. And now you want us to rush to your aid?'

'Yes, yes, I understand all that,' said Mahajan anxiously, leading Menon in, 'and we can talk about it at length later, but now is not the time to discuss the past. We need to look to the future. Kashmir is in dire straits. The raiders...they're only about 45 miles away.' He looked beseechingly at the colonel and the wing commander, as if they had the ability to magically airlift Kashmir out of the mess. 'And we...our state forces...the Muslim soldiers...most of them...' he gasped, 'they've deserted and joined the raiders–'

'What sort of a diwan are you?' Menon cut him short. 'This is no time to get cold feet! You and your maharaja are hoping for the best, but you continue to do nothing!'

Hurricane lantern in hand, ADC Captain Diwan Singh guided the visitors in. 'Please wait here...' The deputy prime minister of Jammu and Kashmir, M.L. Batra, intercepted them in the hallway. 'I'll inform the maharaja.'

Through a latticed wooden wall, Menon could see Hari Singh in his prayer room, eyes closed, hands folded before a host of family deities on a raised marble platform lit by three flickering *diyas*. When M.L. Batra whispered to him, the maharaja turned around, his broad forehead furrowed with worry. Halting his prayers, he rose to meet the visitors. Only a few hours earlier the palace had been alight and abuzz with Dussehra festivities, and then the lights had suddenly gone out, leaving the palace enveloped in darkness and fear.

'Good evening, Your Highness...' Menon greeted the maharaja as they took their seats. 'As Mahajan must have conveyed to you already, India is willing to come to your aid if Kashmir accedes. Sardar has asked me to convey that Kashmir's interest lies in joining India without delay.'

The maharaja nodded grimly, visibly on edge, his eyes flitting nervously from face to face, his ears straining, alert to the smallest sound outside the window.

'Menon, I must speak frankly,' he began in a low voice, 'my forces...are on the back foot. Both in numbers and in morale.' His face was ashen and his eyes moist as he continued, 'The raiders are only a short distance from here. I...frankly...I'—he struggled to get the words out—'I don't know how much longer I can hold the fort.'

Menon exchanged uneasy glances with Colonel Manekshaw. For a head of state, there could be no greater humiliation than an open admission of his inadequacy. They would have to return to Delhi with a bleak report. 'I understand things are grave,' he said, 'but India cannot come to your aid without your signing the Instrument of Accession.'

'I am willing to sign it,' Hari Singh said haltingly. 'Jammu and Kashmir will accede to India.'

Finally! Menon sighed heavily. 'I'm glad you've decided to join India,' he responded sombrely. 'I would also advise Your Highness to leave Srinagar and go to Jammu immediately.'

'What? Abandon my kingdom?' The maharaja was affronted. 'Out of the question!'

'Please understand...' Menon explained, 'as long as the raiders are unable to get to you and force you to join Pakistan, Kashmir will not fall into their hands. This is the only course left.'

'Also, Your Highness,' interjected Colonel Sam Manekshaw, 'what is the latest information you have? And for how long can your forces hold the raiders back?'

'The last we heard, the raiders had reached Baramulla,' the maharaja turned to Batra, who nodded in agreement. 'I'd say about two days from Srinagar.'

'We don't have much of a choice then,' Menon stood up, facing the maharaja's ADC. 'Make preparations to leave Srinagar immediately.'

'Please...no...I...' The maharaja sprang forward and clutched Menon's hand, desperate, undecided, unsure. *Leave his own capital under cover of darkness, like a thief in the night?* 'I cannot... I must not...'

'You've got to listen to me, Your Highness,' insisted Menon. 'Leave for Jammu immediately; and leave the rest to me. India will fight for Kashmir to the last ditch!'

❋ A Dangerous Game of Bluff ❋

Despite the chilly wind, Maqbool Sherwani felt beads of perspiration on his brow as he dismounted from his white horse beneath a skeletal and leafless walnut tree. Struggling up the short rocky incline, he hauled himself over the edge and on to the winding mountain road, recoiling instantly in horror at the cold, blank stare of a bloodied corpse. He stared at the contorted face. '*Ha Khodaya!*' he gasped in shock. It was Abdul Aziz, the spiced-*kahwa* man from the market. Sherwani closed his eyes. The raiders had hacked Abdul Aziz down for giving refuge to Hindus and Sikhs. '*Inna lillahi wa...*' he began reciting the *dua* for the good-natured soul, a shiver running down his spine.

Rubbing his hands for warmth inside his woollen *pheran*, Sherwani recalled the slogan: *Hamlavar, khabardar, Hum Kashmiri hain tayyar*! Reciting those words imbued him with strength, as he stumbled over more corpses, some with pulverized faces, others with their guts spilling out. Bloodstained shoes lay scattered on the ground, bullet magazines littered the sparse patches of grass, and empty food packets blocked the drain. Covering his nose and mouth with his hand to fight the bile rising from the pit of his stomach, Sherwani advanced.

Over the last few days, Baramulla had turned from a bustling town to a deserted graveyard, its 14,000 or so inhabitants reduced to no more than a thousand. Many people were missing. Several more had fled. Men had been hacked down in front of their children. Women had been torn away from their families and girls kidnapped. Shops had been plundered and houses burnt down. The whole town was a smouldering mound of fire and ash; the waters of the Jhelum ran red with blood.

Mustering up his courage, Sherwani approached the three muscular men with guns dangling from their shoulders, brawling in Pashtu over their haul of brassware plundered from the bazaar. Standing a few feet away from the intimidating Pathans, he brought up an unsteady hand in a salaam. They didn't see him.

Slowly, he edged closer to them, his heart beating wildly. The tall, stocky men carried big guns with long barrels. All he had was a slingshot tucked into his trousers. He noticed splotches of blood on the young man's kaftan. The other had a bloody slash across his left eye. The third had only a stub of an arm, visible under his shawl. *Would these battle-hardened men of the Frontier think twice before shooting him dead?* The hair on the nape of his neck rose.

'Indian Army'—Sherwani struggled to find the right words, although he had rehearsed them over and over—'Indian Army...outside Varmul!' he blurted out the words, first in Kashmiri, then in Urdu, making use of hand gestures to indicate his alarm.

COURAGEOUS YOUNG MAQBOOL SHERWANI: HAMLAVAR, KHABARDAR!

The men stopped arguing. The one-armed man fixed him with narrowed eyes. The taller one approached him, rolling up his sleeve. Glaring at Sherwani, he grabbed him by the scruff of his long *pheran*.

'Indian Army...many trucks... soldiers...I see...outside Varmul!' Sherwani told them, terrified, but earnest, eager to convey this message, even as his skinny legs dangled midair, his feet a few inches above the ground.

'Are you speaking the truth?' the beefy six-footer demanded in broken Urdu. 'Else, I'll hack you into a hundred pieces and feed you to the fish in the river!' he dropped Sherwani in a heap to the ground.

'Truth, *janaab*...I swear,' Sherwani rubbed the back of his neck, his mouth dry. 'I show you different road to Srinagar...' he said through quivering lips.

'What road?' the man demanded in Pashtu, bringing Sherwani to his feet, but still eyeing him like a tiger holding its prey.

'Other road...smaller road...Indian Army no find you...' Sherwani managed to say slowly, still conveying more with gestures than words. 'I show you other way, *janaab*,' he said again. 'I help you reach Srinagar quickly...'

The three men glanced at one another, then spoke rapidly in Pashtu, looking suspiciously at their informer. The tribes had earned the wrath of Sairab Khan for wasting crucial time looting and plundering the bazaars of Muzaffarabad. News of a shorter road would certainly please their commander.

Sherwani chewed his lip, looking up at the vultures circling overhead in the grey skies, wondering whether his bluff was going to work.

'*Allahu Akbar*,' exclaimed the one-eyed man, smirking through tobacco-stained teeth. 'Come. We will celebrate Eid in Srinagar.'

❋ These Are No Tribal Raiders! ❋

'Muzaffarabad is in ruins,' Menon began, putting down his glass of water. 'Domel has fallen; so has Uri. In Baramulla...' he paused, horrified at the unspeakable atrocities perpetrated by the raiders, 'they have been on a rampage – burning houses, looting shops, ransacking bazaars, kidnapping children, raping women–' he struggled to finish. 'They didn't even spare the nuns at the Franciscan Missionary...'

Nehru felt a lump in his throat. A tear rolled down his cheek. A loquacious orator on most days, Nehru was rarely at a loss for words, always having plenty to say. But, devastated by the news Menon had brought to the Emergency Defence Committee meeting on Sunday, he could barely speak.

'The raiders have taken control of the Mahura powerhouse and cut off the electricity supply,' Menon went on. 'They will soon be outside Srinagar.'

'You call them raiders? What sort of tribal raiders carry machine guns and mortars and Mark-V mines?' Sardar glanced up from the intelligence report. 'It is the Pakistani Army masquerading as tribal invaders!' He shot a glare at General Lockhart, commander-in-chief of the Indian Army, who had received news about the invading marauders a few days ago from his counterpart's office in Pakistan.

'What about the maharaja? Is he safe?' Lord Mountbatten, who was now India's governor general, asked Menon.

'I told him to leave Srinagar immediately. He has gone to his winter palace in Jammu.'

'Wise call,' nodded the governor general, even as Patel grimaced, fearing the press would have a field day over the maharaja's flight from the capital.

'The maharaja has pleaded for help from India,' Menon conveyed the ruler's desperate message.

'It would be utter folly to send in troops into a neutral state,' remarked the governor general, turning to the three military chiefs for affirmation.

They nodded quickly in agreement.

'Pakistan could do exactly the same,' continued Lord Mountbatten, 'and that would result in certain war.'

'The maharaja is willing to accede to India,' said Menon, 'and to have a democratic constitution in place.' Looking at Nehru, he added, 'and to include Abdullah in the administration.'

'All our conditions are met then,' said Defence Minister Baldev Singh. 'As soon as the maharaja signs the Instrument of Accession, Kashmir will become a part of India, and nothing can stop us from sending in our forces to defend our borders.'

'Hmm...' Mountbatten nodded thoughtfully, 'but this accession is taking place under strained conditions, and I think it ought to be ratified by the people once things return to normal,' he added. 'A referendum must be held as soon as the invaders are driven out. I would urge that India do the right thing...follow the correct legal formalities.'

Patel exchanged glances with a dejected Nehru. The situation in Kashmir could not be seen in isolation; the aftermath of Pakistan's claim to the Hindu-majority state of Junagadh was still playing out in another part of the country.

'Menon, I know you have only just returned from Srinagar,' Sardar placed a gentle hand on the state secretary's shoulder, 'but you must leave for Jammu now. We must have the maharaja's formal accession before we can proceed.'

Menon took a deep breath. After sending off the maharaja from Srinagar, he had been awoken in the dead of night with the news that the raiders were camping at Chhatabal, on the outskirts of Srinagar. He had wanted to leave immediately, but the maharaja hadn't left behind a single car. With great difficulty, Menon and his colleagues had managed to find a vehicle to get to the airport and return to Delhi along with Mahajan. He was exhausted – he hadn't had a proper meal or slept a wink in days. His tired eyes turned to a worried

Nehru and an anguished Patel. For months, these men had abandoned all thoughts of rest and relaxation, battling crisis after crisis to keep the Indian ship afloat. And for weeks hereafter, they were going to be locked in endless defence committee meetings to make preparations – from arranging aircraft to requisitioning military supplies – for what was to be code-named Operation JAK. *Where was the choice?*

'Yes, Sardar,' Menon nodded, 'I'm ready to leave.'

❋ Shoot Me Dead! ❋

'The maharaja is sleeping,' Captain Diwan Singh tried to forestall Menon's entry, as the state secretary tore past the living room of the winter palace in Jammu and into the corridor. 'He has been driving all night and day from Srinagar.'

'Don't I know that?' Menon paused at the bottom of the staircase and spun around. 'I put you both in the car last night, remember? This cannot wait,' he rushed up the steps to the maharaja's private chambers.

Captain Diwan Singh followed close behind Menon, then reluctantly knocked on the door. There was no response. He knocked again. Nothing.

Growing restless, Menon pounded on the teak door with his fist. 'Please open the door, Your Highness,' he hollered, ignoring the ADC's glare.

The door opened. The beleaguered maharaja emerged in a striped night suit, with a silk robe thrown over his shoulders. Dark circles around his eyes, shoulders slumped, face unshaven, hair unkempt, Hari Singh looked a wreck.

'The Government of India is willing to send in the army,' Menon broke the news.

A wave of relief washed over the maharaja's tense face.

'...after you sign the Instrument of Accession,' Menon completed the sentence.

'I...I...am ready...I told you I'm ready to sign...immediately,' the maharaja gripped Menon by his arm, 'but the army must save Kashmir.'

Menon took out the papers from his briefcase. 'As soon as I return with these papers.'

Grabbing the papers from Menon's hand, Hari Singh walked across to a desk. Captain Diwan Singh switched on a table lamp. Menon held out a pen. The maharaja sat down, scanning the document one last time.

> Whereas the Indian Independence Act, 1947, provides that as from the fifteenth day of August 1947, there shall be set up an independent dominion known as INDIA...
>
> ...Now, therefore, I, Shriman Indar Mahandar Rajrajeshwar Maharajadhiraj Shri Hari Singhji, Jammu Kashmir, ruler of Jammu and Kashmir State, in the exercise of my sovereignty in and over my said State do hereby execute this my Instrument of Accession...

Nodding in satisfaction, the maharaja brought down pen to paper, and signed.

> Given under my hand this *26th* day of ~~August~~ *OCTOBER*, Nineteen hundred and forty seven.
>
> Hari Singh [Signed]
>
> Maharaja dhiraj of Jammu and Kashmir State

Menon sighed in relief. *Finally! Jammu and Kashmir was finally a part of India.*

The maharaja stared at the page in silence for a moment. 'Please take a letter from me to the governor general,' he gestured to his ADC, who hurried into the study to bring it to

Menon. 'In it, I have formally asked the Government of India for help.'

'Right...I will leave immediately,' replied Menon calmly. 'Sardar will be waiting for me at the airport, and we will go straight into a defence committee meeting'—he laid out the next steps. 'As soon as the accession is formally accepted by the Indian government, the army will be sent to Srinagar.'

'Time is of the essence, Menon,' the maharaja pleaded. 'Hurry. Please.'

Menon nodded slightly, putting the documents into his briefcase. *If only the maharaja had realized this earlier!* An invasion from Pakistan. Betrayal by his soldiers. Rebellion in Poonch. The state in turmoil. Too much had happened too soon.

'I will do the best I can,' he assured the maharaja, and left as quickly as he had arrived.

***

As soon as Menon was gone, the maharaja reached into the pocket of his dressing gown and brought out a revolver.

'Wake me up tomorrow if the Indian Army has landed in Srinagar,' he placed the gun in his ADC's hands. 'If not, shoot me dead in my sleep!'

❋ Operation JAK ❋

Palam airport in Delhi was normally silent at this hour - but nothing about 27 October 1947 was normal.

Lieutenant Colonel Dewan Ranjit Rai of the First Battalion The Sikh Regiment looked at his watch. It was 4 a.m. Barely six hours since he had received orders to lead the operation to airlift troops into Srinagar, immediately after Maharaja

Hari Singh had signed the Instrument of Accession. Out on the tarmac, the Dakotas of the Royal Indian Air Force were preparing to be airborne, as a battalion and one company assembled hurriedly at the Delhi–East Punjab Headquarters.

'If radio communication with the airfield in Srinagar is not established and you are not given permission to land, you are not to land in Srinagar but go to Jammu,' his radio crackled to life with a message from the army headquarters.

The lieutenant colonel listened as he took one last look at the map charting the course he had been ordered to take towards Baramulla after landing – if they could land, that is. He then rolled up the map and stowed it in place.

If the runway at Srinagar had fallen into the hands of the Pakistanis, as seemed likely, the Indian forces would be compelled to take the slow and hazardous land route. With snow blocking the roads and raiders having seized pockets of the state, that would mean indefinite delays, giving the attackers plenty of time to take over the whole of Kashmir. Reconnaissance flights had not sighted raiders in Srinagar thus far. But the last report was nearly twelve hours old.

Just outside the aerodrome, Jawaharlal Nehru watched dozens of civilian aircraft that had been brought in to aid the critical operation. His trust in British officers heading the armed forces fast waning, he wanted his own eyes and ears on the ground.

'You will be my liaison officer,' the prime minister instructed Brigadier Hira Lal Atal, the director of personal services at the army headquarters, 'and report to me in code.'

'Yes, sir,' Brigadier Atal replied crisply.

'LION, if you find the situation under control when you land in Srinagar, and if you think more troops can be sent in,' said the prime minister. 'JACKAL, if you think it's dangerous to land more men.'

'Copy that, sir.' the brigadier saluted Nehru and marched out to the waiting Dakota, conscious that the success of Operation JAK hinged on one crucial linchpin – had the Pakistanis captured the Srinagar airfield?

❋ Khushamdeed! ❋

The bird's-eye view of the rising sun casting its golden glow over the snow-peaked Himalayas was spectacular. But, as the Dakota carrying the First Battalion of The Sikh Regiment descended into the valley that cold October morning, Lieutenant Colonel Rai and his men had no time to soak in the glorious view.

'Colonel,' shouted Wing Commander K.L. Bhatia over the roar of the propellers, 'should we check for movement on the Baramulla–Srinagar road first?' If the raiders were approaching Srinagar, the convoy of their vehicles would be snaking through the arterial road.

'No!' Rai hollered back. 'Troop landing first.'

The wing commander steered the Dakota towards Budgam airport. It was 0900 hours. As instructed, they were to circle the city and check if it was safe to land. The first officer handed Lieutenant Colonel Rai a pair of binoculars. Drawing its strap over his head, Rai leaned close to the glass pane. He could hear his own heartbeat.

The plane dropped altitude, hovering over the city. Lieutenant Colonel Rai brought the binoculars to his eyes, spotting the crystal-blue Dal Lake first, then the Shankaracharya Hill and the Hari Parbat Fort. Gradually, the dusty and unkempt airstrip came into view.

'Colonel,' the first officer's voice sounded edgy as his eyes restlessly scanned the area for vehicular movement. 'Look there,' he pointed to the undulating ground around the airstrip.

Pressing the binoculars to his eyes, Lieutenant Colonel Rai adjusted the focal length. His eyes widened in astonishment. A multitude of people were emerging from the ditches and charging towards the airfield.

'Are they...' the first officer's voice trailed off. *Was this an ambush by the Pakistanis?* He wiped his sweaty palms on his trousers.

Every eye in the Dakota was glued to the little figures moving towards the airstrip, squinting at what appeared like an army of crawling ants. Nobody said a word.

'They are locals,' Lieutenant Colonel Rai broke the silence after a few tense moments of gazing intently into his binoculars, his lips curving into a slight smile.

Wing Commander Bhatia's fingers hovered gingerly over the landing controls. 'Are you sure?'

'Yes...they're not Pakistani raiders,' the lieutenant colonel smiled, pointing to the joyous crowds rushing towards the airstrip. 'They are Kashmiris.'

Down below, hundreds of men, women and children in colourful *pherans* swarmed the airstrip; their hands raised to the sky, waiting for the plane to descend much like an angel sent from heaven to rescue them.

The Dakota bumped down on the rough airstrip. Wing Commander Bhatia scrunched his face as he applied the brakes and narrowly avoided the rushing people. As the doors were thrown open, Lieutenant Colonel Rai inhaled the scented air of Srinagar, saying a silent prayer of gratitude. Operation JAK had begun well. He turned to his wireless operator, asking for a message to be sent to the army headquarters in code.

The message Delhi was waiting for anxiously went out on 27 October 1947 at 10 a.m.

'LION IMMEDIATE'

Outside, the misty morning air was filled with delighted shrieks, as hundreds lined the streets with flowers in their hands.

'Welcome, Indian Army.'

'Thank you, India.'

'*Khushamdeed!*'

WELCOME, INDIAN ARMY!

♦♦♦♦♦♦♦♦♦♦♦♦♦♦♦♦♦♦♦

Postscript

♦♦♦♦♦♦♦♦♦♦♦♦♦♦♦♦♦♦♦

On 15 August 1947, Jammu and Kashmir was neither a part of India nor Pakistan.

Maharaja Hari Singh signed the Instrument of Accession, identical to those signed by the other princely kingdoms of India, on 26 October 1947, by which Jammu and Kashmir legally became a part of India. This accession was contested by Pakistan, claiming that it had been obtained fraudulently by India.

Both Brigadier Rajinder Singh and Lieutenant Colonel Rai lost their lives in battle. They were among the first recipients of the Maha Vir Chakra in 1950. The brave fight put up in Uri by Brigadier Singh, which delayed the advance of the raiders by a day, posthumously earned him the gallantry award for his conspicuous valour in the presence of the enemy. Lieutenant Colonel Rai, who led the First Battalion of the Sikh Regiment into the Kashmir Valley, was also awarded the honour, the nation's second-highest military decoration for bravery in wartime.

Colonel Sam Hormusji Manekshaw, popularly known as Sam Bahadur (Sam the Brave), went on to become India's first field marshal. Mehr Chand Mahajan, the diwan during those critical days, went on to serve as the third Chief Justice of India in the Supreme Court.

The day the army landed in Srinagar – 27 October – is celebrated as Infantry Day in the Indian Army.

When the Pakistani raiders realized that Maqbool Sherwani had misguided them, they had him nailed to a wooden cross in front of a firing squad and shot him dead. Legend has it that before he was killed he was ordered to shout '*Pakistan zindabad*'. He refused to do so, shouting '*Hindustan zindabad*' instead. After Baramulla was liberated by the Indian Army, Prime Minister Nehru is said to have visited and paid homage at Sherwani's grave.

In a letter in November 1947, Sardar Patel wrote:

> The maharaja came to us very late. Had he delayed by a day, things would have been beyond redemption altogether.

That one day was undoubtedly won by the sacrifice of courageous men like Brigadier Rajinder Singh, Shaheed Maqbool Sherwani and many others.

On 31 October, an emergency administration was created in the state by the Government of India, empowering Sheikh Abdullah to take over the administration. Maharaja Hari Singh later handed over the reins of administration to his son, Karan Singh - who was appointed governor or *Sadr-i-Riyasat* of the state - and left Kashmir for Bombay, never to return. Karan Singh later joined the Indian government and was India's ambassador to the USA.

The war of 1947-48 dragged on for many months. The dispute was finally referred to the United Nations by Prime Minister Nehru at the behest of Lord Mountbatten and a UN-imposed ceasefire was announced on 1 June 1948. The ceasefire line is called the LoC or the Line of Control beyond which lies Pakistan-occupied-Kashmir (PoK) and Muzaffarabad is treated as its capital.

At Mountbatten's suggestion, a plebiscite had also been promised in Jammu and Kashmir by which its people could decide on the matter as soon as normalcy was restored to the Valley. Ironically, Jinnah repeatedly rejected the offer of plebiscite as the popular opinion in Kashmir, after the invasion, was anti-Pakistan and pro-India.

Starting in the 1980s, Pakistan began a sustained campaign to encourage separatists and militants in the Valley, which led to increasing communal tensions and the mass exodus of the Hindu population out of the region. Kashmir remains a thorn in the relations between India and Pakistan to this day.

While much water has flowed down the Jhelum since the events narrated in this chapter, terrorism and military presence have turned the beautiful valley of Kashmir, in which poets and emperors had seen paradise, into a bloody battleground. With no end in sight to the dispute, the words of Pandit Kalhana, considered as India's first historian, in his treatise *Rajatarangini*, make for a poignant reminder:

Kashmir, by the power of the spirit... Yes.
Kashmir, by the power of the sword... Never.

♦♦♦♦♦♦♦♦♦♦♦♦♦♦♦♦♦♦

Did It Really Happen This Way?

♦♦♦♦♦♦♦♦♦♦♦♦♦♦♦♦♦♦

The opening scene is reconstructed based on Mountbatten's record in The Transfer of Power 1942–7, Vol. XII.

The meeting in jail between Sheikh Abdullah and his family has been recreated based on the way his daughters describe him in In a State of Violent Peace: Voices from the Kashmir Valley *by Meera Khanna, speeches made by him and his autobiography,* Flames of the Chinar: An Autobiography.

The discussion between the viceroy and the Indian leaders over the Kashmir situation and Nehru's reactions are based on the minutes recorded in The Transfer of Power 1942–7, Vol. XII *and Nehru's correspondence found in* Nehru Papers, 2nd Series, Vol. II.

Details of the meeting between Kak and Jinnah are based mainly on an essay titled 'Kak and Sheikh' by A.G. Noorani *in* Frontline *(magazine from* The Hindu, 28 *August*–10 *September),* Vol. 27, Issue XVIII.

The description of Gandhi's visit to the state is a compressed version of various events that took place during his tour described in Mahatma: The Life of Mohandas Karamchand Gandhi, Vol. 8 *by D.G. Tendulkar, while some events are drawn from Sheikh Abdullah's* Flames of the Chinar: An Autobiography.

The letter Jinnah receives with reports about the fighting tribes can be found in the Quaid-i-Azam Mohammad Ali Jinnah Papers, Vol. 1, Part 1.

A visit by Jinnah's emissaries to the maharaja, the blockade by Pakistan and the rebellion at Poonch have been mentioned in various sources including, among others, in Kashmir: The Unwritten History by Christopher Snedden.

The discussion between Nehru and Sardar Patel about news of a possible infiltration from Pakistan is based on a letter written by Nehru to Patel. The preparations made by India anticipating an imminent attack are also mentioned in various books, chiefly Mehr Chand Mahajan's autobiography, Looking Back.

The subsequent exchange between Sardar and Mahajan is also in the form of letters. Details about Mahajan's visit to Delhi and the meetings of the defence committee are drawn from Kashmir: A Disputed Legacy, 1846–1990 by Alastair Lamb.

Sheikh Abdullah's release from jail and events subsequent thereto find detailed mention in Abdullah's autobiography entitled Flames of the Chinar: An Autobiography.

Details about Maharaja Hari Singh's personality emerge from various books including those written by his son, Karan Singh, An Examined Life: Essays and Reflections (edited by Raghav Verma) and Heir Apparent: An Autobiography.

The story of Shaheed Maqbool Sherwani, the young boy who thwarted the raiders' attempts by misdirecting them, finds mention in several sources. The character of Abdul Aziz, tea-stall owner, who was murdered by the raiders for giving refuge to Hindu and Sikh women, is based on a report by a member of the National Conference of Muzaffarabad.

Dussehra celebrations at the palace on the eve of the attack are mentioned in From Partition to Operation Bluestar: Tales of a Journalist, Bureaucrat, Spy by Som Nath Dhar, which also describes the invasion. Details of the invasion are taken from various sources, including Tribal Invasion and Kashmir: Pakistani Attempts to Capture Kashmir in 1947, Division of Kashmir and Terrorism by Dr Shabir Choudhry, which sets out, *among other things, evidence of the involvement of Pakistan's government in the operation.*

The names and identities of the Pathan attackers have been imagined to put a face to the Frontier tribes who attacked Kashmir. The news broadcast by All India Radio and Pakistan Radio, and local reactions are based on the account of those events in the book Gilgit Rebellion: The Major Who Mutinied over Partition of India *by William Brown.*

The account of Menon's visit to Srinagar is based mostly on his own account in Integration of the Indian States, *with some minor modifications (e.g., he first visited Mehr Chand Mahajan, the diwan, and then the maharaja; this has been merged into one meeting, to keep the narrative succinct).*

While the accession episode is narrated as per V.P. Menon's account, there are alternative narratives that contradict the sequence of events cited by Menon. For instance, Sheikh Abdullah's autobiography mentions that the signed accession papers were taken to Delhi by Mahajan. The author has chosen to go with Menon's version on this, which does not, in any manner, seek to discredit other sources/versions.

Events describing the start of Operation JAK, with which the chapter ends, are taken mainly from Air Marshal Bharat Kumar's book An Incredible War: IAF in Kashmir War, 1947–1948, *with some alterations for the sake of brevity.*

♦♦♦♦♦♦♦♦♦♦♦♦♦♦♦♦♦♦♦

Special Note to the Reader

♦♦♦♦♦♦♦♦♦♦♦♦♦♦♦♦♦♦♦

Of all the chapters in this book, Kashmir alone is a story that is still unravelling, and is the cause of much pain and anguish to many, in particular to the people of Jammu and Kashmir (many of whom have been forced to flee the state) as also to India's armed forces. The conflict of 1947–48 continued beyond the point where the chapter in this book comes to a close, and involved many other brave officers and soldiers. Several other conflicts have taken place over Kashmir after October 1947, where the story of this chapter ends. These events are outside the purview of the story of the accession of princely states, which is the subject of this book.

The writing of this chapter required condensing and simplifying several complex episodes and may cause the reader to take several long jumps. Nothing mentioned or omitted seeks to either promote or belittle the narrative of any party involved in the struggle. Interested readers are advised to refer to updated sources for a fuller understanding of the current situation in Jammu and Kashmir.

13

The Crawling Caterpillar

THE STORY OF HYDERABAD

PRINCELY STATE OF HYDERABAD IN 1947:
in present-day Telangana
(some parts in Karnataka and Maharashtra)
AREA: 82,313 square miles (213,189 square kilometres)
POPULATION: 16,338,534
RULER: Nizam Sir Mir Osman Ali Khan Siddiqui Asaf Jah
DIWANS: 1. Sir Mirza Ismail;
2. Nawab of Chhatari; 3. Laiq Ali
21-gun-salute state

❋ Richest Man in the World ❋

Sir Mir Osman Ali Khan Siddiqui Asaf Jah, the seventh nizam of Hyderabad, loosened the yellowing collar of his sherwani as he threw another glance at the last lines of his diwan Sir Mirza Ismail's letter of resignation:

> ...there is no alternative for me but to ask to be relieved...I shall always pray that God in His mercy may protect the Asaf Jah crown from the dangers that I see looming ahead.

Placing the 185-carat Jacob diamond paperweight on the letter, the nizam sat back, surveying the long, rectangular treasury of the King Kothi. A blanket of dust covered the steel safes and trunks, each of which was filled with exquisite pearls and rare gems, and fitted with five-shilling locks. Bags of cash and piles of gold bars lay strewn about. Silver coins, precious metals, jade collections, antique pieces, priceless paintings - all of which were but a small fraction of his astounding wealth.

The nizams traced their origin to Mughal times, to a general in Mughal emperor Aurangzeb's army, whose son had established the Asaf Jahi dynasty in the Deccan. For over 200 years, Hyderabad had been the most prominent of all princely states in India. Titles such as 'His Exalted Highness' and 'The Faithful Ally', bestowed on the nizam by the British, stood testimony to his special position.

And yet, the summer of 1947 found the nizam a worried man. So far, he had been cocooned within the protection afforded by paramountcy. But with the British Raj withdrawing, diverse forces were staking their claim to fill the void. The Majlis-e-Ittehadul Muslimeen (MIM), a party that had risen with his support, was pushing for Muslim domination over the Deccan, even as members of the Arya Samaj movement were resisting them with force. The communists had begun spreading their red banner of revolution across the countryside, while the state Congress looked to strike its roots in Hyderabad.

While many other princes appeared to have reconciled to the idea of joining India, the nizam worried that he would have no future under Congress rule. He owned vast properties – palaces, gardens, markets, mosques, tombs, forts and millions of acres of prized land, which yielded a staggering income. *How could he align with a party that was avowedly anti-monarchy*?

In 1949, the *New York Times* reported that the wealth of the nizam of Hyderabad could not be accurately calculated but had been estimated at being in excess of 2 billion US dollars. It was said that the nizam's collection of pearls alone would fill an Olympic-sized swimming pool. One finds several references which claim that the nizam was the richest man in the world at the time.

The world's most famous diamond – the Koh-i-noor – came from the Golconda mines that fell in the nizam's territory.

The dangers that I see looming ahead: the last words in the letter of his diwan – now former diwan – echoed in his ears. Mirza had been an able, unbiased administrator, but hardliners had hounded him out. With Mirza gone and his own grip over the state loosening, the nizam needed a suitable adviser – someone who understood the stakes. Someone he could trust.

Only one name came to mind – Muhammad Ali Jinnah.

❋ The Tables Turned ❋

Taking the monocle off his eye, Jinnah peered at the rows of petunias in his garden. He would soon leave this house in Delhi and head to Karachi, but the flowerbed bothered him. He called out to the gardener, barking out instructions about symmetry and alignment. Small things mattered.

The Muslim League leader walked over to the wicker chair in the lawn, thinking about the letter he had received from the nizam. The ruler of Hyderabad had showered him with grand epithets: *cynosure of all eyes, life giver for Muslims.* As Jinnah reached for his cork-tipped cigarette, a memory flickered in his mind.

About a year ago, when the liberal Sir Mirza had been appointed diwan of Hyderabad, Jinnah had visited the nizam. Stretching out his legs casually, Jinnah had conveyed his disapproval of the nizam's choice. The monarch had been outraged, accustomed as he was to his submissive courtiers – who never showed him their backs, let alone their shoes!

'I don't want any interference in my state!' the nizam had bellowed, rebuking Jinnah sternly, when told that the Muslim League would not support Hyderabad if he ignored their counsel. The outburst had prompted Jinnah to retract his legs and apologize. As he now deposited himself in a

THE NIZAM: I DON'T WANT ANY INTERFERENCE IN MY STATE!

chair with bitter memories of that insulting rebuff, Jinnah smiled smugly as he mulled over the contents of the nizam's latest letter. In just a year, how the tables had turned!

Sir Mirza Ismail had resigned of his own accord as Hyderabad's prime minister, and the nizam was sending Jinnah letter after letter to seek his views. Whether they liked it or not, they had all finally come around to admitting that he, Muhammad Ali Jinnah, was the undisputed leader of Indian Muslims.

Truth be told, he bore nothing but disdain for the monarch - oriental, medieval and feudal, dallying in Urdu poetry - and yet, he had to accept the nizam's olive branch. Osman Ali Jah was after all, the richest Muslim - and indeed among the wealthiest men - in the world.

What better ally for the soon-to-be-born Pakistan?

❋ Azad Hyderabad ❋

'Ala Hazrat'—an attendant entered the nizam's study, bowing in customary salutation, and announced, 'Monckton Sahib is here to see you.'

'*Shab-e-Barat*...' the nizam mumbled, his eyes squeezed shut in concentration. Kneeling by his side, his ustad scribbled down the composition, trying to fit the words into the desired metre.

Sir Walter Monckton entered the study and stood by the door, framed by Picassos on either side. He glanced at the short, spare ruler with narrow, hunched shoulders - polishing his poem - a soiled, dandruff-dusted fez on his head, a moth-eaten scarf dangling from his neck, ill-fitting trousers hanging loosely above his ankles, and on his feet, a pair of clumsy, grey slippers. *Who would ever believe that this shabbily dressed man was so fabulously wealthy*?

'Ah!' The nizam opened his eyes. 'Mr Monckton, please come in...' He stood up slowly, shifting his weight on to his brown walking stick, his little eyes glinting as he greeted his constitutional adviser.

Monckton offered his salutations as the nizam dismissed his ustad. 'Now that the British are leaving,' said the nizam, sitting down, his unkempt moustache fluttering above his narrow lips, 'I'm anxious about Hyderabad's future.'

Sir Walter took a seat. Hyderabad's future was on his mind too. It bothered him that the British were unilaterally withdrawing from inviolate treaties.

'What is your position on the Indian states remaining in the British Commonwealth after the British leave?' the nizam asked pointedly in his curiously accented English. 'You see, I would not like to break ties with His Majesty's government.'

Monckton stiffened. 'Your Exalted Highness, it has been made quite clear that only India and Pakistan – but not the princely states – will be granted Commonwealth membership.'

The nizam's face shrank. When the British needed men or materials for their war chest, Hyderabad had poured in its resources: 25 million pounds sterling during the First World War; three squadrons of warplanes and much more during the Second World War. And yet, now they were favouring the Congress that had opposed them, instead of the ally who had stood by them. 'They discussed all these matters with the Congress,' the nizam protested, 'while none of this was mentioned to the states...when *we* have been the loyal friends.'

Monckton nodded. He couldn't agree more.

'What reason do I have to trust the Congress?' The nizam rocked back and forth in his chair in contemplation. 'One moment they say they won't force the states to join the Union. The next moment they pressurize the states that refuse to join them. You tell me...how do I trust them?'

By no means were the nizam's worries unfounded. Having taken responsibility for Hyderabad's defence, the British had prevented the state from raising an adequate army of its own. *How was the nizam to suddenly fend for himself?*

'I will speak to the viceroy...' Monckton offered to make amends for the British betrayal.

'I have been in talks with Mr Jinnah,' revealed the nizam. 'I wish for you to go to Delhi and meet him before meeting the viceroy. And I intend to issue a *firman*,' he added firmly, 'from 15 August, Hyderabad will become an independent nation.'

❋ Cancer in India's Belly ❋

The only air conditioner in Delhi was operating on full blast, but did little to bring respite to the men in the viceroy's study, inspecting the nizam's *firman*. The previous day, Travancore had declared its independence, Bhopal was threatening to follow suit, and Kashmir had decided to keep out. The nizam's order was yet another blow.

Nehru straightened up, infuriated by Sir Conrad's handling of the states. 'The political department has been keeping us completely in the dark,' he grumbled. 'They work as a kind of *imperium in imperio* – an empire within an empire.'

'Hyderabad will be like a cancer in India's belly,' Sardar's voice was terse, 'cutting off north from south.'

'A mini-Pakistan within India,' mumbled Menon.

Apart from Hyderabad, the nizam was also claiming Berar and the mineral-rich Bastar, located within Indian territory.

'The state has a large Muslim population...we hardly need another cause of communal conflict,' lamented Nehru.

'Negotiations with Hyderabad are more delicate than with other states,' agreed the viceroy. 'Compulsions of geography aside, even going by history, language, culture – Hyderabad is an indissoluble part of India, and the nizam will come around. But he may need more time.'

'Hmm...' mumbled senior bureaucrat N. Gopalaswami Ayyangar. 'We should not give Mr Jinnah a chance to accuse India of being hostile to Muslim rulers,' he said, certain that Jinnah would rush to make the most of any action by the Indian government that appeared to be against the nizam.

'Swami Ramananda Tirtha and Dr Melkote came to meet me,' said Nehru, referring to the Congress leaders from Hyderabad working to bear pressure on the nizam. 'I've encouraged them to arrange a public rally in support of accession to India.'

'Let me handle the nizam,' Lord Mountbatten told the Indian leaders. 'Hyderabad's constitutional adviser Sir Walter Monckton is one of the finest lawyers in all England, an entirely earnest and capable man. I am certain that he will be able to bring the nizam on board.'

Drumming his fingers restlessly on the table, Sardar exhaled deeply. He had no doubts about the capabilities of Mountbatten,

GOPALASWAMI AYYANGAR: WE SHOULD NOT GIVE MR JINNAH ANY LEEWAY...

Monckton or Melkote, but he had mountains of misgivings about the nizam. 'Go ahead,' he told the viceroy, 'but mark my words: in the end, I am certain the nizam will let you down.'

❋ Hail Hussain! ❋

Jinnah studied the bespectacled constitutional adviser of Hyderabad, seated across from him at his study table. 'So, Sir Walter'—he poured his distinguished guest tea, then looked around at the other delegates—'I have warned the viceroy that if the Congress attempts to pressurize Hyderabad, Muslims across India – 100 million of them – will rise as one to defend the oldest Muslim dynasty in India.'

'To be honest, our exalted nizam is all for Pakistan,' said the nawab of Chhatari, Hyderabad's new diwan, 'but we are landlocked within the most Hindu part of Hindustan. Geography alone compels the nizam to deal with India. He worries he may not get good terms from India after 15 August.'

Jinnah sat back in his swivel chair. He had been compelled to swallow the bitter pill of a compromised Pakistan by conceding half of Bengal and Punjab, turning India into the regional giant. But all was not lost – not yet. *The weaker he could render India, the better it was for Pakistan.* 'I hope the nizam is firm in his decision to not accede to India...'

'Absolutely,' Nawab Ali Yavar Jung, Hyderabad's minister for constitutional affairs, assured the Quaid. 'A treaty with India is only for practical purposes.'

'Do you propose to conclude a treaty with India on defence and external affairs?' asked Jinnah pointedly. 'One should die fighting rather than yield on principles.'

'Mr Jinnah,' the nawab of Chhatari cut in, 'as Pakistan and Hyderabad grow stronger, we will review the position and reduce our ties with India over time.'

'The nizam would like to know,' Monckton steered the conversation to practical matters, 'how Pakistan will assist Hyderabad. Will Pakistan guarantee the supply of food, oil and other provisions to Hyderabad in case India creates an economic blockade?'

'And will Pakistan be in a position to supply Hyderabad with arms and equipment?' enquired Nawab Jung.

'It is not possible to give you any undertaking'—Jinnah waved away the query—'but there's no doubt that Pakistan will help Hyderabad.'

The nizam's representatives continued to appear sceptical.

'Look...if Hyderabad is short of petrol or kerosene, it would not matter,' Jinnah continued, tapping his cigarette on the ashtray. 'What matters is an abundance of perseverance and courage. The Russians were threatened by a blockade - did they not go on to win the war? If India puts pressure, like the great martyr Imam Hussain, Hyderabad should rather immolate itself than sacrifice its independence!'

As Jinnah deftly dodged and evaded every attempt of the Hyderabad delegation to obtain clear and concrete assurances, by delivering sermons on courage and conviction, Monckton exchanged dubious glances with the nawab of Chhatari. It was plainly evident to him that Jinnah's guns were aimed at India, but he was doing his utmost to shoot off the nizam's shoulders!

❋ Negotiation ❋

Drained after the entirely futile talk with Jinnah, the nizam's delegation found itself locking horns with the Indian side. 'The nizam wishes to make clear that Hyderabad does not want to join India,' Monckton declared emphatically to the viceroy.

'We've seen the nizam's *firman*...' noted Menon.

'Look...the states can remain independent after 15 August,' replied the viceroy, 'but the Indian Independence Bill will not recognize Hyderabad with dominion status.'

'The nizam wishes to convey his disappointment that Britain should abandon its most trusted ally in this manner,' retorted Hyderabad's diwan, the nawab of Chhatari, reminding the viceroy of Hyderabad's steadfast support to Britain in every war.

'May I also point out that, under our agreement of 1936,' Monckton argued, 'Britain cannot terminate the arrangement without consulting Hyderabad. You consulted the Congress and the Muslim League, but did not care to consult the princes who have stood by Britain all along.'

'We have some other concerns too...' the nawab of Chhatari interjected, 'you see...about 8,000 Indian troops are stationed in the state. If they remain in Hyderabad after 15 August, it would, in effect, be an army of occupation!'

'And there's also the matter of Berar,' added Sir Sultan Ahmed, an adviser to the Chamber of Princes, and another member of the nizam's delegation, 'the nizam wishes the Indian government to recognize that the region of Berar, which is being claimed as part of the Central Provinces in British India, is actually a part of Hyderabad.'

'Look, the Congress is looking at the larger picture,' Menon cut in. 'After Partition, we don't want India to be broken up further. If the nizam helps in maintaining unity, the Indian government could consider some of his demands, as it has done for some other states.'

'But Hyderabad is not just another state,' protested Monckton. 'It is the premier state of India with a 21-gun salute. As big as France. More populous too.'

'Nearly twenty of the fifty-odd member nations of the United Nations are smaller than Hyderabad, and sixteen have less income,' the nawab of Chhatari reinforced Monckton's argument.

'But think of the geography, gentlemen,' argued the viceroy. 'It will be impossible to come to your aid should you require it. I can predict disaster...'

'Your observations suggest that the nizam has no real choice in the matter,' grunted Monckton.

'Look...' said Menon, 'should Hyderabad accede to India, except for defence, external affairs and communications, the nizam will continue to enjoy all his rights.'

Monckton shook his head. 'As I've conveyed to you before, His Exalted Highness will not compromise his sovereignty,' he said. 'Can we not have an agreement in place of accession?'

Conrad Corfield from the political department, silent so far, leaned forward. 'Would the nizam be more willing to sign the accession papers if he were given the right to secede and break away from India after a year?' he suggested. 'The option can be kept open along with perhaps a three-year Standstill Agreement to maintain functional ties?'

'Out of the question! India will not enter into the Standstill Agreement with a state that does not sign the Instrument of Accession as it is!' baulked Menon, brushing aside Corfield's insidious idea. 'These are the terms being offered to all states. No exceptions can be made for the nizam.'

'Hyderabad is not just another state, Mr Menon,' reiterated Walter Monckton, locking eyes with the states' secretary, 'and if you press the nizam too hard'—he stood up to leave—'I'm afraid you'll be pushing Hyderabad to join Pakistan.'

❋ The Razakars Rise ❋

The MIM had been founded in Hyderabad some years ago, to unite Muslims in support of the nizam. And, as the summer of 1947 rolled on, the strength of the organization across its 500-odd branches had swelled to a staggering 900,000 members, thousands of whom had gathered in the vast Parade Grounds one fine morning to take an oath of allegiance to their ruler.

'I do hereby promise to fight to the last to maintain Muslim supremacy in the Deccan!' swore row upon row of young men in khaki, palm upon chest.

From a raised platform at the far end of the ground, Kasim Razvi, the belligerent leader of the MIM, looked on in satisfaction, pleased to have revived and energized the Razakars, the organization's military wing that had been established to mobilize forces during the Second World War. If India even considered flexing its muscles against the nizam, his Razakar forces were ready to lay down their lives for Hyderabad.

'India is a geographical notion, Hyderabad is a political entity,' thundered Razvi into the microphone after the cadre had taken their pledges. 'The nizams have ruled Hyderabad for over 200 years in an unbroken line. Are you prepared to sacrifice the reality of Hyderabad for the idea of India?'

Reporters scribbled away furiously, hanging on to Razvi's every word even as loud applause greeted the leader's speech.

'The delegation that claims to represent our interests in Delhi'—Razvi stroked his beard thoughtfully—'should Ala Hazrat, Our Exalted Nizam, place any trust in them?' He paused to allow the thought to take hold. 'The nawab of Chhatari - a rich zamindar from up north! Ali Yavar Jung? A stooge of Nehru and Patel,' he dismissed them contemptuously, 'and Mr Monckton... the viceroy's friend who's out to sell our interests. Traitors, all of them!' he roared. 'What is the team going to Delhi for? What is the meaning of "negotiating for our rights"?' he thundered on 'I say we bargain to buy mangoes or onions! At no cost do we bargain for our principles!'

KASIM RAZVI: WE BARGAIN TO BUY MANGOES AND ONIONS, NOT FOR OUR PRINCIPLES!

Dozens of trucks pulled up at the edge of the ground – men in short kurtas and ankle-length trousers, sporting skullcaps, jumped out of the vehicles – some brandishing swords, others with muzzle-loaders strapped across their shoulders. Some pumped bullets into the air, others distributed pamphlets with bold Urdu lettering that read 'Free Hyderabad for Hyderabadis!'

'*Kasim Razvi zindabad*!' The ground resounded with claps. '*Kasim Razvi zindabad*!'

'Let's not forget one of our primary tenets – loyalty to the Ala Hazrat who is'—Razvi looked heavenward—'the Shadow of God. He has a divine right to rule...' insisted the firebrand Aligarh-trained lawyer. 'It is shameful that those so-called "freedom fighters" in Delhi have no respect for *our* freedom!'

Slogans of '*Ala Hazrat zindabad*' and '*Kasim Razvi zindabad*' filled the air.

'If they understand us...well and good'—Razvi shrugged nonchalantly—'else, we are prepared – one and all – to defend Hyderabad to our last breath!'

❃ Blowing Hot, Blowing Cold ❃

While the atmosphere heated up in Hyderabad, the viceroy prepared to cool things down in Delhi.

Standing before the mirror as his valet dressed him, Mountbatten was confident he would be able to persuade most of the rudderless rulers to do his bidding at the banquet he had arranged for them. But the clock was ticking, and he knew he would need to work harder to bring in problematic states like Hyderabad and Bhopal.

'Hyderabad's war minister, Mr Jung, is in London to work out a secret arms deal with Czechoslovakia!' Hastings Ismay broke into the viceroy's thoughts with the latest news.

Mountbatten's eyes narrowed; he stared at his chief of staff in the mirror.

'Sir Christopher Courtney of the Royal Air Force was also approached secretly to help Hyderabad raise an air force,' Ismay continued as an attendant placed the Order of the Garter across the viceroy's chest.

Mountbatten turned around. 'This can turn into an embarrassing situation...' he mumbled.

'Indeed...' Alan Campbell-Johnson, the viceroy's press secretary, entered with two glasses of sherry. 'London has indicated that Britain's aim would be to obtain its long-term strategic requirements from India and Pakistan – not so much from the states.'

'Hmm...' nodded the viceroy, sticking out his arms for his valet to fasten his cufflinks. 'So, we are not to support the nizam in this then...'

LORD MOUNTBATTEN: HOW WILL HISTORY JUDGE ME?

'Well...not entirely...' Johnson offered Ismay a glass of sherry and then took a small sip from his own. 'London wants you to keep the doors open for obtaining help from the princely states.'

The viceroy sighed in frustration. For years, Britain's Asia policy had been designed to guard against Soviet Russia's expansionist ambitions. Even as they were about to withdraw from the subcontinent now, it was necessary to have a fallback option to exert their influence in the area in the event that their relations with India or Pakistan soured in the future. *And what better than Hyderabad, Britain's trusted and wealthy ally?*

'Also, we don't want Hyderabad to turn to the USA for business and aid,' Johnson brought the viceroy up to date with London's instructions. 'With our economy in a shambles, Britain can't afford to antagonize a friend like the nizam, nor disgruntle India or Pakistan.'

Mountbatten turned back to the mirror, admiring himself in his full regalia. *How would posterity judge him?* The question he often worried about reared its head again. *Would it appreciate the precarious nature of his predicament?* He was being asked to get off the horse but to keep the saddle ready for Britain to hop on, any time she wished to ride – not one, not two, but three horses all together!

❋ Indians Are Our Brothers ❋

With a week to go until 15 August, in keeping with Nehru's suggestion, the Hyderabad state Congress, led by Swami Ramananda Tirtha, had launched 'Join the Indian Union Day' to counter Kasim Razvi who had organized 'Independent Hyderabad Day' celebrations on 27 July.

'We belong to India,' the saffron-clad Tirtha addressed the vast crowds assembled for the state Congress session, 'whether the nizam likes it or not!'

The minarets of the Charminar stood as silent sentries, witnessing men in khadi kurtas, sporting Gandhi topis, and women in white hand-spun sarees, milling about with Congress flags in hand.

'We note with regret the *firman* issued by the nizam, declaring the independence of Hyderabad,' lamented the Swami. 'No decision can be accepted unless it is endorsed

SWAMI RAMANANDA TIRTHA: LET'S HOIST THE INDIAN FLAG IN HYDERABAD ON 15 AUGUST!

by the people. The people of Hyderabad – whether Hindu or Muslim, Telugu, Marathi or Kannadiga – they come from the same stock as their brethren outside Hyderabad,' he continued. 'The country has achieved freedom by the sacrifice and suffering of the people of India. Our future lies naturally in the Indian Union.'

A thunderous applause welcomed the Swami's words. '*Mahatma Gandhi ki jai!*' the crowd raised the popular slogan, defying murderous glares from the nizam's police standing by.

The fiery Razvi had sold his followers a vision of Muslim supremacy and domination; the courageous Tirtha was boldly challenging it, with calls for unity and inclusion. He was Gandhi's disciple after all, possessing nothing more than a bowl, a blanket, the *Bhagavat Gita* and a staff. With little to lose, he had nothing to fear.

'Remember, our actions may lead to the loss of lives...' Tirtha warned Congress workers, aware that arrest was imminent for such a brazen challenge to the nizam and the MIM, 'but go out and hoist the Indian flag on 15 August. Resist the nizam's autocratic regime. Let the sovereignty of the people be established in Hyderabad.'

'*Bharat Mata ki jai!*' the crowds screamed.

'*Swami Ramananda Tirthaji ki jai!*' the gathering responded with gusto, as the air filled with charged slogans and rallying cries.

Freedom for India was just around the corner, but the battle for Hyderabad was only just beginning.

❋ Freedom at Midnight ❋

As Jawaharlal Nehru took the oath as the first prime minister of free India in New Delhi, the Bombay–Madras Express train neared Gulbarga Railway Station in Hyderabad, the hiss of steam from its engine drowned out by slogans of jubilation from its coaches.

'*Vande Mataram!*' roared the passengers as the train chugged into the station.

'*Bharat Mata ki jai!*' Children waved the tricolour through the windows.

Standing beneath an awning at the station, Sub-Inspector Yusuf glared at the Indian flag pasted upon compartment after compartment of the incoming train. 'Nab each one with that flag,' he yelled, as the train came to a halt. 'Arrest anyone flying a flag other than the nizam's Asaf Jahi standard.'

Yusuf's men rushed into the train with buckets of water, sticks, stones, dry leaves – just about anything they could lay their hands on. And they got to work – scrubbing, erasing, wiping – cleaning all traces of the Indian tricolour.

Inside the train, policemen barked threats at the hapless passengers and snatched the flags from the children.

'Why are you destroying our flag?' demanded the mother of a frightened little boy.

'This is not our flag,' Yusuf snarled, ripping apart the tricolour. 'Go fly your flag in your country, madam,' he growled. 'This is Hyderabad. Not India!'

❋ We the People ❋

India had just shrugged off two centuries of British occupation. And yet, the men at the helm of affairs in Delhi grappled with grim news coming in almost daily – this time, from Hyderabad.

'We are sunk.' Lord Mountbatten, viceroy no more but independent India's first Governor General, stared at the telegram in his hand before passing it on to Menon. 'Sir Walter Monckton has resigned,' he said, and sat back in his chair.

'The nawab of Chhatari and Ali Yavar Jung as well,' Menon said, shaking his head in disbelief. 'They have all stepped down.'

'I'm told Walter won't retract his resignation unless the nizam condemns Razvi's continued scurrilous attacks on him.'

'What...now?' asked a worried Menon, thrown by the sudden stepping down of the nizam's most credible and reliable representatives.

'I'll write to the nizam,' said Mountbatten gloomily. He turned to Sardar, still hopeful that things could be salvaged. 'He is reluctant to cede power, but what if we changed the terms slightly...uh...if we renamed it *Articles* or *Agreement of Association* instead of *Accession*...' his voice trailed off.

'Out of the question,' Sardar dismissed the idea promptly. 'It will be a breach of faith with other states. And, besides, would that not imply that India will offer better terms to those who challenge us rather than those who are with us?' he asked, peeved that the royals had rushed to help the British against the Germans – to defend freedom and democracy on foreign shores – but refused to apply those very same principles in their own kingdoms.

'Well, we have given Hyderabad a two-month extension...' Mountbatten shrugged.

'And that is quite adequate,' snapped Sardar tersely. 'I am certain that these two months will be used by Hyderabad for preparations rather than negotiation. Recent activities of the MIM are creating terror among non-Muslims there.'

The men sipped their tea in sombre silence for a few minutes.

'All right...here's a via media I can offer,' Sardar suggested as he put down his cup. 'Let's submit this issue to the people of Hyderabad for a referendum,' he said, confident that the Hindu-majority state would vote to join India. 'Let the nizam agree to abide by the wishes of his people...the Government of India will accept the result.'

❋ Blissful Oblivion ❋

'Never,' the nizam shot down the suggestion outright. 'No referendum!'

While Delhi grew anxious, the nizam appeared to be blissfully oblivious, rolling out garden parties with a sixty-piece string orchestra playing waltzes and foxtrots on one day, and composing ghazals and love poems for publication in Hyderabadi newspapers the next. As far as India was concerned, he had simply had enough. At Mountbatten's behest he had condemned the press attack on Monckton, reappointed him as constitutional adviser, even reinstated the others who had resigned. Furthermore, he had agreed to distance himself from Razvi and the MIM. But this latest suggestion to take the matter to the people through a referendum was preposterous! He was the ruler after all – the sovereign paramount power in Hyderabad with the divine right to rule – not the ordinary people.

'No accession to India,' the nizam declared. 'Either we have a treaty, or nothing.'

Back from a short absence after his sudden resignation and quick reinstatement, Monckton fidgeted impatiently on the dusty, worn-out chair. 'Excuse my forwardness, Your Exalted Highness, but I think one would be entirely mistaken to be led by Mr Jinnah,' he conveyed his honest opinion. 'His advice is coloured by what benefits Pakistan –

SIR WALTER MONCKTON: MR JINNAH'S ADVICE IS COLOURED BY WHAT BENEFITS PAKISTAN – NOT HYDERABAD...

not Hyderabad. We should press for a treaty with India – short of accession but preserving independence in legal terms...'

The nizam rocked back and forth. Back-channel talks had been initiated with London; arms deals were being negotiated with the Czechs. He was trying to purchase Goa from the Portuguese so that Hyderabad could have a seaport, and Pakistan had assured help to tide through any economic blockade from India. 'I am prepared...' he conceded, 'for Hyderabad to be associated with India for certain purposes... but foreign relations and defence will be under my government.'

The nizam rose and hobbled to the window. Down below in the garage stood dozens of vintage cars covered with grubby canvas sheets, their insides stacked with gold biscuits. *Had he amassed all this wealth just to hand it over to the two-penny men in Delhi?* 'Go to Delhi with the delegation once again,' he directed Monckton. 'Tell them that if they keep pressurizing me like this to accede, I'll cut off all negotiations with India.'

❋ Same Old! Same Old! ❋

Back in Delhi upon the nizam's instructions, Monckton and his delegation sat across from Mountbatten and Menon, around copious cups of tea.

'What's all this I hear about an order for arms you have placed with Czechoslovakia?' the governor general put the question bluntly before the delegation.

The nawab of Chhatari, now back as Hyderabad's diwan after a short period of resignation, shifted uncomfortably in his seat. 'Er...this has been done by the minister of war without my knowledge and...uh...I've no intention of giving it my sanction. But, you see, the Government of India had stopped the normal supply of arms to Hyderabad, and our request that India withdraw its troops from Hyderabad has remained unanswered.'

'Supply of arms has been temporarily halted to all states,' replied Lord Mountbatten. 'You do realize that it would be difficult for Hyderabad to deal with defence, communications and external affairs on its own.'

'I understand...' the nawab admitted, 'but the nizam is agreeable only to a treaty...not accession.'

'Also,' Nawab Ali Yavar Jung cut in, 'he fears that if Hyderabad accedes, the Muslim population will not tolerate it.'

Menon clicked his tongue, tired of the same old arguments and replies repeated *ad nauseam.*

'The nawab of Bhopal and Rampur had the same apprehensions,' pointed out Lord Mountbatten, 'but their fears turned out to be baseless, didn't they?'

'You tell me, sir,' said Menon, nearly at his wits' end, 'if the Hindu population in Hyderabad is suffering and dying, do you expect the Government of India to just sit back and watch?'

'A large proportion of the Hindus are loyal to the nizam,' pointed out Monckton. 'It is the nizam's declared policy to treat his Muslim and non-Muslim subjects impartially and without discrimination.'

Menon raised his eyebrows. If anything, the threat of the Razakars had made the position of the Hindus in Hyderabad most precarious.

'The nizam fears that signing the Instrument of Accession would mean merging his identity with India,' reiterated Monckton for the umpteenth time.

'On the contrary,' explained Lord Mountbatten, also for the umpteenth time, 'signing it would prevent obliteration. I am trying to get the Indian government to make a good offer to Hyderabad, to secure the continuance of his existing rights and internal sovereignty,' he said earnestly. 'But you too must meet them halfway.'

'I have prepared a revised draft of the agreement'—Monckton handed a document to Menon—'a compromise of sorts.'

Menon leafed through it as Mountbatten's staff meticulously noted down the minutes of the proceedings.

'It proposes an association for six months to help both parties gain confidence in each other,' explained Monckton. 'It will help the nizam understand the benefits of accession.'

'These terms are most unsatisfactory.' Menon placed the document on the table, feeling drained. 'All states have transferred legislative power over defence, external affairs and communications to India,' he repeated tiredly. 'Hyderabad wishes to retain those powers. It is not acceptable. Why, the nizam has never exercised these rights even in the past!'

'Mr Menon,' the nawab of Chhatari interjected, 'may I suggest you visit Hyderabad and meet the nizam?'

Menon turned to the governor general. Mountbatten responded with a mere shrug.

'All right...I'll speak to Sardar about that.' Menon heaved a laboured sigh, hopeful that perhaps a direct discussion with the nizam may finally help to make some headway.

But, sometimes, no matter how sincere the effort, things were simply not destined to move forward. Sometimes, no matter how earnest the attempt, things just drifted about endlessly in circles.

❋ Second Best Is Best ❋

'They invited you to Hyderabad just two days ago, isn't it?' demanded an infuriated Sardar. 'So, what do you mean they retracted the invitation?'

Menon made no reply as he followed Patel down the staircase of the office building towards his car. One step forward, two steps back. That was what the Hyderabad debacle had been all about since the beginning.

'Break off all negotiations with Hyderabad,' Sardar thundered, marching down the corridor to the entrance. 'What have we achieved in these three months? Didn't I warn you that all this would lead nowhere?'

'Sardar...from what I am told, the nizam seems to have a problem with the word "accession",' explained Menon. 'If we can get the substance of accession into an agreement... something can be worked out.'

'This has been going on for far too long,' Sardar said, calming down. Although he had let Mountbatten handle the state, reports had reached him from Aravamudu Ayyangar, former minister of Hyderabad, who was still in the nizam's inner circle. He knew that the nizam was accumulating arms with an eye to seizing the region of Berar in Central India, and gradually being drawn into Razvi's fanatical grip. 'He wants the Government of India to yield to him, but he himself will not give an inch. How can one be so unreasonable?' he asked, spreading out his hands.

As they reached the foyer of the building, Menon gazed out at the evening sky. Undoubtedly, the nizam was weaving webs of intrigue, but abandoning talks could only make matters worse. 'Sardar...if we agree to this request, at least we'll be assured that Hyderabad won't accede to Pakistan...' he whispered into Patel's ear. 'With the present situation in Kashmir and Junagadh, do we want to open up one more front of confrontation with Pakistan and...'

'What do you have in mind, Menon?' asked Sardar, as a white car pulled up at the foyer.

'If you and Panditji agree to accept a Standstill Agreement with Hyderabad for now, without an accession, it may provide some respite and buy us some time.'

As an orderly held open the door of the car, Sardar looked up at the rising moon. He had decided not to sign the Standstill Agreement with any state that did not accede. But this, if any, Sardar reckoned, was the time to bend.

'What you say is right'—he placed a hand on Menon's shoulder, grateful for his foresight and initiative—'sometimes in politics - second best is indeed the best.'

❋ Light at the End? ❋

Monckton stepped into the shabby room in King Kothi, littered from end to end with all sorts of Victorian-age paraphernalia. Other delegation members shuffled in, bowed low before the nizam and took their seats.

'I appreciate your coming here straight from the airport,' the nizam greeted them.

'We have promised Lord Mountbatten to be back in Delhi with your decision in four days,' said Monckton, getting straight to the point. 'India has made an exception for Your Exalted Highness and agreed to sign a Standstill Agreement with Hyderabad as a temporary truce.'

The nizam raised his eyebrows; he hadn't expected this.

'It has taken much effort to arrive at this'—Monckton straightened his necktie. Taking out an envelope from his attaché case, he placed it before the nizam. 'This draft now has the approval of Pandit Nehru, Sardar Patel and Lord Mountbatten,' he said. 'We all think it is the best deal for Hyderabad.'

The nizam looked at the document, then at the delegation members. 'You have all looked at it carefully?'

They nodded as one.

'I see...' The nizam sighed. 'Thank you, gentlemen. Let the draft be placed before the executive council. I shall adhere to the decision my government advises me to take.'

Monckton exhaled in relief. As did the other delegation members. With a nod from Delhi and the approval of the nizam, the official decision of the executive council now was no more than a mere formality.

For the first time in months, it felt like they were finally approaching the end of a dark, long and winding tunnel.

They couldn't have been more wrong!

❋ A Costly Postponement ❋

There is more to empty formality at times than meets the eye. As it happened on that warm day of October 1947, when members of Hyderabad's executive council awaited an audience with the nizam to convey their final decision.

'The council members are here to see you, Ala Hazrat,' announced the nizam's ADC, as the ruler emerged from the prayer room after his *namaz*.

Nodding away, the man, among the wealthiest in the world, headed towards the council hall, muttering the names of various herbs, potions and Unani concoctions to be prescribed for his begum who was unwell. Entering the hall cluttered with faded statues, he greeted the council members peremptorily.

'Your Exalted Highness,' the nawab of Chhatari began, 'this is the formal report with our decision.' He handed over a folder.

'Very well,' the nizam said as he sat back in his chair, while liveried waiters, bearing trays of tea and Osmania biscuits, entered the room. 'I would like you all to express your views frankly.'

Aravamudu Ayyangar, member of the nizam's council, stepped forward. 'With your permission, I wish to put a few questions to the learned gathering.'

The nizam nodded.

'Let's say a conflict arises between India and Hyderabad, how long could we hold out?' asked Ayyangar.

All eyes turned to Syed Ahmed El Edroos, the six-foot giant of a commander who headed the nizam's army. He scratched his nose. 'I'd say...uh...not more than four days.'

'Bah!' the nizam scoffed, 'make that two.'

Monckton exchanged glances with Sir Sultan Ahmed, adviser to the Chamber of Princes. Unlike the maharajas and nawabs of other princely states who were well travelled, the nizam spent much of his time immersed in the books in his library. A few weeks ago, when someone had arranged for a radio in the palace to hear Pandit Nehru's speech, the nizam had jumped in fright, wondering whether the Indian prime minister had hidden himself inside the black box! But, despite being cocooned in the palace, the nizam had a very real estimate of Hyderabad's relative military weakness against the Indian Army.

'The wisest course, then,' Ayyangar shrugged, 'would be to sign the Standstill Agreement, isn't it? We have secured much better terms than the other states.'

'Hmm...so what is the final vote of the council?' asked the nizam.

'Six in favour, three against,' the diwan replied.

'Ala Hazrat, Abdur Rahim and I are against signing,' Council Member Moin Nawaz Jung raised his hand. 'We believe that joining India would mean an end to our Deccani way of life.'

'So...the majority advises me to go ahead, then?' the nizam stroked his chin. 'Very well. The decision is made. I will sign the agreement tomorrow!'

'But, Ala Hazrat...' the nawab of Chhatari said hesitantly, 'we're leaving for Delhi tomorrow morning.'

'I'm aware...' the nizam nodded. 'Tomorrow.' He rose to leave.

As the nizam hobbled out of the room, the befuddled delegation members looked at one another in puzzlement.

Why had the nizam postponed the signing? What could change in one night?

As it turned out – just about everything!

❋ Midnight Mayhem ❋

Walter Monckton awoke with a start. A distant hum was growing louder and getting closer.

He glanced at the clock by his bedside. It was past midnight. Jumping out of bed, he dashed to the window and swore under his breath.

'What in heaven's name is going on?' gasped Lady Monckton, grabbing her husband's arm.

A mob was approaching their house. With torches. And sticks. And guns.

Rushing to the telephone, perspiration beading his brow, Monckton dialled the police. No answer. He tried again.

'What do they want?' Lady Monckton drew on her robe and hastily bolted the windows. The crowd was swelling in numbers. People were pouring in – in trucks and cars, armed with spears and swords, shouting into loudspeakers.

'Burn down the houses.'

'No pact with India.'

Throat dry, fingers fumbling, Monckton dialled his neighbour, the nawab of Chhatari.

'Hello!' a nervous voice answered from the other end.

'A mob...more than a thousand...men with guns...they...they have surrounded Lake View,' Monckton stuttered in panic.

'I know. I...uh...I've contacted army headquarters,' the nawab said. 'They're sending help. The mob will leave. Razvi has got an undertaking from the nizam.'

'Undertaking?' exclaimed Monckton. 'What undertaking?'

NO PACT WITH INDIA!

'The nizam,' sighed the nawab of Chhatari, 'has agreed to back out of the agreement.'

❋ Back to Square One ❋

'This tuppenny-halfpenny man has gone mad,' the nizam muttered. 'Razvi's actions are shameful,' he growled bitterly. 'The Standstill Agreement ought to have been accepted. I'm determined to accept it.'

Monckton glared at the nizam through his thick glasses. Whether the old man was putting on a charade or felt genuine remorse for the midnight mayhem, he couldn't tell.

There was a knock on the door. Razvi entered and bent low before the nizam. 'Ala Hazrat asked for me?'

'Yes,' the nizam's voice was stern. 'Why have you objected to the agreement when my executive council has approved it?

'If Ala Hazrat signs the Standstill Agreement, it will mean the end of Hyderabad,' Razvi declared matter-of-factly. 'This delegation is weak,' he scoffed, glancing scornfully at Monckton. 'If they had insisted on the original terms, the

Government of India would have accepted what we wanted. This delegation is no good!'

'Your Exalted Highness,' the nawab of Chhatari felt compelled to address the nizam out of turn, 'the earlier terms have been rejected by Sardar Patel. There is no possibility of altering this agreement any further.'

'Ala Hazrat, give me a chance to form a new delegation,' Razvi refuted the diwan.

'No delegation can hope to achieve the treaty as earlier proposed,' Monckton shot back. 'We have pressed every point. Patel has already granted Hyderabad a concession. He will not reopen negotiations.'

'Give us one reason why you think you will fare better.' Sir Sultan Ahmed sniggered.

'Well, so many reasons,' Razvi said, his eyes darting about the room. 'For one: India is fully preoccupied with the trouble in Kashmir. It is in no position to refuse our demands.'

The nizam cracked his knuckles nervously. With reports about an imminent Pakistani attack on Kashmir and the deployment of the Indian Army in the Valley, the nascent Indian government was on a weak footing.

'Ala Hazrat'—Razvi played to the nizam's mood—'the timing is crucial. The Indian government is cracking under the strain of external and internal troubles. The government will soon fall,' he prophesied with the flair of a fortune teller. 'India is growing weaker every day. It cannot afford to take action against Hyderabad. This,' he said emphatically, 'this is the time to break off talks and put pressure on India while we consolidate our position.'

The nizam paced the room with his hands linked behind him. Razvi followed. 'If we sign the Standstill Agreement now,' Razvi pressed home his advantage, 'that would settle things for now and accession talks will be postponed for a year. But, by then, India would have emerged from its difficulties, making the road harder for us. India is weak now. This is the time to hold out, not give in!'

Monckton rolled his eyes in disbelief. Razvi was misleading the nizam towards a wholly illusory and disastrous path. Hyderabad stood absolutely no chance against the Indian Army, be it now or a year later.

'We have a solid case in law,' Razvi argued, glaring at Monckton contemptuously. A failed lawyer Razvi may have been, but lawyer he was nonetheless, and would put his legal prowess to test even before the world's finest. 'We have inalienable rights and powerful allies. Jinnah is supporting us. The Tory leaders in Britain back us – why, Mr Churchill himself... Ala Hazrat, give me a chance,' he pleaded, 'one chance to negotiate with Delhi and the rest we put in Allah's hands.'

'And what exactly will you negotiate with Delhi?' asked Sir Sultan Ahmed derisively. 'Everything has been thrashed out over and over again! So many meetings. So many drafts have already exchanged hands. This agreement was the culmination of all that.'

'One must always negotiate from a position of strength,' Razvi retorted. 'Hyderabad has its own currency, its own post and telegram, railways and airline. We have our own state bank and public hospitals. You wish for all this to be liquidated and merged into India? What for?' He turned to the nizam. 'We're prepared to deal with India on matters like trade, customs duties, taxes and so on. On these matters we are ready to negotiate...how hard is that to understand?'

The sorcerer had cast his spell, leaving the old man spellbound. The nizam's lips quivered. He nodded.

'I'm afraid I cannot be party to this!' Monckton pulled out a letter from his coat pocket and handed in his resignation for the second time in two months. 'I resign!'

'I must step down as well,' Sir Sultan Ahmed said staidly.

'I resign too!' added the nawab of Chhatari.

As the little stack of resignation letters piled up on the table, Razvi's eyes twinkled and his lips curved into a smile. *They could do their best to cast him off. But he was going to stick on like a leech! Things were going exactly as he wanted!*

❋ Fire and Ice ❋

'Sardar...the nizam has selected a new delegation,' Menon held out a slip, finding a moment to brief Patel in the corridor of the secretariat, as the states minister juggled between crucial meetings. 'And they want to come to Delhi for another round of negotiations.'

Sardar's eyes widened as he perused the names on the list. He hadn't wished to carry on negotiations even with the old committee comprising men of stature like Sultan Ahmed and Walter Monckton. *What could he even begin to say about this one?*

'Ah, I see that the nawab of Chhatari has resigned as diwan again,' he sighed heavily. 'And the nizam has appointed the pro-Pakistan Laiq Ali in his place.'

'This new delegation is Razvi's choice,' Menon shrugged, 'who, by the way, wants an appointment to meet you.'

'Meet me? What for?' Sardar grunted, turning to check the wall clock. The defence council was scheduled to meet shortly to decide the course of action in Kashmir. He had no time to waste with this lot. 'Send him and his delegation back by the very same plane they come on!'

***

Sometimes, when the line between passion and madness begins to blur, no refusal, rejection or rebuff can make a man see reason. The year 1947 had witnessed many dramatic moments and was to see the rise of yet another impassioned rebel in Kasim Razvi, who was not the sort to take no for an answer.

'Salaam!' the leader of the Razakars greeted Sardar and then V.P. Menon with a wry smile as he entered the office of the States Department in Delhi. They could try as they might to stonewall him, but he wasn't going to back down.

'What do you want?' demanded Sardar tersely, with little patience for niceties.

'A change of heart from you'—Razvi pulled up a chair.

'A change of heart is necessary only when one's heart is full of poison!' retorted Sardar.

'Why don't you let Hyderabad remain independent?'

'You are aware that I have conceded to Hyderabad what I did not concede to any other state.'

'You have to understand Hyderabad's difficulties,' insisted Razvi, his eyes darting wildly from Sardar to Menon, then from floor to ceiling like a man possessed.

'I don't see any difficulty'—shrugged Sardar—'unless you have come to some understanding with Pakistan. I would advise you to see sense before it is too late.'

'*Tch!*' Razvi clicked his tongue. He had come to Delhi to negotiate; not to obtain advice. 'If you do not consider our problems, we will not yield,' he warned, before launching into a tirade about his willingness to shed blood for his sovereign and the Almighty.

Sitting stoically still, Sardar took note of Razvi's body language - the man's feet tapped the floor restlessly; his fingers impatiently drummed his knee; his fez was worn at a rakish angle; and his words gushed in a torrent.

'We shall fight!' declared the demagogue, his voice on edge and his hands trembling, 'and we're prepared to die to the last man.'

SARDAR PATEL: MR RAZVI, I CAN ONLY ADVISE YOU TO STOP BEING FOOLISH...

Sardar rose from his seat, seeing little point in wasting time with a fanatic intent on spewing venom – a man who had come uninvited to have a dialogue, and then stayed on to deliver a sermon. 'Mr Razvi, I can only advise you to stop being foolish,' he said, pointing to the door. 'But, if you've decided to commit suicide,' he said calmly, 'I'm afraid I cannot stop you from jumping into the fire.'

***

'How can you even suggest reopening negotiations on a document already rejected by the Government of India?' argued Lord Mountbatten, his face reddening.

'Besides'—an exasperated Menon stood up—'the new agreement had been drawn up upon repeated requests from Hyderabad. The nizam and his executive council had already accepted it.'

'I understand...' Moin Nawaz Jung, Hyderabad's Minister for Police and Information, who was leading the Nizam's new delegation chosen by Razvi, tried to pacify the annoyed men across the table. 'If you could tell me why the agreement was rejected earlier, perhaps I can provide a new perspective.'

'That is not my job,' Mountbatten barked. 'Do your homework! Find out from your original delegation.'

Unperturbed, Jung coolly opened a folder. 'His Exalted Highness has asked for new terms to be inserted into the agreement,' he said, placing a letter before the governor general and Menon.

'Absolutely not'—Lord Mountbatten shook his head. 'I'd do well to alert you not to make the mistake of assuming that India is too preoccupied to give Hyderabad its full attention.'

'Look...the Indian government appreciates the difficulties of the nizam with the MIM,' Menon pressed on, bunching his fingers together. 'That is precisely why we agreed to a compromise. After all that, how can the nizam expect new terms?'

'Mr Menon...we're grateful to the Government of India for the indulgence, but if we go back now without any change in the agreement, it will be very embarrassing...'

'That is a problem created by the nizam'—Menon threw up his hands. 'Is the state being ruled by him or Razvi?'

There was a moment of silence, filled only by the whirring of the ceiling fan and the clickety-clack of typewriter keys.

'The truth, Mr Jung, is this - and allow me to put it bluntly and candidly before you, once and for all,' said Menon, now nearly at the end of his tether. 'If the nizam fails to sign the agreement, it would be a minor inconvenience for India. But for Hyderabad'—he raised an admonitory index finger—'for Hyderabad, it will be an irrevocable disaster!'

Laiq Ali sat back, slowly beginning to realize that the Indian government would not bend any further than it already had. The next few days would see him return to Hyderabad to tell the nizam so; following which the nizam would finally sign the Standstill Agreement, agreeing to keep in place all the existing arrangements.

'Phew! So at least we will have peace for one year,' Nehru would exclaim to Menon with relief later that week. For just about everyone knew it was no more than a temporary truce. The saga of Hyderabad was far from over.

❋ A Dangerous Plan ❋

Peering into All-Saints Lane, Narayan Rao Pawar's hand sat lightly over the revolver tucked into his belt. A daredevil of barely twenty-one, he had given up his legal career for the cause of India's freedom and was now about to give up his life. He checked his pocket watch. It was time.

His eyes scanned the road under cover of the twilight shadows. His partners, Gandaiah Arya and Jagdish Arya from the Arya Samaj, had taken their positions up ahead at Boggulkunta, each equipped with countrymade bombs and revolvers, and even a bottle of poison to end their own lives if the need arose. The burly constable patrolling the marketplace down the street appeared to be sufficiently distracted.

As the clock struck six, the nizam's old and rusty car appeared around the bend, on its way back to King Kothi after his customary evening visit to Mecca Masjid and his mother's tomb. Pawar was confident that as soon as Osman Ali was eliminated, his sons Azam and Moazzam would turn on each other in a chaotic battle for succession, giving India a chance to get a foot in the door. To him, it was a cause worth dying for. Drawing in a deep breath, he recalled Netaji Subhas Chandra Bose's slogan calling Indians to the Azad Hind Fauj: *Give me blood and I will give you freedom!* The words reassured him.

Emerging from the shadow, Pawar began walking briskly towards the approaching vehicle.

As the black car drew near, the nizam's dusty fez became visible through the window.

But when the vehicle was only metres away, it suddenly stopped. Spotting a sudden movement on his left, the driver had instinctively pressed the brakes.

Raising his hand up high, Pawar lunged forward and hurled a bomb at the nizam's car.

Alarmed, the driver responded swiftly - stepping hard on the accelerator, then swerving to his right.

BOOOOOOM!

A huge explosion rocked the street, which soon filled with shattered glass, screaming people and billowing smoke. The patrolling constable came charging down the avenue.

Thrown back by the blast, Pawar steadied himself and rubbed his eyes. Before he knew it, the constable had pinned him down and kicked him hard in the side. Immobilized, Pawar peered through the haze of smoke.

At the far end of the street, the nizam's rattling tinpot of a car zipped past Pawar's two partners who had also failed to hit the target.

Negotiation. Revolution. Assassination.

Somehow, the nizam had managed to get past it all!

❋ Agent General ❋

Growing increasingly worried that the Hyderabad mess was only getting messier, Sardar paid a visit to his guide and mentor, who had changed the course of his life. Sitting beside Gandhi on the low cushion, spinning wheel at hand, Sardar discussed the many complexities in the nizam's state.

'Munshi'—Sardar turned to his friend and confidant, Kanaiyalal Maneklal Munshi, who also happened to be visiting Gandhi at the time—'will you go to Hyderabad?'

Gandhiji stopped scribbling with his pencil stub and turned to his visitors.

Kanaiyalal Munshi looked up at Sardar in surprise. 'Me?'

Sardar began spinning again, continuing to share his thoughts with Gandhi. 'Under the Standstill Agreement that we have finally managed to sign with Hyderabad, the Indian government has the right to appoint an agent there. I want Munshi to go as India's representative.'

Munshi leaned on the bolster cushion. For many months now, the lawyer's every waking hour had been consumed in putting together India's Constitution. Now, all of a sudden, Sardar wanted to send him into the fox's den?

'The agreement has bought us peace for a year, but we need a permanent solution,' Sardar explained, twisting the yarn he had spun.

Munshi took off his glasses, wiped them clean and put them on again. 'The Constituent Assembly work,' he mumbled. 'I'm in the middle of...'

'That'll be taken care of...' Sardar brushed away his concern.

'Bapu...*tamne su lage chhe* [what do you think]?' Munshi turned to his guiding light.

Gandhi nodded. 'You mustn't refuse. It is not merely a commission, it is your dharma.'

'But,' Munshi protested, 'it's a difficult situation.'

'If capable people like you hesitate to undertake difficult jobs, how are we to make any progress?' Gandhi peered at him from over his glasses. 'Of course, Razvi's group will not like you...but I know you won't fail.'

Buoyed somewhat by Gandhi's bracing words, Munshi turned to Sardar. They had been associates for two decades – had worked together, been imprisoned together – and yet, he was uncertain.

'Give me some time to decide...' said Munshi.

'What's to decide?' Sardar waved him off. 'You only need to tell me this...' he said, placing the yarn in a basket and standing up, 'when can you leave?'

That day, Sardar left Gandhi's residence in a buoyant mood. He'd be back to meet the Mahatma soon – but that visit would see Sardar in a very different frame of mind.

❋ Fast unto Death ❋

As India began taking her first steps as an independent nation, and Sardar sought to make changes to rein in Hyderabad, his relationship with Gandhi was undergoing a dramatic shift too. Many years ago, being inspired by Gandhi's thoughts and words, he had given up his legal practice, discarded his Western clothing and thrown himself headlong into the freedom struggle. Ever since, he had been a courageous foot soldier and follower of the Mahatma. But suddenly, even that source of light and comfort was fading, with Gandhi turning up the pressure on the Indian government to release the money it owed Pakistan.

'I ask you to bless the effort and to pray for me,' began Gandhi, his voice a soft whisper. 'My indefinite fast begins from the first meal tomorrow. It will end when and if I am satisfied that there is a reunion of hearts and an awakened sense of duty.'

If India and Pakistan, Hindus and Muslims, Sardar and Jinnah could not sort out their differences, seventy-eight-year-old Gandhi had decided to employ the only weapon in his hand – fasting – until he had had his way.

'I am ready to do anything you wish,' Sardar whispered, crouched by Gandhi's bedside, Nehru sitting to his right, senior Congress leader Maulana Azad to his left. The entire Indian Cabinet was at Gandhi's feet in Birla House.

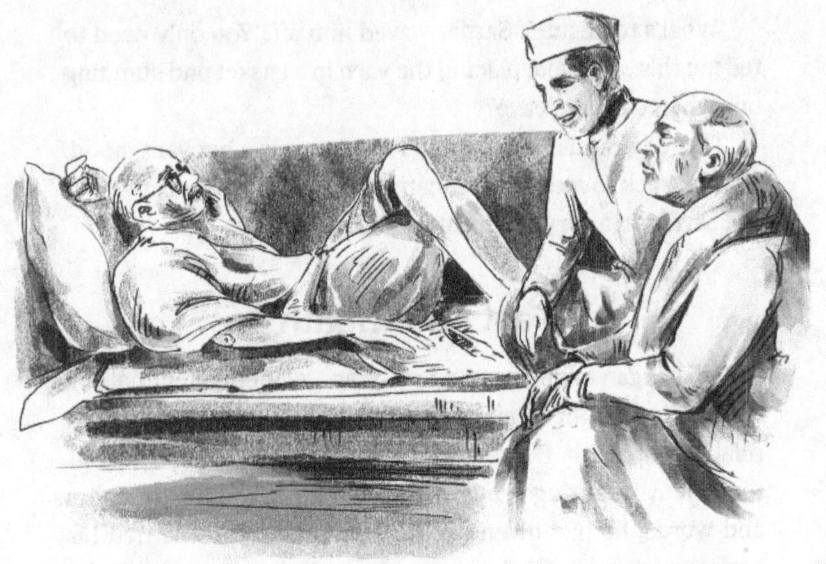

GANDHI: INDIA SHOULD RELEASE THE FIFTY-FIVE CRORE RUPEES DUE TO PAKISTAN

'Then release the money you are withholding from Pakistan,' Gandhi whispered back.

'Bapu...Pakistan will use that money to buy weapons...to kill Indians,' Sardar explained. 'You know what they are doing in Kashmir. We also have reports that they are smuggling arms into Hyderabad.'

'What they do with it is not in our hands'—Gandhi's voice was faint. 'We can only hope and pray that good sense prevails. The money belongs to them, and you are withholding it wrongfully. India is acting dishonourably.' Turning to Sardar, he asked sadly, 'Is this your decision?'

Sardar sighed. The decision to withhold the money due to Pakistan after Partition had been the entire Cabinet's. Mountbatten had put this idea of 'dishonesty' into Gandhi's head. And somehow Gandhi believed it was done at Sardar's behest. Sardar looked up at Nehru and at the other ministers.

Hadn't Nehru himself expressed the view that India ought not transfer the funds to Pakistan? Their silence hurt him.

'Yes,' he nodded, pained to be singled out as the villain for what had been a collective call. 'It is my decision.'

Gandhi looked away. Over the last few weeks, a mountain of misunderstanding had arisen between him and his devoted disciple of decades.

Sardar sat stone-faced, staring at the floor. Differences with Prime Minister Nehru had made it virtually impossible for them to function together; and now even Gandhi suspected him of communal bias. Perhaps, he thought, he ought to step down. Deciding to try again one last time, he leaned forward. 'Bapu...the matter of the money is not isolated...I beg you to withdraw your fast,' he pleaded in Gujarati, with folded hands. Language was one of the many bonds he shared with Gandhi, bonds that were suddenly fraying. 'These things can be discussed later.'

'My first condition to withdraw the fast'—Gandhi held up his frail hand—'is that India should release the fifty-five crore rupees due to Pakistan.'

Sardar closed his eyes. As the saint of Sabarmati, Gandhi could ideate and pontificate, sermonize and philosophize at length about morals and ethics. But he, Sardar, was no saint – he couldn't afford to be. He was the home minister of India, and the responsibility of the nation's security sat squarely and heavily upon his shoulders.

The decision was not going to be easy. But Sardar already knew he had no choice.

❋ A Report from Hyderabad ❋

'Keep watch on the movement of all goods entering Hyderabad,' Sardar instructed Balasaheb Gangadhar Kher,

It may appear strange that Balasaheb Kher is being called prime minister of Bombay in this episode, but that was how it was back then. Diwans of princely states were also referred to as prime ministers. Furthermore, the head of a province of British India too was referred to as prime minister. This nomenclature continued until 1950, when the Constitution of India was adopted, after which only the premier at the Centre was called the prime minister, while the premier of the state was called the chief minister.

prime minister of Bombay. 'No arms, trucks, military vehicles or machinery of any kind to be allowed without sanction,' he said, pressing the telephone receiver to his ear.

The list of Sardar's woes was just as long today as it was on any other morning. People were blaming him for Gandhi's fast and his deteriorating condition. The press was blaming him for lawlessness in Delhi and for the recent bomb blast in Birla House. Gandhi was blaming him for making 'communal' speeches and betraying his values.

But what could he do if Bapu refused security? What was inappropriate in urging Muslims staying back in India after Partition to be loyal to India? What did Gandhi find so communal about that statement? Sardar sat back, feeling dejected.

'Mr Munshi is on the line,' Shankar said, handing Sardar the phone again, just moments after the previous call.

'Ah...Munshi...*kem chhe* [how are you]?' Sardar leaned into the earpiece. 'Is the Exalted Highness taking good care of my Exalted Agent?' he chuckled.

Munshi grunted. In the two weeks since he had taken up his posting in Hyderabad, the nizam's administration had already driven him up the wall.

K.M. MUNSHI: THE NIZAM SAYS INDIAN CURRENCY IS NOT LEGAL TENDER IN HYDERABAD...

'Not good at all,' Munshi replied, 'he's trying to purchase Goa.'

'Hmm...' Sardar closed his eyes, worried that Goa could soon become a funnel for landing arms into Hyderabad. He asked Shankar to make a note of this.

'The Congress leaders are in jail...the MIM is growing in strength...the Hindus here are petrified!' Munshi continued with his litany of woes. 'Razvi's Razakars are spreading terror. The comic irony, if any, is that they call their headquarters "Darussalam", which means the Abode of Peace!'

Sardar sipped water, glad to have his own eyes and ears on the ground.

'Razvi thinks the Indian government is unstable and the army ill-organized to act against Hyderabad. And'—Munshi paused, his tone turning more serious—'Hyderabad has been violating the Standstill Agreement with impunity.'

'How so?'

'The nizam plans to advance a twenty-crore-rupee loan to Pakistan...and he has declared that Indian currency is not legal tender in Hyderabad. He has also banned gold export into India.'

'This is in complete breach of the agreement,' said Sardar. 'Surely Razvi and the Razakars are lulling the nizam into a false sense of security and into believing that he can get away with anything.'

'Sardar, my honest assessment is this...' said Munshi, 'the Razakars will not be eliminated by persuasion – they can only be liquidated by force!'

❋ The Light Goes Out ❋

'I am saddened by your resignation...' Gandhi placed a trembling hand on Sardar's shoulders. 'I understand...that there are differences between you and Jawahar, but this is not the solution.'

Sardar listened patiently, glad to have finally found a moment alone with Bapu. Visits to Birla House were part of his daily routine, but Gandhi was always surrounded by dozens of people, many of whom poisoned his ears against Patel. Little did he know then that the one hour he would spend with Gandhi that afternoon would be the last that Gandhi would spend with anyone.

'You both must work together,' Gandhi insisted after hearing Patel out. 'There are mounting problems. India needs you both to work together.'

Sardar smiled, his heart suddenly lighter. As a young Britain-returned barrister in Ahmedabad, he had scoffed at Gandhi and his unusual methods. But ultimately Bapu's ways had won him over, turning him into one of Gandhi's most steadfast disciples. He listened attentively, replied frankly, and spoke his heart and mind, as a tray of food arrived. Gandhi had his milk and boiled vegetables, and offered Sardar an orange as they continued to discuss the misunderstandings and tensions that had created a rift between the Congress leaders.

'It's ten past five...' Gandhi's daughter-in-law reminded him it was time for the prayer meeting. Hundreds had gathered outside, as they did every day, to hear the Mahatma.

Sardar rose to leave, then turned to examine the guards and cordons he had ordered to be set up around the premises after the bomb scare ten days ago.

Gandhi was running late, something he didn't like. 'We will meet tomorrow'—he patted Sardar's arm before placing his hands on the shoulders of Abha, his nephew's wife, and Manu, his grand-niece. 'You, Jawahar and I – the three of us – we will meet tomorrow and talk this over.'

Sardar nodded as he watched Gandhi's frail figure disappear through the rear door into the gardens, glad that the ice between them seemed to have thawed somewhat. 'Yes...' he murmured, feeling a huge sense of relief after days, '...we will meet tomorrow.'

But that tomorrow would never come. For, in less than an hour, the Father of the Nation would succumb to the murderous bullets of a man named Nathuram Godse.

Much less than meeting the following day, the following hour would find Sardar seated beside Gandhi's lifeless body, a weeping Nehru by his side. Holding hands, they would sob like children over a dead father.

Sardar, as he always did, would give in to Gandhi's wishes, patch up his differences with Nehru, and withdraw his resignation.

Nehru, as he always did, would find the right words to describe the historic moment: 'The light...' the prime minister would tell the grieving nation on All India Radio later that night, '...has gone out of our lives!'

❋ The Tension Rises ❋

Even as the nation mourned the Mahatma, an armed struggle was picking up momentum in Hyderabad. Forming what they called *dalams*, or special volunteer squads, members of the Telangana Armed Struggle roamed the nizam's territory, rabble-rousing, capturing vehicles, seizing property. Equipped with guns and muzzle-loaders, they fought the Razakars, and resisted the police with the mission of overthrowing the exploitative landlords, corrupt administration and autocratic nizam.

Eyes pinned upon their red flag of rebellion overhead, the song 'Jang-e-Azadi' on their lips, the spirited guerrilla squads marched on with zeal.

Woh jung hi kya, woh aman hi kya,
Dushman jisme taraaj na ho,
Woh duniya, duniya kya hogi
Jis duniya mein swaraj na ho!
Woh azadi, azadi kya,
Mazdoor ka jisme raaj na ho!

[What is that battle, what is that peace,
Where the foe is not destroyed?
What is that world, in which
There is no autonomy?
What sort of a freedom is that,
Where the worker doesn't rule?]

They sang verses, penned by Communist Party leader Makhdoom Mohiuddin, that voiced their dreams, before lining up to take the solemn oath: 'I pledge that I am joining the guerrilla force,' swore a lanky young boy. 'I pledge with determination to destroy the exploiters' rule and establish the people's Raj...'—his eyes sparkled as he glanced at the stash of shotguns, country-made rifles and *jambias* looted from the local police station—'...prepared to give my life...I take this pledge in front of the red flag.'

Thousands took similar oaths across Telangana, where messages of the Communist Party of India were spreading like wildfire. They were marching across villages with lathis, hoisting the national flag alongside red flags, breaking open the granaries of rich landlords and distributing rice to the people. Land units of over 200 acres owned by a single person was forcibly taken away and distributed among the landless. Wages were raised. Tanks dug. Canals built. Widow remarriages arranged. Night schools set up. A new political consciousness was taking shape in the countryside of the nizam's kingdom.

Barbers and blacksmiths, washermen and weavers, potters and *palki*-bearers – they had all served wealthy landowners for years without pay. They would accept it no more.

Yeh jung hai jung-e-azadi, azadi ke parcham ke taley,
Dekho parcham lahrata hai...azadi ka, azadi ka!

[This battle is a war for independence, under the flag of freedom,
Look, the flag of freedom is fluttering high, of freedom, of freedom!]

They marched on fearlessly, shoulder to shoulder with their armed comrades. As the months rolled on, the very air of Hyderabad was charged with rebellion.

***

On the one hand, the communist wave threatened to engulf Hyderabad, and on the other, the Razakar tsunami prepared to wreak its own havoc.

'If the goal is not Quranic, it only leads to disaster,' Razvi roared into the microphone. With his stranglehold over the nizam complete, the leader of the MIM felt confident he was more powerful than the king – he was now the kingmaker. 'Hyderabad is an Islamic state founded by the blood and money of Muslim rulers, and we are prepared to shed every last drop of our blood to maintain our state, whether India likes it or not.'

'*Allahu Akbar*!' the crowd chanted in unison to welcome his words.

'*Kasim Razvi zindabad*!'

Critics might have labelled him a fanatical demagogue, but few could deny the zeal he had injected into the Razakars. Following in the footsteps of the first caliph, Abu Bakr Siddiq, he had even donated all his property to the cause, earning him the title Siddiq-e-Deccan.

'If India insists on a plebiscite,' Razvi's voice simmered with rage, knowing full well that a people's vote in Hyderabad, with its Hindu-majority population, would go India's way, 'the final arbiter will be the sword. I urge the Muslims of Hyderabad to march forward with the Quran in one hand and a sword in the other,' he exhorted. 'Rise, my brothers. The day is not far when the waves of the Bay of Bengal will be washing the feet of Our Exalted Sovereign and the Asaf Jahi flag will flutter from the ramparts of the Lal Qila in Delhi.'

❋ Heart Attack ❋

Putting aside the newspaper filled with articles about Razvi's nasty, rabble-rousing speeches, K.M. Munshi picked up his pen to report to Delhi.

The Razakar menace has strengthened the communists... he began, describing the alarming situation he had witnessed during his troubled tour of Vijayawada. Things were worsening rapidly by the day. The MIM newspapers had stepped up psychological propaganda against India, attacking the Indian government and its agent general one day, and the prime minister and home minister the next. Radio Pakistan fuelled the anti-India sentiment, claiming that the Indian Army was losing ground in Kashmir. There were more Pakistani newspapers in Hyderabad – than Indian ones – feeding its people with a steady stream of vitriolic propaganda – more fuel for Razvi's fire.

Villagers fearing the Razakars are taking refuge with the communists, Munshi wrote on. *Krishna, Guntur, East Godavari, Nalgonda, Warangal – the communists have strengthened their hold everywhere.*

A distant hum was heard outside the window. Munshi's ears pricked up.

The communists are in complete control of the Telugu-speaking districts, Munshi continued his report, '*and plan on taking the entire Andhra province.*

The noise outside appeared to be drawing closer. And it sounded like a mob. Munshi put down his pen.

'Have you seen what's going on outside?' His wife, Lilavati, came rushing into the study, ADC Major Randhir Singh following close behind her. Rising from his table, Munshi went over to the window.

'Oh, I cannot bear to hear this'—Mrs Munshi covered her ears as the voices of hundreds of Razakars, marching with flags and banners, became louder and clearer. They were chanting offensive slogans – threatening to force Nehru to bow at the nizam's feet; to bury Patel and Munshi in their graves.

Pulling closed the window shutters, Munshi led his wife into the living room at the far end of the house, trying to calm her down. The poor lady was already having a tough time with daily reports doing the rounds of atrocities against women by the Razakars. She even carried a bottle of cyanide in her purse, to end her life with dignity if it ever came to that.

Munshi sat beside his wife, 'Come, let's talk to Sardar – you will feel better,' he said, instructing his personal secretary, Raghupati, to put a call through to Delhi. At times when they felt most disheartened, conversations with Sardar in Gujarati, that were filled with comforting rustic wisdom and idioms, lifted their spirits. Waiting for the call to be connected, Munshi spotted a Hali Sikka on the coffee table, the currency of the state. As the slogans outside reached fever pitch, even that inoffensive little coin seemed to him like a bold act of defiance, screaming out that Hyderabad would not bend before India.

'What?' Raghupati cried in alarm into the phone.

'What's the matter?' Munshi turned to his secretary.

'Mr Shankar on the line, sir,' Raghupati's voice quavered. 'Sardar...Sardar has suffered a heart attack!'

Munshi held his breath. Lilavati sank into the sofa, hands over her mouth. They had barely overcome their grief of losing Bapu – and now this!

The road to Hyderabad appeared longer and bleaker than ever before.

❃ Goodbye, India ❃

Later, it would be said that Sardar had lost his will to live after Gandhi's death; bitterly blaming himself for failing to intercept the assassin; for letting the Mahatma fall to the bullet. As he recuperated in the hills from a serious attack of thrombosis, he would often be found remarking that Bapu was calling him, and that his time too had come.

Yet Sardar's work in the world was incomplete. Under the care of his ever-vigilant daughter Maniben, his secretary Shankar, and the watchful eyes of his attending doctors, not to mention the cheerful song of the thrush and the *bulbul*, he had moved steadily from bed to wheelchair; and from wheelchair to his feet. Gradually, he started attending to phone calls, reading reports, writing letters, even receiving visitors. So, on a misty June morning, when a row of Rolls-Royces from Delhi pulled up outside Doon Court, where he was convalescing, he was able to welcome the entourage with a warm smile.

'The hills have turned you into a young man,' Nehru said, hugging his friend affectionately. With Sardar away in Dehradun, the prime minister had been shouldering an excessively greater share of the burden over the last few months. The strain was beginning to show.

'We're off in a week,' Edwina Mountbatten held Patel's hands. 'We couldn't leave without saying goodbye to you.'

'I'm touched that you should all come here to meet me,' Patel smiled graciously.

'A goodbye visit mixed with work, of course,' quipped the governor general, whose term was at its close. 'I have come to show you the latest draft sent by Hyderabad. It has the nizam's approval.'

At the governor general's insistence, Sardar leafed through the document, then sighed. The nizam was now refusing to allow India the right to make overriding laws for Hyderabad. *How much more rope was he expected to give Hyderabad?* He glanced at his colleagues. Nehru, Rajkumari Amrit Kaur, Defence Minister Baldev Singh, N. Gopalaswami Ayyangar, V.P. Menon, Defence Secretary H.M. Patel – all of whom had come to meet him. Their unanimous silence said it all.

'This appears to be the only solution to the deadlock,' Mountbatten noted sombrely.

'Impossible,' Patel handed the papers back. 'Laiq Ali came to see me last month,' he told his visitors, 'and I put four conditions before him. I told him the nizam must bring the Razakars under control, release the Congress leaders from jail, bring all communities into the government and, lastly, introduce democratic reforms,' Sardar recounted. 'They don't appear to have adhered to any of our terms.'

'Well, if it helps...the nizam has assured us,' Mountbatten said as they made their way to the lunch table, 'that Hyderabad will not accede to Pakistan.'

Patel said nothing. He had never trusted the nizam, and the one year of constant evasion and manipulation had snuffed out even the tiniest speck of confidence he had in the man.

Lunch arrived. They ate, speaking about things less pressing...the hills, the weather and shared memories.

'India will miss you,' Sardar said to the viceregal couple when it was time for them to leave. 'Your work with the refugees,' he told Edwina Mountbatten, 'will always be remembered. And your help in these difficult times'—he shook the viceroy's hand—'how can I show you my gratitude?'

A GOODBYE VISIT MIXED WITH WORK

'If you really wish to say thanks'—Mountbatten pulled out the agreement again—'sign this.'

Taken aback, Sardar stared quizzically at him.

The governor general nodded. He had arrived over a year ago, dismantled the British Empire, divided a single nation into two. If he could help consolidate what remained of India into a single and united entity, posterity would perhaps judge him kindly.

'Very well,' Sardar relented, as a token of his gratitude and respect for the governor general. Taking the papers from Mountbatten, he affixed his signature on the papers, accommodating Hyderabad yet again, in the hope that the nizam would meet him halfway.

But soon, the nizam would do what he did best - yet another volte-face, extinguishing the last faint flicker of hope that remained. In the days to come, Hyderabad would escalate matters further, by taking the issue to the United Nations; Razvi would continue spewing venom on the streets; and Laiq Ali, the pro-Pakistan diwan, would begin preparations to go to war with India.

❋ A Crumbling House ❋

As 1948 rolled on and the issue of Kashmir simmered at the United Nations, Hyderabad's reference to the Security Council outraged India, an embarrassment at the international forum being the last thing the fledgling government needed.

But, even as pressure was building up far away, things were reaching boiling point at the epicentre within the walls of King Kothi in Hyderabad.

'Give me five crore rupees,' Prince Moazzam demanded, frustrated by his father's indecision and inaction. 'I want to leave Hyderabad.'

'Surely you don't mean that,' protested the nizam in anguish.

'Sir Mirza was a well-wisher, Monckton was a friend,' fumed the prince, openly charging his father with Hyderabad's destruction. 'They left us in disgust. Lord Mountbatten was Hyderabad's friend...you drove him away. Mr Munshi came here as a friend...and you alienated both him and Pandit Nehru.'

The nizam stiffened. He was already having enough trouble with his older son, Azam, whose every act caused him embarrassment. Azam's wife had left for Europe, taking with her the nizam's beloved grandsons, Mukarram and Muffakham. To add to the nizam's woes, Azam insisted on calling himself the official head of Hyderabad's army, prompting his capable commander, Major General El Edroos, to offer his resignation. And now, to hear the wiser of his two sons, his favourite child, Moazzam, speak in this manner, pained him deeply.

THE NIZAM AND HIS SON MOAZZAM CROSS SWORDS...

'Despite being turned away, Sir Mirza continues to care about you. He has been writing to you, imploring that you do the right thing! But you have continued to ignore every piece of sagacious advice! Please listen – if you make peace with India,' said Prince Moazzam, 'the people of Hyderabad will be happy...'

'Son, I am doing all this for your future...' the nizam said with a grimace. 'India will annihilate our dynasty.'

'Only making peace with India can save our dynasty, Father,' exclaimed Prince Moazzam with increasing frustration. 'I don't know when you will understand this. Only peace with India can save Hyderabad.'

❋ Raining Guns! ❋

An inky black sky above. Pitch darkness below. No radar. Zero communication.

Any other pilot would have broken into a sweat. But Sidney Cotton, the blue-eyed Australian who had spent the war years flying combat missions for the Allies, was humming his favourite song as he looked forward to completing yet another arms-smuggling operation for Hyderabad.

It was turning out to be easier than he had imagined. In over a dozen trips in two months, he had airlifted arms from Karachi to Hyderabad – over 500 tonnes of machine guns and grenades, mortars and anti-aircraft guns; besides smuggling in five second-hand Lancaster bombers. He had even flown Hyderabad's emissaries out to meet the rulers of Hejaz, Trans-Jordan and Egypt to purchase arms. But the Indians had failed to smell a rat.

'*Bringing in some fruit tonight*,' the message would go out to those concerned.

'*The vegetables have arrived.*'

'*The cheese is ready for delivery.*'

Fruits. Vegetables. Cheese. Clever code names for arms, ammunition and anti-aircraft guns, to stay undetected.

Approaching the landing station at Bidar with yet another consignment of heavy bombers from Pakistan, Cotton felt it was getting too easy, woefully mundane. He noticed the unmarked airstrip down below, which his radio assistant, Frederick Rowan, had illuminated with kerosene lamps.

Cotton dropped altitude, keeping in mind the Tempests, the pride of the Indian Air Force, that had failed to intercept his gunrunning operations for months.

Cocky and confident, Cotton reached for the radio set. Clandestine operations weren't half as thrilling when the enemy had no clue that they were being duped. Smiling, he sent out a message to the Indian prime minister.

'Where are your Tempests?'

❋ The End of Patience ❋

The daring radio signal from Sidney Cotton was only the latest of several triggers to set off alarm bells in New Delhi.

Ghastly reports poured in daily, of atrocities by the dreaded Razakars, of violence by the revolutionary communists. Of merciless killings, horrific rapes, brutal kidnappings. Of arson, of loot, of mayhem.

Of helpless Hindus fleeing the state; of Pathans pouring in from the north.

Of violent border raids into neighbouring territories. And harassment of railway passengers transiting across the state.

Of Congress workers – over 10,000 of them – languishing behind prison walls.

Of arms purchases; of gunrunning from Pakistan.

Of police inaction. Of the complete and utter collapse of law and order.

Of anarchy. Of terror.

And the news only seemed to get worse.

Pakistan was encashing its twenty-crore-rupee loan from Hyderabad. The Indian government responded with an urgent ordinance, declaring all its securities held by the nizam to be non-transferable without approval. The nizam protested; Pakistan complained. But India remained firm by slapping

Hyderabad with an economic blockade, banning gold and silver exports into the state, and withdrawing its currency chest from the nizam's territory.

The nizam had escalated the matter and petitioned the United Nations Security Council, sending his delegation to Paris via Karachi. Nehru had declared the dispute a purely domestic issue. The nizam had requested Britain and the United States of America to intervene; Menon had asked the Cabinet's defence committee to step in.

India had tried every approach there was: cajoling, conciliation, compromise. Only one course now remained.

❋ Fat in the Fire ❋

'Our army has got to occupy Hyderabad,' pressed Menon, handing the prime minister a draft proclamation, 'that's the only way to stop the chaos there.'

Nehru browsed through the document, his eyebrows knitted together. *Call in the military on one's own people?* The idea outraged the Gandhian in him.

Menon turned towards an ailing and sombre Sardar, sitting impassively at the end of the table. Over a year ago, Patel had expressed his strong suspicion about the nizam. His fears had been vindicated, and just as he had warned, despite much ado, the States Department had been unable to make any headway in the nizam's territory. 'The army?' Nehru huffed. 'You want India to send in the army?' He tore up the proclamation, shredding the draft over which Menon had laboured all night. 'Do you not have any regard for India's international reputation and standing? India has never committed such a crime...'

Principles. One holds them dear to the heart and lives by their guiding light. But sometimes life confronts the best of us with a confounding dilemma, when values wrestle with survival, and morality battles necessity. The solution being proposed had shaken Nehru.

'Sir, all efforts at negotiation with Hyderabad have failed...' Menon reminded the prime minister.

'All of you...you have mishandled the nizam and Hyderabad,' the prime minister blasted Menon, thumping his palms on the table, launching a tirade against the States Department.

Shocked, Menon stared at Nehru. *Surely, the prime minister of India was no stranger to the patient and repeated attempts made by the department to resolve the Hyderabad issue!*

'I...sir...' he mumbled, affronted that Nehru should lay the blame at his door after all he had done to resolve the deadlock. But Nehru went on, hurling accusations of inefficiency and incompetence. Menon felt his temper rise.

As the prime minister ranted on, Menon suddenly realized that Nehru was not speaking to him at all! He was addressing Sardar through him. It made his blood boil.

However, unlike the temperamental and loquacious prime minister, Sardar Patel preferred to see himself as a man of action rather than words. In the past, upon Gandhi's insistence, he had reconciled with Nehru and put aside his differences. But there came a point when patience ran out.

Sardar rose from his seat, fixed Nehru with a stare; then without another word, he stormed out of the room.

***

'The fat is in the fire, VP,' a worried C. Rajagopalachari, India's new governor general known popularly as Rajaji, telephoned Menon an hour later. 'Sardar has resigned.'

'I am resigning too,' Menon retorted, seething over the morning's events. 'I have served three viceroys, sir! At no time have I been treated like this.' He began punching out his resignation letter on his typewriter.

'My dear man,' C. Rajagopalachari tried to pacify Menon over the telephone, 'the prime minister is under immense pressure...'

'And I'm not exactly on a holiday here!' Menon shot back tersely, in a manner completely uncharacteristic of him.

'I'm sorry to hear about what happened, but could you please speak to Sardar and persuade him to come back? I believe he has already called for a meeting of the Congress members.'

'Come back?' Menon flung up his hand in a gesture of surrender. 'After all that's happened! And, if Sardar leaves... trust me, there will be not a single man who can stand up to Nehru.'

'My God! Please, VP'—the governor general's voice was shaky—'you've got to do something. Speak to Sardar.'

'You are senior to me, sir,' Menon said, in no mood for a compromise. 'You go and ask him!'

And yet, within the hour, Menon would go to meet Sardar, who was lying in his oxygen tent after having suffered palpitations on account of the showdown with Nehru. Setting aside his ego, Menon would persuade Sardar to meet Nehru one last time before deciding to step down.

Then, putting aside seniority and ego, Sardar would relent, yet again.

Together, they would make one more attempt to fight for Hyderabad. Together, they would try one last time.

***

'I am sorry...terribly sorry...about my behaviour this morning,' Nehru apologized, walking straight up to Menon.

After much persuasion, Rajaji had managed to get all the men back in the room. 'You know how I am!' he said, looking genuinely remorseful.

Menon locked eyes with the prime minister but said nothing. The overworked Nehru was known for his mood swings and temper tantrums. And yet, such rude and aggressive behaviour was unacceptable.

'Let's sit down and discuss this,' the governor general patted a pale Sardar. 'Hyderabad needs our full attention.'

Sardar took his seat with a sigh. Through laboured breathing, he explained the situation in Hyderabad calmly to the governor general, a situation that could have been prevented if they had all listened to him a year ago in the first place.

Menon handed the governor general a plan with the dates; they began discussing specifics.

Still smarting over the morning's insult, Sardar glared at Nehru. Feelings he had buried deep came bubbling to the fore. 'You think you made the Congress?' he asked the prime minister sharply. 'We are all co-builders of the party.'

Taken aback by the sudden outburst, Nehru stared grimly at Sardar. Rajaji and Menon paused their discussion. One could have heard a pin drop.

SARDAR: YOU THINK YOU MADE THE CONGRESS?

'Do you think I want your position?' Sardar fumed. 'If I did, I would not have resigned my presidentship and asked Bapu that you should take over! I told him I would stand down, and I have no interest in taking your place!' he hollered, in a rare display of emotion.

The governor general stared at the plan before him, deeply embarrassed. Red-faced, Nehru cracked his knuckles and looked away. Picking up his files, Menon beat a quick retreat.

Patel sat back with a sigh. *Hyderabad would find a resolution. And it would find it his way!*

❋ Taking Stock ❋

As tempers flared and leaders sparred in Delhi, the nizam set out to find his bearings in Hyderabad.

'We are in an utterly hopeless situation, Ala Hazrat,' Major General El Edroos apprised the nizam. As commander of the Hyderabad Army, he had an accurate estimate of the strength of his forces. 'Any clash of our troops with the advancing Indian Army will make our terms of surrender harder.'

'We must continue our attempts to purchase arms...' the nizam mumbled.

'It's nearly impossible to do that in the international market now...' lamented the major general. 'Even if we manage to purchase ammunition, it will be impossible to bring them in, because the Indian government has closed all seaports linked to Hyderabad. Even Goa is under close surveillance. Nobody recognizes Hyderabad as an independent country.'

The nizam looked at him crossly. Hyderabad had a large army of its own, numbering over 20,000 regulars. Put together with hired mercenaries, customs and constabulary, the police force, home and civil guards and the Razakars, their numbers were well beyond 200,000 men. 'What is it you propose then?'

'Your Exalted Highness,' said the towering six-footer standing submissively before the frail ruler, 'I have submitted my plan to the government, but Prime Minister Laiq Ali has rejected it. He has instructed me to hold the Indian Army at bay for three months.' The commander Major General El Edroos appeared baffled. 'He believes Pakistan will come to Hyderabad's aid after that.'

The nizam cracked his knuckles. Razvi too seemed to have great confidence in Pakistan's promises to rush to Hyderabad's aid, as also in the Razakars' ability to hold fort against India. But, deep inside, he knew El Edroos was the level-headed man he could trust. 'Tell me...what is your opinion of the Razakars?'

The major general stiffened. 'They must be disarmed, Your Exalted Highness,' he replied crisply, miffed over reports in the Indian press that the Hyderabad army was in league with Razvi's brigands.

The nizam looked at him in horror, shocked that his commander was asking him to do India's bidding. 'I've been advised not to take such drastic action'—he turned his face away. 'It might lead to bloodshed.'

El Edroos pursed his lips, anguished that the nizam's decision should be guided by fear. 'If I had a free hand, Ala Hazrat,' he told his master confidently, 'I'd render the Razakars completely powerless.'

❋ An Unremarkable Death ❋

Miles away from the tumult in Hyderabad, on the dusty roads of Karachi in Pakistan, a military ambulance coughed and sputtered on its way out of Mauripur airport into the city, before breaking down and grinding to a complete halt even as a frantic Fatima Jinnah held her brother's trembling hand in hers.

A few weeks ago, an overworked and ailing Muhammad Ali Jinnah had been shifted from Karachi to Quetta for a break.

At first his health had improved among the fruit trees and birdsong in the hills; yet he passed every moment agonizing over his beloved Pakistan, the situation in Kashmir and the new constitution. He had spent the better part of his life working fourteen-hour days, smoking fifty cigarettes daily; these excesses had taken their inevitable toll. His body was now drained, and his lungs diseased with tuberculosis. The altitude in Quetta having triggered a haemorrhage, he had been advised to return immediately to the plains.

'I was born in Karachi,' Jinnah coughed, barely audible, as they waited by the side of the road for another ambulance to arrive. 'It is only right that I am buried there.'

Fatima Jinnah held his shaking hands in hers. Cars and buses sped past outside, oblivious to the identity of the man inside the broken-down ambulance.

'Jin...' his sister who had been his lifelong companion, squeezed his hand, 'you will be all right.'

'Fati... *Khuda hafiz*,' he whispered, as life slowly ebbed from his veins.

The Indians had lost the Father of their Nation earlier that year; the Pakistanis would lose theirs later that day. On 11 September 1948, after a year of tumult, as India finally prepared to launch a military strike on Hyderabad, Muhammad Ali Jinnah breathed his last.

❋ The Goddard Plan ❋

It would be given many names. Operation Polo. Operation Caterpillar. Police Action.

In essence, however, it was the Goddard Plan – a military strategy drawn up by Lieutenant General Eric Goddard, the Indian Army's commander-in-chief, Southern Command – to be put into action by Lieutenant General Maharaj Rajendrasinhji Jadeja. A plan made against the strictest protestations by the man at the top – General Roy Bucher, commander-in-chief of the Indian Army. Bucher had pleaded with Sardar to desist, predicting years of conflict with the Hyderabad army and revolt by Muslims across the nation.

Munshi had sent warnings too, of rumours about Hyderabad's Peacock Airborne Division that comprised fifty bombers in Pakistan or Iraq, which were being kept ready to bomb Ahmedabad and Bombay in the event India attacked Hyderabad.

But the Iron Man of India had stood firm.

There were to be two major thrusts: a western incursion through the Sholapur–Hyderabad axis and an eastern one along the Vijayawada–Hyderabad route. Major General Jayanto Nath Chaudhuri was to lead the march from Sholapur, and Major General Ajit Rudra was to lead the advance from Vijayawada. Given the fear of violence by the Razakars, keeping the campaign brisk was key to its success.

At Bucher's insistence, a frantic Nehru called a sleeping Patel on the eve of the operation. The army was already engaged in Kashmir. Besides, news of Jinnah's demise had just come in. Perhaps not the best time to launch an offensive.

'Bucher is asking me to call it off,' an anxious Nehru conveyed his last-minute cold feet to the states minister over a late-night telephone call. 'What do I do?'

Sardar looked at the clock and rubbed his eyes. *Was this any hour to rethink*? 'I'd advise you...' he said to Nehru in his trademark style, '...to go to sleep.'

A few hours later, after over a year of dithering and delaying, fumbling and floundering, the Government of India set out to stake its claim over Hyderabad.

❋ Seven Loaves of Bread ❋

On Friday, 17 September 1948, the executive in charge of Deccan Radio in Hyderabad received strict instructions – the daily dose of propagandist news was not to be broadcast; only music. City after city had given in before the advancing Indian Army; neither El Edroos's forces, nor Razvi's Razakars had been able to hold the fort. Operation Polo had begun on Monday; by Friday, the Indian Army had arrived at the gates of Hyderabad city.

At King Kothi, the nizam had been locked in hectic consultations with his diwan, having finally realized that Hyderabad stood no chance.

An ominous family prophecy whispered in his ears:

> Over two hundred years ago, the first nizam of Hyderabad was returning from a hunting trip.
>
> 'Won't you feed a poor old man?' a grey-haired fakir with wrinkled skin hobbled over to him.
>
> Feeling sorry for the tramp, the nizam plucked out seven *kulchas* from his saddlebag and handed them to him.
>
> The old fakir blessed the nizam for his kindness. 'For each loaf of bread that you have given me, your dynasty shall flourish!'
>
> Seven loaves. Seven descendants. There would be no eighth.

Nizam Osman Ali, the seventh nizam of Hyderabad, felt his stomach churn. Monckton, Mountbatten, Mirza, Munshi, Moazzam...they had all counselled him and counselled him well. But he had allowed the likes of Razvi and Laiq Ali and Jinnah to lead him astray. With a heavy heart, he began dictating a letter to the Indian agent general, K.M. Munshi:

> My government has tendered its resignation and asked me to take the political situation into my hands completely...I have

> ordered a ceasefire to my troops by this evening and also ordered to disband the Razakars...

He sat back after dictating the letter, wounded and worried. After threatening to unfurl the Asaf Jahi flag over the Red Fort in Delhi, have the waters of the Bay of Bengal kiss the nizam's feet, and bury Sardar and Munshi in their own graves, Razvi's ragtag bunch of Razakars had fallen to the Indian Army in a little over a hundred hours.

Happy to hear the nizam's message, a delighted Munshi rushed to make a jubilant announcement on the radio about it.

Displeased by Munshi's decision, Sardar berated him in his typical fashion for a hasty acceptance of the Nizam's olive branch. 'This is a surrender, not a tea party!' he reprimanded India's agent general. 'I want a proper surrender of the Hyderabad forces!'

On 18 September 1948, Major General El Edroos surrendered formally before the Indian Army's Major General J.N. Chaudhuri. In the end, while Jinnah did not live to see it, Sardar Patel would rest contented at having finally pieced together a united India, from Kashmir to Kanyakumari.

♦♦♦♦♦♦♦♦♦♦♦♦♦♦♦♦♦♦♦

Postscript

♦♦♦♦♦♦♦♦♦♦♦♦♦♦♦♦♦♦♦

Despite the posturing by Razvi, Hyderabad fell in 108 hours after the beginning of Operation Polo. On the evening of 18 September 1948, the nizam formally announced Hyderabad's surrender on radio. K.M. Munshi thereafter assured the people that India was one secular nation that could not be broken again.

Upon the surrender, power was taken over by Major General J.N. Chaudhuri. In November 1949, the nizam issued a *firman* accepting India's Constitution drafted by the Indian Constituent Assembly as the constitution for Hyderabad. After the police action, the Indian government took various steps to put an end to the Razakar and the communist movements in the state.

The agent general to Hyderabad, K.M. Munshi, continued his role as a member of the committee that drafted India's Constitution; he also later became a Union minister and was one of the founding members of the Bharatiya Vidya Bhavan.

Congress leader Swami Ramananda Tirtha was a mentor to P.V. Narasimha Rao, who later became prime minister of India.

In 1950, convicted in a dacoity and murder case, Razvi was sentenced to prison, after which he anointed one Abdul Owaisi as his successor, before moving to Pakistan, where he lived the rest of his life setting up a legal practice among Partition refugees in Karachi. The MIM is an active political party in Hyderabad to this day, and is now called the All India Majlis-e-Ittehadul Muslimeen (AIMIM).

Laiq Ali, the industrialist-turned-state prime minister, was put under house arrest after Operation Polo. However, he made a dramatic escape to Pakistan by duping the guards.

In a significant cameo in this spectacle, Sidney Cotton, the man who secretly smuggled weapons into Hyderabad, described variously as conman, secret agent and war hero, became the inventor of colour photographic film and the father of modern aerial reconnaissance photography. What's more, Cotton is said to be the inspiration behind the iconic character James Bond.

Questions have been raised about the Indian government terming the army operation as a 'police action'. It was claimed to be a peaceful operation. However, there are reports citing brutal atrocities after the army operation.

The nizam died in 1967, after which his grandson, Mukarram Jah, became the titular head of Hyderabad. He settled down in Australia.

♦♦♦♦♦♦♦♦♦♦♦♦♦♦♦♦♦♦♦

Did It Really Happen This Way?

♦♦♦♦♦♦♦♦♦♦♦♦♦♦♦♦♦♦♦

Descriptions of the nizam, his wealth and personality are all based on historical sources. Details about the characters in this chapter – as also of the prevailing conditions in the state – are based on sources including The Last Nizam: The Rise and Fall of India's Greatest Princely State *by John Zubrzycki,* My Public Life *by Sir Mirza Ismail,* Mission with Mountbatten *by Alan Campbell-Johnson,* End of an Era: Hyderabad Memories *by K.M. Munshi and* Once a Prince of Sarila *by Narendra Singh Sarila.*

The people's movements – both those of the communists and the Congress party – are also based on accounts by those involved in the struggle, some sources for which are Memoirs of Hyderabad Freedom Struggle *by Swami Ramananda Tirtha,* The 30 Years Political Struggle of Hyderabad *by K. Krishna Swamy Mudiraj and* Telangana People's Struggle and Its Lessons *by Putchalapalli Sundarayya. Parts of the resolution passed at the Congress session in Hyderabad have been reproduced here as Swami Ramananda Tirtha's speech.*

The scene of the assassination attempt on the nizam is based on details in Uma T.'s PhD thesis, 'Accession of Hyderabad State to the Indian Union: A Study of the Political and Pressure Groups (1945–1948)'.

Correspondence between the nizam and Jinnah can be found in the Jinnah Papers, Vol. 1. *What appears in this story is a condensed version of their letters. The account of Jinnah's meeting with the delegation is also drawn from those letters as also from an essay by* A.G. Noorani *entitled 'Jinnah and the Nizam of Hyderabad – A Tragic Liaison'. Some references are also found in Sir Mirza Ismail's autobiography.*

The episode about Sardar initially taking a back seat and the scene of Nehru's explosive outburst are based on Narayani Basu's book V.P. Menon: The Unsung Architect of Modern India. *Discussions including delegation meetings are compressed accounts of multiple meetings and lengthy correspondence. The nizam postponed signing the Standstill Agreement with India multiple times, but it has been cut down to avoid repetition.*

Mountbatten's discussion with Hastings Ismay about Britain's military interest in the subcontinent is found in a report sent to the viceroy from Britain's India Office in The Transfer of Power 1942–7, Vol. XII. *This has been included here specifically to throw light on Britain's outlook.*

That Delhi was being kept informed by a member of the nizam's council is attested to by a series of letters written by Aravamudu Ayyangar, with information contained for Sardar. They can be found in Sardar Patel's Correspondence, Vol. VII.

The speeches of Razvi and details about the Razakars are taken from sources mentioned above including from October Coup: A Memoir of the Struggle for Hyderabad *by Mohammed* Hyder. *Sardar's last meeting with Gandhi and the episode of Gandhi's assassination are based on the account in Vishnu Shankar's* My Reminiscences of Sardar Patel.

Details about the arms deals and meetings between Commander El Edroos and the nizam are drawn from references to passages in Major General El Edroos's book, Hyderabad of 'the Seven Loaves' *(the book itself is hard to find).*

The scene of Jinnah's last hours is as described by his sister, Fatima Jinnah, in her book, My Brother.

Details of the army operation are taken from sources including a paper titled, 'September 17, 1948, Hyderabad Liberation Day – A Misnomer', *by Captain Lingala Reddy and some online sources like journalist Narendra Luther's archive, and the informative Instagram page thathyderabadiboy.*

V.P. Menon's Integration of the Indian States *remains the backbone of not just this chapter, but of all the stories narrated in this book.*

Epilogue 1

Carving out the map of India in the manner that it stands today was a formidable task and a monumental achievement.

Accession on the three key matters of defence, external affairs and communications, was the beginning, not the end. The states were thereafter integrated and brought into the Union of India. Different regions were bunched together. Democratic reforms introduced in princely kingdoms. The states were reorganized. This process of integration and merger also presented huge hurdles - from the churlish to the challenging.

All in all, behind the map of India we see today is a story of grit. A story seldom told. A story we must know.

Twenty-three years after India gained independence, Prime Minister Indira Gandhi introduced a bill in the Parliament, seeking to abolish the princely privileges that had been agreed to.

While the bill failed to sail through both houses of Parliament with the requisite majority, a midnight Presidential Order was issued withdrawing all princely privileges. This was subsequently challenged in the Supreme Court by the rulers, who got some respite, but ultimately the princes were stripped of their titles, their privileges and their privy purses under the Constitution (Twenty-sixth Amendment) Act, 1971 (*see Epilogue 2 for details*).

Looking back, we may see the rajas and nawabs as feudal, entitled and extraordinarily privileged. Some accounts of their fabulous wealth and shocking deeds seem hard to believe. The writer Rudyard Kipling once observed: *Providence created the maharajas to offer mankind a spectacle.*

Yet it is important to remember that there were several rulers who were forward-looking and reform-oriented as well; and save a few, most of them agreed – perhaps willingly, perhaps grudgingly – but they agreed to join forces with the Indian Dominion – resulting in the map of India we have today: a single, undisrupted, united geographical entity. Sardar Patel called it 'a bloodless revolution affecting destinies of millions'.

The credit for this historically unprecedented task of unification goes to the stellar team of States Minister Sardar Patel and States Secretary V.P. Menon, as also to Prime Minister Nehru and Viceroy Mountbatten, and the many rulers, their diwans, advisers, and a number of other bureaucrats, including officials of the States Department, who worked tirelessly to make it happen, against all odds and despite the severe paucity of time. Together they exerted strong efforts and overcame multiple obstacles in ensuring that the generations to come would have a unified and consolidated India to call Home.

Epilogue 2

End of Princely India and the Landmark 'Privy Purses' Case

In July 1947, Sardar Patel had promised to scrupulously respect the autonomy of the princely states, and Viceroy Mountbatten had guaranteed that the Government of India would not encroach on the sovereignty of the states. Satisfied with the assurances, rulers of over 500 states had agreed to accede to India.

Starting in 1948, the Indian Government entered into new agreements with the rulers, for the integration and merger of the states.

In return for the rulers handing over their states to India, the Government of India agreed to pay them a sum of money – known as the privy purse – fixed based on a certain formula and intended to cover the ruler's living expenses.

While the ruler of a large state like Mysore was granted an annual privy purse of 26 lakh rupees, the ruler of the tiny state of Katodia in Saurashtra was paid 192 rupees per year. The total cost to India of privy purse payments was about 5 crore rupees. In return, India obtained vast tracts of land, property, assets and cash balances worth several times more. India also gained a railway network of several thousands of kilometres running through the princely states.

From the start, several people within the Congress party objected to the payment of the privy purse on the grounds that many rulers had done little to support the freedom struggle, and on the contrary, had acted as stooges of the British. (After the Mutiny of 1857, Governor General Lord Canning had famously called the princes 'breakwaters in the storm' for their role in protecting the British during the uprising). Even Prime Minister Nehru had written to Sardar Patel in 1949, stating that he was 'a little surprised and taken aback' that the privy purses were tax-free and payable in perpetuity.

Defending the policy, Sardar Patel tried persuading the Constituent Assembly in October 1949 to adopt a provision in the Constitution for the payment of privy purses. He called it a 'small price' India had paid for 'the bloodless revolution which has affected the destinies of millions'. Sardar further said: 'Let us do justice to them; let us place ourselves in their position and then assess the value of their sacrifice. The rulers have now discharged their part of the obligations by transferring all ruling powers and by agreeing to the integration of their states. The main part of our obligation under these agreements is to ensure that the guarantees given by us in respect of privy purses are fully implemented. Our failure to do so would be a breach of faith and seriously prejudice the stabilization of the new order.'

As a result, Article 291 was inserted in the Constitution of India to guarantee the payment of privy purses to former rulers. Article 362 recognized the rights and privileges of the rulers.

After Patel's death in 1950, and later, Congress leaders continued to demand the abolishment of princely privileges.

While Prime Minister Nehru considered privy purses 'too bloated' and requested rulers to voluntarily reduce them, being principally in agreement with Sardar Patel's view that the Government of India ought not break its promise, he did not withdraw princely privileges during his lifetime.

❋ A New Era ❋

When Indira Gandhi became prime minister, the demand to abolish princely privileges continued to raise its head. Several members of princely families had entered politics (more than one-third by some accounts) and some stood for elections against the Congress Party. Being popular, princely candidates were invited by all political parties, and often went on to win elections by huge margins. For instance, Maharani Gayatri Devi of Jaipur earned a place in the *Guinness Book of Records* for winning an election with a whopping margin of 1.75 lakh votes as a candidate of the Swatantra Party in 1962.

Heeding the clamour of voices within the Congress to cut the princely order to size, and as a part of bringing in populist reforms, Prime Minister Indira Gandhi introduced a bill in September 1970 to delete Articles 291 and 362 from the Constitution of India. Terming the princely privileges as not being 'in harmony with a society striving for equality and social justice', she said that history was replete with instances where 'what was sacrosanct in one age was considered inhuman in another'.

The bill was passed in the Lok Sabha but failed to get the requisite two-thirds majority in the Rajya Sabha. Bizarrely, one of the reasons attributed for the failure was the absence of a Congress member during the vote, as he was taking a toilet break! Embarrassed by the debacle, the Cabinet held an emergency meeting in the evening, after which an Indian

Air Force plane was sent to President V.V. Giri in Hyderabad to get his immediate signature on a Presidential Order to end privy purses. This was signed on 6 September 1970, by which recognition of all rulers was withdrawn with immediate effect.

This midnight order was challenged in the Supreme Court of India by a group of rulers in *Madhav Rao Scindia v Union of India*, more popularly known as the Privy Purses Case, regarded as one of the landmark cases of Indian Constitutional Law.

After listening to detailed arguments, the Supreme Court struck down the Presidential Order as being unconstitutional.

Subsequently, having won a convincing mandate in the general elections of 1971, the Congress party once again introduced a bill to abolish privy purses. This time, the princes reached out to Lord Mountbatten for help, who in turn appealed to Indira Gandhi to be 'generous' in the name of her father. But with a decisive majority in Parliament, Indira Gandhi was able to get the bill through without difficulty and all princely privileges were abolished. (The following year, Zulfikar Ali Bhutto – son of the diwan of Junagadh in 1947 – had a presidential order issued to put an end to privy purses in Pakistan.)

The passing of the Constitution (Twenty-sixth Amendment) Act, 1971, brought the curtain down on all the privileges of the princes, and with that, princely India faded into oblivion. Titles like *Maharaja* and *Nawab*, *Highness* and *Exalted* would from then on be forever relegated to history books, and the princely order would dissolve into the pool of common citizens.

Epilogue 3

Princely States in Pakistan

Not all princely states of the subcontinent acceded to India; around a dozen states joined Pakistan. While some of these unions began choppily, Pakistan's problems were minuscule compared to what India had to contend with, both in terms of scale and complexity.

For starters, the states – Amb, Bahawalpur, Chitral, Dir, Hunza, Kalat, Khairpur, Kharan, Las Bela, Makran, Nagar, Phulra and Swat – were territorially within Pakistan. Secondly, they all had Muslim rulers. Further, they had a Muslim-majority population. Given this numerical, geographic, political and demographic profile, the Pakistani leaders showed no urgency regarding accession. As a result, none of the princely states had acceded to Pakistan by 14 August 1947 (Pakistan's Independence Day). In contrast, on 15 August 1947, nearly all 565 states on the Indian side had joined India.

Pakistan too faced challenges regarding accession. The nawab of Bahawalpur considered declaring independence, or acceding to India, even as the ruler of Dir threatened to join

Afghanistan. When Chitral acceded to Pakistan, Maharaja Hari Singh claimed that its ruler had no right to do so, as it was a part of Kashmir. Not wanting to antagonize the maharaja of Kashmir, Pakistan did not accept Chitral's accession for months. The case of Kalat was the most contentious of all, where the Khan was reportedly in secret talks with India, although that was denied by Nehru and Menon.

While Pakistan attempted to claim princely states within India like Rampur and Junagadh, the Indian stand was made clear by Menon in his letter dated 17 July 1947, enclosing a brief for Viceroy Mountbatten about the matter, where he pointed out that the 'rightful place' of princely states like Bahawalpur and Khairpur, ruled by Muslim rulers and with a predominantly Muslim population, was in Pakistan. In his letter Menon stated that the principle that India and Pakistan ought to follow was '...render unto Caesar that which is Caesar's and unto God that which is God's'.

Speaking of Bahawalpur, which shared borders with Bikaner, Jaisalmer and Ferozepur, Menon said there was 'no question of it being absorbed by the dominion of India' and that 'its rightful place is with Pakistan'. Khairpur too, said Menon, 'should obviously form part of the dominion of Pakistan'.

Decoding the Jargon

ACCESSION

Cede power to

The process by which the princely states would hand over some of their powers to either India or Pakistan. So, for instance, if a princely state acceded to India in respect of defence, it would mean that the Government of India would from then on be responsible for the defence of that state.

BOUNDARY AWARD

Decision on boundary line

After the decision to partition India, two commissions were set up to mark the boundary line in Punjab and Bengal respectively, with Sir Cyril Radcliffe as their chairman. The commissions' decision was called the Boundary Award. The dividing boundary line is hence also called the 'Radcliffe Line'.

COMMONWEALTH

Association of British colonies

The British Commonwealth is an association of British colonies.

As Britain began granting self-government to some of its colonies in the early twentieth century, this umbrella association was formed to maintain ties between Britian and her former colonies.

DIWAN

Chief minister of a princely state

Every princely state had a minister who assisted the ruler in administering the kingdom – the Diwan or Prime Minister. Many of them were highly educated and some, like the illustrious M. Visvesvaraya (Diwan of Mysore, early twentieth century), played a key role in transforming the destiny of their states.

DOMINION STATUS

Full Nationhood within British Commonwealth

It meant complete freedom to a nation under the umbrella of the Commonwealth. In 1947, the British made it clear that only India and Pakistan would be granted Dominion Status, and not the princely states. This irked many princes as they wished to have Commonwealth membership and stay connected to the British Crown.

GOVERNOR GENERAL

Head of State

The governor general was the head of the nation state.

Upon Independence, Lord Mountbatten was India's first governor general.

Muhammad Ali Jinnah was the first governor general of Pakistan.

INSTRUMENT OF ACCESSION

Legal document to accede

The princes could transfer their rights to manage three matters - defence, communications and external affairs - in respect of their kingdoms to the Indian government by signing a document. That document was known as the Instrument of Accession.

INTERIM GOVERNMENT

Temporary government

In 1946, a temporary government was put in place to make way for the transition from colonial rule to independence.

Jawaharlal Nehru was the interim prime minister of India during 1946–47 after which he became independent India's first prime minister.

LAPSE OF PARAMOUNTCY

End of paramountcy

When the British decided to leave India, they also decided that the arrangement of paramountcy with the princely states would end. The states would no longer be obliged to accept the British monarch as their supreme power. As a result, the princely states would be free once again. All the rights they had ceded to the British Crown would revert to them.

PARAMOUNTCY

Supreme power

Under treaties, Indian princely states had accepted the British Crown as their supreme power and handed over many of their powers to the Crown. In return, they were paid an annual compensation and allowed to rule their kingdoms.

PARTITION

Division of India

India was divided into India and Pakistan in 1947.

Partition is the process by which the country was divided, and entailed the mass migration of people, settlement of accounts and distribution of resources between the two nations.

Over a million people lost their lives during Partition violence, thousands of families were separated and several millions left homeless.

PRINCELY STATES

Kingdoms

Parts of the Indian subcontinent ruled by hereditary rulers like rajas and nawabs.

In 1947, there were about 565 princely states comprising over 40 per cent of the Indian subcontinent. About 25 per cent of the Indian population lived in princely states at that time.

PRIVY PURSE

Payment to princes

In return for ceding their powers to India, the Government of India agreed to pay the princes an annual sum of money. That amount is referred to as the privy purse.

REFERENDUM/ PLEBISCITE

Voting

A process by which the will of the people is ascertained through voting.

In 1947, referendums were held in the North West Frontier Province and in Sylhet to decide about joining India or Pakistan.

STANDSTILL AGREEMENT

Agreement to maintain status quo

Railway lines, water canals, roads and post and telegraph networks criss-crossed various states and provinces.

By signing the Standstill Agreement, the princely states and the Government of India would ensure that all such matters continued to run smoothly even after paramountcy ended.

STATES DEPARTMENT

Ministry for dealing with the princely states

The States Department (later States Ministry) was set up in July 1947 to look into the problem of the princely states. Sardar Patel was appointed the minister of states. The secretary of the department was V.P. Menon.

TREATY

An agreement between states

An agreement signed by two or more states or countries.

Over the years, the British Crown had entered into several treaties with the Indian princely states with regard to water canals, railway lines and so on. If the British were to end all those treaties abruptly, it would lead to chaos.

VICEROY

Representative of the British Crown

The British monarch appointed a viceroy as his/her representative in India. Mountbatten was the last viceroy of India, till 15 August 1947, and the governor general from August 1947 to June 1948. That's why he is called viceroy in some places, and governor general in others.

OPPOSING FORCES

PAKISTAN

Why was Jinnah wooing the Hindu states?

Jinnah's initial idea of Pakistan was a bigger swathe of territory stretching across much of north India.

With Punjab and Bengal divided in half, and Kashmir sitting on the fence, Jinnah felt he was getting what he called a 'moth-eaten' Pakistan.

In order to compensate for the loss of these territories, he began to approach the rulers of several states to join Pakistan.

PRINCES

Why did many princes dislike the Congress?

The princes ruled under a system of monarchy.

The Congress party advocated democracy.

It encouraged people to demand more democratic governance and reform from their rulers. Naturally, many of the rulers did not like or trust the Congress and its leaders.

In early 1947, when it became clear that the British were leaving, many of the princes did not wish to partner with the Congress as they believed the Congress was against the princely order.

Select Bibliography

❋ Princely India and Accession ❋

Allen, Charles and Dwivedi, Sharda. *Lives of the Indian Princes*. Eswar, 1998.

Binodini, M.K., trans. Roy, L. Somi. *The Maharaja's Household: A Daughter's Memories of Her Father*. Zubaan Books, 2015.

Bond, J.W., and Wright, Arnold. *Indian States: A Biographical, Historical, and Administrative Survey*. Asian Educational Services, New Delhi, 2006.

Copland, Ian. *State, Community and Neighbourhood in Princely North India, c. 1900–1950*. Palgrave Macmillan, 2005.

Copland, Ian. *The Princes of India in the Endgame of Empire, 1917–1947*. Cambridge University Press, 2002.

Corfield, Conrad. *The Princely India I Knew: From Reading to Mountbatten*. Indo British Historical Society, 1975.

Devi, Gayatri. *A Princess Remembers: The Memoirs of the Maharani of Jaipur*. Rupa Publications India, 1994.

Jeffrey, Robin, ed. *People, Princes and Paramount Power: Society and Politics in the Indian Princely States*. Oxford University Press, 1978.

Menon, V.P. *Integration of the Indian States*. Orient BlackSwan, 2014.

Pillai, Manu S. *False Allies: India's Maharajas in the Age of Ravi Varma*. Juggernaut, 2021.

Phadnis, Urmila. *Towards the Integration of Indian States: 1919–1947.* Asia Publishing House, 1968.

Ramusack, Barbara N. *The New Cambridge History of India: The Indian Princes and Their States.* Cambridge University Press, 2003.

Sarila, Narendra Singh. *Once a Prince of Sarila: Of Palaces and Tiger Hunts, of Nehrus and Mountbattens.* IB Tauris, 2008.

Sorabjee, Soli J. and Datar, Arvind P. *Nani Palkhivala: The Courtroom Genius.* LexisNexis, Butterworths Wadhwa, 2012.

Taraporewala, Soonoo. *Tiger Warrior: Fateh Singh Rathore of Ranthambhore.* Penguin Books, 2012.

Vaikuntanath, Y., ed. *People's Movements in the Princely States.* Manohar, 2004.

White Paper on Indian States, 1950.

Zubrzycki, John. *Dethroned: Patel, Menon and the Integration of Princely India.* Juggernaut, 2023.

❋ Correspondence ❋

Gandhi, M.K., *Letters to Sardar Vallabhbhai Patel by Gandhi.* Navjivan Publishing House, Ahmedabad.

Nandurkar, G.M., ed. *Sardar's Letters – Mostly Unknown – II, Birth Centenary, Vol. V, Years 1947–48: Part One.* Sardar Vallabhbhai Patel Smarak Bhavan, Ahmedabad, 1978.

Mansergh, Nicholas, ed. *Transfer of Power: 1942–47* – Vols X, XI, XII.

Quaid-i-Azam Mohammad Ali Jinnah Papers, Vol. 1, Part 1.

Selected Works of *Jawaharlal* Nehru, 2nd series, Vol. 2, Jawaharlal Nehru Memorial Fund.

❋ Biographies ❋

Agarwal, Purshottam, ed. *Who is Bharat Mata? On History, Culture and the Idea of India: Writings by and on Jawaharlal Nehru.* Speaking Tiger Publishing Pvt. Ltd, 2019.

Al Mujahid, Sharif, ed., and Jinnah, Fatima. *My Brother.* Quaid-e-Azam Academy, 1987.

Basu, Narayani. V.P. *Menon: The Unsung Architect of Modern India.* HarperCollins India, 2021.

Gadgil, Madhav. *The God Who Failed: An Assessment of Jawaharlal Nehru's Leadership.* Rupa Publications Pvt. Ltd, 2014.

Gandhi, Rajmohan. *Patel, A Life.* Navjivan Trust, 2011.

Johnson, Alan Campbell. *Mission with Mountbatten.* Penguin Books Ltd. 1985.

Krishna, B. *India's Bismarck.* Indus Source Books, 2008.

Mountbatten, Pamela and Hicks, India. *India Remembered: A Personal Account of the Mountbattens during the Transfer of Power.* Pavilion, 2007.

Nanda, B.R. *Road to Pakistan: The Life and Times of Mohammad Ali Jinnah.* Routledge India, 2013.

Nandurkar, G.M., ed. *Sardar Patel – In Tune with the Millions – Birth Centenary,* Vol 3. Sardar Vallabhbhai Patel Smarak Bhavan Ahmedabad, 1976.

Rajgopal, P.V. ed. *I Was Nehru's Shadow: From the Diaries of K.F. Rustamji, IP, Padma Vibhushan.* Wisdom Tree Publishers, 2015.

Sarvepalli, Gopal. *Jawaharlal Nehru, A Biography,* Vol. 1, 1889–1947, Oxford University Press, 1976. Schofield, Victoria. *Wavell: Soldier and Statesman.* Pen and Sword Military, 2011.

Sengupta, Hindol. *The Man Who Saved India: Sardar Patel and His Idea of India.* Penguin Viking, 2018.

Shankar, V. *My Reminiscences of Sardar Patel,* Vols 1 and 2. The Macmillan Company of India Limited, 1975.

Tendulkar, D.G. *Mahatma: Life of Mohandas Karamchand Gandhi,* Vol. 8. Publications Division, Government of India, 1969.

Tharoor, Shashi. *Nehru: The Invention of India.* Penguin Random House, 2018.

Warner, Philip. *Auchinleck: The Lonely Soldier.* Pen and Sword Military, 2006.

❋ Independence and Partition ❋

Ahmed, Ishtiaq. *The Punjab – Bloodied, Partitioned and Cleansed: Unravelling the 1947 Tragedy through Secret British Reports and First-Person Accounts.* Oxford University Press, 2012.

Butalia, Urvashi. *The Other Side of Silence: Voices from the Partition of India*. Duke University Press, 2000.

Dhar, Som Nath. *From Partition to Operation Bluestar: Tales of a Journalist, Bureaucrat, Spy*. HarperCollins, 2013.

Dwarkadas, Kanji. *Ten Years to Freedom*. Popular Prakashan, 1968.

Gandhi, Rajmohan. *Revenge and Retaliation: Understanding South Asian History*. Penguin India, 2000.

Gandhi, Rajmohan. *Punjab: A History from Aurangzeb to Mountbatten*. Aleph Book Co. Pvt. Ltd, 2013.

Gandhi, Rajmohan. *Understanding the Muslim Mind*. Penguin India, 2000.

Guha, Ramchandra. *India after Gandhi*. Ecco, 2019.

Hajari, Nisid. *Midnight's Furies: The Deadly Legacy of India's Partition*. Mariner Books, 2016.

Hamid, Major General Shahid. *Disastrous Twilight: A Personal Record of the Partition of India*. Lee Cooper, 1993.

Hodson, H.V. *The Great Divide: Britain, India, Pakistan*. Oxford University Press, 1986.

Khan, Yasmin. *The Great Partition: The Making of India and Pakistan*. Yale University Press, 2017.

Lapierre, Dominique and Collins, Larry. *Freedom at Midnight*; 2nd edition. HarperCollins, 1997.

Mosley, Leonard. *The Last Days of the British Raj*. Harcourt, Brace & World, Inc, New York, 1961.

Sarila, Narendra Singh. *Shadow of the Great Game: The Untold History of India's Partition*. HarperCollins, 2009.

Singh, Khushwant. *A History of the Sikhs*, Vols 1 & 2; 2nd edition. Oxford University Press, 2005.

von Tunzelmann, Alex. *Indian Summer: The Secret History of the End of an Empire*. Simon and Schuster, 2007.

White-Spunner, Barney. *Partition: The Story of Indian Independence and the Creation of Pakistan*. Simon and Schuster, UK, 2017.

Zakaria, Anam. *The Footprints of Partition: Narrative of Four Generations of Pakistanis and Indians*. HarperCollins India, 2015.

❋ Additional Resources for Specific Princely States ❋

TRAVANCORE

Menon, Sreedhara. *Triumph and Tragedy in Travancore: Annals of Sir CP's sixteen years*. DC Books, 2019.

Panikkar, K.M., trans. Krishnamurthy, K. *An Autobiography*. Oxford University Press.

Pillai, Manu S. *The Ivory Throne: Chronicles of the House of Travancore*. HarperCollins India, 2016.

GWALIOR

Farooqui, Amar. *Scindias and the Raj: Princely Gwalior C. 1800–1850*. Primus Books, 2011.

Kidwai, Rasheed. *The House of the Scindias: A Saga of Power, Politics and Intrigue*. Roli Books, 2021.

Palit, Major General D.K. *Musings and Memories*, Vol. 1. Lancer Publishers and Distributors, 2004.

Scindia, Vijaya Raje. *The Last Maharani of Gwalior: An Autobiography*. State University of New York Press, 1987.

Srinivasan, M.A. *Of the Raj, Maharajas and Me*. Speaking Tiger Books, 2022.

BIKANER

Panikkar, K.M., trans. Krishnamurthy, K. *An Autobiography*. Oxford University Press.

BARODA AND NAWANAGAR

Bhattacharya, Anuradha. *The Second Homeland: Polish Refugees in India*. Sage Publications Pvt. Ltd, 2013.

PATIALA

Panikkar, K.M. *The Indian Princes in Council: A Record of the Chancellorship of His Highness the Maharaja of Patiala, 1926–1931 and 1933–1936*. Oxford University Press, 1936.

Singh, Khushwant. A *History of the Sikhs*, Vol. 1, 2nd edition. Oxford University Press, 2005.

Singh, Khushwant. *Captain Amarinder Singh, The People's Maharaja, An Authorized Biography*. Hay House India, 2017.

Singh, Khushwant. *The Sikhs*. HarperCollins India, 2020.

Souvenir on Master Tara Singh, Sant Sipahi Panth, 1981.

The Sikh Sansar USA–*Canada Canada*, Vol. 3, No. 4, December 1974. *Maharajadhiraj Sir Yadavindra Singh of Patiala Memorial Issue*. Sikh Digital Library, 1974.

TRIPURA

Bhaumik, Subir. *Insurgent Crossfire: North-East India*. Spantech and Lancer, 1995.

Dutta Ray, B. and Agarwal, S.P., eds. *Re-organisation of North-East India Since 1947*. Concept Publishing Company, 1996.

Gan-Chaudhuri, Jagdish. A *Constitutional History of Tripura*. Parul Prakashani, 2021.

Ghoshal, Anindita. *Refugees, Borders and Identities: Rights and Habitat in East and Northeast India*. Routledge India, 2020.

Prakash, Col Ved. *Encyclopaedia of North-East India*, Vol. 8. Atlantic, 2006.

KASHMIR

Ali, Tariq et al. *Kashmir: A Case for Freedom*. Verso Books, 2011.

Brown, William. *Gilgit Rebellion: The Major Who Mutinied over Partition of India*. Pen and Sword Military, 2014.

Butalia, Urvashi. *Speaking Peace: Women's Voices from Kashmir*. Zubaan Publishers Pvt. Ltd, 2002.

Choudhry, Dr Sabir. *Tribal Invasion and Kashmir: Pakistani Attempts to Capture Kashmir in 1947, Division of Kashmir and Terrorism*. Author House UK, 2013.

Das, Durga, ed. *Sardar Patel Correspondence, Vol. 1, New Light on Kashmir*. Navjivan Publishing House, 1971.

Dhar, Som Nath. *From Partition to Operation Bluestar: Tales of a Journalist, Bureaucrat, Spy*. Harper India, 2013.

Haqqani, Husain. *Pakistan: Between Mosque and Military*. Carnegie Endowment for International Peace, 2005.

Khanna, Meera. *In a State of Violent Peace: Voices from the Kashmir Valley*. *Harper*Collins India, 2015.

Kumar, Air Marshal Bharat. *An Incredible War:* IAF *in Kashmir War* 1947–48. K.W. Publishers Pvt. Ltd, 2013.

Lamb, Alaistair. *Kashmir:* A *Disputed Legacy*, 1846–1990. Roxford Books, 1991.

Mahajan, Mehr Chand. *Looking Back: The Autobiography of Mehr Chand Mahajan: Former Chief Justice of India*. Har-Anand Publication Pvt. Ltd, 2018.

Singh, Karan. *Heir Apparent: An Autobiography*. Oxford University Press, 1983.

Singh, Khushwant, trans. *Flames of the Chinar: An Autobiography of Sheikh Abdullah*. Penguin Books India, 1995.

Snedden, Christopher. *Kashmir, the Unwritten History*. HarperCollins India, 2013.

Verma, Raghav, ed. *An Examined Life: Essays and Reflections of Karan Singh*. HarperCollins India, 2019.

Zakaria, Anam. *Between the Great Divide:* A *Journey into Pakistan-Administered Kashmir*. HarperCollins India, 2018.

Zia, Ather and Bhat, Javed Iqbal, eds. A *Desolation Called Peace:* Voices *from Kashmir*. Harper India, 2019.

HYDERABAD

Hyder, Mohammed. *October Coup:* A *Memoir of the Struggle for Hyderabad*. Roli Books Pvt. Ltd, 2012.

Ismail, Sir Mirza. *My Public Life*. Allen and Unwin, 1954.

Kulkarni, V.B. K.M. *Munshi (Builders of India Series)*. Publications Division, Government of India, 1959.

Mudiraj, Krishna Swami. The 30 *Years Political Struggle of Hyderabad*, 1st edition, English. Shri K. Krishna Swamy Mudiraj Memorial Trust Hyderabad, 2011.

Munshi, K.M. *End of an Era: Hyderabad Memories*. Bharatiya Vidya Bhavan, 1957.

Sundarayya, P. *Telangana People's Struggle and Its Lessons*. Cambridge University Press India Pvt. Ltd, 2006.

Tirtha, Swami Ramananda. *Memoirs of Hyderabad Freedom Struggle*. Popular Prakashan, 1961.

Zubrzycki, Jacob. *The Last Nizam: An Indian Prince in an Australian Outback*. Pan Macmillan, 2006.

❋ Plays ❋

Brenton, Howard. *Drawing the Line* (NHB Modern Plays). Nick Hern Books, 2014.

Joshi, Shashi. *The Last Durbar: A Dramatic Presentation of the Division of British India*. Lotus/Roli Books, 2007.

❋ Others ❋

Austin, Granville. *Working a Democratic Constitution: A History of the Indian Experience*. Oxford University Press India, 2000.

Luthra, H.R. *Indian Broadcasting*. Publications Division, Government of India, 1986.

Raghavan, Srinath. *War and Peace in Modern India*. Palgrave Macmillan, 2010.

NOTE: The above bibliography lists the books that formed part of the reference material. Several research papers, websites, newspaper articles, magazines and other sources were also referred to, which are not included in the list above. Many of the books mentioned above are available on www.archive.org.

Acknowledgements

My gratitude to:

Prof Sunthar in IIT Bombay for taking me on as the curator and content writer on the NVLI project on Sardar Patel. It opened my eyes to the story I knew so little about. Thank you for the opportunity to visit Ahmedabad and Karamsad to research Sardar's life. It was then, roaming the streets near Lal Darwaza in Ahmedabad, when I was asking people the way to Patel's office and was met with blank stares, that I made up my mind to do my bit, to take this story to a wider audience, especially youngsters.

Author Vinitha Ramchandani for encouraging me to be more unabashed about approaching publishers. It was vital advice for me back then. And for suggesting that I write to Hachette. Many thanks. It worked!

Vatsala Kaul Banerjee, Publisher, Hachette India, for your faith in this story, and for being so responsive and thorough, encouraging and positive. Thank you for making this book your baby too.

Arati Desai, librarian at the Nehru Centre in Mumbai. Thank you for allotting me a research desk and for access to your vast catalogue. This wouldn't have been possible without access to all the material I had at the wonderful library.

All my friends who read initial drafts – thank you for your honest inputs and regular enquiries about the progress of the book.

Aneez Alangadan, for managing to source books, despite the COVID-19 pandemic. Prarthana Patil for material on the dress and appearance of royalty. Harveen Choudhary for help with the Punjabi words and Hemendra Arya for the Marwari words.

Sangeeta Pawar, whose help around the house allowed me time and energy to research and write.

Amma, Appa, my late Pati, Aaji and Athai – for believing in me always and for the values with which I was raised. Words can never say enough to express my gratitude.

Shashi – for being such a rock of constant support, for the happiness and security that allow me to explore an alternative and creative career. It wouldn't have been possible without you.

Karthik and Kabir – my journey as a writer began because of you. Thank you for new beginnings.

Tatha, my late grandfather, who instilled in me an interest in Indian history. The books you left me, their margins filled with scribbled notes, way beyond my understanding back then, speak to me today – years after you're gone. I hope this work meets your standards.

To end, very grateful to Rana Safvi and Dr Shashi Tharoor for giving the book a read despite tight schedules and for the wonderful words of encouragement.